h Butler Reader

The Judith Butler Reader

Edited by
Sara Salih
with Judith Butler

Blackwell
Publishing

BLACKWELL PUBLISHING
350 Main Street, Malden, MA 02148-5020, USA
9600 Garsington Road, Oxford OX4 2DQ, UK
550 Swanston Street, Carlton, Victoria 3053, Australia

First published 2004 by Blackwell Publishing Ltd

12   2013

Library of Congress Cataloging-in-Publication Data

Butler, Judith.
  The Judith Butler reader/edited by Sara Salih with Judith Butler.
        p.cm.
  Includes bibliographical references and index.
    ISBN 978-0-631-22593-5 (alk. paper) – ISBN 978-0-631-22594-2 (pbk.: alk. paper)
  1. Feminist theory. 2. Feminist theory—Political aspects. 3. Structuralism.
  4. Postmodernism—Social aspects. I. Salih, Sara. II. Title.

HQ1190. B883 2003
305.42′01—dc22

                                                                2003021493

A catalogue record for this title is available from the British Library.

Set in 10.5 / 12.5 pt Bembo
by Kolam Information Services Pvt. Ltd, Pondicherry, India
Printed and bound in Singapore
by COS Printers Pte Ltd

For further information on
Blackwell Publishing, visit our website:
www.blackwellpublishing.com

Contents

Acknowledgments

The editor and publisher gratefully acknowledge the permission granted to reproduce the copyright material in this book:

1 Judith Butler, "Variations on Sex and Gender: Beauvoir, Wittig, Foucault," pp. 128–42 and 185 (notes) from Seyla Benhabib and Drucilla Cornell (eds.), *Feminism as Critique: Essays on the Politics of Gender in Late Capitalist Societies*. Oxford: Polity Press, 1987. Reprinted by permission of Blackwell Publishing Ltd/Polity Press.

2 Judith Butler, preface to 1999 edition, pp. vii–xvii, and chapter 1, "Desire, Rhetoric and Recognition in Hegel's *Phenomenology of Spirit*," pp. 17–59, 240–4 (notes), from *Subjects of Desire: Hegelian Reflections in Twentieth-Century France* (originally published 1987; reprinted in paperback 1999 by Columbia University Press, New York). Reprinted by permission of Columbia University Press.

3 Judith Butler, preface to 1999 anniversary edition, pp. xiv–xxvi, 191–3 (notes), and chapter 3, "Subversive Bodily Acts," pp. 163–80, 215–16 (notes), from *Gender Trouble: Feminism and the Subversion of Identity* (originally published 1990; reprinted 1999 by Routledge, New York). Reproduced by permission of Routledge, an imprint of Taylor & Francis Books, Inc.

4 Judith Butler, "Imitation and Gender Insubordination," pp. 13–31 from Diana Fuss (ed.), *Inside Out: Lesbian Theories, Gay Theories*. New York: Routledge, 1991. Reproduced by permission of Routledge, an imprint of Taylor & Francis Books, Inc.

5 Judith Butler, chapter 2, "The Lesbian Phallus and the Morphological Imaginary," pp. 57–91, 257–65 (notes) from *Bodies That Matter: On the Discursive Limits of "Sex."* New York: Routledge, 1993. Reproduced by permission of Routledge, an imprint of Taylor & Francis Books, Inc.

6 Judith Butler, "The Force of Fantasy: Mapplethorpe, Feminism, and Discursive Excess," pp. 105–25 from *differences: A Journal of Feminist Cultural*

Studies 2:2 (1990). Bloomington: Indiana University Press. © 1990 by Indiana University Press. All rights reserved. Used by permission of the publisher.

7   Judith Butler, "Endangered/Endangering: Schematic Racism and White Paranoia," pp. 15–22 from Robert Gooding-Williams (ed.), *Reading Rodney King/Reading Urban Uprising*. New York: Routledge, 1993. Reproduced by permission of Routledge, an imprint of Taylor & Francis Books, Inc.

8   Judith Butler, chapter 1, "Burning Acts, Injurious Speech," pp. 43–69, 169–73 (notes) from *Excitable Speech: A Politics of the Performative*. New York: Routledge, 1997. Reproduced by permission of Routledge, an imprint of Taylor & Francis Books, Inc.

9   Judith Butler, chapter 5, "Melancholy Gender/Refused Identification," pp. 132–50, 211–12 (notes) from *The Psychic Life of Power: Theories in Subjection*. Stanford: Stanford University Press, 1997. Originally published in *Psychoanalytic Dialogues* 5:5.2 (1995), pp. 165–94. Reprinted by permission of the Analytic Press as copyright holder and publisher.

10   Judith Butler, extracts from "Competing Universalities," pp. 143–8, 151–8, 159–62, 175–81 in Judith Butler, Ernesto Laclau, Slavoj Žižek, *Contingency, Hegemony, Universality: Contemporary Dialogues on the Left*. London: Verso, 2000. Reprinted by permission of Verso.

11   Judith Butler, chapter 3, "Promiscuous Obedience," pp. 57–82, 92–7 from *Antigone's Claim: Kinship Between Life and Death*. New York: Columbia University Press, 2000. Reprinted by permission of Columbia University Press.

12   Judith Butler, "What Is Critique? An Essay on Foucault's Virtue," pp. 212–26 from David Ingram (ed.), *The Political*. Oxford: Blackwell, 2001. Reprinted by permission of Blackwell Publishing Ltd.

13   Judith Butler, interview with Gary A. Olson and Lynn Worsham, "Changing the Subject: Judith Butler's Politics of Radical Resignification," pp. 731–65 from *jac* 20:4 (2000). Reprinted by permission of Lynn Worsham and Gary A. Olson.

Every effort has been made to trace copyright holders and to obtain their permission for the use of copyright material. The publisher apologizes for any errors or omissions in the above list and would be grateful if notified of any corrections that should be incorporated in future reprints or editions of this book.

Introduction
Sara Salih

I

What does it mean to offer a critique? Who will be a subject and what will count as a life? These are the questions with which Judith Butler begins and concludes "What Is Critique?" her recent essay-lecture on Foucauldian virtue as a mode of self-stylization. That the text is titled and framed by questions is significant, since it is quickly apparent that the reader will not be offered the reassurance of definite answers. "This is, of course, not to say what withdraws reassurance is, by definition, not an answer," Butler writes, commenting on Foucault. "Indeed, the only rejoinder, it seems to me, is to return to a more fundamental meaning of 'critique' in order to see what may well be wrong with the question as it is posed and . . . to pose the question anew, so that a more productive approach to the place of ethics within politics might be mapped."[1] The ethical-political stance Butler takes up, in other texts as well as this one, requires patience from readers who may well find the absence (indeed, the removal) of epistemological anchors disorienting. So, like Nietzsche, Butler semi-humorously advises her readers to follow the example of cows and learn "the art of slow rumination" in their textual practices. As Nietzsche puts it, reading is an art for which one must place oneself in a state that is "practically bovine," but this by no means implies an attitude of passivity and contentment; rather, readers should learn not to expect what Butler calls "radical accessibility" when they encounter texts that have set themselves the difficult task of rethinking and reconfiguring the possible within political theorizing.[2]

By "possible" Butler means the possibly "human," possible configurations of the social world and possible modes of doing. In fact, she calls for nothing less than the transformation of the social world as it is currently constituted, since it is a place in which responses to the question "What is a human?" come far too easily, and where defining difference invariably entails the violence of exclusion. On the other hand, living in the midst of the unknowable is a nonviolent, ethical response to otherness that aims to bring about a transcendence of simple, simplistic identity categories.[3] As radical democratic practices, rumination and critique deliberately eschew straightforward definitions; nor do they propose easy solutions to the issues they raise since the category of "the human" and the socially-defining norms within which it is located must be built up over time. For this reason, Butler's work continues to challenge the frames of reference within which people speak, think, and live subject categories. Throughout her career as a published academic, Butler has theorized the subject as opaque, unknown to itself, characterized by what she calls its "unbearable relationality" to the other. The contingent, self-incoherent subject is dependent upon the recognition of the other, which means that, as Butler puts it, "we are, from the start, ethically implicated in the lives of others."[4] Although Butler has resisted the so-called "return to ethics" because she worries that it constitutes both an escape from politics and a heightening of moralism, she writes eloquently about the problem of navigating ethical ambivalence in ways that will establish a basis for ethical responsibility.[5] To argue that the subject is opaque, non-self-identical, unknown to itself is not an admission of ethical failure; rather, it is a theory of subject-formation that works in the service of ethics by acknowledging the limits of "the self"/self-knowledge, while insisting on the importance of those intersubjective bonds through which "humans" are connected to one another.[6]

It is never easy – or indeed, wise – to gauge the "success" of a political-theoretical project such as this, and yet it would certainly be true to say that Butler's work has had an enormous impact in numerous fields. Widely translated and taught, her texts continue to provoke important debates on philosophical and political issues concerning identity, the subject, gender, sex, sexuality, and "race."[7] Recognizing that "politics has a character of contingency and context to it that cannot be predicted at the level of theory," Butler is an activist-theorist who is engaged at a grass-roots level with many of the struggles she writes about.[8] For example, she has campaigned for affirmative action and academic freedom in various contexts, and she supports a wide range of causes, from rights for illegal immigrants to the Intersex Society of North America. She is also on the Advisory Board of Faculty for Israeli-Palestinian Peace. Many readers will know Butler as the philosopher who, at an early stage in her career as a published academic, developed the radical and politically far-reaching insight that identity is a contingent construction which assumes multiple forms even as it presents itself as singular and stable.[9] From this point on, Butler has remained centrally concerned with how heterosexual and racial imperatives are secured together, and her work continues to probe the ways in which identity norms are taken up and subject positions assumed. The theorization of identity categories as "originating activit[ies] incessantly taking place,"[10] means that it will be possible to subvert, disrupt, and refuse those activities, thus de-instating dominant heterosexual and racial epistemes and forcing them into crisis. Behind such resignifications and redeployments lies a fundamental commitment to extend and expand the category of "the human," so that subjects who do not conform to its hetero-normative, racialized imperatives need no longer suffer the violence of social exclusion. As part of this commitment, Butler continues to represent the rights of "sexual minorities" (the term is Gayle Rubin's) – "all kinds of people who for whatever reason are not immediately captured or legitimated by the available norms" – with the long-term goal of transforming the delimiting power structures which currently prescribe what counts as "human."[11] This is a particularly pressing impetus, given that the norms by which "humans" live are largely unavailable to groups such as gays, lesbians, transsexuals, "racial minorities," and other others who are condemned to the social death of extra-normativity. Moreover, Butler is fully aware that normative heterosexuality is not the only regulatory regime at work in the discursive production of identity, and she sees racial and heterosexual imperatives as simultaneously operative in reproductive sexing and gendering practices. Sexual and racial differences are not discrete axes of power, and sex and gender are by no means prior to race. "What appear within such an enumerative framework as separable categories are, rather, the conditions of articulation *for* each other," Butler writes: "How is race lived in the modality of sexuality? How is gender lived in the modality of race? How do colonial and neo-colonial nation-states rehearse gender relations in the consolidation of state power?"[12]

Addressing (but not necessarily answering) this question, Butler's interrogative mode of political philosophizing seeks to suspend the ontological certainties currently pertaining to the category of "the human," thereby facilitating a more capacious understanding of difference. Like Emmanuel Levinas, Butler invites us to approach the other in a spirit of openness and questioning, repeatedly asking the other, "Who are you?" without expecting or hoping for a conclusive answer. We will never be able absolutely to understand the other, and the other herself may change from one time of asking to the next.[13] This is Butler's post-Hegelian revision of the scene of desire and recognition as an ethical project in which desire and recognition will necessarily remain unsatisfied. Post-Hegel, the other must not be overcome (sublated) for the sake of the self, but the ethical stance means permitting the other to live in its alterity in the full knowledge that one's notions of self-coherence and self-identity will be interrupted by the difference that one embraces.[14]

Such openness and open-endedness are characteristic of Butler's work, where the strategy of interrogation without resolution that characterizes "What Is Critique?" is frequently and effectively deployed. For Butler as for

Foucault, the posing of "difficult" questions and the deliberate withholding of reassuring answers is not an epistemological evasion; it is a crucial element of critical subversion, a political mode that is designed to produce a sense of alienation and discomfort in the reader so that newness may enter and alter a defamiliarized world. Accordingly, as Butler has pointed out, the work of the critical intellectual is always and inevitably political, since it involves working hard on difficult texts in order to encourage the reader to adopt a questioning attitude towards the world s/he thought s/he knew.[15] Critique is not deployed merely for the pleasure of the question; far from it, since if anything may be said to characterize Butler's work as a whole, it is its ethical impetus to extend the norms by which "humans" are permitted to conduct liveable lives in socially recognized public spheres. To this end, Butler has argued for rupture and resignification as means of agency, while her "critical genealogy of gender categories" is an ongoing political project which, in its deconstruction of gender, sex, and "race," has as its urgent incentive the survival that Butler regards as the necessary background to gender trouble – itself a means of social and ontological survival.[16]

In Butler's genealogical theorizations, the subject, which has neither origin nor end, comes into conflict with and defines itself against other subjects and existing regimes of power, through processes involving loss and melancholia.[17] This is Butler's Foucauldian and psychoanalytical appropriation of Hegel's subject as a performative, melancholic agent that assumes its social identity inside rather than outside existing power structures.[18] Hegel's account of desire, recognition, and the progress of consciousness in *Phenomenology of Spirit* continues to influence Butler's work, which, as she puts it, takes place "within the orbit of a certain set of Hegelian questions."[19] Butler has acknowledged the importance of dialectic to her thinking, although it is dialectic without ultimate synthesis, or "supplemented" dialectic,[20] and yet she breaks with Hegel through Foucault and psychoanalysis, while her work also engages with a wide array of thinkers and critical-theoretical fields, including psychoanalysis, feminism, poststructuralism, and Marxism. Other phenomenological frameworks – specifically, Husserl's understanding of consciousness as a constituting activity in which the object is built up through a series of intentional acts – inform Butler's conceptualization of gender as a sequence of performative acts, while her contention that gender's "interior essence" is retroactively installed derives from "Devant la loi," Derrida's essay on Kafka,[21] and Derrida's account of the iterability and citationality of the linguistic sign in "Signature Event Context" informs *Bodies That Matter* and *Excitable Speech*.[22]

In crucial ways these texts, along with the critical frameworks cited above, complicate what might be called Butler's Hegelian inheritance. "I began my philosophical career within the context of a Jewish education, one that took the ethical dilemmas posed by the mass extermination of the Jews in World War II, including members of my own family, to set the scene for the thinking of ethicality as such," Butler recalls in her essay, "Ethical Ambivalence."[23] Having avoided Nietzsche's texts until a friend brought her to Paul de Man's class on *Beyond Good and Evil*, Butler claims that to this day she is less familiar with the work of contemporary queer theorists than with the Jewish thinkers she read from an early age – thinkers including Maimonides, Spinoza, Arendt, and Benjamin.[24] In the 1999 preface to *Subjects of Desire* (reprinted here, pp. 00–0) Butler recalls that by the 1970s and early 1980s, her interests lay primarily with continental philosophy (Hegel, Marx, Nietzsche, Heidegger, Kierkegaard, Merleau-Ponty, and the Frankfurt School), and as a postdoctoral fellow she became receptive to the French theory she had previously resisted. In particular, Paul de Man, Michel Foucault, and Jacques Derrida are of obvious and continuing significance to her thought. From one of her earliest articles ("Foucault and the Paradox of Bodily Inscriptions," 1989) right through to her recent essay on critique, Foucault is a consistent presence in Butler's work, and his historically contextualized analyses of the discursive production of sex and sexuality inform her own theorizations of identity categories as unfixed, constructed entities.

All the same, while Butler sometimes identifies aspects of her work as "poststructuralist," the designation does not adequately capture the multiplicity of her theoretical provenances, and to call Butler a poststructuralist (or a postmodernist – a label she does not consider appropriate) would elide the feminist, psychoanalytic, and Marxist frameworks within which her work is also located.[25] So, for example, Butler's two early essays on sex and gender take Simone de Beauvoir's feminist existentialism as a starting point, while the 1999 preface to *Gender Trouble* acknowledges that the book "is rooted in 'French Theory'," including the ideas of Monique Wittig, Julia Kristeva, and Luce Irigaray, together with Lacanian psychoanalysis.[26] Indeed, it is impossible to underestimate the importance of psychoanalysis to Butler's work generally, and specifically to her theorizations of melancholic identity. Key texts include Freud's "Mourning and Melancholia" (1917) and *The Ego and the Id* (1923), while Butler's psychoanalytically inflected rereading of the significatory investment of body parts addresses Lacan's "The mirror stage as formative of the function of the I as revealed in psychoanalytic experience" (1949) and "The signification of the phallus" (1958).[27] Additionally, Althusser's doctrine of interpellation as formulated in "Ideology and Ideological State Apparatuses" (1969) informs her discussions of the interpellative functioning of discourse and the law, particularly in *Bodies That Matter*, *Excitable Speech*, and *The Psychic Life of Power*.

Butler's theoretical eclecticism is part of what constitutes the challenge, the radicalism, and indeed, the richness of her work. Theoretical formulations such as Althusserian interpellation, Kristevan abjection, and Freudian melancholia are re-cited and relocated to produce stunning and innovative juxtapositions – a good example is the Foucauldian reading of melancholia as one of power's operations in chapter 5 of *The Psychic Life of Power* (reprinted here, pp. 000–0), where melancholia is also identified as a potential site of subversion and agency. Readers will find Butler returning to certain thinkers and texts in order to revise and develop her ideas, sometimes in direct response to criticism or comment, and always in the spirit of critique.[28] Like the ontological subject she theorizes, Butler's writings are necessarily open-ended, but this does not mean that they are politically "promiscuous" (although other forms of promiscuity are valorized in *Antigone's Claim*; see p. 00). Butler's work is always politically and ethically motivated, and her autocritiques valorize contingency, unknowingness, and unrealizability themselves as components of a radical democratic project that seeks both to resist and to extend the discursive norms by which subjects are currently defined. For as Butler observes in *Contingency, Hegemony, Universality*, democracy itself must remain unrealizable in order to be "democratic."[29]

II

The suspension of ontological certainties and the withholding of definitions and answers is a risky undertaking that may produce "vertigo and terror" in the subject who interrogates existing configurations of power,[30] and from certain responses to Butler's work, it is also clear that this practice sometimes exposes the questioner to denunciation and abuse. Perhaps the discomfort certain readers have experienced is unsurprising, since even for those who do not consciously challenge gendered/sexed/"raced" hegemonies, Butler leaves little room for belief in identity categories as stable, self-evident, or "natural." Her interrogations and destabilizations of exclusionary norms start out from the premise that the subject-effect, as she dubs it, is not a self-evident entity, but is retroactively installed by and in discourse; in other words, the subject is the result of its deeds rather than the initiator of them. Friedrich Nietzsche's insight that "there is no 'being' behind doing, acting, becoming; the 'doer' is merely a fiction imposed on the doing – the doing itself is everything" prompts Butler to offer the following gendered corollary in *Gender Trouble*: "There is no gender identity behind the expressions of gender; that identity is performatively constituted by the very 'expressions' that are said to be its results."[31] Together Nietzsche's causal reversal, Althusserian interpellation, and Austinian performativity inform Butler's insight that that the subject is retroactively, performatively "hailed" into gender in much the same way that Austin's ship is named and Althusser's "man on the street" assumes his subject-position in response to the policeman's call.[32] In *Bodies That Matter*, Butler substitutes Althusser's "Hey, you there!" with the statement "It's a girl!" uttered as an infant emerges from the womb or when a fetus is seen for the first time on an ultrasound scan. These words do not merely describe the infant, but they constitute the subject in the act of naming it. "[I]n that naming the girl is 'girled'," Butler writes, "brought into the domain of language and kinship through the interpellation of gender."[33] This "girling" of the girl does not happen once, but the initial interpellation is reiterated over time so that the "naturalized effect" of sex and gender is reinforced and/or contested; as Butler puts it, "[t]he naming is at once the setting of a boundary, and also the repeated inculcation of a norm."[34]

If anything may be said to be "essential" to the performative subject Butler theorizes, it would appear to be loss – not just the loss of notions of self-identity and autonomy, but the more fundamental loss of primary desire. Recently, Butler acknowledged that she may have "moved too quickly" to accept Nietzsche's punitive scene of inauguration of the subject in *The Pyschic Life of Power*, although in that book she does accept the validity of accounts of homosexuality that do not have repudiation as their basis.[35] And yet as early as *Subjects of Desire*, the subject is characterized as an intersubjective, melancholic entity which comes into self-consciousness through its recognition of the other, its desire for the other, and its concomitant loss of self. Developing these concepts in the important second chapter of *Gender Trouble* ("Prohibition, Psychoanalysis and the Production of the Heterosexual Matrix"), Butler argues that primary homosexual desire is foreclosed by the taboo against homosexuality, so that all gendered and sexed identities are marked by a primary loss of desire – literally "marked," since prohibited homosexual cathexes are incorporated on the surface of the body as "sex."[36] "Sex" is thus symptomatic of the same-sex desire that must be abandoned if one is to count as a subject, so that as Butler asserts in *The Psychic Life of Power*, "the 'truest' lesbian melancholic is the strictly straight woman, and the 'truest' gay male melancholic is the strictly straight man" (see below, p. 254).

Here Butler draws from Freud's schematizations of melancholia and incorporation in *Mourning and Melancholia*, along with his follow-up essay, "The Ego and the Id." The latter describes how the infant's ego is formed through the loss of primary desire for its parents, but whereas Freud asserts that the infant's innate sexual "dispositions" determine whether it desires the parent of the same or the opposite sex, Butler argues that the primary sexual dispositions posited and unaccounted for by Freud are no more than the effects of the law – specifically here, the taboo against homosexuality which, crucially, precedes the taboo against incest. The infant's identification with one or other of its parents is not innate or "natural," but occurs within (and is to some extent determined by) a "heterosexual matrix of desire."[37] The taboos and laws within this matrix are generative, which means that far from repressing homosexuality, the taboo against homosexuality produces the desire it is supposed to proscribe; indeed, homosexuality is produced *in order* to repress it, so that a "natural" homosexuality is crafted even as it is foreclosed, thereby rendering heterosexuality both intelligible and secure.[38]

Butler's Foucauldianism is once again implicit in her brilliant readings of Freudian taboo as proliferative and productive, and it informs her insight that the subject is by no means a suffering melancholic doomed to a lifetime of anhedonia and loss. The melancholic subject does not flee the law in pursuit of an ontological "freedom" which resides somewhere outside discourse, for there is no such space. Rather, the subject is inevitably and passionately attached to the law upon which it depends for its very being. To theorize this relationship between the subject and the law, Butler frequently returns to the complex and fraught Hegelian encounter between lord and bondsman, crystallizing as it does the two-way nature of subjection and subjectivation.[39] Here as elsewhere, power does not operate straightforwardly from the top downwards, but the lord and his bondsman are mutually reliant, mutually constituting entities who cannot live without each other. Butler's post-Hegelian subject is a fundamentally social being that depends on the other and its constitutive address, which means that the notion of self-identity must be relinquished in favor of an ecstatic relation to the other in which the "I" is placed outside itself in its recognition of the other and its acceptance of its own intersubjective alterity and opacity. As Butler puts it, "the subject of recognition is one for whom a vacillation between loss and ecstasy is inevitable. The possibility of the 'I' . . . resides in a perspective that dislocates the first-person perspective whose very condition it supplies."[40]

Such ontological sociality clearly has ethical implications, as, post-Hegel, recognizing the other and one's relation to it will involve letting the other live – partly for one's own sake. The melancholic subject's non-totalizing incoherence and interdependency are constitutive of its ethical connection to others, while self-opacity is not a form of "poststructuralist nihilism," but an acknowledgment of social responsibility. By accepting the loss of its primary homosexual cathexes, the subject embraces its own incompletion and alterity, thus facilitating the epistemological, nonviolent encounter with the other that is crucial for both subjects' psychic survival. For as Butler argues in *The Psychic Life of Power*, it is only by recognizing oneself as and in the other that one will become anything at all.[41] A new sense of ethics thus emerges from the subject's failure to define itself on its own terms, and conceding the limits of self-knowledge gives rise to a disposition of humility, generosity, and forgiveness of the other for whom one is also responsible.[42]

III

As Butler has recently expressed it, the subject is both subjected to the norm and to the agency of its use, so that if subject-formation is the repeated inculcation of a norm, it will be possible to repeat and re-repeat that norm in unexpected, unsanctioned ways. Performative identity norms resemble the sign as it is characterized by Derrida, and they are vulnerable to precisely the same "grafting," recitation, and semantic excess. The performatively and linguistically constituted subject is not ultimately defined by the interpellative "call to gender"; neither is the subject fully determined or radically free to deploy discourse at will. Steering a careful middle course between voluntarism and determinism, Butler distances herself from the strategic deployment of "essential" identity categories as a political practice. "[S]trategies always have meanings that exceed the purposes for which they are intended," she asserts in *Gender Trouble*, a concern that she reiterates in "Changing the Subject."[43] Similarly, in *Contingency, Hegemony, Universality*, Butler expresses doubts about the political efficacy of subverting dominant norms by occupying them, since she now suspects that this practice will effectively strengthen those norms. The performative appropriations Butler advocated in her early work give way to what she calls a performativity proper to refusal, in other words, the strategic *rejection* rather than occupation of some (but by no means all) hegemonic, heterocentric, and racist norms, depending on whether they are entrenched or vulnerable to resignification.[44]

Rejection and resignification are key components of "affirmative deconstruction," the political mode Butler describes in her concluding contribution to *Contingency, Hegemony, Universality*, where she insists that "a concept may be put under erasure *and* played at the same time."[45] Crucially, the deconstruction of the subject is by no means equivalent to its destruction,[46] since as Butler argues in her introduction to *Bodies That Matter*, "[t]o claim that the subject is itself produced in and as a gendered matrix of relations is not to do away with the subject, but only to ask after the conditions of its emergence and operation."[47] Seeking out the instabilities of discourse, language, and the constitutive terms of identity will force them into epistemic crisis, revealing the limits of knowledge and being, discourse and the law, along with the inevitable opacity of a subject that will always fail ultimately to define itself. Like Homi K. Bhabha, Butler sees melancholia as a potential means of subversion and agency, a site of refusal and revolt rather than uniquely a scene of suffering. For although the intersubjective, interdependent, melancholic subject may not be autonomous, s/he is certainly an agent, since s/he is not inevitably bound to respond to the names by which s/he is addressed. *The Psychic Life of Power* finds potential for agency in the subject's responses to an interpellative call that "regularly misses its mark,"[48] while elsewhere Butler insists that there are any number of ways in which the subject may "turn around" in response to the call of the law.[49] By acknowledging his or her own incompletion and redeploying the terms of discourse, the subject may exploit the productive nature of melancholia, language, and the law to subversive ends in order to stage unforeseen and unsanctioned modes of identity. So agency, Butler repeatedly insists, begins where sovereignty wanes (or where sovereignty is given up), and it always resides within a law that is multiple, myriad, and self-proliferating.[50]

Since performativity and melancholia contain the political promise of radical disruption and subversion, Butler focuses on those moments in which the subject exceeds the terms that constitute her/him. Indeed, her own appropri-ation of Freudian melancholia effects such an "exceeding" at a theoretical level; by reinscribing homosexual cathexis within a heterosexual matrix of power and arguing that homosexual desire is constitutive of the "straight" subject, Butler calls heterosexual priority into question, panicking heterosexuality by revealing that it is imitative and derivative. In this analysis, heterosexuality is unreal, the parodic effect of abandoned desires (indeed, *all* gender identities are imitative and unreal), a copy of a copy without an original. The disruptive "playing" and proliferation of gender categories releases them from the binarisms in which they are currently mired,[51] thus de-instating heterosexual hegemony by claiming it as a field of theoretical operation. In "Changing the Subject," Butler herself engages in the catachrestic deployment of the "I" when she claims and re-cites the term "lesbian," revealing the term's undeniability, inadequacy, and contingency in her playful appropriations, while also prac-ticing the radical resignifications she has described elsewhere in her work.[52]

Discerning political potential in such stagings of ontological insufficiency, Butler is drawn to figures who exemplify the "virtuous disobedience" that she identifies as an effective strategy of subversion. So *Antigone's Claim* analyzes the ways in which Antigone's nonconformity and refusal to obey her uncle, King Creon, reveal the instability and contingency of the sexual and kinship norms that she flouts, while elsewhere, Butler describes how Herculine Barbin's dually-sexed body confounds the univocal, binary nature of existing sex/ gender systems.[53] Antigone and Barbin's disobedience and nonconformity throw into sharp relief what Butler identifies as a "promising fatality" at the heart of heterosexual and kinship norms, even as these norms present them-selves as univocal, "natural," immutable, and above all, exclusive. And yet, while Butler insists that Foucauldian proliferation always takes place within existing power structures, this by no means implies that subjects can autonomously reinvent themselves. If genders and sexes are "chosen" in some sense, the choosing is always constrained by existing cultural norms, while no account of the self can take place outside the interpellative structure of address, even if the addressee remains implicit and anonymous. Performativity certainly sustains theoretical connections to theater as well as linguistic theory,[54] but when Butler characterizes gender as performative she is not positing the existence of an autonomous "actor" who gets up in the morning to survey a wardrobe from which s/he selects a gender costume for the day.[55] The point is not to replace one volitional, self-identical subject with another, and panicking heterosexuality by seeking out and exposing its aporia certainly does not support the comforting illusion of ontological stability and "wholeness." Instead, it constitutes what Butler in another context calls a politics of discomfort that is designed to maximize self-alienation to ethical and democratic ends.[56]

So, as Barbin and Antigone demonstrate, radical resignificatory practices are not deployed merely for the pleasure of spectacle or play, but they have as their impetus a normative aspiration towards livability and survival. This is a particularly pressing motive, given the threat of violence and death under which many subjects currently exist. In particular, Butler has described the violence (both state and individual) against transgendered subjects, and others "who live, or try to live, on the sexual margins."[57] Butler points out that the desire to kill someone for not conforming to the gender norms by which subjects are supposed to live means that "life" itself requires the norm, while living outside the norm involves placing oneself at risk of death – sometimes actual death, but more frequently the social death of delegitimation and non-recognition.[58] Certainly, Antigone is threatened with execution for disobeying King Creon, and ultimately she takes her own life, but for sexual minorities, living outside the bounds of heterosexual normativity and what is considered its appropriate morphology does not inevitably result in physical death. Non-normative subjects who are forced to conduct an existence at one remove from life and its recognized norms suffer the protracted pain of social exclusion, as nonconformity is punished with a life in de-realized mode, neither fully (socially) living nor fully (physically) dead.

For Butler then, "survival" is not only a matter of averting physical violence and death, but it also means being able to consider that one's life is possible and viable, so that one is permitted to exist and to operate freely in public spaces with all the attendant norms of recognition. Butler is acutely aware of the threat of physical violence and actual death under which many nonconforming subjects live, yet her work is more extensively concerned with averting social death through radical resignificatory practices and political/philosophical critique.[59] The ethical question that repeatedly arises in what Butler has called her "philosophy of freedom" (and it is a question that applies to "race" as much as gender, since gender norms are always racialized) is how to encounter the gendered/sexed/"raced" differences that do not slot into existing grids of intelligibility, without killing or sublating those differences.[60] Resignification is one way of opposing violence against "differently constituted" subjects, and yet Butler is acutely aware that resignification may be deployed by activists on the political left *and* the right.[61] Accordingly, she is careful to distinguish the operation of resignification in the service of radical democratic politics from its right-wing counterpart. Whereas those on the right use the violence of exclusion to narrow the categories by which subjects "qualify" for human status, those on the left actively counter the violence of exclusion through the interrogation and resignification of existing norms. As Butler defines it, a radical democratic politics works to open up the norms which sustain viable life, making those norms available to communities that have previously been disenfranchised, excluded, subjected to violence. So, as part of a collective struggle to increase the possibilities of "life" for sexual minorities, Butler's work continues to identify those moments in which subjects may performatively assert their right to a livable life where there has been no such prior authorization.

Butler's work may have a normative impetus, but it is never prescriptive. In a recent interview she wryly explains why she does not offer "five suggestions on how to proceed" in which the reader will learn "What is to be Done."[62] Such prescriptiveness would foreclose context and contingency, whereas Butler expresses the belief that political decisions are made in a "lived moment" that cannot always be theoretically anticipated.[63] Indeed, Butler recognizes that "life" itself is a site of contest and an unstable term whose meanings are multiple and debatable, so rather than setting out to define "life," her works prompt another fundamental question: what do humans require in order to maintain and reproduce the conditions of their own livability?[64] The impetus towards livability (again, it is a normative one) involves conceptualizing possible lives and arranging for their institutional acceptance and support. In this sense, "to live," as Butler defines it, is to live a life politically – in other words, to recognize one's relation to others, one's relation to power, and one's responsibility to strive for a collective, more inclusive future. This does not mean that the direction of radical democratic politics is known or foreclosed in advance, and Butler continues to insist on the ethical values of openness and "unknowingness," since living in the challenge of difference without attempting to kill or sublate it will also mean remaining open to the tensions and instabilities of democratic politics and the fundamental categories it interrogates and contests. This is a kind of political and philosophical negative capability, which Butler identifies as the need "to know unknowingness at the core of what we know, and what we need," once again validating incompletion as an ethical condition of radical democracy.[65]

IV

The continuing importance of Butler's formulations of identity, subjectivity, sexuality, and gender makes the publication of a selection of her texts particularly timely. Just a glance at Eddie Yeghiayan's excellent, exhaustive bibliography of Butler's works and those which reference or draw from her (there are literally hundreds of the latter), reveals the extent of her influence in, among other fields, queer theory, feminist theory, "race" studies, film studies, literary studies, sociology, politics, and philosophy.[66] Many critics have acknowledged the impact of Butler's ideas:[67] for example, Lois McNay describes the crucial role of Butler's work in pushing feminist understandings of gender identity beyond the polarities of the essentialist debate, while the "Judith Butler" entry in the *Biographical Dictionary of Twentieth-Century Philosophers* identifies the importance of performativity in a number of critical fields, again including feminist theory.[68] This assertion is borne out in (among others) Vikki Bell's article "Mimesis as Cultural Survival," where Butler's theorizations of gender identities as performative and mimetic are intelligently and usefully deployed in the contexts of race, racism, and ethnicity.[69]

Many readers who have had no direct contact with Butler's works are likely to have encountered her ideas in other contexts, and it is hoped that this *Reader* will encourage a fuller knowledge of both familiar and lesser-known formulations. Where possible, whole texts have been included, while an attempt has also been made to represent the range of Butler's political, philosophical, and theoretical engagements. Butler herself has been actively involved in selecting the texts included here, so that if there is some sense in which this book is "doing Butler" it might also be said that she is "doing herself." Of course, this is not to imply that the *Reader* is an exercise in self-presentation, nor is Butler attempting to have the last word on her ideas and how readers interpret them. As she acknowledges at the end of *Bodies That Matter*, one of the consequences of the theoretical decentering of the subject is a concomitant decentering of the author herself, whereby her writing becomes "the site of a necessary and inevitable expropriation." And yet Butler is also fully aware of the political corollaries of yielding intellectual ownership; as she puts it: "the taking up, reforming, deforming of one's words does open up a difficult future terrain of community, one in which the hope of ever fully recognizing oneself in the terms by which one signifies is sure to be disappointed."[70] One of the aims of this *Reader* is to open up new, "difficult" terrains of community which may lead to the productive, proliferative appropriations Butler acknowledges in her characterization of critical writing and response, as well as in her theorizations of the ontological subject.

The chronological arrangement of texts (apart from the articles on Robert Mapplethorpe and Rodney King, which accompany the extract from *Excitable Speech*) is not intended to imply that Butler's ideas have unfolded and developed according to a straightforward, teleological line of thought. As much as anything, the *Reader* has been structured to facilitate ease of reference, although it will be useful to bear in mind the implicit "framing" that occurs when texts are decontextualized, abbreviated, relocated – in short, edited. Accordingly, I would draw attention to the fact that although where possible the principle of completeness has been followed in editing this *Reader*, a number of the texts are selections taken from books, articles, or chapters which were too long to reproduce in their entirety. It is hoped that the republication of lesser-known but nonetheless important pieces will prove useful and convenient, and yet notwithstanding the benefits of textual accessibility, it must be said that there is no "quick route" to Butler's work that will substitute for the careful, ruminative method of reading that, like Nietzsche, she recommends as a vital practice in the ongoing task of critique.

Notes

1   "What Is Critique?" See pp. 302–22.
2   Friedrich Nietzsche, *On the Genealogy of Morals*, 5: "If this text strikes anyone as unintelligible and far from easy listening, the blame, as I see it, does not necessarily rest with me. The text is clear enough, assuming in the first place, as I do, that one has put some effort into reading my earlier writings ... Admittedly, to practise reading as an *art* ... requires one thing above all, and it is something which today more than ever has been thoroughly unlearnt – a fact which explains why it will be some time before my writings are 'readable' – and it is something for which one must be practically bovine and certainly *not* a 'modern man': that is to say, rumination." For Butler's comments on reading, writing and "difficulty," see also "Changing the Subject," pp. 327–8 below.
3   *Gender Trouble*, preface to anniversary edition, p. xxvi. See also p. 103 below.
4   "Giving an Account of Myself," Spinoza Lecture 2002. Forthcoming in *Diacritics*.
5   "Ethical Ambivalence," in *The Turn to Ethics*, ed. Marjorie Garber, Beatrice Hanssen, and Rebecca L. Walkovitz (New York: Routledge, 2000), 15, 26–7.
6   "Giving an Account of Myself," 4.
7   Butler's work has been translated into over 20 languages. *Gender Trouble* alone has been translated into German, Japanese, Korean, Romanian, Dutch, Croatian, Slovenian, Hungarian, Spanish, Chinese, Slovakian, Serbian, Finnish, Ukranian, Portuguese, Turkish, Norwegian, Bulgarian, Russian.

8 "On Speech, Race and Melancholia. An Interview with Judith Butler," *Theory, Culture & Society* 16: 2 (1999), 167–74.
9 See "Variations on Sex and Gender. Beauvoir, Wittig, Foucault," 1987, reprinted below pp. 23–38.
10 "Variations on Sex and Gender," p. 26 below.
11 "Changing the Subject," p. 339 below; *Gender Trouble*, pp. xxii, xxvi.
12 *Bodies That Matter*, 18, 116–17.
13 The point is Dominic Rainsford's: he argues that Butler takes a step beyond the "endless waiting and listening of the Levinasian stance" by not simply ceding to the other, but asking the other "who are you?" Dominic Rainsford, "Solitary Walkers, Encountering Blocks: Epistemology and Ethics in Romanticism and Lord Art," *European Journal of English Studies*, special issue on Ethics and Literature, 7:2 (2003), 177–92.
14 In "Giving an Account of Myself."
15 "Changing the Subject," p. 328 below.
16 *Gender Trouble*,
17 For Butler on genealogy, see "Revisiting Bodies and Pleasures," *Theory, Culture & Society* 16:2 (1999), 15.
18 See below pp. 245–56 for a fuller discussion of melancholia. Performativity, melancholia, and agency are also considered in the individual introductions to Butler's texts.
19 See preface to the paperback edition, reprinted below, p. 47.
20 See "Gender as Performance," in *A Critical Sense*, 116.
21 Jacques Derrida, "Devant la loi," in *Philosophy and Literature*, ed. A. Phillips Griffiths, (Cambridge: Cambridge University Press, 1984).
22 Butler occasionally uses the term "deconstruction" to describe her theorizations of the subject; see for example *Bodies That Matter*, 30, *Contingency, Hegemony, Universality*, 264.
23 "Ethical Ambivalence," 17.
24 "Ethical Ambivalence," 16–17.
25 For example, Butler calls *Bodies That Matter* "a poststructuralist rewriting of discursive performativity as it operates in the materialization of sex." *Bodies*, 12. For Butler on "postmodern," see "For a Careful Reading," in *Feminist Contentions*, 133.
26 "Sex and Gender in Simone de Beauvoir's *Second Sex*" and "Variations on Sex and Gender. Beauvoir, Wittig, Foucault"; *Gender Trouble*, 1999 edition, x.
27 Jacques Lacan, *Écrits. A Selection* (1977).
28 See, for example, the preface to the 1999 Anniversary edition of *Gender Trouble*, pp. 94–103 below.
29 *Contingency, Hegemony, Universality*, 41, 174, 267.
30 The phrase is from "Variations".
31 *On the Genealogy of Morals*, 29; *Gender Trouble*, 25.
32 For performative utterances, see J. L. Austin, *How to Do Things With Words* (Cambridge: Harvard University Press, 1962); for interpellation see Louis Althusser,

"Ideology and Ideological State Apparatuses," in *Lenin and Philosophy and Other Essays*, trans. Ben Brewster (London: New Left Books, 1969).

33   *Bodies That Matter*, 7.

34   *Bodies That Matter*, 8.

35   "Giving an Account of Myself"; *The Pyschic Life of Power*, 164.

36   See *Bodies That Matter*, 2–3.

37   See *Gender Trouble*, 63. Freud writes that after relinquishing her father as a primary love-object the girl "will bring her masculinity into prominence and identify with her father (that is, with the object that has been lost) instead of with her mother. This will clearly depend on whether the masculinity in her disposition – *whatever that is* – is strong enough [i.e. to identify with her father]." *The Ego and the Id*, 372, my emphasis.

38   *Gender Trouble*, 77.

39   The Hegelian scene is analyzed in the first chapter of *Subjects of Desire* (reprinted below, pp. 48–89), and again in chapter 1 of *Psychic*, where Butler gives a psychoanalytic reading of Foucault and a Foucauldian reading of psychoanalysis.

40   "Giving an Account of Myself".

41   *The Psychic Life of Power*, 195–6.

42   "Giving an Account of Myself".

43   See "Changing the Subject," p. 333 below, where Butler asserts that "the semantic life of the term will exceed the intention of the strategist and . . . as it travels through discourse it can take on new ontological meanings and become established in ways one never intended."

44   See *Contingency, Hegemony, Universality*, 177.

45   Ibid., 264.

46   See *Excitable Speech*, 16, *Bodies That Matter*, 30, "Contingent Foundations," 15 (in *Feminists Theorize the Political*).

47   *Bodies That Matter*, 7.

48   For the failure of interpellation, see *The psychic Life of Power*, 129, 197; *Bodies that Matter*, 122.

49   *Gender Trouble*, xxvi.

50   *Bodies That Matter*, 122–3; "Construction is not opposed to agency; it is the necessary scene of agency," *Gender Trouble*, 147; and "Contingent Foundations," 15.

51   See "Variations on Sex and Gender," pp. 23–37 below.

52   See "Variations" and "Changing the Subject."

53   For Butler's discussions of Herculine Barbin see "Foucault and the Paradox of Bodily Descriptions," 607; "Variations on Sex and Gender," pp. 33–4 below; *Gender Trouble*, 31–2, 120, 123–35.

54   For discussions of theatre and identity, see Sue-Ellen Case, *Feminism and Theatre* (Basingstoke: Macmillan, 1988); Sue-Ellen Case (ed.), *Performing Feminisms: Feminist Critical Theory and Theatre* (Baltimore: Johns Hopkins University Press, 1990); Ann Pellegrini, *Performance Anxieties: Staging Psychoanalysis, Staging Race* (New York: Routledge, 1997).

55 See the preface to *Bodies That Matter* where Butler explicitly rejects this analogy. *Bodies That Matter*, x.

56 See "Sexual Inversions."

57 See preface to the anniversary edition of *Gender Trouble*, reprinted below, p. 103.

58 Cf. also Emmanuel Levinas on killing and death: "[T]here are a variety of ways to kill. It isn't always just a mater of killing, say, with a knife. The everyday killing with a good conscience, the killing in all innocence – there is such a thing as well!" "Being-Toward-Death," 132, in *Is It Righteous to Be? Interviews with Emmanuel Levinas*, ed. Jill Robbins (Stanford: Stanford University Press, 2001).

59 For Butler on physical death, see "Sexual Inversions."

60 "The symbolic – that register of regulatory ideality – is also and always a racial industry, indeed, [it is] the reiterated practice of *racializing* interpellations," *Bodies That Matter*, 18.

61 In the preface to the anniversary edition of *Gender Trouble*, Butler also warns that subversive practices risk becoming "deadening clichés" when they are repeated in a commodity culture where "subversion" possesses a certain market value. See p. 99 below.

62 "On Speech, Race and Melancholia. An Interview with Judith Butler," 167.

63 Ibid.

64 "See for example Judith Butler, *Precarious Life: The Powers of Mourning and Violence* (London and New York: Verso, 2004 forthcoming)", "What Is Critique?", 20.

65 "The End of Sexual Difference." In *Feminism at the End of the Millennium*, ed. Elizabeth Bronfen and Misha Kavka (New York: Columbia university Press, 2001).

66 For Yeghiayan's bibliographies, see http://sun3.lib.uci.edu/individual/scctr/Wellek/butler/html.

67 For critics on Butler's influence, see for example Bruce Robbins, review of *Subjects of Desire*, in *London Review of Books*, November 2, 2000; Jonathan Dollimore, "Bisexuality, Heterosexuality, and Wishful Theory," *Textual Practice* 10:3 (1996), 533; Susan Bordo, *Unbearable Weight: Feminism, Western Culture, and the Body* (Berkeley: California University Press, 1993), 290; Sally O'Driscoll, "Outlaw Readings: Beyond Queer Theory," *Signs: Journal of Women in Culture and Society* 22:1 (1996), 31.

68 Margrit Shildrick, "Judith Butler," in Stuart Brown, Diané Collinson, Robert Wilkinson (eds.), *Biographical Dictionary of Twentieth-Century Philosophers* (Oxford: Blackwell, 1996). Lois McNay "Subject, Psyche and Agency: The Work of Judith Butler," *Theory, Culture & Society* 16.2 (1999), 175.

69 Vikki Bell, "Mimesis as Cultural Survival: Judith Butler and Anti-Semitism," *Theory, Culture and Society* 16:2 (1999), 133–61.

70 *Bodies That Matter*, 241–2.

Part I

Sex, Gender Performativity, and the Matter of Bodies

Variations on Sex and Gender:
Beauvoir, Wittig, Foucault (1987)

Introduction

Even if one accepts Simone de Beauvoir's postulation that "one is not born, but rather becomes a woman," received wisdom would apparently still have it that sex is an immutable essence, so that it should at least be possible to say that people are born male or female. Not according to Butler in this early article and in another, similar piece published a year earlier, both of which start out from the premise that gender is unnatural, a cultural construction (see "Sex and Gender in Simone de Beauvoir's *Second Sex*," 1986). Reading Beauvoir through Monique Wittig and Michel Foucault, in "Variations on Sex and Gender" Butler provides what she calls "a schematic outline of a theory of gender invention," although throughout the article she is careful to emphasize that to talk in terms of gender's "inventiveness" is not to imply that it is a radical act of creation. Rather, gender is "an originating activity incessantly taking place," a construct, a process, a project occurring in a culture where it is impossible to be "without" (i.e. lacking or outside) gender. Jean-Paul Sartre's ambivalence towards the Cartesian mind/body dualism leads Butler to argue that the body is neither static nor self-identical but something that is lived and experienced in specific contexts. As Beauvoir puts it, consciousness *exists* one's body, which, in the context of culture, involves "becoming" one's gender.

One way of overcoming the Cartesian mind/body dualism is to argue that sex is *already* gender, since the body/mind split no longer makes sense if you claim, as both Butler and Beauvoir do, that gender is a way of "doing" the body. As Butler puts it, we can only know sex *through* gender, and although we "become" our genders, there is no place outside gender which precedes this becoming. Sex, as Butler will claim in *Gender Trouble*, is always already gender: the body does not antedate or "cause" gender, but it is an effect of genders which can only be taken up within existing cultural norms, laws, and taboos which constrain that taking up or "choice."

Clearly, gender is not a static entity, and Butler analyzes how gender identities are taken on and disavowed by subjects who are not, however, engaged in radical acts of

From Seyla Benhabib and Drucilla Cornell (eds.), *Feminism as Critique: Essays on the Politics of Gender in Late Capitalist Societies*, pp. 128–42 and 185 (notes). Oxford: Polity Press, 1987. Reprinted by permission of Blackwell Publishing Ltd/Polity Press.

creation. The moments of gender dislocation which both Butler and Beauvoir acknowledge, reveal the contingency of existing gender identities, and yet the recognition
of gender's instability also brings with it what Butler identifies as the "vertigo and
terror" of losing or leaving one's sanctioned social place. Butler insists that inventiveness
or innovation is more effective than the transcendence of sex and gender for which
Monique Wittig calls in *The Lesbian Body*: this is not the Marcusean dream of sexuality
without power (a dream Wittig appears to entertain), but the subversion and dispersal of
existing forms of power. Indeed, Butler sees Wittig's call for the eradication of sex as
profoundly humanistic, and an unwitting reinforcement of the binaries she seeks to
transcend.

   On the other hand, what Butler calls "postmodern relations of power" present opportunities for the subversion and destabilization of existing gender hierarchies from within
those structures. "[T]he power of binary opposition is diffused through the force of
internal ambiguity," Butler argues, citing as an example Herculine Barbin, the nineteenth-century "hermaphrodite" whose translated journals are published with an introduction by Michel Foucault. By confounding rather than transcending univocal sex and
the binary sex/gender system, Herculine reveals the ways in which anatomy is invested
and defined within binary terms, although Butler appears to concur with Wittig that
sexual difference is created when it is restricted to certain body parts that are pronounced
and identified at birth. The facticity of the body is by no means refuted, and the "vertigo
and terror" generated by a body such as Barbin's which cannot be defined according to
existing binaries, reveals both the mythology and the multiplicity of heterosexuality, even
as it attempts to present itself as univocal and "natural."

   In conclusion, Butler acknowledges that the Foucauldian proliferation of existing power
structures might indeed seem to imply the possibility of radical invention, yet viewed
through a Marxist psychoanalytic lens, it is clear that gender identities are circumscribed
and socially constituted. Gender may be "chosen" only from within the parameters of
culturally available terms which always preexist the subject. To acknowledge, as Marxists
and psychoanalysts do, that the subject is not free to create herself or himself at will,
necessitates scrutinizing language in order to reveal the ontological assumptions underlying terms such as "woman" that disguise and preclude productive gender dissonance
and multiplicity. Again, Marxist and psychoanalytic models constitute a challenge to
current configurations of sexed and gendered identities, while Gayle Rubin's reading of
psychoanalysis as a reconfiguring of kinship structures leads Butler to suggest that
tracing the history of gender may reveal its gradual release from the binary restrictions
within which it has been mired.

   Butler's later work continues to describe gender and sex, the subject and the body, as
effects rather than causes, products of a law (characterized here as a binary or
"dimorphic" gender system) which precedes, produces – indeed *effects* – the subject.
This early article displays many of the philosophical and theoretical preoccupations of
Butler's later work, where psychoanalytic, Foucauldian, and Marxist insights continue to
underpin her theories of gender, sex, and performativity.

"One is not born, but rather becomes, a woman"[1] – Beauvoir's now-famous formulation asserts the noncoincidence of natural and gendered identity. Because what we become is not what we already are, gender is dislodged from sex; the cultural interpretation of sexual attributes is distinguished from the facticity or simple existence of these attributes. The verb "become" contains, however, a consequential ambiguity. Not only are we culturally constructed, but in some sense we construct ourselves. For Beauvoir, to *become* a woman is a purposive and appropriative set of acts, the gradual acquisition of a skill, a "project" in Sartrian terms, to assume a culturally established corporeal style and significance. When "become" is taken to mean "purposefully assume or embody," Beauvoir's declaration seems to shoulder the burden of Sartrian choice. If genders are in some sense chosen, then what happens to the definition of gender as a cultural interpretation of sex, that is, what happens to the ways in which we are, as it were, already culturally interpreted? How can gender be both a matter of choice and cultural construction?

Beauvoir does not claim to be describing a theory of gender identity or gender acquisition in *The Second Sex*, and yet her formulation of gender as a *project* seems to invite speculation on just such a theory. Monique Wittig, a French feminist who wrote an influential article "One is Not Born a Woman" (1978), extends Beauvoir's theory on the ambiguous nature of gender identity, i.e. this cultural self that we become but which we seem to have been all along. The positions of Beauvoir and Wittig, though different in crucial respects, commonly suggest a theory of gender that tries to make cultural sense of the existential doctrine of choice. Gender becomes the corporeal locus of cultural meanings both received and innovated. And "choice" in this context comes to signify a corporeal process of interpretation within a network of deeply entrenched cultural norms.

When the body is conceived as a cultural locus of gender meanings, it becomes unclear what aspects of this body are natural or free of cultural imprint. Indeed, how are we to find the body that preexists its cultural interpretation? If gender is the corporealization of choice, and the acculturation of the corporeal, then what is left of nature, and what has become of sex? If gender is determined in the dialectic between culture and choice, then what role does "sex" serve, and ought we to conclude that the very distinction between sex and gender is anachronistic? Has Beauvoir refuted the original meaning of her famous formulation, or was that declaration more nuanced than we originally guessed? To answer, we must reconstruct Beauvoir's distinction between sex and gender, and consider her theory's present life in the work of Monique Wittig who, in fact, considers the distinction anachronistic. We will then turn to Michel Foucault's rejection of the category of "natural sex," compare it with Wittig's position, and attempt a reformulation of gender as a cultural project.

Sartrian Bodies and Cartesian Ghosts

The notion that we somehow choose our genders poses an ontological puzzle. It might at first seem impossible that we can occupy a position outside of gender in order to stand back and choose our genders. If we are always already gendered, immersed in gender, what sense does it make to say that we choose what we already are? Not only does the thesis appear tautological, but in so far as it postulates a choosing self prior to its own chosen gender, it seems to adopt a Cartesian view of the self, an egological structure that lives and thrives prior to language and cultural life. This view of the self runs counter to contemporary findings on the linguistic construction of personal agency and, as is the problem with Cartesian egos everywhere, their ontological distance from language and cultural life precludes the possibility of their eventual verification. If Beauvoir's claim is to have cogency, if it is true that we "become" our genders through some kind of volitional and appropriative set of acts, then she must mean something other than an unsituated Cartesian act. That personal agency is a logical prerequisite for *taking on* a gender does not presuppose that this agency is itself disembodied; indeed, it is our genders that we become, and not our bodies. If Beauvoir's theory is to be understood as freed of the Cartesian ghost, we must first establish her view of embodied identity, and consider her musings on the possibilities of disembodied souls.

Whether consciousness has any discrete ontological status apart from the body is a question that Sartre answers inconsistently throughout *Being and Nothingness*.[2] This ambivalence toward a Cartesian mind/body dualism reemerges, although less seriously, in Beauvoir's *The Second Sex*. In fact, in *The Second Sex* we can see an effort to radicalize the one implication of Sartre's theory concerned with establishing an embodied notion of freedom. The chapter on "The Body" in *Being and Nothingness* contains the echoes of Cartesianism which haunt his thinking, but also gives evidence of his own efforts to expel the Cartesian ghost. Although Sartre argues that the body is coextensive with personal identity (it is a "perspective" that one lives), he also suggests that consciousness is in some sense beyond the body ("My body is a *point of departure* which I *am* and which at the same time I surpass"). Instead of refuting Cartesianism, Sartre's theory assimilates the Cartesian moment as an immanent and partial feature of consciousness; Sartre's theory seeks to conceptualize the disembodied or transcendent feature of personal identity as paradoxically, yet essentially, related to consciousness as embodied. The duality of consciousness as both embodied and transcendent is intrinsic to personal identity, and the effort to locate personal identity exclusively in one or the other is, according to Sartre, a project in bad faith.

Although Sartre's references to "surpassing" the body may be read as pre-supposing a mind/body dualism, we need to understand this self-transcendence as itself a corporeal movement, and thus rethink both our usual ideas of "transcendence" and of the mind/body dualism itself. For Sartre, one may surpass the body, but this does not mean that one definitively gets beyond the body; the subversive paradox consists in the fact that the body itself is a surpassing. The body is not a static or self-identical phenomenon, but a mode of intentionality, a directional force and mode of desire. As a condition of access to the world, the body is a being comported beyond itself, referring to the world and thereby revealing its own ontological status as a referential reality. For Sartre, the body is lived and experienced as the context and medium for all human strivings.[3] Because for Sartre all human beings strive after possibilities not yet realized, human beings are to that extent "beyond" themselves. This *ek-static* condition is itself a corporeal experience; the body is thus experienced as a mode of becoming. Indeed, for Sartre the natural body only exists in the mode of being surpassed: "We can never apprehend this contingency as such in so far as our body is *for us*; for we are a choice, and for us to be is to choose ourselves... this inapprehensible body is precisely the necessity that *there be a choice*, that I do not exist *all at once*."[4]

Beauvoir does not so much refute Sartre as take him at his non-Cartesian best.[5] Sartre writes in *Being and Nothingness* that "it would be best to say, using 'exist' as a transitive verb, that consciousness *exists* its body."[6] The transitive form of "exist" is not far removed from Beauvoir's disarming use of "become," and Beauvoir's concept of becoming a gender seems both a radicalization and concretization of the Sartrian formulation. In transposing the identification of corporeal existence and "becoming" onto the scene of sex and gender, Beauvoir appropriates the ontological necessity of the paradox, but the tension in her theory does not reside between being "in" and "beyond" the body, but in the move from the natural to the acculturated body. That one is not born, but rather becomes, a woman does not imply that this "becoming" traverses a path from disembodied freedom to cultural embodiment. Indeed, one is one's body from the start, and only thereafter becomes one's gender. The movement from sex to gender is internal to embodied life, a sculpting of the original body into a cultural form. To mix Sartrian phraseology with Beauvoir's, we might say that to "exist" one's body in culturally concrete terms means, at least partially, to become one's gender.

Although we "become" our genders in Beauvoir's view, the temporal movement of this becoming does not follow a linear progression. The origin of gender is not temporally discrete precisely because gender is not suddenly originated at some point in time after which it is fixed in form. In an important sense, gender is not traceable to a definable origin because it itself is an originating activity incessantly taking place. No longer understood as a product of cultural and psychic relations long past, gender is a contemporary way of organizing past and future cultural norms, a way of situating oneself in and through those norms, an active style of living one's body in the world.

Gender as Choice

One chooses one's gender, but one does not choose it from a distance, which signals an ontological juncture between the choosing agent and the chosen gender. The Cartesian space of the deliberate "chooser" is fictional, but if the distanced deliberations of the spectator are not the choices whereof Beauvoir speaks, then how are we to understand the choice at the origin of gender? Beauvoir's view of gender as an incessant project, a daily act of reconstruction and interpretation, draws upon Sartre's doctrine of prereflective choice and gives that abstract epistemological structure a concrete cultural meaning. Prereflective choice is a tacit and spontaneous act which Sartre terms "quasi-knowledge." Not wholly conscious, but nevertheless accessible to consciousness, it is the kind of choice we make and only later realize that we have made. Beauvoir seems to rely on this notion of choice in referring to the kind of volitional act through which gender is assumed. Taking on a gender is not possible at a moment's notice, but is a subtle and strategic project, laborious and for the most part covert. Becoming a gender is an impulsive yet mindful process of interpreting a cultural reality laden with sanctions, taboos, and prescriptions. The choice to assume a certain kind of body, to live or wear one's body a certain way, implies a world of already established corporeal styles. To choose a gender is to interpret received gender norms in a way that reproduces and organizes them anew. Less a radical act of creation, gender is a tacit project to renew a cultural history in one's own corporeal terms. This is not a prescriptive task we must endeavor to do, but one in which we have been endeavoring all along.

By scrutinizing the mechanism of agency and appropriation, Beauvoir is attempting, in my mind, to infuse the analysis of women's oppression with emancipatory potential. Oppression is not a self-contained system that either confronts individuals as a theoretical object or generates them as its cultural pawns. It is a dialectical force that requires individual participation on a large scale in order to maintain its malignant life.

Beauvoir does not address directly the burden of freedom that gender presents, but we can extrapolate from her position how constraining gender norms work to subdue the exercise of gender freedom. The social constraints upon gender compliance and deviation are so great that most people feel deeply wounded if they are told that they exercise their manhood or womanhood improperly. In so far as social existence requires an unambiguous gender affinity, it is not possible to exist in a socially meaningful sense outside of established gender norms. The fall from established gender boundaries initiates a sense of radical dislocation which can assume a metaphysical significance. If human existence is always gendered existence, then to stray outside of established gender is in some sense to put one's very existence into question. In these moments of gender dislocation in which we realize that it is hardly necessary that we be the genders we have become, we confront the burden of choice intrinsic to living as a man or a woman or some other gender identity, a freedom made burdensome through social constraint.

The anguish and terror of leaving a prescribed gender or of trespassing upon another gender territory testifies to the social constraints upon gender interpretation as well as to the necessity *that there be* an interpretation, i.e., to the essential freedom at the origin of gender. Similarly, the widespread difficulty in accepting motherhood, for example, as an institutional rather than an instinctual reality expresses this same interplay of constraint and freedom. The effort to interpret maternal feelings as organic necessities discloses a desire to disguise motherhood as an optional practice. If motherhood becomes a choice, then what else is possible? This kind of questioning often engenders vertigo and terror over the possibility of losing social sanctions, of leaving a solid social station and place. That this terror is so well known gives the most credence to the notion that gender identity rests on the unstable bedrock of human invention.

Embodiment and Autonomy

Beauvoir's analysis of the body takes its bearings within the cultural situation in which men have traditionally been associated with the disembodied or transcendent feature of human existence and women with the bodily and immanent feature of human existence. Her own view of an embodied identity that "incorporates" transcendence subscribes to neither position. Although she occasionally seems to embrace a view of authority modeled on the disembodied transcendence of consciousness, her criticism of this disembodied perspective suggests that another version of autonomy is implicitly at work in her theory.

Women are "Other" according to Beauvoir in so far as they are defined by a masculine perspective that seeks to safeguard its own disembodied status through identifying women generally with the bodily sphere. Masculine dis-embodiment is only possible on the condition that women occupy their bodies as their essential and enslaving identities. If women *are* their bodies (to be distinguished from "existing" their bodies, which implies living their bodies as projects or bearers of created meanings), if women are only their bodies, if their consciousness and freedom are only so many disguised permutations of bodily need and necessity, then women have, in effect, exclusively monopolized the bodily sphere of life. By defining women as "Other," men are able through the shortcut of definition to dispose of their bodies, to make themselves other than their bodies – a symbol potentially of human decay and transience, of limita-tion generally – and to make their bodies other than themselves. From this belief that the body is Other, it is not a far leap to the conclusion that others *are* their bodies, while the masculine "I" is a noncorporeal soul. The body rendered as Other – the body repressed or denied and, then, projected – reemerges for this "I" as the view of others as essentially body. Hence, women become the Other; they come to embody corporeality itself. This redundancy becomes their essence, and existence as a woman becomes what Hegel termed "a motionless tautology."

Beauvoir's dialectic of self and Other argues the limits of a Cartesian version of disembodied freedom, and criticizes implicitly the model of autonomy upheld by these masculine gender norms. The pursuit of disembodiment is necessarily deceived because the body can never really be denied; its denial becomes the condition of its emergence in alien form. Disembodiment be-comes a way of existing one's body in the mode of denial. And the denial of the body – as in Hegel's dialectic of master and slave – reveals itself as nothing other than the embodiment of denial.

The Body as Situation

Beauvoir suggests an alternative to the gender polarity of masculine disembodi-ment and feminine enslavement to the body in her notion of the body as a "situation." The body as situation has at least a twofold meaning. As a locus of cultural interpretations, the body is a material reality that has already been located and defined within a social context. The body is also the situation of having to take up and interpret that set of received interpretations. As a field of interpretive possibilities, the body is a locus of the dialectical process of interpreting anew a historical set of interpretations which have already informed corporeal style. The body becomes a peculiar nexus of culture and choice, and "existing" one's body becomes a personal way of taking up and reinterpreting received gender norms. To the extent that gender norms function under the aegis of social constraints, the reinterpretation of those norms through the proliferation and variation of corporeal styles becomes a very concrete and accessible way of politicizing personal life.

If we accept the body as a cultural situation, then the notion of a natural body and, indeed, a natural "sex" seem increasingly suspect. The limits to gender, the range of possibilities for a lived interpretation of a sexually differentiated anatomy, seem less restricted by anatomy than by the weight of the cultural institutions that have conventionally interpreted anatomy. Indeed, it becomes unclear when we take Beauvoir's formulation to its unstated consequences, whether gender need be in any way linked with sex, or whether this linkage is itself cultural convention. If gender is a way of existing one's body, and one's body is a situation, a field of cultural possibilities both received and reinterpreted, then both gender and sex seem to be thoroughly cultural affairs. Gender seems less a function of anatomy than one of its possible uses: "the body of woman is one of the essential elements in her situation in the world. But that body is not enough to define her as woman; there is no true living reality except as manifested by the conscious individual through activities and in the bosom of society."[7]

The Body Politic

If the natural body – and natural "sex" – is a fiction, Beauvoir's theory seems implicitly to ask whether sex was not gender all along. Monique Wittig formulates this challenge to natural "sex" explicitly. Although Wittig and Beauvoir occupy very different sides of the feminist political spectrum in contemporary France, they are nevertheless joined theoretically in their refusal of essentialist doctrines of femininity. Wittig's article, "One is Not Born a Woman," takes its title from Beauvoir's stated formulation, and was initially presented at the Simone de Beauvoir conference in New York City in 1979. Although that piece does not mention Beauvoir after the first few paragraphs, we can nevertheless read it as an effort to make explicit Beauvoir's tacit theory of gender acquisition.

For Wittig, the very discrimination of "sex" takes place within a political and linguistic network that presupposes, and hence requires, that sex remain dyadic. The demarcation of sexual difference does not *precede* the interpretation of that difference, but this demarcation is itself an interpretive act laden with normative assumptions about a binary gender system. Discrimination is always "discrimination," binary opposition always serves the purposes of hierarchy.

Wittig realizes that her position is counterintuitive, but it is precisely the political education of intuition that she wants to expose. For Wittig, when we name sexual difference, we create it; we restrict our understanding of relevant sexual parts to those that aid in the process of reproduction, and thereby render heterosexuality an ontological necessity. What distinguishes the sexes are those anatomical features, which either bear on reproduction directly, or are construed to aid in its eventual success. Hence, Wittig argues that erogeneity, the body's sexual responsiveness, is restricted through the institutionalization of binary sexual difference; her question: why don't we name as sexual features our mouths, hands, and backs? Her answer: we only name sexual – read, feel sexual – those features functional in reproductive activity.

Her claim is counterintuitive because we see sexual difference constantly, and it seems to us an immediate given of experience. She argues:

> Sex . . . is taken as an "immediate given," a sensible given, "physical features," belonging to a natural order. But what we believe to be a physical and direct perception is only a sophisticated and mythic construction, an "imaginary formation," which reinterprets physical features (in themselves as neutral as others but marked by a social system) through the network of relationships in which they are perceived.[9]

Like Beauvoir, Wittig understands gender as a proscription and a task; in effect, gender is a norm that we struggle to embody. In Wittig's words, "We have been compelled in our bodies and our minds to correspond, feature by feature, with the *idea* of nature that has been established for us."[9] That we experience ourselves or others as "men" and "women" are political categories and not natural facts."

Wittig's theory is alarming for a number of reasons, foremost among them the intimation that discourse about sex creates the misnomer of anatomy. If this were Wittig's point, it would seem that sexual difference has no necessary material foundation, and that seeing differences among bodies, which turn out to be binary, is a deep delusion indulged in by cultures in an almost universal fashion. Luckily, I do not think this is Wittig's claim. Surely, differences do exist which are binary, material and distinct, and we are not in the grips of political ideology when we assent to that fact. Wittig contests the social practice of valorizing certain anatomical features as being definitive not only of anatomical sex but of sexual identity. She points out that there are other kinds of differences among people, differences in shape and size, in earlobe formation and the lengths of noses, but we do not ask when a child enters the world what species of earlobe it has. We immediately ask about certain sexually differentiated anatomical traits because we assume that those traits will in some sense determine that child's social destiny, and that destiny, whatever else it is, is structured by a gender system predicated upon the alleged naturalness of binary oppositions and, consequently, heterosexuality. Hence, in differentiating infants in the ways that we do, we recapitulate heterosexuality as a precondition for human identity, and posit this constraining norm in the guise of a natural fact.

Wittig thus does not dispute the existence or facticity of sexual distinction, but questions the isolation and valorization of certain kinds of distinctions over others. Wittig's *Lesbian Body* is the literary portrayal of an erotic struggle to rewrite the relevant distinctions constitutive of sexual identity. Different features of the female body are detached from their usual places, and remembered, quite literally. The reclamation of diverse bodily parts as sources of erotic pleasure is, for Wittig, the undoing or rewriting of binary restriction imposed at birth. Erogeneity is restored to the entire body through a process of sometimes violent struggle. The female body is no longer recognizable as such; it no longer appears as an "immediate given of experience"; it is disfigured, reconstructed, and reconceived. The emancipation of this consists in the dissolution of the binary framework, in the emergence of essential chaos, polymorphousness, the precultural innocence of "sex."

It might well seem that Wittig has entered into a utopian ground that leaves the rest of us situated souls waiting impatiently this side of her liberating imaginary space. After all, the *Lesbian Body* is a fantasy, and it is not clear whether we readers are supposed to recognize a potential course of action in that text, or simply be dislocated from our usual assumptions about bodies and pleasure. Has Wittig decided that heterosexual norms are cultural norms while lesbian norms are somehow natural? Is the lesbian body that she posits as somehow being prior to and exceeding binary restrictions really a body at all? Has the lesbian preempted the place of the psychoanalytic polymorph in Wittig's particular sexual cosmogony?

Rather than argue for the superiority of a nonheterosexual culture, Wittig envisions a sexless society, and argues that sex, like class, is a construct that must inevitably be deposed. Indeed, Wittig's program seems profoundly humanistic in its call for an eradication of sex. She argues that

> a new personal and subjective definition for all humankind can be found beyond the categories of sex (man and woman) and that the advent of individual subjects demands first destroying the category of sex, ending the use of them, and rejecting all sciences which still use these categories as their fundamentals (practically all social sciences).[10]

On the one hand, Wittig calls for a transcendence of sex altogether, but her theory might equally well lead to an inverse conclusion, to the dissolution of binary restrictions through the *proliferation* of genders.

Because the category of "sex" only makes sense in terms of a binary discourse on sex in which "men" and "women" exhaust the possibilities of sex, and relate to each other as complementary opposites, the category of "sex" is always subsumed under the discourse of heterosexuality. Hence, Wittig argues that a lesbian is not a woman, because to be a woman means to be set in a binary relation with a man. Wittig does not argue that the lesbian is another sex or gender, but claims that the lesbian "is the only concept I know which is beyond the category of sex."[11] But even as Wittig describes the lesbian in relation to this binary opposition of "man" and "woman," she underscores the fact that this being beyond opposition is still a way of being related to that opposition, indeed a binary relation at that. In order that the lesbian avoid being caught up in another binary opposition, i.e., the opposition to heterosexuality itself, "being lesbian" must itself become a multiple cultural phenomenon, a gender with no univocal essence. If binary oppositions imply hierarchies, then postulating a sexual identity "beyond" culture promises to set up yet another pair of oppositions that, in turn, suggest another hierarchical arrangement; hegemonic heterosexual culture will stand as the "Other" to that postcultural subject, and a new hierarchy may well replace the old – at least on a theoretical level. Moreover, to define culture as necessarily preoccupied with the reproduction of binary oppositions is to support a structuralist assumption that seems neither valid nor politically beneficial. After all, if binary restrictions are to be overcome in experience, they must meet their dissolution in the creation of new cultural forms. As Beauvoir says, and Wittig should know, there is no meaningful reference to a "human reality" outside the terms of culture. The political program for overcoming binary restrictions ought to be concerned, then, with cultural innovation rather than myths of transcendence.

Wittig's theory finds support in Foucault's first volume of *The History of Sexuality* which holds improbable but significant consequences for feminist theory. In that Foucault seeks to subvert the binary configuration of power, the juridical model of oppressor and oppressed, he offers some strategies for the subversion of gender hierarchy. For Foucault, the binary organization of power, including that based on strict gender polarities, is effected through a multiplication of productive and strategic forms of power. Hence, Foucault is interested no longer in the Marcusean dream of a sexuality without power, but is concerned with subverting and dissipating the existing terms of juridical power. In this sense, Wittig is paradoxically closer to Marcuse's theory of sexual emancipation as she does imagine a sexual identity and a sexuality freed of relations of domination. In effect, Foucault writes in the disillusioned aftermath of Marcuse's *Eros and Civilization*, rejecting a progressive model of history based on the gradual release of an intrinsically liberating *eros*. For Foucault, the *eros* which is liberated is always already structured culturally, saturated with power dynamics, thus implicitly raising the same political dilemmas as the repressive culture it was meant to liberate. Like Wittig, however, Foucault does reject "natural sex" as a primary given, and attempts to understand how "the deployment of sexuality... was what established this notion of 'sex'."[12] The category of sex belongs to a juridical model of power that assumes a binary opposition between the "sexes." The subversion of binary opposites does not result in their transcendence for Foucault, but in their proliferation to a point where binary oppositions become meaningless in a context where multiple differences, not restricted to binary differences, abound. Foucault seems to suggest "proliferation" and "assimilation" as strategies to diffuse the age-old power game of oppressor and oppressed. His tactic, if that it can be called, is not to transcend power relations, but to multiply their various configurations, so that the juridical model of power as oppression and regulation is no longer hegemonic. When oppressors themselves are oppressed, and the oppressed develop alternative forms of power, we are in the presence of postmodern relations of power. For Foucault, this interaction results in yet new and more complicated valences of power, and the power of binary opposition is diffused through the force of internal ambiguity.

For Foucault, the notion of natural sex is neither primary nor univocal. One's "sex," i.e., one's anatomically differentiated sexual self, is intimately linked to "sex" as an activity and a drive. The word compromises a variety of meanings that have been clustered under a single name to further certain strategic ends of hegemonic culture:

> The notion of "sex" made it possible to group together, in an artificial unity, anatomic elements, biological functions, conducts, sensations, and pleasures, and it enabled one to make use of this fictitious unity as a causal principle, an omnipresent meaning, a secret to be discovered everywhere: sex was thus able to function as a unique signifier and as a universal signified.[13]

Foucault no more wants to dispute the material reality of anatomically discrete bodies than does Wittig, but asks instead how the materiality of the body comes to signify culturally specific ideas. Hence, he imagines at the close of volume I of *The History of Sexuality* "a history of bodies [which shows] the manner in which what is most material and most vital in them has been invested."[14]

Foucault conducts a phenomenology of such an "investment" in publishing the journals of Herculine Barbin, a nineteenth-century hermaphrodite whose anatomical ambiguity culminates in an eventual "confession" and suicide.[15] In his introduction Foucault insists upon the irrelevance of established gender categories for Alexina's (Herculine's) sexual life:

> One has the impression, at least if one gives credence to Alexina's story, that everything took place in a world of feelings – enthusiasm, pleasure, sorrow, warmth, sweetness, bitterness – where the identity of the partners and above all the enigmatic character around whom everything centered, had no importance. It was a world in which grins hung about without the cat.[16]

Herculine seems to have escaped univocal sex, and hence the binary system governing sex, and represents for Foucault the literalization of an ambiguity in sex and sexual identity which is the suppressed potential of every proper and univocal sex or gender. Herculine Barbin, our hermaphrodite, is neither here nor there, but neither is she in some discrete third place. She is an amalgamation of binary opposites, a particular configuration and conflation of male and female. Because of her uncanny intrusion into the male domain, she is punished and banished by the Church authorities, designed univocally as a male. Herculine does not transcend sex as much as she confuses it, and while we can see her fate as to a certain extent anatomical, it is clear that the legal and medical documents that address her anatomical transgression reveal an urgent social need to keep sex down to just the usual two. Hence, it is not her anatomy, but the ways in which that anatomy is "invested," that causes problems. Her plight reveals in graphic terms the societal urge and strategy to discover and define anatomy within binary terms. Exploding the binary assumption is one of the ways of depriving male hegemony and compulsory heterosexuality of their most treasured of primary premises. When, on the other hand, binary sexual difference is made a function of ontology, then the options for sexual identity are restricted to traditional heterosexual terms; indeed, heterosexuality is itself reduced to a mythical version of itself, disguising its own potential multiplicity beneath a univocal presentation of itself.

Conclusion: Embodying Dissonance

In conclusion, it seems important to note that the challenge to a dyadic gender system that Beauvoir's theory permits and that Wittig and Foucault help to formulate, is also implicitly a challenge to those feminist positions that maintain sexual difference as irreducible, and which seek to give expression to the distinctively feminine side of that binary opposition. If natural sex is a fiction, then the distinctively feminine is a purely historical moment in the development of the category of sex, what Foucault calls, "the most speculative, most ideal, and most internal element in a deployment of sexuality organized by power in its grip on bodies and their materiality."[17]

The schematic outline of a theory of gender invention that I have been sketching here does not overcome the existential pitfalls of Sartrianism by the mere fact of its cultural application. Indeed, with Foucauldian proliferation at hand, we seem to have moved full circle back to a notion of radical invention, albeit one that employs and deploys culturally existent and culturally imaginable conventions. The problem with this theory seems twofold, and in many senses the objections that will surely be raised against these visions are ones that have, in altered form, been raised against the existential thesis from both Marxist and psychoanalytic perspectives. The Marxist problem may be understood as that of the social constitution of personal identity and, by implication, gender identity. I not only choose my gender, and not only choose it within culturally available terms, but on the street and in the world I am always constantly constituted by others, so that my self-styled gender may well find itself in comic or even tragic opposition to the gender that others see me through or with. Hence, even the Foucauldian prescription of radical invention presupposes an agency which, à la Descartes, definitionally eludes the gaze of the Other.

The psychoanalytic objection is perhaps the most trenchant, for psychoanalytic theories of gender identity and gender acquisition tend to insist that what we become is always in some sense what we have always been, although the process of becoming is of oedipal necessity a process of restricting our sexual ambiguity in accord with identity-founding incest taboos. Ambiguity, whether described in the discourse of bisexuality or polymorphousness, is always to be presupposed, and established gender identity both contains and conceals this repressed ambiguity. The proliferation of gender beyond binary oppositions would thus always constitute a return to a pre-oedipal ambiguity which, I suppose, would take us outside of culture as we know it. According to the psychoanalytic perspective, the normative ideal of multiplicitous genders would always be a peculiar mix of memory and fantasy to be understood in the context of an oedipally conditioned subject in an affective quarrel with the incest taboo. This is the stuff of great literature, perhaps, but not necessarily practicable in the cultural struggle to renovate gender relations as we know them. In effect, speaking within this point of view, what I have provided here is a pre-oedipal fantasy that only makes sense in terms of a subject who can never realize this fantasy. In this sense, both the hypothetical Marxist and the psychoanalytic objection would charge that the theory I have presented lacks a reality principle. But, of course, such a charge is tricky, because it is unclear whether the principle governing this reality is a necessary one, or whether other principles of reality might well be "invented," as it were, and whether such counterintuitive principles as these are part of the cultural fantasies that ultimately do come to constitute new organizations of reality. It is not clear to me that reality is something settled once and for all, and we might do well to urge speculation on the dynamic relation between fantasy and the realization of new social realities.

A good deal of French feminist scholarship has been concerned with specifying the nature of the feminine to settle the question of what women want, how that specific pleasure makes itself known, or represents itself obliquely in the rupture of logocentric language. This principle of femininity is sought in the female body, sometimes understood as the pre-oedipal mother and other times understood naturalistically as a pantheistic principle that requires its own kind of language for expression. In these cases, gender is not constituted, but is considered an essential aspect of bodily life, and we come very near the equation of biology and destiny, that conflation of fact and value, which Beauvoir spent her life trying to refute. In an article entitled, "Women can never be defined," Julia Kristeva remarks that "the belief that 'one is a woman' is almost as absurd and obscurantist as the belief that 'one is a man'."[18] Kristeva says "almost as absurd" because there are practical, strategical reasons for maintaining the notion of women as a class regardless of its descriptive emptiness as a term. Indeed, accepting Wittig's argument that "women" is a political category, Kristeva goes on to consider whether it might not be a *useful* political category at that. This brings us back to the Marxist objection proferred above, and yet Kristeva is prepared to forfeit the term altogether when its political efficacy is exhausted. Hence, she concludes, "we must use 'we are women' as an advertisement or slogan for our demands. On a deeper level, however, a woman cannot 'be'; it is something which does not even belong in the order of *being*."[19] Women is thus a false substantive and univocal signifier that disguises and precludes a gender experience internally varied and contradictory. And if women are, to return to Beauvoir, such a mode of becoming that is arrested prematurely, as it were, through the reductive imposition of a substantializing nomenclature, then the release of women's internally complex experience, an experience that would make of the very name "women's experience" an empty signification, might well become released and or precipitated. And here the task is not simply to change language, but to examine language for its ontological assumptions, and to criticize those assumptions for their political consequences. In effect, to understand woman to exist on the metaphysical order of *being* is to understand her as that which is already accomplished, self-identical, static, but to conceive her on the metaphysical order of *becoming* is to invent possibility into her experience, including the possibility of never becoming a substantive, self-identical "woman." Indeed, such substantives will remain empty descriptions, and other forms of active descriptions may well become desirable.

It is not surprising that Beauvoir derives her philosophical framework from existential philosophy, and that Wittig seems more indebted to Beauvoir than to those French feminists who write either for or against Lacan. Nor is it surprising that Foucault's theory of sexuality and his history of bodies is written against the background of Nietzsche's *Will to Power* and the *Genealogy of Morals* whose method of existential critique regularly revealed how values that appear natural can be reduced to their contingent cultural origins.

The psychoanalytic challenge does well to remind us of the deep-rootedness of sexual and gender identity and the Marxist qualification reinforces the notion that how we are constituted is not always our own affair. It may well be that Wittig and Foucault offer (a) new identity/ies which, despite all their qualification, remain utopian. But it is useful to remember Gayle Rubin's reading of psychoanalysis as the reconstruction of kinship structures in the form of modern gender identities.[20] If she is right to understand gender identity as the "trace" of kinship, and to point out that gender has become increasingly free of the vestiges of kinship, then we seem justified in concluding that the history of gender may well reveal the gradual release of gender from its binary restrictions. Moreover, any theoretical effort to discover, maintain, or articulate an essential femininity must confront the following moral and empirical problem: what happens when individual women do not recognize themselves in the theories that explain their unsurpassable essences to them? When the essential feminine is finally articulated, and what we have been calling "women" cannot see themselves in its terms, what then are we to conclude? That these women are deluded, or that they are not women at all? We can argue that women have a more inclusive essence, or we can return to that promising suggestion of Simone de Beauvoir, namely, that women have no essence at all, and hence, no natural necessity, and that, indeed, what we call an essence or a material fact is simply an enforced cultural option which has disguised itself as natural truth.

Notes

1 Simone de Beauvoir, *The Second Sex* (New York: Vintage Press, 1973), 301. Parts of the discussion of Simone de Beauvoir's *The Second Sex* are taken from the author's article "Sex and Gender in Beauvoir's *Second Sex*," *Yale French Studies* 72 (1986).

2 Monique Wittig, "One is Not Born a Woman," *Feminist Issues*, 1, 2 see also "The Category of Sex", *Feminist Issues*, 2, 2.

3   See Thomas W. Busch, "Beyond the Cogito: The Question of the Continuity of Sartre's Thought," *The Modern Schoolman*, LX (March 1983).
4   Jean-Paul Sartre, *Being and Nothingness: An Essay in Phenomenological Ontology*, tr. Hazel E. Barnes (New York: Philosophical Library, 1947), 329.
5   Beauvoir's defense of the non-Cartesian character of Sartre's account of the body can be found in "Merleau–Ponty et le Pseudo-Sartrisme," *Les Temps Modernes*, 10, 2 (1955).
6   Sartre, *Being and Nothingness*, 329.
7   Beauvoir, *The Second Sex*, 41.
8   Wittig, "One is Not Born a Woman," 48.
9   Ibid., 47.
10 Wittig, "The Category of Sex," 22.
11 Wittig, "One is Not Born a Woman," 53.
12 Michel Foucault, *The History of Sexuality* (New York: Random House, 1980), vol. I: *An Introduction*, tr. Robert Hurley, 154.
13 Ibid.
14 Ibid., 152.
15 Michel Foucault (ed.), *Herculine Barbin, Being the Recently Discovered Memoirs of a Nineteenth Century Hermaphrodite*, tr. Richard McDougall (New York: Pantheon, 1980).
16 Foucault, *Herculine Barbin*, xiii.
17 Foucault, *The History of Sexuality*, vol. I, 155.
18 Julia Kristeva, "Women can Never be Defined," in Elaine Marks and Isabel de Courtivron (eds.), *New French Feminisms*, 137.
19 Ibid.
20 See Gayle Rubin, "The Traffic in Women: The Political Economy of Sex," in Rayna R. Reiter, *Toward an Anthropology of Women* (New York: Monthly Review Press, 1975), 178–92.

Desire, Rhetoric, and Recognition in Hegel's *Phenomenology of Spirit* (1987)

Introduction

Submitted as a dissertation at Yale University in 1984, revised in 1985–6, and published in 1987, *Subjects of Desire* originally dealt with the reception of G. W. F. Hegel by French philosophers of the 1930s and 1940s. The preface to the 1999 paperback edition of the book provides a fascinating narrative of Butler's philosophical trajectory, her study of continental philosophers (Marx, Hegel, Husserl, Heidegger, Kierkegaard, Merleau-Ponty), the Critical Theorists of the Frankfurt School, and German idealist philosophies. It was after this initial philosophical training that Butler was influenced by the work of Michel Foucault and French poststructuralist theory, and when she later revised the dissertation that was to become *Subjects*, she added sections on Lacan, Foucault, Deleuze, and Derrida, touching briefly but significantly on Kristeva at the end of the book.

Chapter 1, "Desire, Rhetoric, and Recognition in Hegel's *Phenomenology of Spirit*," gives an account of the Hegelian Subject's progress through the various stages of consciousness. Characterizing *Phenomenology of Spirit* as a study in fiction-making in which the Quixotic Subject sets off on an impossible ontological pursuit, Butler empha-sizes the centrality of desire to Hegel's accounts of consciousness, self-consciousness, and the movement from one to the other. This process occurs when the subject discovers its alterity through its desire for another, so that as Butler puts it, "self-consciousness is desire in general," while desire itself is characterized by loss – both loss of the self in desiring another, and the Subject's loss of the world in desiring itself. Negation and loss are preconditions of identity, and as in *Gender Trouble* and *Bodies That Matter*, the Hegelian subject is characterized as a melancholic agent who must recognize and overcome the Other (*Aufhebung*) in order to become itself. Self-consciousness is a mode of knowing that is also a mode of becoming, and Butler's analysis of desire in the fourth section of *Phenomenology of Spirit* ("Independence and Dependence of

Preface to 1999 edition, pp. vii–xvii, and chapter 1, pp. 17–59, 240–4 (notes), from *Subjects of Desire: Hegelian Reflections in Twentieth-Century France* (originally published 1987; reprinted in paperback 1999 by Columbia University Press, New York). Reprinted by permission of Columbia University Press.

Self-consciousness: Lordship and Bondage") emphasizes the self-negating, self-estranging principle that is central to the experience of desire. In Hegel's account of lordship and bondage there is no experience without intersubjectivity, as the lord and his bondsman seek to know themselves through the supersession of otherness: the lord "overcomes" the bondsman, while the bondsman labors on an object that is constitutive of his identity. Again, in later work intersubjectivity and exclusion prove to be crucial to Butler's psychoanalytically inflected formulations of identity (and see also Jessica Benjamin, *The Shadow of the Other: Intersubjectivity and Gender in Psychoanalysis* [New York: Routledge, 1998] for a discussion of Butler's ideas).

After the analysis of Hegel's account of the desiring subject, *Subjects of Desire* considers two generations of French philosophers, their readings of Hegel, and their attempts to reject and revise his theories of subjectivity. Starting with Alexandre Kojève's influential *Introduction à la lecture de Hegel* (*Introduction to the Reading of Hegel*) published in 1941, Butler analyzes the "Hegelian reflections" of Jean Hyppolite and Jean-Paul Sartre, alluding briefly to Jean Wahl, the importance of whose *Le Malheur de la conscience dans la philosophie de Hegel* (1929) is acknowledged in her 1999 preface. It is Butler's contention that in different ways, each of these philosophers attempts to move outside Hegelian dialectic and the Hegelian account of subject-formation, a philosophical move which, as she points out, is itself implicitly dialectical, and therefore continues rather than breaks the Hegelian connection. By taking the subject of desire as the focal point of their analyses, these thinkers remain within a Hegelian theoretical framework, and Butler suggests that they construct a Hegelian subject (and indeed a Hegel) in order to refute it. The pattern is repeated by the next generation of philosophers whose work variously describes the disintegration and dislocation of an apparently self-identical and secure Hegelian subject. Butler argues that both generations of thinkers have misread (or rather, overread) *Phenomenology of Spirit*, a work that has frequently been compared to a *Bildungsroman* because it seems to plot the Subject's journeys through a sequence of ontological stages until it reaches its final destination – Absolute Knowledge. However, the narrative charted in *Phenomenology of Spirit* is not quite so straightforwardly teleological, since in Butler's reading, far from describing "a self-identical subject who travels smugly from one ontological place to another," Hegel's Subject "*is* its travels, and *is* every place in which it finds itself." Clearly the Hegelian Subject is not an entity on its way to completion, and Butler compares him (and she points out that *he* is always masculine) to a cartoon character, a Mr. Magoo who, encountering frequent and drastic reversals, fails, fails again, and fails better in a Beckettian spirit of never-ending and irresolvable ontological enterprise.

If *Phenomemology of Spirit* has been compared to a *Bildungsroman*, then *Subjects of Desire* could be characterized as a *Bildungsroman* in reverse, a narrative of how the Hegelian subject is interrogated, disintegrated, and deconstructed in the work of two generations of twentieth-century French philosophers. "The philosophical narrative of Hegel's reception and reinterpretation in France begins with the self-sufficient yet metaphysically secure Hegelian subject, that omnivorous adventurer of the Spirit who turns out, after a series of surprises, to *be* all that he encounters along his dialectical way," Butler states in her introduction. Hegel's traveler does indeed seem to be shattered and dispersed in French philosophers' accounts of it: while Alexandre Kojève's *Introduction à la lecture de Hegel* rejects what is taken to be Hegel's unified subject, Jean Hyppolite characterizes the Hegelian Spirit as a tragic figure, and Jean-Paul Sartre reveals Hegel's Absolute as an ontological impossibility. Kojève's work constitutes the first Hegelian "moment" in twentieth-century France, and this is followed by Hyppolite's and Sartre's formulations of the subject in terms of its finitude, corporeal boundaries, and temporality. "Third-wave" Hegelians characterize the Spirit as split (Lacan), displaced (Derrida), and eventually dead (Foucault, Deleuze). (See *Subjects of Desire*, p. 175.) In the final chapter of *Subjects of Desire*, Butler raises the question of gender, and her call for a more specific history of bodies than is provided by Foucault in volume I of his *History of Sexuality* anticipates her own future analyses of "concrete bodies in complex historical situations" in *Gender Trouble, Bodies That Matter*, and subsequent work.

In her preface to the 1999 edition of *Subjects of Desire*, Butler acknowledges Hegel's importance to her work which, she claims, centers around the following Hegelian questions: "What is the relation between desire and recognition, and how is it that the constitution of the subject entails a radical and constitutive relation to alterity?" Perhaps this is what distinguishes Butler from the philosophers she discusses in *Subjects of Desire*: namely, that she does not attempt to "overcome" Hegel (a word which of course contains resonances of *Aufhebung*, or sublation), or to synthesize her own theories of the subject of/and desire. Instead what we have is an open-ended, contingent, and temporal mode of reading – or as Butler puts it, "a definition in displacement, for which there is no final restoration" – which resembles the subject as it is theorized by both Hegel and Butler.

The whole of the first chapter of *Subjects of Desire* in which Butler analyzes the progress of Hegel's desiring subject as described in "The Truth of Self-Certainty" and "Lordship and Bondage" in Hegel's *Phenomenology of Spirit*, is included here, as well as the preface to the paperback edition.

Preface to the Paperback Edition (1999)

Subjects of Desire is my 1984 dissertation, revised in 1985–86. I wrote on the concept of desire, concentrating on Hegel's *Phenomenology of Spirit* and some of the central appropriations of that theme in twentieth-century French philosophy. Prior to my graduate studies, I was a Fulbright Scholar studying Hegel and German Idealism at the Heidelberg Universität, attending the seminars and lectures of Dieter Henrich and Hans-Georg Gadamer. As a graduate student in the Department of Philosophy at Yale University in the early 1980s, I trained in the tradition of continental philosophy, studying Marx and Hegel, phenomenology, Heidegger, Kierkegaard, Merleau-Ponty, and the Frankfurt School. I wrote the dissertation under Maurice Natanson, a phenomenologist who generously supported my scholarship, but let me know that French philosophy met its reasonable limit in the work of Sartre and selected writings of Merleau-Ponty. Studying at Yale in the late '70s and early '80s, I certainly knew about poststructuralist thought, but tended to place it outside the sphere of the continental philosophical tradition I meant to study. I occasionally attended a seminar by Derrida, and more often audited Paul de Man's lectures, but for the most part worked in the traditions of phenomenology, hermeneutics, and the Frankfurt School while seeking to acquire a background in German Idealism. It was in the context of a women's studies faculty seminar that I encountered the work of Michel Foucault. And it was not until I left Yale and became a visiting faculty member and then a postdoctoral fellow at Wesleyan University from 1983–86 that I became open to French theory in a way that I mainly resisted while at Yale. At the Center for the Humanities, I was exposed to critical theory in the French vein, and it was in the initial stages of that exposure that I revised the dissertation as *Subjects of Desire: Hegelian Reflections in Twentieth-Century France*, published by Columbia University Press in 1987. The final chapters on Deleuze, Lacan, and Foucault were not part of the dissertation proper, and they represent first forays into material that I have since come to understand deserves a more complex consideration.

I published the book too early, pressured by the job market, and I republish it now too late to make revisions. Any revised version of this work would be a new work altogether, one that I am not prepared to embark upon at this time. In 1985–86, I was not quite prepared to make the theoretical moves that I begin in the final chapters and that I subsequently made in the writing of *Gender Trouble*, published in late 1989. Although at the time of this writing I am not yet ancient, the book reads to me – to the extent that I can read it – as my juvenilia, which means that I ask the reader to approach it with abundant forgiveness in reserve.

The text is neither a comprehensive account of French Hegelianism nor a work in intellectual history.[1] It is a critical inquiry into a relation repeatedly figured between desire and recognition. If it were to have been a comprehensive treatment, it most certainly would have included a chapter on the work of Georges Bataille.[2] *Subjects of Desire* would have also considered the influence of Hegel's *Logic* in greater detail, especially on the work of Jean Hyppolite in which the *Logic* provides validation for the essential truths revealed in subjective experience in the *Phenomenology*.[3] To the extent that *Subjects of Desire* focuses on the *Phenomenology*, it could have included as well a consideration of Hegel's chapter, "Freedom of Self-Consciousness: Stoicism, Scepticism, and the Unhappy Consciousness." This key chapter's appropriation by Jean Wahl might reasonably be said to be the first major work on Hegel in twentieth-century France, indeed, it is the chapter through which the twentieth-century

French reception of Hegel began. Wahl's short text, *Le Malheur de la conscience dans la philosophie de Hegel* (Monfort, 1929), established an appropriative reading of Hegel, bringing the internally divided consciousness to bear on both religious and existential themes, and emphasizing the *negativity* of consciousness that plays such a prominent role in the subsequent readings provided by Kojève and Hyppolite.

In 1995, I published an essay, "Stubborn Attachment, Bodily Subjection: Rereading Hegel on the Unhappy Consciousness," which constitutes a continued reflection on the Hegelian subject.[4] There I sought to show that Hegel offers a sequel to the Lordship and Bondage chapter that is rarely considered by those who prize the apparently emancipatory conclusion of the former chapter. Hegel offers a configuration of the subject in which subjection becomes a psychic reality, one in which oppression itself is articulated and entrenched through psychic means. My suggestion is that Hegel begins to explain the inversions of power that take place as it acquires the status of psychic reality, an explanation that allies him with insights usually credited to Nietzsche and Freud.

This text relies on available English translations of Hyppolite, Kojève, and Sartre, and works with selected essays in French with the consequence that the bulk of Kojève's untranslated writings (including the full version of his *Introduction à la lecture de Hegel*) remain largely unconsidered. His lectures, offered from 1933–39 at the École des Hautes Études, include extensive discussions of Hegel's relation to Kant, the place of poetic language, tragedy, and religion in the *Phenomenology*, and an extended discussion of the figure of Christ and the meaning of Christianity that did not survive into the abridged English translation.[5]

Kojève remains a difficult author to understand, claimed on the one hand by the Straussian tradition of Allan Bloom, Stanley Rosen, and Francis Fukuyama, and heralded on the other hand as a Marxist by Pierre Macheray and others.[6] Even as Kojève insisted that Hegel's text is open to a set of historical appropriations unanticipated in Hegel's time, so his own reading of Hegel has become open to widely conflicting readings. And this predicament may well be the result of the kind of "reading" that Kojève himself put into place, one that sought less to be faithful to the letter of Hegel's text than to produce new interpretations that reflect the changed historical circumstance of reading itself. Hegel's text, as it moves through time, thus continually re-poses the question of its own readability, most clearly because the end of history that he foretells is not the end of time and not the end of the temporality of reading.[7] Thus Hegel's text, perhaps despite itself, opens up the question of the relation between time and readability. The future is, for Kojève, no longer constrained by teleology, and the future that Hegel anticipates is in some ways precisely the one that Kojève mourns as lost idealism. Kojève's "reading" brings into relief the temporality of Hegel's text, showing that the temporality into which it has survived demands a different kind of reading, one that does not move progressively with the same confidence. This predicament of temporality post-Hegel has lead some of the Straussians to conclude that history itself must resolve into "perennial" themes, and it has also led Althusserians to conclude that a structuralist analysis of society relieved of the conceits of diachrony is the preferable conclusion. But another perspective can be derived from Kojève, one that insists that temporality is irreducible to historicity, and that neither is reducible to teleology. The temporality of the concept is neither static nor teleological, but requires a doubly inverted reading that knows no closure, which will no doubt offend the avatars of common sense, but without which no approach to Hegel is possible.

The speculative sentence that Hegel outlines in the *Logic* underscores this problem of temporality as a predicament of reading. We cannot expect that language will transparently show the truth of what it says, but neither can we expect that this truth will be found outside of language. The truth is not the same as the narrative that the *Phenomenology* provides, and yet it is made manifest only through its exposition. The sentence moves in such a way that the familiar is rendered unfamiliar, and this pertains to the familiar grammar of the sentence itself. This becomes especially true when we consider the grammatical place of "negation," a term that not only undergoes semantically important shifts in meaning, but that also "acts" in essential ways in the unfolding of essential truths.

These functions of "negation" elicit the usual jokes on Hegel by contemporary analysts who insist that Hegel either be made plain or be rejected once and for all. Hegel has other plans in mind when he claims, for instance, in the *Phenomenology* that the speculative proposition destroys the general nature of the proposition (Miller 38). But the question is not what logical sense can be made of negation in Hegel, but how the very use of negation in Hegel calls into question our understanding of logical relations.

In the *Phenomenology*, negation emerges in a number of ways, and not merely in the service of an assimilating or domesticating conceptual operation that subdues the alterities it confronts. In the section, "The Truth of Self-Certainty," consciousness negates its objects by consuming them; in Lordship and Bondage, negation appears first as the effort of both figures to annihilate one another and then transmutes into relations of domination and servitude. What does it mean that negation "appears" through these various figures? And how are we to understand the transmutations that the appearance of negation undergoes?

My suggestion is that in the *Phenomenology*, figures emerge to describe a state that has not yet achieved a stable logical status; indeed, the figure marks the instability of logical relations. Conversely, though, every logical relation assumes a shape or an appearance that is figural. If we are to read Hegel, what will this reading do to a grammar that is preconceived to express logical relations (the conceit of Husserl's *Logical Investigations* and the early Wittgenstein alike)? One reads along in the *Phenomenology* with the assumption that a stable reality is being described only to come up against the obduracy of descriptive language itself. We think we know at any given textual moment what negation "is" and what it does, only to find out by following the course of its action, indeed, by reading it, that our former convictions were unfounded. It is the term, in other words, that constantly undermines our own knowingness. The language we thought was reporting on the reality of negation turns out to take part in the activity itself, to have its own negating function and, indeed, to be subject to negation itself. The language of the text thus exhibits its own rhetoricity, and we find that the question of logic and that of rhetoric are indissociable from each other. Similarly, no claims of cognition can be made apart from the practice of reading: the temporality of the concept is not finally separable from the temporality of reading.

One of the more recent French readers of Hegel, Gérard Lebrun, in his *La patience du Concept: Essai sur le discours hégélien*, makes a similar point as he disputes the possibility of a Hegelian dogmatism and shows that Hegelian discourse actively initiates the reader into a new mode of philosophical thought.[8] Just as for Kojève, the reading of Hegel must traverse a temporality that is past (an idea of the future that is past), so the reading of Hegel's grammar according to the demands of the speculative sentence can be read "forward" only to find that the presuppositions that animated the reading must themselves be read in turn, compelling a reversal that does not quite undo what has been done (and that, at the very level of grammar, enacts a notion of negation proper to reading itself).

Jean-Luc Nancy makes this point in a different way in his recently published *Hegel: L'inquiétude du négatif.*[9] For him, the subject is not recoiled into itself, but is defined fundamentally as an act by which the self overcomes itself in its passage toward and into the world. The subject disperses itself into its world, and this self-surpassing is precisely the operation of its negativity. Nancy's work releases Hegel from the trope of totality, insisting that the "disquiet" of the self is precisely its mode of becoming, its final nonsubstantiality in time, and its specific expression of freedom. Nancy's work is rhetorically significant as well because in the place of a systematic exegesis of Hegel's work it provides a discontinuous set of meditations on the *Phenomenology* through the key terms by which the question of freedom is approached. Those who expect Hegel's *Phenomenology* to illustrate a clear teleology will be productively confounded by such a text.[10]

In fact, the status of teleology seems significantly contentious in the reconsideration of the twentieth-century French appropriation of Hegel. Although it

was within the context of French theory, after all, that Hegel became synono-
mous with totality, teleology, conceptual domination, and the imperialist
subject, the French appropriation of Hegel also puts the totalizing and teleological presumptions of Hegel's philosophy into question. Indeed, often the
marks of a distinctively "post-Hegelian" position are not easy to distinguish
from an appropriative reading of Hegel himself. Kojève's writings are especially
pertinent here to the extent that they interrogate the time that emerges after
the end of history, thus signaling a closure to teleology that is not precisely a
teleological closure, an ending that is more on the lines of a break, interruption,
and loss. Although Althusser once termed Kojève's work "silly," he takes
seriously Kojève's effort to recast teleology in Hegel as anthropocentrism.[11]
Althusser's early reflections on Hegel develop an immanent critique of
Kojève's view, arguing that Kojève develops the subjective dimension of
negativity to the exclusion of the objective one.[12] The attempt to reduce the
workings of negativity to the subjective is bourgeois revisionism, affirming the
individual at the expense of his objective situation. And where objectivity
returns via Hegel, it is always devoid of its specifically onomic content, which
leads it to valorize a philosophically abstracted notion of equality and democracy at the expense of one wrought from the class struggle. To the extent that
Kojève's Hegel is read through the lens of the young Marx, and both Hegel
and Marx are understood to affirm a subjective dimension of negation,
"Kojève's existentialist Marx is a travesty in which Marxists will not recognize
their own" (172).

Although Althusser devotes several essays to the reconsideration of Hegel in
his *Écrits philosophiques et politiques*, where he offers a critique of Hegelian
abstraction and begins through the practice of immanent critique to articulate
a totality without a subject, he is quick to insult Hegel and French Hegelianism
in particular. He commends Kojève's book with ambivalence: "His book is
more than an *Introduction to the Reading of Hegel*: it is the resurrection of a
corpse, or, rather, the revelation that Hegel, a thinker dismantled, torn to
pieces, trampled underfoot, and betrayed, profoundly haunts and dominates an
apostate age" (171). And later, he remarks in the same vein that despite the
discrediting of Hegel's philosophy, "this dead god, covered with insults and
buried a hundred times over, is rising from the grave" (174). Finally, Althusser
not only accuses Hegelian philosophy of providing a philosophical glorification
of the bourgeois status quo, but of supplying a revisionism "of a fascist type"
(183).

Pierre Macheray's recent book, *Hegel ou Spinoza*,[13] is clearly influenced by
Althusser, but takes the critical potential of Hegel's philosophy more seriously.[14] By counterposing Spinoza to Hegel, and by asking how each philosophical position defines the necessary limit of the other, Macheray argues for a

dialectical conception of history relieved of the teleological presumption, in which there is a "struggle of tendencies that do not carry in themselves the promise of a resolution . . . a unity of contraries, but without the negation of negation."[15] Moreover, Macheray considers, contra Althusser, the sense of a Hegelian subject that remains irreducible to its ordinary use as a bearer of predicative judgements. The Hegelian subject is one for whom the stable relation between subject and predicate within ordinary grammar becomes undone (248). Thus, as a reader in the Althusserian tradition, Macheray nevertheless yields an interpretation that converges with that of Lebrun and Nancy in that he acknowledges that the subject is only the term for the process that it accomplishes, is nonsubstantial, and is one whose illimitability destroys its ordinary grammatical function.

The revision of *Subjects of Desire* that I might have done would have included as well as Derrida's original criticism of the Hegelian concept in "The Pit and the Pyramid," the subsequent revision and restaging of his view in the introduction to Lacoue-Labarthe's *Typographies* and Derrida's own *Glas*.[16] A fuller consideration would also no doubt include a chapter on Luce Irigaray's various engagements with Hegel, especially in "The Eternal Irony of the Community" in *Speculum of the Other Woman*, and in her reflections on Hegel, kinship, and universality in *Sexes et parentés*.[17] One of my future projects will be to consider Frantz Fanon's engagement with Hegel in *Black Skin, White Masks* on the problem of recognition within the dynamics of hierarchical racial exchange. Fanon's treatment of Hegel can be read as an important appropriation of Kojève's thesis of the centrality of desire to the struggle for recognition and the constitution of the subject (and the problematic mimimization of labor as a constitutive condition of recognition).[18]

My interest in the Hegelian legacy was not precisely overcome through the early publication of this book. I have taught courses on Hegel and contemporary theory, and continue to be interested in the way that Hegel is read and misread at the advent, institution, and dissemination of structuralism. In a sense, all of my work remains within the orbit of a certain set of Hegelian questions: What is the relation between desire and recognition, and how is it that the constitution of the subject entails a radical and constitutive relation to alterity?

I am currently at work on a book to be published as part of the Wellek Library Lectures series that centrally engages Hegel's writing on Antigone in the *Phenomenology, The Philosophy of Right*, and the *Aesthetics*.[19] In it I am as much concerned with the way in which Antigone is consistently misread by Hegel as with his provocative way of understanding her criminal act as an eruption of an alternate legality within the sphere of public law. Whether Antigone functions as a subject for Hegel remains a compelling question for me, and raises the question of the political limit of the subject, that is, both the limitations imposed upon subjecthood (who qualifies as one), and the limits of the subject as the point of departure for politics. Hegel remains important here, for his subject does not stay in its place, displaying a critical mobility that may well be useful for further appropriations of Hegel to come. The emergent subject of Hegel's *Phenomenology* is an ek-static one, a subject who constantly finds itself outside itself, and whose periodic expropriations do not lead to a return to a former self. Indeed, the self who comes outside of itself, for whom ek-stasis is a condition of existence, is one for whom no return to self is possible, for whom there is no final recovery from self-loss. The notion of "difference" is similarly misunderstood, I would suggest, when it is understood as contained within or by the subject: the Hegelian subject's encounter with difference is not resolved into identity. Rather, the moment of its "resolution" is finally indistinguishable from the moment of its dispersion; the thinking of this cross-vectored temporality ushers in the Hegelian understanding of infinity and offers a notion of the subject that cannot remain bounded in the face of the world. Misrecognition does not arrive as a distinctively Lacanian corrective to the Hegelian subject, for it is precisely by misrecognition that the Hegelian subject repeatedly suffers its self-loss. Indeed, this is a self constitutively at risk of self-loss. This subject neither has nor suffers its desire, but is the very action of desire as it perpetually displaces the subject. Thus, it is neither precisely a new theory of the subject nor a definitive displacement of the subject that Hegel provides, but rather a definition in displacement, for which there is no final restoration.

Desire, Rhetoric, and Recognition in Hegel's Phenomenology of Spirit

The sun by day and the gods revealed are familiar sights
Shaping the countenance which, by ancients named "one and all,"
Has filled to the brim with free satisfaction the reticent heart,
And first and alone is the source of gratified desire.

Hölderlin, "Bread and Wine"

A consideration of desire in the *Phenomenology of Spirit* requires a preliminary turn to the larger problem of how philosophical themes are introduced and "argued" within the terms of this sometimes tortuous text. I place the verb "argue" within quotations, not to dismiss the kind of argumentation that Hegel pursues, but to draw attention to the idiosyncrasy of its form. After all, the

Phenomenology of Spirit is a *Bildungsroman,*[1] an optimistic narrative of adventure and edification, a pilgrimage of the spirit, and upon immediate scrutiny, it is unclear how Hegel's narrative structure argues the metaphysical case he wants to make. Moreover, Hegel's sentence structure seems to defy the laws of grammar and to test the ontological imagination beyond its usual bounds. His sentences begin with subjects that turn out to be interchangeable with their objects or to pivot on verbs that are swiftly negated or inverted in supporting clauses. When "is" is the verb at the core of any claim, it rarely carries a familiar burden of predication, but becomes transitive in an unfamiliar and foreboding sense, affirming the inherent movement in "being," disrupting the ontological assumptions that ordinary language usage lulls us into making.

The rhetorical inversion of Hegelian sentences as well as the narrative structure of the text as a whole convey the elusive nature of both the grammatical and human subject. Against the Understanding's compulsion to fix the grammatical subject into a univocal and static signifier, Hegel's sentences indicate that the subject can only be understood in its movement. When Hegel states, "Substance is Subject," the "is" carries the burden of "becomes," where becoming is not a unilinear but a cyclical process. Hence, we read the sentence wrong if we rely on the ontological assumptions of linear reading, for the "is" is a nodal point of the interpenetration of both "Substance" and "Subject"; each *is* itself only to the extent that it *is* the other because, for Hegel, self-identity is only rendered actual to the extent that it is mediated through that which is different. To read the sentence right would mean to read it cyclically, or to bring to bear the variety of partial meanings it permits on any given reading. Hence, it is not just that substance is being clarified, or that the subject is being defined, but the very meaning of the copula is itself being expressed as a locus of movement and plurivocity.

The grammatical subject is, thus, never self-identical, but is always and only itself in its reflexive movement; the sentence does not consist of grammatical elements that reflect or otherwise indicate corresponding ontological entities. The sentence calls to be taken as a whole, and in turn indicates the wider textual context in which it itself is to be taken. But the way in which this context is "indicated" is less referential than rhetorical; Hegel's sentences *enact* the meanings that they convey; indeed, they show that what "is" only is to the extent that it is *enacted*. Hegelian sentences are read with difficulty, for their meaning is not immediately given or known; they call to be reread, read with different intonations and grammatical emphases. Like a line of poetry that stops us and forces us to consider that the *way* in which it is said is essential to *what* it is saying, Hegel's sentences rhetorically call attention to themselves. The discrete and static words on the page deceive us only momentarily into thinking that discrete and static meanings will be released by our reading. If we refuse to give up the expectation that univocal meanings linearly arranged will unfold from the words at hand, we will find Hegel confused, unwieldy, unnecessarily dense. But if we question the presumptions of the Understanding that the prose asks us to, we will experience the incessant movement of the sentence that constitutes its meaning.

Hegel's sentences are never completed in that they never offer up "what is meant" in some final and digestible form. "Substance is Subject" suggests not only what substance is, what the subject is, and what the meaning of the copula is, but also that no ratiocination of possible meanings could capture all of the meanings that the sentence suggests. All three terms signify indefinitely inasmuch as each calls for continual concretization and revision. To know the meaning of that sentence is to know the meaning of Hegel's system, and that meaning cannot be known once and for all by any living subject. Hence, Hegel's sentences send us forth, as it were, into a journey of knowledge; they indicate what is not being expressed, what must be explored for any given expression to acquire meaning. As sentential narratives, they are cyclical and progressive at once, reflecting and enacting the movement of consciousness by which they might be comprehended. Because Hegel's rhetoric defies our expectations of a linear and definite philosophical presentation, it initially obstructs us (no one reads Hegel quickly), but once we have reflected upon the assumptions that Hegel wants to release us from, the rhetoric initiates us into a consciousness of irreducibly multiple meanings which continuously determine each other. This multiplicity of meanings is not static, according to Hegel, but is the essence of becoming, of movement itself.[2] In reading for multiple meanings, for plurivocity, ambiguity, and metaphor in the general sense, we experience concretely the inherent movement of dialectical thinking, the essential alteration of reality. And we also come to understand the role of our own consciousness in constituting this reality inasmuch as the text must be read to have its meaning enacted.

This last point is made especially clear in the *Phenomenology*, which is specifically concerned with the point of view of the human subject. Like the grammatical subject of Hegel's metaphysical remarks, the human subject is never simply and immediately there. As soon as we get a grammatical indication of his location, he travels forth and becomes something different from what he was when we first got wind of it.[*] More than the rhetorical strategy of Hegel's sentential narratives, the organizing narrative structure of the

---

[*] Although Hegel's subject is a fictive personage, and clearly without recognizable gender, I will refer to this fiction as "he." This procedure ought not to be taken as an identification of the universal with the masculine, but is intended to avoid an unwieldy grammatical situation.

Phenomenology narrows the distance between philosophical form and content. Hegel's narrative is designed to seduce the reader, to exploit his need to find himself in the text he is reading. The *Phenomenology* requires and effects the imaginative identification of the reader with the traveling subject so that reading becomes a philosophically instructive form of travel.

Identifying with Hegel's protagonist is no easy matter. We begin the *Phenomenology* with a sense that the main character has not yet arrived. There is action and deliberation, but no recognizable agent. Our immediate impulse is to look more closely to discern this absent subject in the wings; we are poised for his arrival. As the narrative progresses beyond the "this" and the "that," the various deceptions of immediate truth, we realize slowly that this subject will not arrive all at once, but will offer choice morsels of himself, gestures, shadows, garments strewn along the way, and that this "waiting for the subject," much like attending Godot, is the comic, even burlesque, dimension of Hegel's *Phenomenology*. Moreover, we discover that simply waiting is not what is expected of us, for this narrative does not progress rationally unless we participate in thinking through the logical necessity of every transition. The narrative purports to develop inexorably, so we must test the necessity of its every move.

Although Hegel's *Bildungsroman* does not address his reader directly, as does Diderot's *Jacques le fataliste*,[3] the narrative strategy of the *Phenomenology* is to implicate the reader indirectly and systematically. We do not merely witness the journey of some other philosophical agent, but we ourselves are invited on stage to perform the crucial scene changes. At the close of the *Phenomenology*, the philosopher is no longer "Other" to ourselves, for that distinction would announce an "outside" to that ostensibly all-inclusive unity. Indeed, we recognize *ourselves* as the subjects we have been waiting for inasmuch as we gradually constitute the perspective by which we recognize our history, our mode of becoming, through the *Phenomenology* itself.

Thus, the *Phenomenology* is not only a narrative about a journeying consciousness, but is the journey itself. The narrative discloses and enacts a strategy for appropriating philosophical truth; it sets the ontological stage in a variety of ways, compels our belief in the reality of that staged scene, encourages our identification with the emergent subject that the scene includes, and then asks us to suffer the inevitable failure of that subject's quest for identity within the confines of that scene. The subject fails – and we, imaginatively, with him – precisely because he took seriously the ontological commitments that the scene required; hence, his demise is revealed again and again as a function of a tragic blindness, although, for Hegel, tragic events are never decisive. There is little time for grief in the *Phenomenology* because renewal is always so close at hand. What seems like tragic blindness turns out to be more like the comic myopia of Mr. Magoo whose automobile careening through the neighbor's chicken coop always seems to land on all four wheels. Like such miraculously resilient characters of the Saturday morning cartoon, Hegel's protagonists always re-assemble themselves, prepare a new scene, enter the stage armed with a new set of ontological insights – and fail again. As readers, we have no other narrative option but to join in this bumpy ride, for we cannot anticipate this journey without embarking on it ourselves. Time and again the *Phenomenology* compels our belief in an ontological scene, a picture of what the world is like and where the Absolute can be found, only to reveal that picture finally as a systematically induced deception.

It makes no more sense for the reader to reject the particular configurations of the world that the *Phenomenology* offers than it would to refuse to accept a novel as true. Hegel's provisional scenes, the stage of self-certainty, the struggle for recognition, the dialectic of lord and bondsman, are instructive fictions, ways of organizing the world which prove to be too limited to satisfy the subject's desire to discover itself as substance. These scenes are thus consistently undermined by that which they unwittingly exclude, and are forced to re-assemble as more complicated arrangements, now including that which brought the previous scene to dissolution. As readers who accept each scene as true, we identify imaginatively, but every effort at identification is finally subverted. What initially compels our belief turns out to be a false premise, but this falsehood immediately indicates a truer and more inclusive premise by which it might be replaced. Hegel's subject does not rest easily with any partial conception of its relationship with the world of substance, and every exclu-sionary ontological commitment engenders a "return of the repressed." Hegel's subject suffers no permanent bout of bad faith or debilitating repression of what is real. Every deception immediately releases a broader conception of truth by which it might be transcended. This subject journeys with compulsive meta-physical honesty toward his ultimate dialectical harmony with the world. No matter how many times his world dissolves, he remains infinitely capable of reassembling another world; he suffers the negative, but is never wholly engulfed by it. Indeed, suffering only enhances his synthetic powers. The negative is always and only useful – never debilitating in any final sense. Hegel's subject is thus a fiction of infinite capability, a romantic traveler who only learns from what he experiences, who, because infinitely self-replenishing, is never devastated beyond repair.

The dramatic metaphysical hope of Hegel's subject prompted Kierkegaard to ask whether such a person might really be said to exist. After all, how do we account for the relentless desire not merely to survive but to profit from suffering, illness, loss? For Hegel, this desire is presuppositional, so that a metaphysical finesse obscures the existential and psychological difficulties at work. But how often does suffering prompt the reconstruction of a world on yet firmer ground, and how often does suffering simply erode whatever ground there is, producing anxiety about the very possibility of a coherent world? Clearly, Hegel's subject has a very fine director working for him, one who monitors those scene changes carefully and makes sure that every transition is survived. But as Kierkegaard once asked about existence, "where is the director? I should like to have a word with him."[4]

If we accept Kierkegaard's existential critique of Hegel's subject, what becomes of the *Phenomenology's* claim to be experiential truth? If Hegel's subject is fictional, can he perhaps still have a meaning for us? Consider that the narrative of the *Phenomenology* is a series of deceptions which prove to be the *via negativa* of philosophical truth, that these successive fictions form the history of a consciousness which, in turn, constitutes its substance, the circle of its being. The deceptive pursuit of the Absolute is not a vain "running around in circles," but a progressive cycle which reveals every deception as permitting some grander act of synthesis, an insight into yet more regions of interrelated reality. The substance that is known, and which the subject *is*, is thus an all-encompassing web of interrelations, the dynamism of life itself, and, consequently, the principle that all specific determinations are not what they appear to be. And yet, as beings who must be cultivated to the absolute standpoint, we begin with the determinate, the particular, and the immediate, and treat it as if it were absolute, and then learn through that misplaced certainty that the Absolute is broader and more internally complicated that we originally thought. The history of these deceptions is a progressive one inasmuch as we understand how these deceptions imply each other as necessary consequences, and that together they reveal that the *insufficiency* of any given relationship to the Absolute is the basis of its *interdependence* on other relationships, so that the history of deception is, finally, the unity of internal relations which is the Absolute. Absolute truth in the *Phenomenology* is thus something like the dramatic integrity of a comedy of errors. In Nietzsche's comparable view, " 'Truth': this, according to my way of thinking, does not necessarily denote the antithesis of error, but in the most fundamental cases only the posture of various errors in relation to one another."[5]

In this sense, the *Phenomenology* is a study in fiction-making which shows the essential role of fiction and false belief in the quest for philosophical truth. According to such a reading, the fictional status of Hegel's subject takes on a new set of possible meanings. We might read this subject as a trope for the hyperbolic impulse itself, that frantic and overdetermined pursuit of the Absolute which *creates* that place when it cannot be found, which projects it endlessly and is constantly "foiled" by its own projection. As a being of metaphysical desires, the human subject is prone to fiction, to tell himself the lies that he needs to live.[6] Reading Hegel in this Nietzschean fashion, we can take the *Phenomenology* as a study of desire and deception, the systematic pursuit and misidentification of the Absolute, a constant process of inversion which never reaches ultimate closure. The subject becomes a locus of ever more sophisticated forms of deception, and thus learns about ever more insidious appearances of the Absolute which turn out to be partial, fictional, and false. Hence, if Hegel's subject cannot be located in existence, perhaps we ought not to be surprised at his fictional reality. Like Don Quixote, Hegel's subject is an impossible identity who pursues reality in systematically mistaken ways. As readers of his text, accepting time and again the terms of his journey, we indulge in the same exorbitant desires; we become makers of fiction who cannot sustain belief in our creations, who wake to their unreality, but only to dream more shrewdly the next time.

The Ontology of Desire

Hegel's explicit discussion of desire begins in the section, "The Truth of Self-Certainty," which initiates the transition between consciousness and self-consciousness. The appearance of desire at this juncture is curious, for if the progress of the *Phenomenology* is impelled by desire, why does desire emerge as an explicit theme only in the fourth chapter of the text? Indeed, what does it mean that desire "appears" at a given stage in the *Phenomenology* at all?

Desire *appears*, but the moment of appearance is not necessarily the initial moment of its efficacy. In a sense, nothing comes into existence *ex nihilo* for Hegel; everything comes into explicit form from a potential or implicit state; indeed, everything has, in a sense, been there all along. "Appearance" is but one explicit or actual moment in the development of a phenomenon. In the *Phenomenology*, a given phenomenon appears in the context of a given configuration of the world. In the case of desire, we must ask, what kind of world makes desire possible? What must the world be like for desire to exist?

When we ask after the conditions or features of the world that make desire possible, we are not asking a preliminary question which, once answered, will allow us to continue the investigation with ease. Nor is it the Kantian inquiry into the transcendental conditions of desire's appearance. For Hegel, the preconditions of desire are the object of the inquiry itself, for desire in its articulation always thematizes the conditions of its own existence. When we ask, what is desire "after," we can give a partial answer: the illumination of its own opacity, the expression of that aspect of the world that brought it into being. This is part of what is meant by the *reflexivity* that desire is said to embody and enact. Eventually, the reflexivity enacted by desire will be identical with absolute knowledge itself. As Stanley Rosen remarks, "In analytical terms, part of the self is encountered outside oneself; the desire to assimilate the desire of the Other is thus an effort to grasp analytically the preanalytic or indeterminate structure of absolute reflection."[7] Desire is *intentional* in that it is always desire *of* or *for* a given object or Other, but it is also *reflexive* in the sense that desire is a modality in which the subject is both discovered and enhanced. The conditions that give rise to desire, the metaphysics of internal relations, are at the same time what desire seeks to articulate, render explicit, so that desire is a tacit pursuit of metaphysical knowledge, the human way that such knowledge "speaks."

At the juncture in the *Phenomenology* where desire emerges as a central theme, we are in the midst of a quandary. The subject has not arrived, but a predecessor is on the scene: consciousness. Consciousness is marked by its assumption that the sensuous and perceptual world it encounters is fundamentally different from itself. The "world" it encounters is a natural world, spatiotemporally organized, exhibiting discrete empirical objects. Consciousness contemplates this world, convinced that it is the Absolute and that it is external, or ontologically different from, itself. The sensuous and perceptual world is self-generating and self-subsisting; it has no need of consciousness. Consciousness finds itself in exile from the Absolute, believing its own powers of apprehending the world to be unrelated to that world. Consciousness here is pure intentional enthrallment with the world, but is not identified with the world, and in no way determines the truth or objective existence of that world. A paradox arises within this stage of experience because the fact remains that the sensuous and perceptual world is *delineated in* consciousness, and this delineation suggests that consciousness itself participates in the determination of that world's truth. This may not seem initially clear, but when we consider that the sensuous and perceptual world only *becomes actual* or determinate through its mediation in alterity, we recognize that consciousness is this Other which reflects and, thus, actualizes the truth of that world. Seen from this point of view, consciousness all of a sudden returns from its exile and now plays a major ontological role in determining Absolute reality. This sudden reorganization of the world requires a revision of basic concepts: what must consciousness be like if it "mediates" the world, and what meaning can we give to "alterity" and "actualization"? How did the dissolution of this particular world give rise to edifying philosophical insights?

The role of externalization and alterity in the determination of something as true is made clear partially through the introduction of the notion of Force. Appearing in the final section of Part 1 of "The Truth of Self-Certainty," Force is said to prefigure the Concept (*Begriff*), a mode of consciousness which, Hegel argues, permits one to "think antithesis within the thesis itself" (¶ 160). Force is essential to the transition from consciousness to self-consciousness because it posits the externality of the world of sensuous and perceptual reality as one that is essentially related to consciousness itself; in effect, Force posits externalization as a necessary moment of thought. In order that consciousness complete its own intentional requirement to think "something," it must become *determinate* thought: it must be a thought "of" something external to itself, and, in turn, become determined by that external something. Hence, by thinking a particular thing, thinking itself becomes particularized, becomes a given *mode* of thought. Thought that remains a purely inner phenomenon is not truly thought at all; it must be related to something outside itself in order to gain an actualized and determinate reality as consciousness. The notion of Force thus distinguishes the inner and outer "moments" of thought inasmuch as Force is a constant movement between an inner reality and a determinate manifestation; in effect, Force is the compulsion that a nascent reality exhibits to find a determinate manifestation for itself — Hegel's reformulation of Spinoza's *conatus*. Force characterizes relations in the physical world as well as within consciousness itself, and thus becomes the ontological basis of consciousness' bond with the sensuous and perceptual world that it initially encountered as ontologically disparate from itself. This compulsion to externalize prefigures the work of the Concept itself which, in Charles Taylor's words, "is the Idea of necessity which necessarily posits its own external manifestation."[8]

Force is that which impels an inner reality to gain determinate form, but it is also that which frustrates the absorption of that inner reality into determinate form. In other words, Force sustains a tension between that which appears and that which does not appear, and in this sense is different from other principles of teleological development. The notion of "inner difference" or the unity of opposites which is so central to Hegel's mode of dialectical thinking is enhanced through the notion of Force. It is not the drive toward determinate shape that would bring all nascent reality to explicit potency, but rather the constant process of giving and superseding determinate form. In a brief discussion of gravity, Hegel claims that without the notion of Force, or inner difference, we might have to think of space and time as only contingently related to one another: "But through the Notion of inner difference, these unlike and indifferent moments, space and time, etc. are a difference which is no difference, or only a difference of what is selfsame, and its essence is unity. As positive and negative they stimulate each other into activity, and their being is rather to posit themselves as not-being and to suspend themselves in the unity. The two distinguished moments both subsist; they are implicit and are opposite in themselves, i.e., each is the opposite of itself; each has its 'other' within it and they are only one unity" (¶ 161).

The "unity" of the phenomenon impelled by Force is not a static unity, but *movement*, incessant and dialectical. The Absolute cannot be identified with the determinate objects of the spatiotemporal world, the *res extensa* of sensuous and perceptual reality; there is always something that is beyond the determinate, some operative negativity, that accounts for the genesis of determinate form as well as for its eventual dissolution. The notion of Force confirms that there is something that does not appear, but that is nevertheless crucial to any given appearance; moreover, it indicates that reality is not coextensive with appearance, but always sustains and is sustained by a hidden dimension. In order to think the object of experience that the sensuous and perceptual world offers up to consciousness, we must relinquish faith in the kind of thinking that can take only determinate beings as its objects; conceptual thinking must replace Understanding, for only the former can think the movement between opposites. The Understanding consistently mistakes stasis for truth, and can only understand movement as a series of discrete moments, not as the vital unity of moments that imply each other endlessly and do not appear simultaneously. The Understanding cannot grasp movement itself; it is always prone to fix its object in a present tense which purports to present exhaustively the full reality of the object at hand. Because consciousness reaches its most sophisticated development in the Understanding, it proves incapable of the kind of thinking that the phenomenon of Force calls upon it to make. In the explication of Force, consciousness proves to be interminably partial; it always indicates a negativity that it itself cannot grasp. Self-consciousness arises, then, as the effort to think inner difference, the mutual implication of opposites, as constitutive of the object itself. Self-consciousness thus portends to conceptualize Force, and Life itself, defined as the constitution and dissolution of shape. Self-consciousness is not the momentary act of a discrete consciousness attending an opposing and discrete world, but a cognitive experience taking place in a developing sense of time; it is, in turn, able to grasp the temporal life of the object itself. Consciousness could think determinate being, but could not think the process of determination and indetermination that is Life itself; it could not think change.

Self-consciousness thus emerges as a kind of knowing that is at once a mode of becoming; it is suffered, dramatized, enacted. Consciousness gives rise to self-consciousness in the bungled attempt to *explain* what it knows: "Appearance, or the play of Forces, already displays infinity... this absolute unrest of pure movement, but it is as an '*explanation*' that it first freely stands forth; and in being finally an object for consciousness, as *that which it is*, consciousness is thus self-consciousness" (¶ 163). Force can be explained as a series of isolated phenomena, but the interrelation between them will never satisfactorily be explained. If this explanation is executed from the point of view of consciousness, it will only be a fracturing of the moments of Force; gravity can be analytically separated from positive and negative electricity, and distance and attraction can be similarly scrutinized in isolation, but the phenomenon itself will be lost, or presented as a lifeless series of internally unrelated attributes. The Understanding lacks reflexivity, and so cannot understand how consciousness' own difference from that which it scrutinizes is itself part of the phenomenon under investigation. Hence, it cannot extrapolate from this experience of "constitutive difference" to the object under investigation in order to know how the play of Forces holds together in the temporalized unity of the phenomenon. And so consciousness fumbles to explain Force, listing the moments of the play of Forces, listing them again, trying to force a synthesis from a series, but lacking the proper cognitive tools. And yet this failed explanation reveals an unexpected clue to the proper formulation of the phenomenon. As an "Explanation," the Understanding comes to be determinately manifest in material form; there is consciousness itself sprawled on the page, formed in letters and words, existing, materially, outside itself. In recognizing the authorship of that explanation, consciousness becomes aware of itself for the first time. No longer enthralled intentionally with a world that ostensibly monopolized reality, consciousness discovers its own reflexivity; it has become other to itself, and knows itself as such: "The reason why explaining affords so much self-satisfaction is just because in it consciousness is, so to speak, communing directly with itself, enjoying only itself; although it seems to be busy with something else" (¶ 163).

Consciousness thus relinquishes itself as consciousness in the process of explaining what it knows. By the time the Explanation is over, neither consciousness nor the object it seeks to explain are the same. The process of Explanation transforms the two poles of experience it was meant to mediate. No longer a tool in the hands of a consciousness intact, Explanation becomes a curious kind of agent that turns on its user and shakes his identity. The object of Explanation becomes curiously ambiguous as well; in being explained, the object is revealed as having certain properties that consciousness itself can elucidate. But what the object reveals, and what consciousness contributes, remain indistinguishable, for the only route to the object is through the Explanation itself, so that we cannot appeal to the object what exists outside this explanation in order to see to what extent the Explanation adequately expresses the object itself. Indeed, the object itself is no different from the object-as-explained; it exists in the form of the Explanation which has become its actuality. Consciousness is thus faced with an unanticipated ambiguity, for it finds itself in the terms of an explanation which is "of" the object of experience; it is both itself and the object under investigation. And if it exists in this double sense, then it must be part of the world it investigates. Consciousness thus learns that what exists in itself also exists in its alterity. This principle allows it to grasp the phenomenon of Force, but also, as an inadvertent discovery, to grasp itself as essentially reflexive. Moreover, it comes to understand that its own reflexivity means that it is constitutive of the reality that it investigates:

> I distinguish myself from myself, and in doing so, I am directly aware that what is distinguished from myself is not different from me. I, the self-same being, repel myself from myself; but what is posited as distinct from me, or as unlike me, is immediately, in being so distinguished, not a distinction for me. It is true that consciousness of an "other," of an object in general, is itself necessarily self-consciousness, a reflectedness-into-self, consciousness of itself in its otherness. (¶ 164)

In distinguishing something as different from consciousness, consciousness makes a determination of something negative. In *stating* "that is not me," a positive reality is born. The fact of the statement seems to undermine the content of the statement, for the statement effects a linguistic relationship between the "I" and the reality that is "other." Clearly, this reality which is ostensibly different from the consciousness that announces itself here is not *so* different that it eludes linguistic reference altogether. Consciousness knows it well enough to negate it, and this piece of "not me" has a linguistic place within the world of consciousness itself. Hence, the question arises, what does it mean to affirm through language that which one seeks to negate? What kind of curious negation is this that lives on in language as an affirmation?

When Hegel's emergent subject, here understood as the mode of consciousness, states or explains its fundamental difference from the world, the mode in which that explanation is made contradicts the explicit intention and content of the explanation. As that which must express what it knows in language, i.e., that which must externalize its knowledge in linguistic form, consciousness is "of" the world, in the sense that it appears in the world. Hence, if consciousness seeks to explain its ontological difference from the world, it can only contradict itself in the process. And yet the rhetoric of Explanation does not completely make a fool of the consciousness that seeks to articulate its onto-logical distinction. Consciousness *is* different from the sensuous and perceptual world that it encounters, but this difference is not an external one; rather, consciousness is internally related to that which it seeks to know, a necessary moment in the hermeneutical circle in which the investigator is implicated in the object of investigation.

The encounter with ostensible ontological disparity and the discovery that interrelatedness exists after all is, here as elsewhere in the *Phenomenology*, effected in the transition from reading literally to reading rhetorically. When the Hegelian subject states or enacts or otherwise externalizes its conviction that it is absolutely other to this or that aspect of the world, the very process of externalizing that conviction works to undermine it, and, eventually, proves that the opposite is true. In stating or dramatizing its truth, negation gains a home in the world, and thus is transformed from an indeterminate negation to a determinate one, one that exists as a moment in a web of interrelatedness, one that has a place.

Significantly, Hegel relies on the rhetorical meanings of linguistic explanation in effecting the transition between consciousness and self-consciousness. Inasmuch as self-consciousness is characterized by reflexivity, i.e., the capacity to relate to itself, this is conditioned by the power of articulation. Moreover, it is not that articulation offers forth a "content" which is then reflected upon by a consciousness doggedly watching from an ontological elsewhere, but consciousness reveals itself as *an articulated phenomenon*, that which only becomes itself *as* articulation. Once articulated, this consciousness is no longer appropriately called by that name, for it has rhetorically refuted the conditions of ontological disparity which that name denoted. In becoming articulated, consciousness becomes itself, but, in classical Hegelian parlance, it does this only by becoming another. In this instance, that Other, which is, yes, its fullest self, is self-consciousness.

The movement of this transition is a *rhetorical* movement; the insight that is finally revealed is first enacted without self-awareness, and it is only once that enactment is completed, the Explanation stated and finished, that consciousness takes a look at this product and recognizes itself as its author. The purpose of the Explanation no longer matters, for consciousness has made an unexpected and more significant discovery: it has the capacity to recognize itself, it is a reflexive structure, and it inhabits a place in the world. As external, consciousness is "other" to itself, which means that it is that which is generally understood as "other" to itself, namely, the world; hence, the inverse of this statement of identity is also true: consciousness of the world is always simply consciousness of itself in its alterity. The rhetorical movement of the transition thus reaffirms the principle of identity, the ontological place of difference, the supporting web of internal relations.

As a rhetorical agency, the Hegelian subject always knows more than it thinks it knows, and by reading itself rhetorically, i.e., reading the meanings it unwittingly *enacts* against those it explicitly *intends*, it recovers ever greater dimensions of its own identity. Rhetoric is thus the condition of deception and of illumination, the way in which the subject is always beyond itself, meaning what it does not necessarily intend but nevertheless externalizes, then reads, and finally recovers for itself.

The rhetorical drama of Explanation we have been following is recapitulated on a more concrete level in the drama of desire. The problem of consciousness, we will remember, is how to conceptualize its relationship with the sensuous and perceptual world. As the advanced form of Understanding, consciousness could delineate the features or "moments" of this world, but could not effect a unity with that world. In effect, consciousness has only a theoretical experience of its object, a notion of what it must be like, but the sensuous and perceptual world remains remote, conjectured, experientially unknown. In the transition to self-consciousness, we are told to expect the following: "the Notion of the object is superseded in the actual object, or the first, immediate presentation of the object is superseded in experience: certainty gives place to truth" *(die Gewissheit ging in der Wahrheit verloren)* (¶ 166).

How then does the sensuous and perceptual world become an experience for self-consciousness, or, in even stronger terms, how is this world experienced *as* self-consciousness? In ¶ 167, the *Phenomenology* begins to answer this question for us by calling on the experience of *desire* as the mode in which self-consciousness requires that sensuous and perceptual world. Hegel introduces the notion of desire casually, at the end of a complicated explanation, as if it were something we should already understand. The problem under consideration is how to make the sensuous and perceptual world a difference that is no difference, that is, how to recapitulate this world as a feature of self-consciousness itself. We have seen that "explaining" the world went part of the way in doing the trick, but the solution there seemed too abstract:

> With the first moment, self-consciousness is in the form of consciousness, and the whole expanse of the sensuous world is preserved for it, but at the same time only as connected with the second moment, the unity of self-consciousness with itself; and hence the sensuous world is for it an enduring existence which, however, is only *appearance*, or a difference which, in itself, is no difference. This antithesis of appearance and its truth has, however, for its essence only the truth, viz, the unity must become essential to self-consciousness, i.e. self-consciousness is Desire in general. (¶ 167)

In the "first moment" or primary thesis – roughly Part 1 of the *Phenomenology* – the sensuous world endures as appearance. But what kind of appearance is this? It is, we learn, ostensibly different from a reality or essence, but then this distinction turns out not to hold: it is "difference which, in itself, is no difference." Consciousness has learned through its powers of explanation that it appears to hold the truth of the opposing world, yet a new disparity arises, namely, that between the *appearance* of that world as external and unreachable, and its *truth* which is evidenced in consciousness' well-wrought Explanation. In order to overcome this particular distinction between appearance and truth, this sensuous and perceptual world must become "unified" with consciousness in some way; if this unity is to take place, and one of the terms of this unity is the sensuous world, then it makes sense to assume that self-consciousness itself must have a sensuous expression. And that the sensuous articulation of self-consciousness "is Desire in general."

The German word for desire, *Begierde*, suggests animal appetite rather than the anthropocentric sense conveyed by the French *le désir* and the English *desire*.[9] Introduced at this juncture in the text, the term clearly acquires the meaning of animal hunger; the sensuous and perceptual world is desired in the sense that it is required for consumption and is the means for the reproduction of life. As we follow the textual development of desire, we learn that human desire is distinguished from animal desire in virtue of its reflexivity, its tacit philosophical project, and its rhetorical possibilities. At this point, however, we are equipped only with the insights that Force and Explanation have provided us; we understand *movement* as the play of Forces, and Explanation as the necessary *alterity* of consciousness itself. Predictably enough, the experience of desire initially appears as a synthesis of movement and alterity.

In desiring some feature of the world, self-consciousness effects the unity with the world that consciousness could only effect theoretically and inadvertently. As an explicit desire for some aspect of the world, self-consciousness not only appropriates the rhetorical accomplishment of consciousness, but follows the syllogism through, as it were, and becomes the sensuous enactment of this unity. Hence, desire becomes the sensuous articulation of a sensuous object which is simultaneously a reflexive pursuit of self-consciousness itself. Immediately following Hegel's remark that "self-consciousness is Desire in general," Hegel explains the ambiguity of the project of desire:

> Consciousness, as self-consciousness, henceforth has a double object, that of sense-certainty and perception, which however for self-consciousness has the character of a negative; and the second, viz, itself, which is the true *essence*, and is present in the first instance only as opposed to the first object. (¶ 167)

Desire is here described in terms of its ambiguous intentional aims, but these two aims are also developmental stages of consciousness: the first aim, the object of sense-certainty and perception, is the conventional object of consciousness, a relationship we have already examined; the second aim, consciousness' reflexive pursuit of itself, is also already known, for that is what we found in the drama of Explanation. Hence, desire is always desire for something other which, in turn, is always a desire for a more expanded version of the subject. The "immediate object...of sense-certainty and perception" appears as "a negative" because it is *not* consciousness. And yet self-consciousness seeks to articulate or thematize itself, and in this "first instance" or initial phase of desire's development, the pursuit of alterity and the pursuit of oneself seem in stark opposition. In effect, we have learned the lessons of Force and Explan-ation, but at this point we can only embody these lessons as an internal paradox. Insofar as we desire, we desire in two mutually exclusive ways; in desiring something else, we lose ourselves, and in desiring ourselves, we lose the world. At this stage in the dramatization of desire, unacceptable impover-ishment seems to be its consequence; either as narcissism or as enthrallment with an object, desire is at odds with itself, contradictory and dissatisfied.

Desire has a "double-object," and, therefore, becomes a source of deception when a single univocal aim becomes the object of "true desire." And yet there is motivation for overcoming this paradoxical situation, for the confrontation with the object of sense-certainty and perception is intrinsically dissatisfying. That object is "other," absolutely different, signifying nothing for conscious-ness except its own ontological limitations. Otherness incites self-consciousness, occasions its articulation as desire, but is also the source of suffering for this emergent subject. Self-consciousness is thus additionally defined by Hegel as "essentially the return from otherness" (¶ 167), in which case desire, as the expression of self-consciousness, is a constant effort to overcome the appear-ance of ontological disparity between consciousness and its world. This dispar-ity initially appears as insurmountable, and this alleged insurmountability pervades the naive experience of our metaphysical traveler; it is a primary phenomenological given, but one that is gradually dissolved through the efforts of desire. In effect, desire does not alter ontological difference, but provides an alternate mode of conceptualizing this disparity, a conceptualization that per-mits the revelation of that disparity in its proper, more fully developed, ontological organization. The world of desire, the countervailing world of consciousness, must not be annihilated, but reconceived and rediscovered as constitutive of self-consciousness. This is effected through an enhanced under-standing of "difference." The negative relation that adheres between the emerging subject and its world not only differentiates, but *binds*. Consciousness is *not* the object of its desire, but this negation is a *determinate* negation, for that object is prefigured by desire, and desire is essentially transformed by that object; in effect, this negation is constitutive of desire itself. In seeking its own return from otherness, desire implicitly attempts to recast absolute differ-ence as determinate negation, to reconcile difference within a unity of experi-ence in which negation is revealed as a relation that mediates. Desire can thus be said to reveal negation as constitutive of experience itself.

We can see, then, that the ontological primacy of negation is both enacted and revealed by desire, that the negation can only be understood as essential to experience through a consideration of the *reflexivity* of self-consciousness. Insofar as all external relations are transformed into internal – or double – relations through the mediated self-reflection of Hegel's emerging subject, all

indeterminate negations or ruptures in the ontology of experience are rediscovered as determinate negations, differences that are contained within the
ontological integrity of experience. In that desire always emerges as a confrontation with a difference that appears ontologically disparate, and is, further, an
effort to overcome this disparity through disclosing a mode of interrelatedness
which has hitherto remained opaque, it seems fair to conclude that desire is
always thematizing – and rendering actual – the ontological preconditions of its
own emergence. Whereas the initial confrontation with otherness enforces a
sense of limitation on consciousness, the satisfaction of desire reveals a more
capable self, one that is able to admit its interdependence, and thereby gain a
more expanded and expansive identity.

But what is meant by satisfaction? We have learned that Hegel's subject
desires the object of sense-certainty and perception, and that this desire
incorporates the two projects characteristic of Force and Explanation. At
first, these two projects appear at odds, and it seems that the subject can
only pursue the object or itself, but never both at once. In an attempt to
reconcile this paradox, consciousness sets the paradox into movement. The
objects of desire are no longer understood as static and ontologically self-
sufficient, but are reconceived as so many *shapes* of Life, where Life is defined
as the incessant consolidation and dissolution of shape. The "play of Force" is
thus recast onto the field of objects at a more sophisticated level of ontological
organization.

The concept of Life appears, then, to reconcile the moments of determinateness and negativity which, conceived from a static point of view, appeared only
paradoxically related. Indeed, this unity is constitutive of Life: "the simple
substance of Life is the splitting up of itself into shapes and at the same time the
dissolution of these existent differences . . . life . . . is just as much an imparting
of shape as a supersession of it" (¶ 171). At this point Hegel's subject concludes
that the proper object of desire is Life, and subscribes to a primitive form of
pantheism which attributes creative powers to the objective world. Excluded
from this dialectic of vitalism, the subject views this active world from a
distance that signals its relapse into ontological exile. This subject desires
Life, but as one who is himself incapable of living, so that desire is mixed
with pathos, the inevitable melancholy which attends the knowledge of irre-
traversible distance. Conceived here as an initial stage of self-consciousness, the
subject is wise to Life without being "of" it.

This form of estrangement is reminiscent of the Emily Dickinson poem
beginning, "I cannot live with You – It would be Life – And Life is over there
–." Like the irony of that poetic voice which so intimately disavows its own
proximity to the living, so Hegel's melancholic self-consciousness vitally refutes any claim to Life. This subject does not yet know its own "livelihood," its

capacity to create and dissolve shape, and, in fact, does not gain that knowledge until the end of the section "Lordship and Bondage"; indeed, the bondsman exists as a "lifeless thing" until he labors on objects that reflect his creative powers. At this juncture, however, the subject is out of work, like a meditative Faust whose sadness turns to frustration and, finally, to destructive envy.[10] Life here appears as a monolith, self-sufficient and impervious, and human desire, a futile and humiliating enterprise. Like Fichte's notion of human reality as an intrinsically insatiable *Sehnsucht* or longing, so desire at this moment in the *Phenomenology* is a constant reminder of the uselessness of human endeavors. Desire is vacuity, a pure for-itself, the "useless passion" which will later appear in Sartre's *Being and Nothingness*.

Either our traveling subject has forgotten his lessons, or he no longer knows how to sustain his new-found identity as a mediating agent in this encounter with Life. Both are doubtless true, difficulty begetting forgetfulness. Because this hapless agency does not participate in the Life that he desires, he seems not to consider himself a living being, and so desire becomes the experience of a kind of death in life, an isolated moment of non-being, what Emily Dickinson's speaker refers to as "my Right of Frost – Death's privilege . . . " Experiencing itself as an essential poverty, self-consciousness becomes a vacuum that must consume Life in order to gain some temporary reality for itself. This subject does not sit with its identity as a static nothingness in the midst of being; indeed, it seems unable to bear the stasis of its own negativity. Thus, without intentionally challenging the presumption of ontological exile, this agent sets its own negativity into motion, becoming an agent of nothingness, an actor whose role is to negate. Thematizing the presumed conditions of its own identity, this subject dramatizes its despair. Instead of a dead being, it becomes an agency of death.

This reflexive appropriation of the conditions of its own identity results in an *enactment* of negativity which, predictably, has paradoxical rhetorical consequences. As an effort to negate, consuming desire seeks to annihilate the independence of some living object (it cannot negate Life in the general sense, so restricts itself to some determinate manifestation of the enemy). By negating *this* living object, rendering this object as nothing, self-consciousness comes to view the object as no longer existing, and accounts for its vanishing from existence in terms of its own actions. Thus, self-consciousness recognizes *itself* as the agency of accomplishment; certain of the nothingness of this object, self-consciousness explicitly affirms that this nothingness is *for itself* the truth of this object. The ontological roles are thus inverted. Through destroying the living object, self-consciousness gives itself positive form as an agency of destruction. Regarding its own agency in this accomplished act, self-consciousness becomes certain of its own reality once again. The lessons gleaned from the drama of Explanation are thus recapitulated in the scene of consuming desire.

Having destroyed an independently living object, self-consciousness now knows itself as an agency of destruction. Its certainty of itself is, of course, dependent on that object that once was and now no longer is. As the effort to consume or destroy life, desire proves to be essentially related to Life, even if only in the mode of negation. The experience of consuming desire makes explicit the mediated relationship of self-consciousness and its object once again, for the experience of desire cannot furnish self-certainty without first relating to an independent object. In effect, a destructive agent has no identity without a world to be destroyed; thus, this being who, convinced of his exile from Life, endeavors to destroy all living things, ends up paradoxically dramatizing his essential dependence on the world of the living.

As a destructive or consuming agency, self-consciousness as desire essays to gain reality through the consumption of a living thing. The reality that it gains, however, is different from the reality that it intended to appropriate: having assumed that the object monopolized Life, this agency sought to consume the object and appropriate Life as an attribute that could be easily transferred from the object to self-consciousness. Now this same agency realizes that having negated the object, it still retains a dependency on that object; moreover, that determinate living object is not the same as Life itself, and so a potentially infinite number of living objects must be negated for self-consciousness to gain the monopoly on Life that it seeks, and this project soon appears endless and futile. Self-consciousness thus concludes that Life and living objects cannot be fully assimilated, that desire must find some new form, that it must develop from destruction to a recognition of the insurpassibility of other living things: "In this satisfaction . . . experience makes it aware that the object has its own independence. . . . It is in fact something other than self-consciousness which is the essence of Desire; and through this experience self-consciousness has realized its own truth" (¶ 175).

The project of consuming desire is itself conditioned by a prior ontological assumption which casts self-consciousness in the role of a pure vacuity, external and unrelated to substantive being. This scheme is disrupted through the dramatization of destruction inasmuch as desire once again determines itself as a positive reality through its own determinate acts. Desire is thus revealed as a *negating negativity*, no longer a lifeless and isolated nothingness. As an active or generative negation, desire is once again articulated as a determinate reality. And insofar as desire in this general sense is self-consciousness, we discover at yet another level of experience the *reflexivity* of self-consciousness as that which dramatizes itself, and the *intentionality* of self-consciousness – the insurpassability of otherness: "Desire and the self-certainty obtained in its gratification are conditioned by the object, for self-certainty comes from superseding this other; in order that this supersession can take place, there must be this other" (¶ 175).

We saw the intentional enthrallment characteristic of consciousness, and here we see it recapitulated as a mediating structure of self-consciousness. As the experience of desire, self-consciousness sustains a necessarily ambiguous relation to that which is other to itself. Desire is always desire "for" something other than self-consciousness (even when what is desired is the obliteration of the other, it is "the obliteration of the other" which remains its intentional object). Moreover, the intentionality of desire is always also informed by its reflexive project; desire always reveals the desiring agent as intrinsically other to itself: self-consciousness is an *ek-static* being, outside itself, in search of self-recovery. The proliferation of objects of desire affirm for self-consciousness the persistent realm of alterity. In order for desire to gain determinate reality, it must continually pursue an indefinite domain of alterity; the reflexive experience of desire is only possible in and through the experience of desirable things. The conclusion drawn by self-consciousness that the world of objects is not consumable in its entirety has an unexpected inverse conclusion: desire requires this endless proliferation of alterity in order to stay alive as desire, as a desire that not only wants life, but *is living*. If the domain of living things could be consumed, desire would, paradoxically, *lose* its life; it would be a quiescent satiety, an end to the negative generativity that is self-consciousness. This agency that once assumed that a counterposing world of being monopolized Life, that "Life is over there," now distrusts self-identical being as death itself, and safeguards its own negativity as the source of its own perpetual life.

The drama of consuming desire proves to be not wholly satisfying. As self-consciousness eats its way through the world, it realizes that this mode of contending with difference is exceedingly tiresome. For a while, this ravenous agent figures that ultimately the domain of external objects will all be consumed, but Life proves to be more prolific than expected, and instead of gradually eliminating the domain of alterity, self-consciousness confronts the infinity of determinate objects and, accordingly, the infinite insatiability of desire. As the constant activity of negation, desire never successfully thematizes itself in and through a given object, for that object is always vanishing into the stomach of desire, as it were, and so vanishes self-consciousness' own experience of itself. Self-consciousness knows itself as that which consumes alterity, but it only knows this indirectly, inferring from the absence of an object its own power of agency. Now convinced of its own status as a living being, self-consciousness becomes weary of its own vanishing act, and comes to wonder whether it might not reconcile Life with some more permanent sense of self. Endeavoring to escape the fate of a purely transient self, self-consciousness develops the notion of a being like itself which might remain independent and offer a more stable experience of reflexivity than the consumption of natural objects could provide. The intentional object of desire thus alters from the infinity of natural objects to the finite Other:

> It is in fact something other than self-consciousness that is the essence of Desire; and through this experience self-consciousness has realized its truth. But at the same time it is no less absolutely *for itself*, and it is so only by superseding the object; and it must experience its satisfaction, for it is the truth. On account of the independence of the object, therefore, *it can achieve satisfaction only when the object effects the negation within itself* [my emphasis]; and it must carry out this negation of itself in itself, for it is *in itself* the negative, and must be *for* the other what it *is*. Since the object is in its own self negation, and in being so is at the same time independent, it is consciousness. (¶ 175)

When Hegel claims that something "other than self-consciousness" must be the essence of desire, he seems to be relying on the previously drawn conclusion that for desire the realm of alterity is insurpassable. And yet the very next sentence casts doubt on this initial claim: "at the same time it [self-consciousness] is no less absolutely *for itself*." The question then emerges, how are we to understand self-consciousness as essentially realized in otherness, and yet as absolutely for itself? What kind of "otherness" must self-consciousness find such that self-realization mediated by this Other results in self-recovery? If desire is realized in otherness, and this otherness reflects itself, then the otherness that desire seeks must be *another self-consciousness*. Hence, the only true satisfaction for desire is to be found in an object that mirrors the reflexive structure of desire itself. The externality of the independent object can only be overcome if intrinsic to that externality is a self-negating or reflexive structure: "on account of the independence of the object, therefore, it can achieve satisfaction only when the object effects the negation within itself."

We might well question whether self-consciousness is the kind of phenomenon that fits this requirement exclusively. Hegel tells us that negation is specified in self-consciousness as "absolute negation" (¶ 178), which distinguishes self-consciousness from other phenomena that embody negation in other ways. Apart from absolute negation, which is equivalently referred to as "Desire" or "negation in another self-consciousness," there is negation as a determinateness or apparent externality, and negation as "the inorganic universal nature of Life," the dynamic of consolidating and dissolving shape already considered (¶ 178). In absolute negation, we find negation operating as the essence and final actualization of a given reality. Like Spinoza's definition of desire as a "final end,"[11] Hegel here characterizes the negativity of desire as the final, fully realized form of self-consciousness. To understand this correctly, we must not assume that negation is nothingness; on the contrary, as a differentiating relation that mediates the terms that initially counter each other, negation, understood in the sense of *Aufhebung*, cancels, preserves, and transcends the apparent differences it interrelates. As the final realization of self-consciousness, negation is a principle of absolute mediation, an infinitely capable subject that is its interrelations with all apparently different phenomena. The human capacity for negation is privileged inasmuch as the work of negation can be thematized and appropriated by the negating agency itself; indeed, thematization and appropriation become essential moments of "the labour of the negative," the work of discovering relations where there seemed to be none. Hence, Hegel claims that only in self-consciousness do we find a "universal independent nature in which negation is present as absolute negation." In the following paragraph, Hegel elaborates: "the immediate 'I' " – the other self-consciousness that is the object of desire – "is itself absolute mediation, it *is* only as a supersession of the independent object, in other words, it is Desire" (¶ 176).

For desire to enact absolute negation, it must find a way to embody absolute negation as an object of experience; and if it *is* absolute negation, it must, therefore, duplicate itself as the object of desire. Only through its duplication as an Other can desire be rendered explicit, realized as its own final end: "a self-consciousness exists *for a self-consciousness*. Only so is it in fact self-consciousness; for only in this way does the unity of itself in its otherness become explicit for it" (¶ 177).

In "The Truth of Self-Certainty," this other self-consciousness is imagined as the logically appropriate object of desire, but not until the following section, "Lordship and Bondage," do we meet such an Other, and only in the course of that section do we become convinced of the necessity of its existence. We have understood desire as the effort of a disembodied consciousness to acquire reality from an ostensibly disparate world of substance, and we have altered our notion of human agency to fit the reflexive requirements of self-consciousness. As a sensuous articulation of consciousness, desire discloses self-consciousness as that which participates in what it investigates. Desire thus constantly widens its intentional aims and thereby expands the domain of reflexivity which it indicates and enacts. Indeed, from Force to Explanation, to the consumption of Life, we have gained insight into the ever widening circumference of reflexivity that constitutes the emerging subject of the *Phenomenology*. In this last dramatic moment, we learn that this subject not only consumes its world, that the mediation of difference is not only the internalization of otherness, but also the externalization of the subject. These two moments of assimilation and projection are part of the same movement, that ever-widening circumference of reality which, in Hegel's words, "unifies" subject and substance, those two related but independent moments which condition the irreducible ambiguity of this emerging identity. Desire is this subject's necessarily ambiguous movement toward the world, consumption and externalization, appropriation and dispersal; the "Life" of the subject is the constant consolidation and dissolution of itself. As desire becomes desire-for-another-desire, this subject hopes to get a self-sustaining picture of himself, an independent embodiment of negation that will reflect his own powers of absolute negation. This subject no doubt expects that this is the end of the journey, that to know oneself as "absolute negation" is to recognize one's own self-sufficiency, the unity of independence – explicit reality – and negativity that one is. But at this point this subject's vision is too narrow, for he mistakenly restricts his dependence to the world of natural objects, and does not anticipate his dependence on the self-consciousness he will meet. He shows no understanding of human embodiment, and he surely underestimates the complexity and consequences of what it means to be reflected in and by another emerging subject. Vain and headstrong, this subject once again travels swiftly toward defeat.

Bodily Paradoxes: Lordship and Bondage

An infernal love . . . aims at subjugating a freedom in order to take shelter in it from the world. – Sartre, *Saint Genet*

Desire is *aufgehoben* in "Lordship and Bondage"; it is canceled yet preserved, which is to say that it is transformed into a more internally complicated mode of human striving. Viewed as the least sophisticated project of self-consciousness, desire is sometimes dismissed as no longer having an ontological role to play in this section;[12] it may be said to be supplanted by the struggle for recognition and the dialectic of lord and bondsman, but the meaning of "supplanted" must be critically attended. As long as we are still within the experience of self-consciousness, and "Desire in general" is its essential character, then the drama of recognition and labor must be seen as permutations of desire; indeed, what we witness in this chapter is the gradual specification of desire: self-consciousness as desire *in particular*. The notion of desire loses its reified character as an abstract universal, and becomes situated in terms of an embodied identity. For Hegel, labor is "inhibited desire" (¶ 195), and recognition becomes the more sophisticated form of reflection that promises to satisfy desire.

The above argument is in some sense superfluous, for it is not finally appropriate to consider whether desire, conceived as some independent agency, is *aufgehoben* or superseded in "Lordship and Bondage." The action of supersession is not applied to desire as a force externally imposed upon a discrete agent; desire is nothing other than the action of supersession itself. Moreover, what it means to "supersede" a given externality itself changes and develops throughout the *Phenomenology*, and *Aufhebung* is only the abstract and logical term for a developing set of experiences which dramatize the negation of difference and thereby posit/reveal ever more encompassing unities or interrelations. The concrete meaning of *Aufhebung* is here understood as the developing sequence: consuming desire, desire for recognition, desire for another's desire. Hence, in asking whether desire is still operative in "Lordship and Bondage," we misunderstand the operative force in the *Phenomenology* at large, its logical motor, as it were, which, embodied by human subjects, is desire itself. The sophistication of desire's intentional aims is at once the enhancement of human conceptual powers, the ever-expanding capacity to discern identity in difference, to expand the hermeneutical circle of Hegel's traveling metaphysician.

In "The Truth of Self-Certainty" we learn that through the experience of desire self-consciousness discovers itself as "essentially negative." Moreover, we come to see how the "difference" between consciousness and its object becomes the ground for a new identity. The effort of desire to appropriate an object, and through that appropriation to assert its own identity, reveals self-consciousness as that which must relate itself to another being in order to become itself. The gradual yet insistent effort of Hegel's journeying subject in the *Phenomenology of Spirit* never relinquishes this project to relate itself to externality in order to rediscover itself as more inclusive being. The insurpassability of externality implies the permanence of desire. In this sense, insofar as Hegel's subject never achieves a static union with externality, it is hopelessly beyond its own grasp, although it retains as its highest aim the thorough comprehension of itself. This thoroughgoing self-determination is the ideal of integrity toward which self-consciousness strives, and this striving is denoted by desire.

On the one hand, we concede that desire alone will never achieve this total self-comprehension for desire alone is the consumption of objects, and we have seen how consumption fails effectively to assimilate externality. On the other hand, we need to ask whether speaking of "desire alone" in Hegel's view makes any sense. After all, desire revealed an implicit intentional aim, namely, to disclose and enact a common ontological structure with the world. Hence, despite the alleged object of desire, i.e., "this piece of fruit," or its more general aim, "the consumption of this brute being which poses as other to me," desire has at base a metaphysical project which, while requiring determinate objects, transcends them as well, i.e., to effect a unity with the realm of externality which both preserves that realm and renders it into a reflection of self-consciousness. The dissatisfaction of desire implies that something *would* satisfy desire, that this something is missing, and that a consideration of the inadequacies of the mode of consumption will provide the criteria for a satisfying object. In the turn to another self-consciousness as a possible object of satisfaction, we can see that it is not desire itself that is superseded, but a *peculiar form* of desire, and that the aim of self-consciousness, even as it leaves the section on self-certainty, is still the satisfaction of desire.

Desire does not merely survive into the section "Lordship and Bondage," but remains essential to the ever-expanding project of negation that structures the *Phenomenology*. Because desire is the principle of self-consciousness' reflexivity or inner difference, and because it has as its highest aim the assimilation of all external relations into relations of inner difference, desire forms the experiential basis for the project of the *Phenomenology* at large. Desire and its satisfaction constitute the first and final moments of the philosophical pursuit of self-knowledge (¶ 165). In this regard, the metaphysical project that informs the entire project of *Geist* finds its original and final measure in the criteria desire sets forth for its satisfaction. Hence, to claim that desire is simply an unsophisticated form of knowing and being in Hegel's system is to misread the standard of truth that governs the *Phenomenology* generally; the gradual sophistication of desire – the expanding inclusiveness of its intentional aims – is the principle of progress in the *Phenomenology*.

Stanley Rosen, a student of Kojève's, argues that desire is the basis of both historical progress and the development of philosophical self-reflection; he places Hegel among those modern philosophers who stress the primacy of desire in human development:

> In the tradition of such modern philosophers as Machiavelli and Hobbes, [Hegel] recognizes desire as the "engine" of world-history (thereby uniting the Platonic Eros with the directedness of historical development). The spirit first knows itself as subjective feeling. When feeling is localized externally, or given an objective status, spirit divides itself into inner and outer world. We become alienated from ourselves or regard our true self as contained in the object outside us, which we desire to assimilate. Desire is thus fundamentally desire for myself, or for my interior essence from which I have become detached. The struggle to satisfy my desires leads to the development of individual consciousness. Since others desire the same things, this struggle is also the origin of the family, the state, and, in general, of world-history.[13]

As Rosen suggests, the dramatic education of Hegel's journeying subject consists of a series of self-alienations which prompt a revision of the subject itself.[14] Every confrontation with an external reality is at once an alienation of the subject; difference threatens the subject with annihilation until the subject can discover that difference as an essential moment of itself. In the section "Lordship and Bondage," Hegel's emergent subject confronts another self-consciousness, and immediately concludes that it, the initial subject, has lost itself. Desire remains defeated until it can find a way of revealing that other subject as essential to its own identity; this way is forged through the struggle for recognition.

The previous section on self-certainty provides a theoretical understanding of the necessity of the Other. Self-consciousness needed to understand itself as self-negation, as a self-determining being. The Other was distinguished from other objects in that it was like the first self-consciousness – an independently subsisting being who exhibited the principle of self-negation. Discovering this Other self-consciousness appears in that section to be the only way that the initial self-consciousness can regard its own essential structure rendered explicit. The task of "Lordship and Bondage" is to demonstrate how this process is effected in experience. The reflection of the subject in and through the Other is achieved through the process of reciprocal recognition, and this recognition proves to be – in the terms of that section – the satisfaction of desire. Our task, then, is to understand the project of desire – the negation and assimilation of otherness and the concomitant expansion of the proper domain of the subject – in the encounter with another subject with a structurally identical set of aims.

The transition from "The Truth of Self-Certainty" to "Lordship and Bondage" is a curious one in that the former section conjectures the existence of the Other as an adequate object for self-consciousness' desire in *theoretical* terms. And yet the progress of the *Phenomenology* is ostensibly necessitated by knowledge gained from experience. The first paragraph of "Lordship and Bondage" reiterates this theoretical conclusion, asserting prior to its demonstration that "self-consciousness exists in and for itself when, and by the fact that, it so exists for another; that is, it exists only in being acknowledged [*anerkannt*]" (¶ 178). Because we cannot expect that self-consciousness has certain knowledge of its own requirements before these requirements are made clear in experience, we are forced to regard the emergence of the Other in the following paragraph as puzzling: "Self-consciousness is faced by another self-consciousness" (¶ 179) – but why? And why has it not happened earlier? Why did the journeying subject of the *Phenomenology* begin its journey alone, and why was its confrontation with the sensuous and perceptual world previous to its confrontation with an Other?

As I noted in my earlier discussion of the "appearance" of desire, the development of the *Phenomenology* suggests that the reader must make a strict distinction between the *appearance* of a given entity and its conceptual reality. The appearance of the Other must be understood as an emergence into explicit reality which has hitherto remained an implicit or nascent being. Before its actual appearance, the Other remains opaque, but not for that reason without reality. Coming into existence – or explicit appearance – is never, for Hegel, a creation *ex nihilo*, but is, rather, a moment in the development of a Concept (*Begriff*). The Other is revealed as an essential structure of all experience in the course of the *Phenomenology*; indeed, there can be no experience outside the context of intersubjectivity. Hence, even as the *Phenomenology* claims to be an experience of the genesis of *Geist*, it is a fictive experience created by and through the text, and must be understood as an experience uniquely philosophical – a sustained inverted world – which delineates in the terms of its own temporality the structures that condition and inform historical experience as we know it.[15]

To say, then, that the Other appears is not to claim that the initial self-consciousness discovers a phenomenon that previously had no ontological status; rather, it is only now that the Other becomes explicit in virtue of its centrality to the initial self-consciousness' pursuit of an identity that encompasses the world. The Other becomes the general object of desire.

The optimism that characterized the closure of "The Truth of Self-Certainty" and the opening paragraph of "Lordship and Bondage" is a function of the purely conceptual nature of the conclusion that mutual recognition is a possible and gratifying object for desire; this possibility, however, must be dramatized in order to be known. Self-consciousness begins this struggle in ¶ 179 where it discovers that the structural similarity of the Other is not an immediate occasion for deriving an adequate reflection of itself in the Other; indeed, the first experience of the Other's similarity is that of *self-loss*.

> Self-consciousness is faced by another self-consciousness; it has come *out of itself.* This has a two-fold significance: first, it has lost itself, for it finds itself as an *other* being; secondly, in doing so it has superseded the other, for it does not see the other as an essential being, but in the other sees its own self. (¶ 178)[16]

The initial self-consciousness seeks to have itself reflected in the other self-consciousness, but finds itself not merely reflected, but wholly absorbed. The initial self-consciousness no longer seeks to consume the Other, as it sought to consume objects, *but is instead consumed by the Other.* Self-consciousness comes out of itself when faced with the Other, where "*ausser sich*" in German not only denotes coming out of oneself, but ecstasy as well as anger.[17] The intentional and reflexive relations to the Other are temporarily lost, and self-consciousness is convinced that the Other has occupied its own essence – self-negation – stolen it even, and in this sense self-consciousness finds itself besieged by the Other. In one respect, self-consciousness discovers that the self-negating principle of self-consciousness itself is a detachable attribute, one that might be extricated from the particular embodiment that the initial self-consciousness is. And insofar as self-negation is its own essence, self-consciousness concludes that essence and embodiment are only contingently related, that the same essence might inhabit different embodiments at different times. That self-consciousness can find its own essential principle embodied *elsewhere* appears as a frightening and even angering experience. And yet the ambiguity of "*ausser sich sein*" suggests that the externality that self-consciousness is now seen to inhabit is not wholly external: in desiring the Other, self-consciousness discovers itself as ecstatic being, a being that has it in itself to become other to itself, which, through the self-surpassing principle of desire, *gives itself up* to the Other even as it charges that the Other has somehow appropriated it. The ambiguity of gift and appropriation characterizes the initial encounter with the Other, and transforms this meeting of two desires into a struggle (*Kampf*).[18]

The first lesson gleaned from the encounter with the Other is that of the essential ambiguity of self-consciousness' externalization. Self-consciousness seeks a reflection of its own identity through the Other, but finds instead the enslaving and engulfing potential of the Other. As desire for a comprehensive identity, self-consciousness initially expects the Other to be a passive medium of reflection for itself; the Other will mirror itself since the Other is like itself. Perhaps extrapolating from its experience with objects, self-consciousness naively expects that the Other will be passive like objects, and differ only insofar as it can reflect self-consciousness' structure. Apparently, this initial self-consciousness did not take seriously enough the extent to which the Other is, indeed, *like* itself, i.e., a principle of *active* negation, and so is scandalized by the independent freedom of the Other. The independence that was to be a passive reflection of the initial self-consciousness is now conceived as an externality which safeguards freedom within the Other, a situation considered threatening by the first self-consciousness who viewed freedom as its own exclusive property.

Self-consciousness' anger – the way in which it is "*ausser sich*" – does not proceed directly from the perceptual experience described above, but as a consequence of its own ecstatic involvement with the Other. The Other embodies its freedom because the initial self-consciousness has forfeited its freedom to the Other. Desire is here understood as ecstatic self-sacrifice, which is in direct contradiction to the overriding project of desire, i.e., to attain an ever more capable identity. Desire thus founders on contradiction, and becomes a passion divided against itself. Striving to become coextensive with the world, an autonomous being that finds itself everywhere reflected in the world, self-consciousness discovers that implicit in its own identity as a desiring being is the necessity of being claimed by another.

The initial encounter with the Other is thus a narcissistic project which fails through an inability to recognize the Other's freedom. This failure of recognition is itself conditioned by the view of the Other's externality as encapsulating, a view that presupposes that the ecstatic involvement of the first self-consciousness is necessarily self-annihilating. The philosophical assumption of this experience is that freedom is an exclusive characteristic of the individual, and that it can inhabit a particular embodiment only as that embodiment's exclusive property. Thus, insofar as it is the body of the Other that is seen to lay claim to freedom, it is that body that must be destroyed. Only through the death of the Other will the initial self-consciousness retrieve its claim to autonomy.

The quandary conditioning the struggle of life and death is that of having to choose between ecstatic and self-determining existence. Not only the bodily exteriority of the Other offends the initial self-consciousness, but its own estrangement from itself. This estrangement is not to be understood solely in terms of the fact of the Other as an independent freedom, but also as *the self-estrangement implicit in the experience of desire*. As an intentional movement, desire tends to eclipse the self that is its origin. Enthralled with its object, the desiring self can only regard itself as estranged. As a movement outside of itself, desire becomes an act of willful self-estrangement even as its overriding project is to establish a more inclusive self. Thus, the effort to overcome the Other is simultaneously an effort to overcome self-consciousness' own otherness to itself.

The ambiguity of the otherness self-consciousness seeks to overcome forms the central theme of "Lordship and Bondage," and it becomes clear that any reflexive relation that self-consciousness seeks to have is itself only possible through an intentional relation to an Other; it can overcome its own self-alienation only through overcoming the externality of the Other's self-consciousness:

> It must supersede this otherness of itself. This is the supersession of the first ambiguity, and is therefore itself a second ambiguity. First, it must proceed to supersede the *other* independent being in order thereby to become certain of *itself* as the essential being; secondly, in so doing it proceeds to supersede its *own* self, for this other is itself. (¶ 180)

The experiential meaning of "supersession" or "overcoming" in the above reveals itself as *recognition (Anerkennung)*. The initial self-consciousness can only retrieve itself from its ecstatic involvement with the Other insofar as it recognizes the Other as also in the process of retrieving itself from its own estrangement in desire. Self-consciousness' predicament, that of having to choose between ecstatic and self-determining existence, is seen to be the predicament of the Other as well. This similarity between the two self-consciousnesses ultimately proves to be the basis of their harmonious interdependence, the discovery of each that "as consciousness, it does indeed *come out of itself*, yet, though out of itself, is at the same time kept back within itself, is *for itself*, and the self outside it, is for *it*. It is aware that it at once is, and is not, another consciousness" (¶ 184). Recognition, once achieved, affirms the ambiguity of self-consciousness as both ecstatic and self-determining. The process of recognition reveals that the self-consciousness which is self-estranged, unrecognizable to itself, is still the author of its own experience: "there is nothing in it of which it is itself not the origin" (¶ 182). When the Other is viewed as the same as the subject, and this subject understands his own act of recognition as having brought the Other into explicitness, then the self is also revealed as the author of the Other. As it becomes clear that the same truths hold true of the Other's relationship to the self, the Other is also viewed as the author of the subject. Desire here loses its character as a purely consumptive activity, and becomes characterized by the ambiguity of an exchange in which two self-consciousnesses affirm their respective autonomy (independence) and alienation (otherness).

The life and death struggle appears as a necessary dramatic move for a self-consciousness that assumes that the Other's embodiment is primarily responsible for thwarting self-consciousness' pursuit of its own identity. Here corporeality everywhere signifies limitation, and the body which once seemed to condition freedom's concrete determination now requires annihilation in order for that freedom to be retrieved. The corporeal externality of each to the other presents itself as an insurpassable barrier, and seems to imply that each subject can be certain only of his own determinate life, but never can get beyond his own life to be certain of the life of the Other. Determinate life itself becomes suspect in this predicament; it thwarts self-consciousness' project to transcend its own particularity and discover itself as the essence of objects and Others in the world. The effort to annihilate the Other is originally motivated by the desire of the initial self-consciousness to present itself as a "pure abstraction"; it seeks to break its dependence on the Other and, hence, prove "that it is not attached to any specific *existence*, not to the individuality common to existence as such, that is, not attached to life" (¶ 187). And yet in order to disenthrall itself from the enslaving externality of the Other, this self-consciousness must stake its own life in the process. The project of "pure abstraction" is quickly foiled as it becomes clear that without determinate existence the initial self-consciousness would never live to see the identity after which it strives. Moreover, the death of the Other would deprive self-consciousness of the explicit recognition it requires.

The life and death struggle is a crucial section in the *Phenomenology's* development of the notion of autonomy; as Hegel claims, "the individual who has not risked his life may well be recognized as a *person*, but he has not attained to the truth of this recognition as an independent self-consciousness" (¶ 187). Although determinate life is a necessary precondition for the project of self-consciousness, desire is never satisfied when it is merely the desire to live. In order to discover itself as a negative or self-surpassing being, self-consciousness must do more than merely live; it must transcend the immediacy of pure life. It cannot stay content with the "first nature" into which it is born, but must engage itself in the creation of a "second nature" which establishes the self, not merely as a presupposition or a point of view, but as an achievement of its own making. Autonomy can be achieved only through relinquishing an enslavement to life.[19]

The life and death struggle is an extension of self-consciousness' initial project to gain unity with the Other, and to find its own identity through the Other. Insofar as the effort to obliterate the Other is a mutual or "two-fold action" (¶ 187), each self-consciousness seeks to destroy the determinate boundaries that exist between them; they seek to destroy each other's bodies. Violence to the Other appears as the most efficient route by which to nullify the Other's body. And insofar as both individuals seek to rid themselves of their dependence on determinate existence, and release the pure freedom which they view as trapped within corporeality, each seeks to merge with the Other as the abstract principle of freedom, "absolute abstraction" (¶ 186), pure being-for-self.

Thus, the life and death struggle is a continuation of the erotic that introduces Hegel's chapter; it is desire once again transformed to destruction, a project that assumes that true freedom exists only beyond the body. Whereas destructive desire in its first appearance sought to internalize otherness into a self-sufficient body, this second appearance of destructive desire endeavors to overcome bodily life altogether, i.e., to become an abstract identity without corporeal needs. Endeavoring to rid the Other of its determinate life, each self-consciousness engages in an anti-corporeal erotic which endeavors to prove in vain that the body is the ultimate limit to freedom, rather than its necessary ground and mediation.

The dynamic of lord and bondsman emerges as an extenuation of the desire to annihilate, but, because annihilation would undermine the project altogether by taking away *life*, this desire is held in check. Domination, the relation that replaces the urge to kill, must be understood as the effort to annihilate within the context of life. The Other must now *live its own death*. Rather than become an indeterminate nothingness through death, the Other must now prove its essential nothingness *in life*. The Other which was at first captivating, now becomes that which must be captured, subdued, contained. Angered at having been captivated by the Other, self-consciousness in pursuit of its own absolute freedom forces this Other to annihilate its own freedom and thus affirm the illusion that the Other is an unfree body, a lifeless instrument.

The lord's reflexive relation must be understood as an internalization of the intentional relation it had toward the Other in the life and death struggle. Self-consciousness' original effort to annihilate the body of the Other entailed the staking of its own bodily life. In dramatizing annihilation, this subject learns that annihilation can be dramatized, that is, given a living form; moreover, the fear and trembling accompanying the risking of his own life teaches him the relief of abstraction. Terror gives rise to dissociation. The lord cannot deny his body through suicide, so he proceeds *to embody his denial*. This internalization of an intentional relation, i.e., its transformation into a reflexive one, itself engenders a new intentional one: the reflexive project of disembodiment becomes linked to the domination of the Other. The lord cannot get rid of the body once and for all – this was the lesson of the life and death struggle. And yet he retains the project of becoming a pure, disembodied "I," a freedom unfettered by particularity and determinate existence, a universal and abstract identity. He still acts on the philosophical assumption that freedom and bodily life are not essential to one another, except that bodily life appears to be a precondition of freedom. But freedom does not, in the tacit view of the lord, require bodily life for its concrete expression and determination. For the lord, bodily life must be taken care of, but just as well by an Other, for the body is not part of his *own* project of identity. The lord's identity is essentially beyond the body; he gains illusory confirmation for this view by requiring the Other to *be* the body that he endeavors *not* to be.

The lord appears at the outset to live as a desire without needs; significantly, the lord is said to "enjoy" *("im Genusse sich zu befriedigen")* the fruits of the bondsman's labor, where enjoyment implies a passive reception and consumption of something other to self-consciousness, as distinct from desire which requires an active principle of negation (¶ 190). The lord desires without having to negate the thing desired, except in the impoverished sense of consuming it; the bondsman, through working on the thing, embodies the principle of negation as an active and creative principle, and thus inadvertently dramatizes that he is more than a mere body, and that the body itself is an *embodying* or expressive medium for the project of a self-determining identity. Through the experience of work, the body is revealed as an essential expression of freedom. And insofar as the bondsman works to create goods that sustain life, the bondsman also demonstrates that desire – rather than expressing a freedom *from* needs – can find fulfillment through the satisfaction of needs. Indeed, insofar as the bondsman creates a reflection of himself through his labor on products, he triumphs as the freedom that, through finding itself expressed in determinate existence (through physical labor on physical things), has found some semblance of recognition for himself as a self-determining agent. And although the lord endeavors to be free of the need for physical life, he can sustain this illusory project only through developing a need for the bondsman. As needed by the lord, the bondsman discovers his action as efficacious. The lord's need thus confirms the bondsman as more than a body; it affirms him indirectly as a laboring freedom. It provides *indirect recognition* of the bondsman's power of self-determination.

At the outset of the struggle of lord and bondsman we know that self-consciousness' desire is, at its most general articulation, a desire to discover itself as an all-inclusive identity, and also a desire *to live*. Desire must arrange for its satisfaction within the context of life, for death is the end of desire, a negativity which, except in the imaginary realms of Augustine's or Dante's hells, cannot be sustained. Desire is coextensive with life, with the realm of otherness, and with Others. Whatever the ultimate satisfaction for desire, we know at this stage that certain preconditions must first be met. We also know from our introductory remarks on Hegel that whatever exists as a precondition of desire serves also as an intentional aim of desire's articulation. The lord acknowledges with reservation and self-deception that he is, indeed, tied to life. Life appears as a necessary precondition for the satisfaction of desire. The bondsman asserts this precondition as the proper end of desire; acting in the face of the fear of death (¶ 194), the bondsman asserts the desire to live.

Both the posture of the lord and the posture of the bondsman can be seen as configurations of death in life, as death-bent desires emerging in the shadows of more explicit desires to die. Domination and enslavement are thus defenses against life within the context of life; they emerge in the spirit of nostalgia over the failed effort to die. In this sense, domination and enslavement are projects of despair, what Kierkegaard termed the despair of not being able to die.[20] Life or determinate existence requires the sustained interrelationship of physical existence and the cultivation of identity. As such, it requires the maintenance of the body in conjunction with the project of autonomous freedom.

The lord and the bondsman turn against life in different ways, but both resist the synthesis of corporeality and freedom, a synthesis that alone is constitutive of human life; the lord lives in dread of his body, while the bondsman lives in dread of freedom. The dissolution of their antagonism paves the way for an embodied pursuit of freedom, a desire to live in the fullest sense. "Life" in this mediated sense is not a merely physical enduring – that was seen as a posture of death in life in the case of the bondsman. The desire to live in the full sense is rendered synonymous with the desire to attain a more capable identity through reciprocal recognition. Hence, the desire to live is demonstrated here not merely as the *precondition* of the pursuit of a self-determining identity, but as its highest achievement. Desire that seeks to rediscover substance as subject is the desire to become the whole of life. Desire is thus always an implicit struggle against the easier routes of death; domination and enslavement are metaphors for death *in life*, the presence of contradictions, that keep one from wanting life enough.[21]

The dialectic of lord and bondsman is implicitly a struggle with the general-ized problem of life. The division of labor between lord and bondsman presupposes a discrepancy between the desire to live and the desire to be free. The lord, displeased with the prospect of having to live, delegates the task to the bondsman. The bondsman takes to working on things, fashioning them into products for human consumption. For the lord, life appears as material exigency, as a limit to his project of abstraction. The lord's desire to be beyond life (the intentionality of his desire) reveals a desire to be beyond desire (the reflexivity of his desire). He does not relish the dialectic of want and satisfaction; his sole project is to remain sated and, hence, to banish desire and its possibilities.

The bondsman, delegated the task of trafficking with life, is originally cast as a mere thing, "the consciousness for which thinghood is the essential charac-teristic" (¶ 190), but this role did not accommodate the repetitive dimension of having to live. The bondsman cannot merely exist as a thing and yet endeavor to live; in fact, the inorganic quality of things is constitutive of their deathlike dimension. Life is not, as the lord assumed, a merely material and, hence, limiting precondition of self-consciousness. It is a task that demands to be taken up again and again. The bondsman cannot be identified with the *Naturwüch-sigkeit* of the things he works upon, precisely because work turns out to be the negation of naturalness: "through his service he rids himself of his attachment to natural existence in every single detail; and gets rid of it by working on it" (¶ 194). The labor of the bondsman emerges as a truncated form of desire: he exhibits the principle of active negation, but does not wholly view himself as the author of his actions; he still works for the lord rather than for himself. In the case of the bondsman, the desire to live, specified as the desire to create the goods to live, cannot become integrated with the desire to be free until he relinquishes his shackles through disobedience and the attendant fear of death.

The division of tasks between lord and bondsman can be seen to explicate two different yet related projects of dissatisfied desire. The lord implicitly restricts desire to the consumption of ready-made goods and thus substi-tutes the satisfaction of desire for the entirety of the process. The bondsman exemplifies the dimension of desire missing from the lord's implicit account; his is a project of survival and activity encompassed by the meaning of labor. The lord's project of disembodiment becomes, ironically, a posture of greed; distanced from the physical world, yet requiring it to live, the lord becomes a passive consumer who, despite his privilege, can never be satisfied.

The lord's project to be beyond need becomes itself a pressing and relentless need; and his requirement to remain always sated ties him irrevocably to particularity and his own body, a tie he originally sought to break. And the bondsman, consigned to the realm of particularity, discovers through laboring on natural things his own capacity to transform the brutely given world into a reflection of his own self. The lord becomes schooled in the lessons of life, while the bondsman becomes schooled in freedom. And the gradual inversion of their initial roles offers lessons in the general structure and meaning of desire.

The project or desire to live and the project or desire to gain autonomous identity can be integrated only in the desire that explicitly takes account of need. The denial of need alienates self-consciousness from itself, and is a key way in which self-consciousness renders part of itself as an externality. As long as need is considered to be a contingency or piece of affective facticity, self-consciousness remains split off from itself, and the possibility of attaining an integrated self is foreclosed. When the satisfaction of needs becomes integrated into the pursuit of identity, we find that needs are but the alienated forms of desire; the need to live, formulated as such, affirms the view of life as mere exigency, and confirms the faulty distinction between the desire to live and the desire to achieve a self-determining identity. When needs are owned, they are experienced as desire.

Desire requires as well the transformation of the particularity of the natural world (the lived body as well as natural objects) into reflections of human activity; desire must become expressed through labor, for desire must give shape or form to the natural world in order to find itself reflected there (¶ 195). Giving form is thus the external determination of desire; in order to find satisfaction, i.e., recognition for itself, desire must give way to creative work. Desire is not wholly canceled through work of this kind, but work is "desire held in check, fleetingness staved off; in other words, work forms and shapes the thing. *The negative relation to the object becomes its form* and something permanent, because it is precisely for the worker that the object has independence" (¶ 195; my emphasis).

The negating or appropriative function of desire is no longer to be construed as consumption, the ecstatic enthrallment with another, nor domination, but as the re-creation of natural objects into reflections of their maker. Desire is to find its satisfaction, the reflection of itself as a self-determining and determinate existence, through effecting a human genesis of the external world. The externality of the world is negated through becoming transformed into a creation of human will. Self-consciousness is to attain to a godlike authorship of the world, "a universal formative activity," not "master over some things, but . . . over the universal power and the whole of objective being" (¶ 196).

I have argued that desire always maintains a reflexive as well as an intentional structure; I must now add that desire's intentionality is twofold: desire is always linked with the problem of recognition of and by another self-consciousness, and desire is always an effort to negate/transform the natural world. The realm of sensuous and perceptual reality relinquished in the discovery of the Other as a self-negating independence is here resurrected in new form. Mutual recognition only becomes possible in the context of a shared orientation toward *the material world*. Self-consciousness is mediated not only through another self-consciousness, but each recognizes the other in virtue of the form each gives to the world. Hence, we are recognized not merely for the form we inhabit in the world (our various embodiments), but for the forms we create of the world (our works); our bodies are but transient expressions of our freedom, while our works shield our freedom in their very structure.

Hegel begins "Lordship and Bondage" with the claim that "self-consciousness exists in and for itself when, and by the fact that, it so exists for another; that is, it exists only in being acknowledged *[als ein Anerkanntes]*" (¶ 178). But what is it that the other recognizes us *as?* The answer is, as a *desiring* being: "Self-consciousness is Desire in general" (¶ 167). We have seen that desire is a polyvalent structure, a movement to establish an identity coextensive with the world. Hegel's discussion of labor begins to show us how the world of substance becomes recast as the world of the subject. Desire as a transformation of the natural world is simultaneously the transformation of its own natural self into an embodied freedom. And yet, these transformations cannot occur outside of an historically constituted intersubjectivity which mediates the relation to nature and to the self. True subjectivities come to flourish only in communities that provide for reciprocal recognition, for we do not come to ourselves through work alone, but through the acknowledging look of the Other who confirms us.

At the close of "Lordship and Bondage" we have the sense that the life of self-consciousness is slowly drawing to an end. With the possibility of mutual recognition, we see the beginnings of Spirit or *Geist*, that collective identity which signifies yet a different set of ontological presumptions. The subject of Hegel's *Phenomenology* emerges not only as a mode of intentional enthrallment and the reflexive pursuit of identity, but as a desire that requires Others for its satisfaction and for its own constitution as an intersubjective being. In the effort to gain reflection of itself through the recognition of and by the Other, this subject discovers its dependency not only as one of many attributes, but as its very self. This interdependence, this new subject, is still desire, but one that seeks metaphysical satisfaction through the articulation of the subject's historical place in a given community.

This reformulation of desire as the articulation of historical identity and historical place forms the philosophical starting point of Alexandre Kojève's introduction of Hegel into twentieth-century French intellectual life. In effect, Kojève halts the *Phenomenology* at the end of "Lordship and Bondage," and retells Hegel's narrative from the point of view of that struggling individual on the brink of collective identity. Kojève's subject retains all the metaphysical impulses of his Hegelian precursor, but is tempered by a Marxian distrust of Hegel's idealism. Hence, self-consciousness emerges decades later in the French language as an historical actor requiring recognition by Others, and fully expecting his sense of immanent metaphysical place to be confirmed therein. In seeking to historicize the metaphysical plan of Hegel's traveler, Kojève unwittingly introduces the possibility that historical action and metaphysical satisfaction may not imply each other mutually. Indeed, as Hegel's subject makes his way across the border into France, and into the twentieth century, we will see that the question of historical agency and historical experience will come to challenge that subject's well-planned itinerary. Indeed, without his progressive journey, it will become unclear whether the traveler himself can survive.

Notes

Preface
1 For an excellent work in intellectual history with a comprehensive bibliography, see Michael S. Roth, *Knowing and History: Appropriations of Hegel in Twentieth-Century France* (Ithaca: Cornell University Press, 1988).
2 For an excellent consideration of the place of Bataille in French Hegelianism, see part 3 of Allan Stoekl, *Agonies of the Intellectual: Commitment, Subjectivity, and the Performative in the Twentieth-Century French Tradition* (Lincoln: University of Nebraska Press, 1992). For an illuminating set of perspectives on Bataille and Kojève, see the special issue of *Parallax*, "Kojève's Paris. Now Bataille" (no. 4, Feb. 1997). See as well Denis Hollier (ed.), *The College of Sociology, 1937–39* (Minneapolis: University of Minnesota Press, 1988).
3 For a clear rendition of this relationship, see Jean Hyppolite, "On the *Logic* of Hegel," in *Studies on Marx and Hegel*, tr. John O'Neill (New York: Basic Books, 1969).
4 David Clarke and Tillotama Rajan (eds.), *Intersections: Nineteenth-Century Philosophy and Contemporary Theory* (Albany: SUNY Press, 1995), reprinted in *Hegel Passé, Hegel à Venir* (Paris: L'Harmattan, 1995); and in my *The Psychic Life of Power: Essays in Subjection* (Stanford: Stanford University Press, 1997).

5   The French edition, originally published by Gallimard in 1947, also contains an important appendix that was not translated with the English edition: "L'idée de la mort dans la philosophie de Hegel." The English edition is *Introduction to the Reading of Hegel: Lectures on the Phenomenology of Spirit*, assembled by Raymond Queneau, ed. Allan Bloom, tr. James H. Nichols, Jr. (1969; reprint, Ithaca: Cornell University Press, 1980).

6   For a recent intellectual biography, see Dominique Auffret, *Alexandre Kojève: La philosophie, l'État, la fin de l'Histoire* (Paris: Grasset, 1990).

7   The contingency of the end of history thesis is indicated by Hegel himself at the end of the *Phenomenology of Spirit* when "infinity" exceeds the historical domain, but also when one reads the *Phenomenology* in the context of the *Logic* and the specific temporality of the concept developed there.

8   Lebrun can be seen to extend the provocative insights offered by Alexandre Koyré in his essay "La terminologie hégélienne." See Lebrun, *La patience du concept* (Paris: Gallimard, 1972), p. 18.

9   (Paris: Hachette Littératures, 1997); in English as *The Restlessness of the Negative*, trans. Jason Smith and Steven Miller (Minneapolis: University of Minnesota Press, 2002). See also Nancy's earlier work on the speculative sentence, *La Remarque spéculative (un bon mot de Hegel)* (Paris: Éditions Galilée, 1973).

10 See as well the translation of Hegel's "How Common Sense Understands Philosophy" by Jean-Marie Lardic and his commentary, which argues that contingency and the radical disorientation of common sense are central to the meaning of the dialectic: *Comment le sens commun comprend la philosophie suivi de la contingence chez Hegel* (Paris: Actes Sud, 1989).

11 Althusser writes, "Hegelian history is neither biological nor providential nor mechanistic, for these three schemas all entail externality. The negative dimension by virtue of which history constitutes itself through and for itself... does not lie outside history, but with the self: the nothingness by means of which history is engendered and then takes possession of itself as it evolves is in history. This nothingness is man." Louis Althusser, *The Spectre of Hegel: Early Writings*, ed. François Matheron, tr. G. M. Goshgarian (London: Verso, 1997), first published in *Écrits philosophiques et politiques. Tome I* (Paris: Stock/IMEC, 1994).

12 Ibid., 171.

13 (Paris: Éditions la Découverte, 1990).

14 See also Jean-Pierre Lefebvre and Pierre Macheray, *Hegel et la société* (Paris: Presses Universitaires de France, 1984). The discussion of Hegel's *Philosophy of Right* in this volume focuses usefully on the inversion of "beginning" and "ending" in the text, confounding usual notions of teleological development.

15 Ibid., my translation, p. 259.

16 I published a brief consideration of Derrida's early views on Hegel as "Response to Joseph Flay's 'Hegel, Derrida, and Bataille's Laughter'" in *Hegel and His Critics: Philosophy in the Aftermath of Hegel*, ed. William Desmond (Albany: SUNY Press, 1989). I highly recommend Tim Walter's book on the idea of "Critique" in Hegel (forthcoming, Stanford University Press) for a consideration of the affinities

between Hegel and Derrida as well as Werner Hamacher's *Premises* (Cambridge: Harvard University Press, 1997) and Rodolphe Gasché's *The Tain of the Mirror: Derrida and the Philosophy of Reflection* (Cambridge: Harvard University Press, 1986).

17 Some of my reflections on Irigaray's work are published in my book on Antigone and contemporary kinship, in the Wellek Library Lectures Series, *Antigone's Claim* (New York: Columbia University Press, 2000).

18 On the question of Hegel, race, and recognition, see also Franz Fanon, *Black Skin, White Masks* (New York: Grove Press, 1967); Valentin Mudimbe, *The Surreptitious Speech: Présence Africaine and the Politics of Otherness, 1947–1992* (Chicago: University of Chicago Press, 1992); Shamon Zamir, *Dark Voices* (Chicago: University of Chicago Press, 1994); Paul Gilroy, *The Black Atlantic: Modernity and Double-Consciousness* (Cambridge: Harvard University Press, 1993).

19 *Antigone's Claim* (see n. 17).

Desire, Rhetoric, and Recognition in Hegel's Phenomenology of Spirit

1 A "psychological novel." See M. H. Abrams, *Natural Supernaturalism*, "Hegel's 'Phenomenology of the Spirit': Metaphysical Structure and Narrative Plot," pp. 225–37.

2 Derrida argues in "The Pit and the Pyramid: An Introduction to Hegel's Semiology," that dialectical movement, in virtue of its circularity, circumscribes a stationary place which precludes the possibility of movement. This leads Derrida to argue that for Hegel, the process of signification is a kind of death-in-life, a posture of stasis which implicitly refutes its own claim to being a kind of movement. Derrida's assumption, however, is that Hegel's system, understood in terms of his semiology, is completed and self-sufficient, when it is precisely that assumption that first requires clarification.

3 Diderot's *Jacques le fataliste* renders a master–slave dialectic which clearly influenced Hegel's own discussion of the dynamic. Diderot implicates his reader directly, exaggerating the polemical purpose of the text, and indirectly setting up the relation between text and reader as its own dialectic of power. Hegel's narrative strategy is less self-consciously polemical, avoiding the direct assertion of pronouns. In part, this narrative strategy appears to conform to his design to show the dramatic emergence of the subject, i.e., the impossibility of simple reference to an "I" or a "you" precisely because we cannot yet be sure what these designations mean.

4 Kierkegaard, *Repetition*, p. 200 (freely interpreted).

5 Nietzsche, *The Will to Power*, ¶ 535.

6 Nietzsche's critique of morality and philosophical abstraction generally reveals one kind of lie that aids in the living of a "slave's existence," but in "Truth and Lie in an Extra-Moral Sense," he argues that the "truth" counterposed to this lie is itself a kind of necessary falsehood. In *Beyond Good and Evil*, it becomes clear that concepts are such necessary falsehoods, that they invariably reduce the multiple significations from which they are generated, i.e., that they are "dead" rather than living, metaphorical, fluid. The stages of the *Phenomenology* can be read as frozen

moments in a necessarily fluid movement; hence, they are necessarily false, but nevertheless informative, if deconstructed into the suppressed multiplicity at their origin.

7   Rosen, *Hegel: An Introduction to the Science of Wisdom*, p. 159.

8   Taylor, *Hegel*, p. 146.

9   See Gadamer, *Hegel's Dialectic: Five Hermeneutical Studies*, p. 62, ff.7.

10 *Goethe's Faust, part 1*, p. 146.

11 Spinoza, *Ethics*, part 4, Preface, p. 88.

12 See Findlay, *Hegel: A Reexamination*, p. 96.

13 Rosen, *Hegel: Introduction to the Science of Wisdom*, p. 41.

14 For a discussion of this notion of self-alienation in terms of the religious concept of ecstasy, see Rotenstreich, "On the Ecstatic Sources of the Concept of Alienation," *Review of Metaphysics*, 1963.

15 The "experience" of the *Phenomenology* ought not be understood as ordinary experience, but, rather, as the gradual and insistent cultivation of philosophical truths embedded in ordinary experience. Werner Marx accounts for the distinction between natural and phenomenal consciousness in *Hegel's Phenomenology of Spirit: A Commentary on the Preface and Introduction*, trans. Peter Heath (New York: Harper and Row, 1975).

16 Although Hegel occasionally claims to begin his phenomenological narrative with ordinary experience [¶ 8: "It has taken such a long time . . . (to) make attention to the here and now as such, attention to what has been called 'experience,' an interesting and valid enterprise"] he also claims that philosophy must now lift Spirit beyond the realm of pure sense. The philosophical cultivation of sensuousness into an all-embracing truth begins not with "ordinary experience" or daily life, but with the philosophical assumptions of ordinary experience. Hence, the "experience" of the *Phenomenology* is never devoid of philosophical appropriation; although the referent is implicitly the ordinary experience of human beings, this referent is never disclosed as outside of the philosophical language that interprets it.

In German: "Es ist für das Selbstbewusstsein ein anderes Selbstbewusstsein; es ist ausser sich gekommen. Dies hat die gedoppelte Bedeutung: erstlich, es hat sich selbst verloren, denn es findet sich als anderes Wesen; zweitens, es hat damit das Andere aufgehoben, denn es sieht auch nicht das Andere als Wesen, sondern, sich selbst im Anderen." Hegel, *Phänomenologie des Geistes*, p. 146.

17 For a subject whose ideal is that of self-sufficiency, self-estrangement might well be understood as a threat to that project and that identity. Anger thus makes sense as a counterpart to ecstasy for such a subject.

18 The struggle for recognition was reconceived a number of times throughout Hegel's early writings, but the *Phenomenology* establishes the struggle as consequent upon the experience of desire for and by another. Although Kojève and Leo Strauss have interpreted this struggle as emerging from a conflict of desires over goods, the scarcity of which sets individual wills against each other, this interpretation has been deftly refuted by the scholarship of Ludwig Siep in "Der Kampf um Anerkennung;" "Zur Dialektik der Anerkennung bei Hegel"; and "Zum

Freiheitsbegriff der praktischen Philosophie Hegels in Jena," pp. 217–28. In his "Der Kampf um Anerkennung" Siep traces the evolving conception of the struggle for recognition throughout the Jena writings, and discovers that Hegel's conception of the struggle between self-consciousness differs significantly from Hobbes' notion of the conflict of interests that forms the basis of contractarian legal theory. While Hobbes understood the conflict of desires to give rise to an artificial state apparatus which would limit the (naturally) limitless freedom of egoistic individuals, Hegel developed the view that the struggle for recognition gave rise to a concept of the individual essentially defined in terms of a larger cultural order, which, rather than limiting the individual's freedom, provided for its concrete determination and expression. In the *System der Sittlichkeit* (1802–3), Hegel viewed the struggle for recognition, not as a pursuit of property or personal honor but of the integrity of the family. The struggle was enacted within the family as a struggle between members who must reconcile their individual wills with the exigencies of collective family life, and as a struggle between distinct families for recognition. The act of recognition ensures that the individual is no longer a discrete entity, but is, rather, "*ein Glied eines Ganzen*" (*System der Sittlichkeit*, p. 50). That recognition aids in the construction of a collective identity is reinforced by Henry Harris' analysis of the *System der Sittlichkeit* in "The Concept of Recognition in Hegel's Jena Manuscripts" Hegel-Studien, Beiheft 20.

In the *Realphilosophie II* (1805–6), Hegel reconceives the struggle for recognition as a pursuit of property and honor, but even here it is not the individual who seeks recognition of his own interests, but, rather, a set of individuals who seek to find recognition for their common identity. Hegel here develops his notion of absolute freedom which calls for the surpassing of individual wills: "die einzelnen haben sich durch Negation ihrer, durch Entäusserung und Bildung zum Allgemeinen zu machen" (*Realphilosophie II*, ¶ 245). The *Realphilosophie II* envisions the struggle for recognition as *following* the breakdown of a contractual agreement; hence, the struggle does not, as it does for Hobbes, signify the need for a contract, but, rather, for an ethical community based on nonartificial, i.e., natural, ties.

In every case in the Jena writings, Hegel conceives of the struggle for recognition as one that is resolved through a discovery of a prior unifying ground which remains concealed throughout the struggle itself. Both of the above cited texts resolve the struggle through positing love or family as its necessary solution. This struggle for a community based on *agape* is prefigured in Hegel's early essay on love (*Die Liebe*), written between 1797 and 1798. By the time of the *Phenomenology* (1806) Hegel views the struggle for recognition as motivated by the demands of reciprocal desire, but the life and death struggle emerges as an intermediary stage of this development. *Siep points out that the struggle for recognition is often misconceived as a struggle that begins with the life and death struggle, but he argues that the life and death struggle is itself precipitated by the prior struggle for recognition implicit in desire:* "Die Bewegung des Anerkennens beginnt nämlich nach Hegel damit, dass es 'ausser sich' ist, sich als 'Fürsichseiendes aufhebt' und sich nur im Anderen anschaut. . . . Diese Struktur entspricht nicht dem Kampf, sondern der Liebe. . . .

Nicht der Anfang der Bewegung des Anerkennens, sondern erst der Schritt des Selbstbewusstseins, 'sein Andersein auf(zu)heben,' ist im Kampf auf Leben und Tod verkörpert" (Siep, "Der Kampf um Anerkennung," p. 194).

The struggle for recognition arises, then, not from a primary competitive attitude toward the other, but from the experience of desire for and by another. Specific desires for property, goods or positions of social dominance must be, according to Hegel's framework, seen as derivative expressions of the desire for a community based on love. Desire is, thus, not originally an effort of acquisition or domination, but emerges in such forms only when a community based on the principles of reciprocal recognition has not yet been developed.

19   See Gadamer, "Hegel's Dialectic of Self-Consciousness," p. 66: "self-consciousness . . . is unable to achieve true being-for-self without overcoming its attachment to life, i.e. without annihilating itself as mere 'life.'"

20   Kierkegaard, *Sickness Unto Death*, p. 18.

21   It is not merely the failure of desire that precipitates the experience of death in life, for desire is *itself* an expression of the negative. The failure to achieve substantial being, which is, strictly speaking, not the failure of desire, but the failure of satisfaction, must be viewed in Hegelian terms as philosophically important. Prefiguring Kierkegaard's frustration with those "too tenacious of life to die a little," Hegel claims in his preface that "the life of the spirit is not the life which shrinks from death and keeps itself untouched by devastation, but rather the life which endures it and maintains itself in it" (¶ 32). Walter Kaufmann's translation of the rest of the paragraph elucidates the project to which devastation, the failure of desire, the experience of death in life, gives rise: "Spirit gains its truth only by finding itself in absolute dismemberment. This power it is – not as the positive that looks away from the negative – as when we say of something, this is nothing or false, and then, finished with it, turn away from it to something else: the spirit is this power only by looking the negative in the face and abiding with it. This abiding is the magic force which converts the negative into being," Kaufmann, *Hegel: Texts and Commentary*, p. 50.

3

Bodily Inscriptions, Performative Subversions (1990)

Introduction

When it was first published in 1990, *Gender Trouble* constituted a significant intervention into a number of fields including gender studies, feminist theory, and queer theory, and many consider this book to be Butler's most important work. Although at first glance it may seem as though Butler has moved away from the phenomenology and existentialism of her early work, *Gender Trouble* marks a continuation of her theorizations of identity and the body rather than a departure or a change of direction. Butler is still working within the framework of the Hegelian questions which she claims structure all her work, questions concerning the relationship between desire, recognition, and the subject's radical and constitutive relation to alterity.[1] Desire, alterity, and identity are still very prominent in *Gender Trouble*, where, in Butler's extended analyses of the constitution of the subject, gender and sex continue to be cast in implicitly dialectical terms, particularly since the book is intended as a contribution to the collective struggle to increase the possibilities of livability for those currently existing on the sexual margins.[2]

It is in *Gender Trouble* that Butler formulates her best-known and most misunderstood theories, including melancholic sexuality, radical parody and drag, and performativity. The "trouble" that *Gender Trouble* sets out to make occurs in the realm of discourse, as Butler continues to interrogate the terms by which our identities are described, constituted, and circumscribed. Unlike a number of feminist theories that assume the existence of a stable but oppressed female subject awaiting emancipation and representation (or emancipation *in* representation), *Gender Trouble* is a Foucauldian, anti-essentialist critique of those identity categories which reify and endorse a repressive heterosexual matrix. This is "a *feminist genealogy* of the category of woman," Butler's use of the word "genealogy" once again underscoring the Foucauldianism of her investigations into the political operations of discourse. Butler's genealogy is not a search for the origins and causes of gender and discourse, since she claims they have neither origin nor cause, but here as in "Sex and Gender," gender is an open-ended process, a sequence of acts or events which does not originate and which is never fully or finally "realized."

Preface to 1999 anniversary edition, pp. xiv–xxvi, 191–3 (notes), and chapter 3, pp. 163–80, 215–16 (notes), from *Gender Trouble: Feminism and the Subversion of Identity* (originally published 1990; reprinted 1999 by Routledge, New York). Reproduced by permission of Routledge, an imprint of Taylor & Francis Books, Inc.

Once again Butler collapses the distinction between sex and gender, asserting that there is no sex that is not always already gender; or as she puts it, "sex by definition will be shown to have been gender all along." This means that, as before, there is no "natural body" which preexists culture and discourse, since all bodies are gendered from the beginning of their social existence. Butler adopts the Beauvoirian position that gender is not something one *is*, but something one *does*, or as she puts it, "[g]ender is the repeated stylization of the body, a set of repeated acts within a highly rigid regulatory frame that congeal over time to produce the appearance of substance, of a natural sort of being." *Gender Trouble* is "a political genealogy of gender ontologies" which will deconstruct these "congealed" substances in order to reveal the myriad ways in which gender is "done" or "produced" within discourse, as well as the ways in which gender "does" the subject.

We know that the unstable, ever-shifting subject Butler described in *Subjects of Desire*, although not explicitly gendered, was constituted by its repeated failures and reversals. This characterization of identity as an ongoing and repeated "failure" is picked up in *Gender Trouble*, where it provides the basis for Butler's theorization of gender as performative. Eve Sedgwick is not alone in considering *Gender Trouble* to be crucial to current work on performativity in relation to sex and gender,[3] but the theory has been widely misinterpreted and Butler has revised and clarified her ideas at least partly in response to criticism. To cast gender in terms of "performativity" is not to imply that it is a piece of theater staged by a knowing actor who selects her/his script at will. Rather, drawing from the speech act theory of J. L. Austin along with Jacques Derrida's critique of Austin, Butler theorizes gender in linguistic and discursive terms (although it must be said that Foucault is more in evidence in *Gender Trouble* than either Derrida or Austin). If gender is a "doing" rather than a "being," a verb rather than a noun, it is not an action that is done by a volitional agent who is free to select her/his gender "styles" (Butler's word). Instead, the subject is "done" by gender; it is the effect rather than the cause of a discourse which is always there first. As in previous works, this reversal of cause and effect is crucial to Butler's theories of identity, and here Butler appropriates Friedrich Nietzsche's insight that "there is no 'being' behind doing, acting, becoming; the 'doer' is merely a fiction imposed on the doing – the doing itself is everything."[4] She offers the following gendered corollary to this formulation: there is no gender identity behind the expressions of gender; identity is discursively *constituted*, the effect rather than the cause of the sequence of acts which give it "the appearance of a substance." There is no actor who performs the sequence of gender acts which constitute its identity: if you like, the actor is *done by* those acts, so that, to return to Nietzsche, "the doing itself is everything."

Performative gender is a complex theory which has been widely misread, but equally important, although sometimes overlooked, are Butler's genealogical readings of structuralist and psychoanalytic accounts of identity in the long second chapter of *Gender Trouble*, "Prohibition, Psychoanalysis, and the Production of the Heterosexual Matrix." Both here and in other works, Butler draws extensively from two essays by Sigmund Freud ("Mourning and Melancholia" [1917] and *The Ego and the Id* [1923]). In the earlier of the two essays Freud distinguishes between mourning, which is the reaction to a real loss, often the death of a loved one, and melancholia, a pathological condition similar to depression in which the melancholic may not actually have lost anything or anyone. The melancholic reacts to this imagined loss by taking the lost object into her/himself (or "introjecting" it) and setting it up as an identification, thereby preserving the lost object in the psyche. Six years later in *The Ego and the Id*, Freud de-pathologizes melancholia by describing all ego formation as a melancholic structure. According to Freud, a child's primary desire for one or other of its parents is transformed into an identification by the interposition of the incest taboo. The infant must abandon its desire (its primary cathexis) for the parent because of the taboo against incest, but like the melancholic who takes the lost object into herself or himself and thereby preserves it, the ego introjects the lost object (the desired parent) and preserves it as an identification. "[A]n object which was lost has been set up again inside the ego," Freud writes, "that is...an object-cathexis has been replaced by an identification." This means that the ego is a repository of prohibited desires, or as Freud puts it, "the character of the ego is a precipitate of abandoned object-cathexes and...it contains the history of those object-choices."[5]

Whether the child desires the parent of the same or the opposite sex depends on what Freud calls its "disposition," but Freud is not altogether clear as to what a "disposition" is or what determines it.[6] Seizing on Freud's uncertainty, Butler wants to know whether "masculine" and "feminine" dispositions can be traced to an identification and where those identifications take place: "What are these primary dispositions on which Freud himself apparently founders?" she asks:

> What aspect of "femininity" do we call dispositional, and which is the consequence of identification?...Moreover, how do we identify a "feminine" or a "masculine" disposition at the outset? By what traces is it known, and to what extent do we assume a "feminine" or a "masculine" disposition as the precondition of a heterosexual object choice? In other words, to what extent do we read the desire for the father as evidence of a feminine disposition only because we begin, despite the postulation of a primary bisexuality, with a heterosexual matrix of desire?[7]

According to Butler, the infant's identification with the parent of the same or the opposite sex is *not* the result of its primary dispositions (i.e. its essential homosexuality or heterosexuality), but the identifications Freud claims stem from these dispositions have *already* taken place within a heterosexual matrix of desire. In other words, primary dispositions are no more than the effects of the law, specifically here, the taboo against homosexuality which Butler, following Gayle Rubin, asserts precedes the taboo against incest. This means that the desire which is preserved as an identification is always same-sex desire, and Butler concurs with contemporary psychoanalysts Nicolas Abraham and Maria Torok that this refused desire is not preserved in the psyche as Freud argues (i.e. it is not introjected) but it is incorporated on the surface of the body, so that the subject literally embodies the homosexual desire it was forced to give up as an infant. As Butler puts it, "[this] is the means by which the body comes to bear 'sex' as its literal truth": once again we return to the notion that sex as much as gender is something that is "borne," i.e. a construct rather than something one is "born" with, a natural fact.

Hegel is an implicit presence throughout *Gender Trouble*, but Butler's argument that the primary sexual dispositions or desires for which Freud is unable to account are the effects of a law which precedes them, is implicitly Foucauldian. What is simultaneously dialectical and Foucauldian about the theory of melancholic sexuality (and it is important to note that *all* sexual identities are melancholic) is Butler's assertion that the law or taboo *creates* the desires it then sets out to repress, or in Hegelian parlance, "overcome," where *Aufhebung* simultaneously means to cancel, to preserve, and to transcend. As in the confrontation between lord and bondsman described in the fourth section of Hegel's *Phenomenology of Spirit*, the heterosexual matrix requires something to negate and sublate:[8] adopting Foucault's critique of the repressive hypothesis, Butler argues that the law which prohibits incestuous and homosexual unions simultaneously invents and invites them in order to establish its own coherence and superiority. "If the incest taboo regulates the production of discrete gender identities, and if that production requires the prohibition and sanction of heterosexuality, then homosexuality emerges as a desire which must be produced in order to remain repressed," she writes. "In other words, for heterosexuality to remain intact as a distinct social form, it *requires* an intelligible conception of homosexuality, and also requires the prohibition of that conception in rendering it culturally intelligible."

This is one of Butler's most brilliant insights, as it introduces a vital instability at the heart of heterosexual norms which are now revealed as vulnerable to what Butler calls "performative surprise."[9] Clearly, it is possible to re-enact gender in ways that work against the heterosexual grain, and subversive performances such as parody and drag reveal ontological inner depths and gender cores as regulatory fictions. It would be a mistake to assume that the imitations to which Butler refers are parodies of an original; rather, the notion of an original *itself* is parodied and exposed as "an imitation without an origin...a production which in effect – that is, in its effect – postures as an imitation." Gender is thus a corporeal style and a copy of a copy. Butler points out that people who fail to "do" their gender correctly, or who do it in ways which accentuate its genealogy and construction, are punished by cultures and laws which have a vested interest in maintaining a stable distinction between surface and depth, sex and gender, the body and the psyche, homosexual and heterosexual, masculine and feminine. However, if there is no gender identity behind the expressions of gender, the question arises as to how much agency this performative subject possesses. Butler insists that construction is not *de*-struction, and that far from being opposed to agency, this is the site through which agency takes place, *within* constraining norms that are worked against themselves. Acknowledging that subversive performances risk becoming "deadening clichés" through their repetition in a commodity culture, Butler refuses to provide prescriptive "guidelines" for subversion. "The effort to name the criterion for subversiveness will always fail, and it ought to," she writes.[10] Rather than setting out prescriptions for "what is to be done,"

Butler's work continues to take part in the ongoing struggle to extend the norms of "livability" to sexual minorities who live their daily lives in the irreducible complexity of identity categories.[11] As part of this collective struggle Butler continues to pose difficult, disquieting, ethically motivated questions about ontological intelligibility, livability, and the presumptions of normativity in determining what does and does not count as "human."[12]

An excerpt from chapter 3 of *Gender Trouble* is included here, along with the preface to the 1999 anniversary edition of the text.

Preface (1999)

[. . .] Much of my work in recent years has been devoted to clarifying and revising the theory of performativity that is outlined in *Gender Trouble*.[1] It is difficult to say precisely what performativity is not only because my own views on what "performativity" might mean have changed over time, most often in response to excellent criticisms,[2] but because so many others have taken it up and given it their own formulations. I originally took my clue on how to read the performativity of gender from Jacques Derrida's reading of Kafka's "Before the Law." There the one who waits for the law, sits before the door of the law, attributes a certain force to the law for which one waits. The anticipation of an authoritative disclosure of meaning is the means by which that authority is attributed and installed: the anticipation conjures its object. I wondered whether we do not labor under a similar expectation concerning gender, that it operates as an interior essence that might be disclosed, an expectation that ends up producing the very phenomenon that it anticipates. In the first instance, then, the performativity of gender revolves around this metalepsis, the way in which the anticipation of a gendered essence produces that which it posits as outside itself. Secondly, performativity is not a singular act, but a repetition and a ritual, which achieves its effects through its naturalization in the context of a body, understood, in part, as a culturally sustained temporal duration.[3]

Several important questions have been posed to this doctrine, and one seems especially noteworthy to mention here. The view that gender is performative sought to show that what we take to be an internal essence of gender is manufactured through a sustained set of acts, posited through the gendered stylization of the body. In this way, it showed that what we take to be an "internal" feature of ourselves is one that we anticipate and produce through certain bodily acts, at an extreme, an hallucinatory effect of naturalized gestures. Does this mean that everything that is understood as "internal" about the psyche is therefore evacuated, and that internality is a false metaphor? Although *Gender Trouble* clearly drew upon the metaphor of an internal psyche in its early discussion of gender melancholy, that emphasis was not brought forward into the thinking of performativity itself.[4] Both *The Psychic Life of Power* and several of my recent articles on psychoanalytic topics have sought to come to terms with this problem, what many have seen as a problematic break between the early and later chapters of this book. Although I would deny that all of the internal world of the psyche is but an effect of a stylized set of acts, I continue to think that it is a significant theoretical mistake to take the "internality" of the psychic world for granted. Certain features of the world, including people we know and lose, do become "internal" features of the self, but they are transformed through that interiorization, and that inner world, as the Kleinians call it, is constituted precisely as a consequence of the interiorizations that a psyche performs. This suggests that there may well be a psychic theory of performativity at work that calls for greater exploration.

Although this text does not answer the question of whether the materiality of the body is fully constructed, that has been the focus of much of my subsequent work, which I hope will prove clarifying for the reader.[5] The question of whether or not the theory of performativity can be transposed onto matters of race has been explored by several scholars.[6] I would note here not only that racial presumptions invariably underwrite the discourse on gender in ways that need to be made explicit, but that race and gender ought not to be treated as simple analogies. I would therefore suggest that the question to ask is not whether the theory of performativity is transposable onto race, but what happens to the theory when it tries to come to grips with race. Many of these debates have centered on the status of "construction," whether race is constructed in the same way as gender. My view is that no single account of construction will do, and that these categories always work as background for one another, and they often find their most powerful articulation through one another. Thus, the sexualization of racial gender norms calls to be read through multiple lenses at once, and the analysis surely illuminates the limits of gender as an exclusive category of analysis.[7]

Although I've enumerated some of the academic traditions and debates that have animated this book, it is not my purpose to offer a full apologia in these brief pages. There is one aspect of the conditions of its production that is not always understood about the text: it was produced not merely from the academy, but from convergent social movements of which I have been a part, and within the context of a lesbian and gay community on the east coast of the United States in which I lived for fourteen years prior to the writing of this book. Despite the dislocation of the subject that the text performs, there is a person here: I went to many meetings, bars, and marches and saw many kinds of genders, understood myself to be at the crossroads of some of them, and encountered sexuality at several of its cultural edges. I knew many people who were trying to find their way in the midst of a significant movement for sexual recognition and freedom, and felt the exhilaration and frustration that goes along with being a part of that movement both in its hopefulness and internal dissension. At the same time that I was ensconced in the academy, I was also living a life outside those walls, and though *Gender Trouble* is an academic book, it began, for me, with a crossing-over, sitting on Rehoboth Beach, wondering whether I could link the different sides of my life. That I can write in an autobiographical mode does not, I think, relocate this subject that I am, but perhaps it gives the reader a sense of solace that there is someone here (I will suspend for the moment the problem that this someone is given in language).

It has been one of the most gratifying experiences for me that the text continues to move outside the academy to this day. At the same time that the book was taken up by Queer Nation, and some of its reflections on the theatricality of queer self-presentation resonated with the tactics of Act Up, it was among the materials that also helped to prompt members of the American Psychoanalytic Association and the American Psychological Association to reassess some of their current doxa on homosexuality. The questions of performative gender were appropriated in different ways in the visual arts, at Whitney exhibitions, and at the Otis School for the Arts in Los Angeles, among others. Some of its formulations on the subject of "women" and the relation between sexuality and gender also made its way into feminist jurisprudence and antidiscrimination legal scholarship in the work of Vicki Schultz, Katherine Franke, and Mary Jo Frug.

In turn, I have been compelled to revise some of my positions in *Gender Trouble* by virtue of my own political engagements. In the book, I tend to conceive of the claim of "universality" in exclusive negative and exclusionary terms. However, I came to see the term has important strategic use precisely as a non-substantial and open-ended category as I worked with an extraordinary group of activists first as a board member and then as board chair of the International Gay and Lesbian Human Rights Commission (1994–7), an organization that represents sexual minorities on a broad range of human rights issues. There I came to understand how the assertion of universality can be proleptic and performative, conjuring a reality that does not yet exist, and holding out the possibility for a convergence of cultural horizons that have not yet met. Thus, I arrived at a second view of universality in which it is defined as a future-oriented labor of cultural translation.[8] More recently, I have been compelled to relate my work to political theory and, once again, to the concept of universality in a co-authored book that I am writing with Ernesto Laclau and Slavoj Žižek on the theory of hegemony and its implications for a theoretically activist Left (published by Verso in 2000).

Another practical dimension of my thinking has taken place in relationship to psychoanalysis as both a scholarly and clinical enterprise. I am currently working with a group of progressive psychoanalytic therapists on a new journal, *Studies in Gender and Sexuality*, that seeks to bring clinical and scholarly work into productive dialogue on questions of sexuality, gender, and culture.

Both critics and friends of *Gender Trouble* have drawn attention to the difficulty of its style. It is no doubt strange, and maddening to some, to find a book that is not easily consumed to be "popular" according to academic standards. The surprise over this is perhaps attributable to the way we underestimate the reading public, its capacity and desire for reading complicated and challenging texts, when the complication is not gratuitous, when the challenge is in the service of calling taken-for-granted truths into question, when the taken for grantedness of those truths is, indeed, oppressive.

I think that style is a complicated terrain, and not one that we unilaterally choose or control with the purposes we consciously intend. Fredric Jameson made this clear in his early book on Sartre. Certainly, one can practice styles, but the styles that become available to you are not entirely a matter of choice. Moreover, neither grammar nor style are politically neutral. Learning the rules that govern intelligible speech is an inculcation into normalized language, where the price of not conforming is the loss of intelligibility itself. As Drucilla Cornell, in the tradition of Adorno, reminds me: there is nothing radical about common sense. It would be a mistake to think that received grammar is the best vehicle for expressing radical views, given the constraints that grammar imposes upon thought, indeed, upon the thinkable itself. But formulations that twist grammar or that implicitly call into question the subject – verb requirements of propositional sense are clearly irritating for some. They produce more work for their readers, and sometimes their readers are offended by such demands. Are those who are offended making a legitimate request for "plain speaking" or does their complaint emerge from a consumer expectation of intellectual life? Is there, perhaps, a value to be derived from such experiences of linguistic difficulty? If gender itself is naturalized through grammatical norms, as Monique Wittig has argued, then the alteration of gender at the most fundamental epistemic level will be conducted, in part, through contesting the grammar in which gender is given.

The demand for lucidity forgets the ruses that motor the ostensibly "clear" view. Avital Ronell recalls the moment in which Nixon looked into the eyes of the nation and said, "let me make one thing perfectly clear" and then proceeded to lie. What travels under the sign of "clarity," and what would be the price of failing to deploy a certain critical suspicion when the arrival of lucidity is announced? Who devises the protocols of "clarity" and whose interests do they serve? What is foreclosed by the insistence on parochial standards of transparency as requisite for all communication? What does "transparency" keep obscure?

I grew up understanding something of the violence of gender norms: an uncle incarcerated for his anatomically anomalous body, deprived of family and friends, living out his days in an "institute" in the Kansas prairies; gay cousins forced to leave their homes because of their sexuality, real and imagined; my own tempestuous coming out at the age of 16; and a subsequent adult landscape of lost jobs, lovers, and homes. All of this subjected me to strong and scarring condemnation but, luckily, did not prevent me from pursuing pleasure and insisting on a legitimating recognition for my sexual life. It was difficult to bring this violence into view precisely because gender was so taken for granted at the same time that it was violently policed. It was assumed either to be a natural manifestation of sex or a cultural constant that no human agency could hope to revise. I also came to understand something of the violence of the foreclosed life, the one that does not get named as "living," the one whose incarceration implies a suspension of life, or a sustained death sentence. The dogged effort to "denaturalize" gender in this text emerges, I think, from a strong desire both to counter the normative violence implied by ideal morphologies of sex and to uproot the pervasive assumptions about natural or presumptive heterosexuality that are informed by ordinary and academic discourses on sexuality. The writing of this denaturalization was not done simply out of a desire to play with language or prescribe theatrical antics in the place of "real" politics, as some critics have conjectured (as if theatre and politics are always distinct). It was done from a desire to live, to make life possible, and to rethink the possible as such. What would the world have to be like for my uncle to live in the company of family, friends, or extended kinship of some other kind? How must we rethink the ideal morphological constraints upon the human such that those who fail to approximate the norm are not condemned to a death within life?[9]

Some readers have asked whether Gender Trouble seeks to expand the realm of gender possibilities for a reason. They ask, for what purpose are such new configurations of gender devised, and how ought we to judge among them? The question often involves a prior premise, namely, that the text does not address the normative or prescriptive dimension of feminist thought. "Normative" clearly has at least two meanings in this critical encounter, since the word is one I use often, mainly to describe the mundane violence performed by certain kinds of gender ideals. I usually use "normative" in a way that is synonymous with "pertaining to the norms that govern gender." But the term "normative" also pertains to ethical justification, how it is established, and what concrete consequences proceed therefrom. One critical question posed of Gender Trouble has been: how do we proceed to make judgments on how gender is to be lived on the basis of the theoretical descriptions offered here? It is not possible to oppose the "normative" forms of gender without at the same time subscribing to a certain normative view of how the gendered world ought to be. I want to suggest, however, that the positive normative vision of this text, such as it is, does not and cannot take the form of a prescription: "subvert gender in the way that I say, and life will be good."

Those who make such prescriptions or who are willing to decide between subversive and unsubversive expressions of gender, base their judgments on a description. Gender appears in this or that form, and then a normative judgment is made about those appearances and on the basis of what appears. But what conditions the domain of appearance for gender itself? We may be tempted to make the following distinction: a *descriptive* account of gender includes considerations of what makes gender intelligible, an inquiry into its conditions of possibility, whereas a *normative* account seeks to answer the question of which expressions of gender are acceptable, and which are not, supplying persuasive reasons to distinguish between such expressions in this way. The question, however, of what qualifies as "gender" is itself already a question that attests to a pervasively normative operation of power, a fugitive operation of "what will be the case" under the rubric of "what is the case." Thus, the very description of the field of gender is no sense prior to, or separable from, the question of its normative operation.

I am not interested in delivering judgments on what distinguishes the subversive from the unsubversive. Not only do I believe that such judgments cannot be made out of context, but that they cannot be made in ways that endure through time ("contexts" are themselves posited unities that undergo temporal change and expose their essential disunity). Just as metaphors lose their metaphoricity as they congeal through time into concepts, so subversive performances always run the risk of becoming deadening clichés through their repetition and, most importantly, through their repetition within commodity culture where "subversion" carries market value. The effort to name the criterion for subversiveness will always fail, and ought to. So what is at stake in using the term at all?

What continues to concern me most is the following kinds of questions: what will and will not constitute an intelligible life, and how do presumptions about normative gender and sexuality determine in advance what will qualify as the "human" and the "livable"? In other words, how do normative gender presumptions work to delimit the very field of description that we have for the human? What is the means by which we come to see this delimiting power, and what are the means by which we transform it?

The discussion of drag that *Gender Trouble* offers to explain the constructed and performative dimension of gender is not precisely *an example* of subversion.

It would be a mistake to take it as the paradigm of subversive action or, indeed, as a model for political agency. The point is rather different. If one thinks that one sees a man dressed as a woman or a woman dressed as a man, then one takes the first term of each of those perceptions as the "reality" of gender: the gender that is introduced through the simile lacks "reality," and is taken to constitute an illusory appearance. In such perceptions in which an ostensible reality is coupled with an unreality, we think we know what the reality is, and take the secondary appearance of gender to be mere artifice, play, falsehood, and illusion. But what is the sense of "gender reality" that founds this perception in this way? Perhaps we think we know what the anatomy of the person is (sometimes we do not, and we certainly have not appreciated the variation that exists at the level of anatomical description). Or we derive that knowledge from the clothes that the person wears, or how the clothes are worn. This is naturalized knowledge, even though it is based on a series of cultural inferences, some of which are highly erroneous. Indeed, if we shift the example from drag to transsexuality, then it is no longer possible to derive a judgment about stable anatomy from the clothes that cover and articulate the body. That body may be preoperative, transitional, or postoperative; even "seeing" the body may not answer the question: for *what are the categories through which one sees?* The moment in which one's staid and usual cultural perceptions fail, when one cannot with surety read the body that one sees, is precisely the moment when one is no longer sure whether the body encountered is that of a man or a woman. The vacillation between the categories itself constitutes the experience of the body in question.

When such categories come into question, the *reality* of gender is also put into crisis: it becomes unclear how to distinguish the real from the unreal. And this is the occasion in which we come to understand that what we take to be "real," what we invoke as the naturalized knowledge of gender is, in fact, a changeable and revisable reality. Call it subversive or call it something else. Although this insight does not in itself constitute a political revolution, no political revolution is possible without a radical shift in one's notion of the possible and the real. And sometimes this shift comes as a result of certain kinds of practices that precede their explicit theorization, and which prompt a rethinking of our basic categories: what is gender, how is it produced and reproduced, what are its possibilities? At this point, the sedimented and reified field of gender "reality" is understood as one that might be made differently and, indeed, less violently.

The point of this text is not to celebrate drag as the expression of a true and model gender (even as it is important to resist the belittling of drag that sometimes takes place), but to show that the naturalized knowledge of gender operates as a preemptive and violent circumscription of reality. To the extent the gender norms (ideal dimorphism, heterosexual complementarity of bodies, ideals and rule of proper and improper masculinity and femininity, many of which are underwritten by racial codes of purity and taboos against miscegenation) establish what will and will not be intelligibly human, what will and will not be considered to be "real," they establish the ontological field in which bodies may be given legitimate expression. If there is a positive normative task in *Gender Trouble*, it is to insist upon the extension of this legitimacy to bodies that have been regarded as false, unreal, and unintelligible. Drag is an example that is meant to establish that "reality" is not as fixed as we generally assume it to be. The purpose of the example is to expose the tenuousness of gender "reality" in order to counter the violence performed by gender norms.

In this text as elsewhere I have tried to understand what political agency might be, given that it cannot be isolated from the dynamics of power from which it is wrought. The iterability of performativity is a theory of agency, one that cannot disavow power as the condition of its own possibility. This text does not sufficiently explain performativity in terms of its social, psychic, corporeal, and temporal dimensions. In some ways, the continuing work of that clarification, in response to numerous excellent criticisms, guides most of my subsequent publications.

Other concerns have emerged over this text in the last decade, and I have sought to answer them through various publications. On the status of the materiality of the body, I have offered a reconsideration and revision of my views in *Bodies that Matter*. On the question of the necessity of the category of "women" for feminist analysis, I have revised and expanded my views in "Contingent Foundations" to be found in the volume I coedited with Joan W. Scott, *Feminists Theorize the Political* (Routledge, 1993) and in the collectively authored *Feminist Contentions* (Routledge, 1995).

I do not believe that poststructuralism entails the death of autobiographical writing, but it does draw attention to the difficulty of the "I" to express itself through the language that is available to it. For this "I" that you read is in part a consequence of the grammar that governs the availability of persons in language. I am not outside the language that structures me, but neither am I determined by the language that makes this "I" possible. This is the bind of self-expression, as I understand it. What it means is that you never receive me apart from the grammar that establishes my availability to you. If I treat that grammar as pellucid, then I fail to call attention precisely to that sphere of language that establishes and disestablishes intelligibility, and that would be precisely to thwart my own project as I have described it to you here. I am not trying to be difficult, but only to draw attention to a difficulty without which no "I" can appear.

This difficulty takes on a specific dimension when approached from a psychoanalytic perspective. In my efforts to understand the opacity of the "I" in language, I have turned increasingly to psychoanalysis since the publication of *Gender Trouble*. The usual effort to polarize the theory of the psyche from the theory of power seems to me to be counterproductive, for part of what is so oppressive about social forms of gender is the psychic difficulties they produce. I sought to consider the ways in which Foucault and psychoanalysis might be thought together in *The Psychic Life of Power* (Stanford, 1997). I have also made use of psychoanalysis to curb the occasional voluntarism of my view of performativity without thereby undermining a more general theory of agency. *Gender Trouble* sometimes reads as if gender is simply a self-invention or as if the psychic meaning of a gendered presentation might be read directly off its surface. Both of those postulates have had to be refined over time. Moreover, my theory sometimes waffles between understanding performativity as linguistic and casting it as theatrical. I have come to think that the two are invariably related, chiasmically so, and that a reconsideration of the speech act as an instance of power invariably draws attention to both its theatrical and linguistic dimensions. In *Excitable Speech*, I sought to show that the speech act is at once performed (and thus theatrical, presented to an audience, subject to interpretation), and linguistic, inducing a set of effects through its implied relation to linguistic conventions. If one wonders how a linguistic theory of the speech act relates to bodily gestures, one need only consider that speech itself is a bodily act with specific linguistic consequences. Thus speech belongs exclusively neither to corporeal presentation nor to language, and its status as word and deed is necessarily ambiguous. This ambiguity has consequences for the practice of coming out, for the insurrectionary power of the speech act, for language as a condition of both bodily seduction and the threat of injury.

If I were to rewrite this book under present circumstances, I would include a discussion of transgender and intersexuality, the way that ideal gender dimorphism works in both sorts of discourses, the different relations to surgical intervention that these related concerns sustain. I would also include a discussion on racialized sexuality and, in particular, how taboos against miscegenation (and the romanticization of cross-racial sexual exchange) are essential to the naturalized and denaturalized forms that gender takes. I continue to hope for a coalition of sexual minorities that will transcend the simple categories of identity, that will refuse the erasure of bisexuality, that will counter and dissipate the violence imposed by restrictive bodily norms. I would hope that such a coalition would be based on the irreducible complexity of sexuality and its implication in various dynamics of discursive and institutional power, and that no one will be too quick to reduce power to hierarchy and to refuse its productive political dimensions. Even as I think that gaining recognition for one's status as a sexual minority is a difficult task within reigning discourses of law, politics, and language, I continue to consider it a necessity for survival. The mobilization of identity categories for the purposes of politicization always remain threatened by the prospect of identity becoming an instrument of the power one opposes. That is no reason not to use, and be used, by identity. There is no political position purified of power, and perhaps that impurity is what produces agency as the potential interruption and reversal of regulatory regimes. Those who are deemed "unreal" nevertheless lay hold of the real, a laying hold that happens in concert, and a vital instability is produced by that performative surprise. This book is written then as part of the cultural life of a collective struggle that has had, and will continue to have, some success in increasing the possibilities for a livable life for those who live, or try to live, on the sexual margins.[10]

Bodily Inscriptions, Performative Subversions

"Garbo 'got in drag' whenever she took some heavy glamour part, whenever she melted in or out of a man's arms, whenever she simply let that heavenly-flexed neck . . . bear the weight of her thrown-back head. . . .

How resplendent seems the art of acting! It is all impersonation, whether the sex underneath is true or not."
—Parker Tyler, "The Garbo Image," quoted
in Esther Newton, *Mother Camp*

Categories of true sex, discrete gender, and specific sexuality have constituted the stable point of reference for a great deal of feminist theory and politics. These constructs of identity serve as the points of epistemic departure from which theory emerges and politics itself is shaped. In the case of feminism, politics is ostensibly shaped to express the interests, the perspectives, of "women." But is there a political shape to "women," as it were, that precedes and prefigures the political elaboration of their interests and epistemic point of view? How is that identity shaped, and is it a political shaping that takes the very morphology and boundary of the sexed body as the ground, surface, or site of cultural inscription? What circumscribes that site as "the female body"? Is "the body" or "the sexed body" the firm foundation on which gender and systems of compulsory sexuality operate? Or is "the body" itself shaped by political forces with strategic interests in keeping that body bounded and constituted by the markers of sex?

The sex/gender distinction and the category of sex itself appear to presuppose a generalization of "the body" that preexists the acquisition of its sexed significance. This "body" often appears to be a passive medium that is signified by an inscription from a cultural source figured as "external" to that body. Any theory of the culturally constructed body, however, ought to question "the body" as a construct of suspect generality when it is figured as passive and prior to discourse. There are Christian and Cartesian precedents to such views which, prior to the emergence of vitalistic biologies in the nineteenth century, understand "the body" as so much inert matter, signifying nothing or, more specifically, signifying a profane void, the fallen state: deception, sin, the premonitional metaphorics of hell and the eternal feminine. There are many occasions in both Sartre's and Beauvoir's work where "the body" is figured as a mute facticity, anticipating some meaning that can be attributed only by a transcendent consciousness, understood in Cartesian terms as radically immaterial. But what establishes this dualism for us? What separates off "the body" as indifferent to signification, and signification itself as the act of a radically disembodied consciousness or, rather, the act that radically disembodies that consciousness? To what extent is that Cartesian dualism presupposed in phenomenology adapted to the structuralist frame in which mind/body is redescribed as culture/nature? With respect to gender discourse, to what extent do these problematic dualisms still operate within the very descriptions that are supposed to lead us out of that binarism and its implicit hierarchy? How are the contours of the body clearly marked as the taken-for-granted ground or surface upon which gender significations are inscribed, a mere facticity devoid of value, prior to significance?

Wittig suggests that a culturally specific epistemic *a priori* establishes the naturalness of "sex." But by what enigmatic means has "the body" been accepted as a *prima facie* given that admits of no genealogy? Even within Foucault's essay on the very theme of genealogy, the body is figured as a surface and the scene of a cultural inscription: "the body is the inscribed surface of events."[1] The task of genealogy, he claims, is "to expose a body totally imprinted by history." His sentence continues, however, by referring to the goal of "history" – here clearly understood on the model of Freud's "civilization" – as the "destruction of the body" (148). Forces and impulses with multiple directionalities are precisely that which history both destroys and preserves through the *Entstehung* (historical event) of inscription. As "a volume in perpetual disintegration" (148), the body is always under siege, suffering destruction by the very terms of history. And history is the creation of values and meanings by a signifying practice that requires the subjection of the body. This corporeal destruction is necessary to produce the speaking subject and its significations. This is a body, described through the language of surface and force, weakened through a "single drama" of domination, inscription, and creation (150). This is not the *modus vivendi* of one kind of history rather than another, but is, for Foucault, "history" (148) in its essential and repressive gesture.

Although Foucault writes, "Nothing in man [*sic*] – not even his body – is sufficiently stable to serve as the basis for self-recognition or for understanding other men [*sic*]" (153), he nevertheless points to the constancy of cultural inscription as a "single drama" that acts on the body. If the creation of values, that historical mode of signification, requires the destruction of the body, much as the instrument of torture in Kafka's "In the Penal Colony" destroys the body on which it writes, then there must be a body prior to that inscription, stable and self-identical, subject to that sacrificial destruction. In a sense, for Foucault, as for Nietzsche, cultural values emerge as the result of an inscription on the body, understood as a medium, indeed, a blank page; in order for this inscription to signify, however, that medium must itself be destroyed – that is, fully transvaluated into a sublimated domain of values. Within the metaphorics of this notion of cultural values is the figure of history as a relentless writing instrument, and the body as the medium which must be destroyed and transfigured in order for "culture" to emerge.

By maintaining a body prior to its cultural inscription, Foucault appears to assume a materiality prior to signification and form. Because this distinction operates as essential to the task of genealogy as he defines it, the distinction itself is precluded as an object of genealogical investigation. Occasionally in his analysis of Herculine, Foucault subscribes to a prediscursive multiplicity of bodily forces that break through the surface of the body to disrupt the regulating practices of cultural coherence imposed upon that body by a power regime, understood as a vicissitude of "history." If the presumption of some kind of precategorial source of disruption is refused, is it still possible to give a genealogical account of the demarcation of the body as such as a signifying practice? This demarcation is not initiated by a reified history or by a subject. This marking is the result of a diffuse and active structuring of the social field. This signifying practice effects a social space for and of the body within certain regulatory grids of intelligibility.

Mary Douglas's *Purity and Danger* suggests that the very contours of "the body" are established through markings that seek to establish specific codes of cultural coherence. Any discourse that establishes the boundaries of the body serves the purpose of instating and naturalizing certain taboos regarding the appropriate limits, postures, and modes of exchange that define what it is that constitutes bodies:

> ideas about separating, purifying, demarcating and punishing transgressions have as their main function to impose system on an inherently untidy experience. It is

only by exaggerating the difference between within and without, above and below, male and female, with and against, that a semblance of order is created.[2]

Although Douglas clearly subscribes to a structuralist distinction between an inherently unruly nature and an order imposed by cultural means, the "untidiness" to which she refers can be redescribed as a region of *cultural* unruliness and disorder. Assuming the inevitably binary structure of the nature/culture distinction, Douglas cannot point toward an alternative configuration of culture in which such distinctions become malleable or proliferate beyond the binary frame. Her analysis, however, provides a possible point of departure for understanding the relationship by which social taboos institute and maintain the boundaries of the body as such. Her analysis suggests that what constitutes the limit of the body is never merely material, but that the surface, the skin, is systemically signified by taboos and anticipated transgressions; indeed, the boundaries of the body become, within her analysis, the limits of the social *per se*. A poststructuralist appropriation of her view might well understand the boundaries of the body as the limits of the socially *hegemonic*. In a variety of cultures, she maintains, there are

> pollution powers which inhere in the structure of ideas itself and which punish a symbolic breaking of that which should be joined or joining of that which should be separate. It follows from this that pollution is a type of danger which is not likely to occur except where the lines of structure, cosmic or social, are clearly defined.
>
> A polluting person is always in the wrong. He [*sic*] has developed some wrong condition or simply crossed over some line which should not have been crossed and this displacement unleashes danger for someone.[3]

In a sense, Simon Watney has identified the contemporary construction of "the polluting person" as the person with AIDS in his *Policing Desire: AIDS, Pornography, and the Media*.[4] Not only is the illness figured as the "gay disease," but throughout the media's hysterical and homophobic response to the illness there is a tactical construction of a continuity between the polluted status of the homosexual by virtue of the boundary-trespass that is homosexuality and the disease as a specific modality of homosexual pollution. That the disease is transmitted through the exchange of bodily fluids suggests within the sensationalist graphics of homophobic signifying systems the dangers that permeable bodily boundaries present to the social order as such. Douglas remarks that "the body is a model that can stand for any bounded system. Its boundaries can represent any boundaries which are threatened or precarious."[5] And she asks a question which one might have expected to read in Foucault: "Why should bodily margins be thought to be specifically invested with power and danger?"[6]

Douglas suggests that all social systems are vulnerable at their margins, and that all margins are accordingly considered dangerous. If the body is synecdochal for the social system *per se* or a site in which open systems converge, then any kind of unregulated permeability constitutes a site of pollution and endangerment. Since anal and oral sex among men clearly establishes certain kinds of bodily permeabilities unsanctioned by the hegemonic order, male homosexuality would, within such a hegemonic point of view, constitute a site of danger and pollution, prior to and regardless of the cultural presence of AIDS. Similarly, the "polluted" status of lesbians, regardless of their low-risk status with respect to AIDS, brings into relief the dangers of their bodily exchanges. Significantly, being "outside" the hegemonic order does not signify being "in" a state of filthy and untidy nature. Paradoxically, homosexuality is almost always conceived within the homophobic signifying economy as *both* uncivilized and unnatural.

The construction of stable bodily contours relies upon fixed sites of corporeal permeability and impermeability. Those sexual practices in both homosexual and heterosexual contexts that open surfaces and orifices to erotic signification or close down others effectively reinscribe the boundaries of the body along new cultural lines. Anal sex among men is an example, as is the radical re-membering of the body in Wittig's *The Lesbian Body*. Douglas alludes to "a kind of sex pollution which expresses a desire to keep the body (physical and social) intact,"[7] suggesting that the naturalized notion of "the" body is itself a consequence of taboos that render that body discrete by virtue of its stable boundaries. Further, the rites of passage that govern various bodily orifices presuppose a heterosexual construction of gendered exchange, positions, and erotic possibilities. The deregulation of such exchanges accordingly disrupts the very boundaries that determine what it is to be a body at all. Indeed, the critical inquiry that traces the regulatory practices within which bodily contours are constructed constitutes precisely the genealogy of "the body" in its discreteness that might further radicalize Foucault's theory.[8]

Significantly, Kristeva's discussion of abjection in *Powers of Horror* begins to suggest the uses of this structuralist notion of a boundary-constituting taboo for the purposes of constructing a discrete subject through exclusion.[9] The "abject" designates that which has been expelled from the body, discharged as excrement, literally rendered "Other." This appears as an expulsion of alien elements, but the alien is effectively established through this expulsion. The construction of the "not-me" as the abject establishes the boundaries of the body which are also the first contours of the subject. Kristeva writes:

> *nausea* makes me balk at that milk cream, separates me from the mother and father who proffer it. "I" want none of that element, sign of their desire; "I" do

not want to listen, "I" do not assimilate it, "I" expel it. But since the food is not an "other" for "me," who am only in their desire, I expel *myself*, I spit *myself* out, I abject *myself* within the same motion through which "I" claim to establish myself.[10]

The boundary of the body as well as the distinction between internal and external is established through the ejection and transvaluation of something originally part of identity into a defiling otherness. As Iris Young has suggested in her use of Kristeva to understand sexism, homophobia, and racism, the repudiation of bodies for their sex, sexuality, and/or color is an "expulsion" followed by a "repulsion" that founds and consolidates culturally hegemonic identities along sex/race/sexuality axes of differentiation.[11] Young's appropriation of Kristeva shows how the operation of repulsion can consolidate "identities" founded on the instituting of the "Other" or a set of Others through exclusion and domination. What constitutes through division the "inner" and "outer" worlds of the subject is a border and boundary tenuously maintained for the purposes of social regulation and control. The boundary between the inner and outer is confounded by those excremental passages in which the inner effectively becomes outer, and this excreting function becomes, as it were, the model by which other forms of identity-differentiation are accomplished. In effect, this is the mode by which Others become shit. For inner and outer worlds to remain utterly distinct, the entire surface of the body would have to achieve an impossible impermeability. This sealing of its surfaces would constitute the seamless boundary of the subject; but this enclosure would invariably be exploded by precisely that excremental filth that it fears.

Regardless of the compelling metaphors of the spatial distinctions of inner and outer, they remain linguistic terms that facilitate and articulate a set of fantasies, feared and desired. "Inner" and "outer" make sense only with reference to a mediating boundary that strives for stability. And this stability, this coherence, is determined in large part by cultural orders that sanction the subject and compel its differentiation from the abject. Hence, "inner" and "outer" constitute a binary distinction that stabilizes and consolidates the coherent subject. When that subject is challenged, the meaning and necessity of the terms are subject to displacement. If the "inner world" no longer designates a topos, then the internal fixity of the self and, indeed, the internal locale of gender identity, become similarly suspect. The critical question is not *how* did that identity become *internalized*? as if internalization were a process or a mechanism that might be descriptively reconstructed. Rather, the question is: From what strategic position in public discourse and for what reasons has the trope of interiority and the disjunctive binary of inner/outer taken hold? In what language is "inner space" figured? What kind of figuration is it, and through what figure of the body is it signified? How does a body figure on its surface the very invisibility of its hidden depth?

From interiority to gender performatives

In *Discipline and Punish* Foucault challenges the language of internalization as it operates in the service of the disciplinary regime of the subjection and sub-jectivation of criminals.[12] Although Foucault objected to what he understood to be the psychoanalytic belief in the "inner" truth of sex in *The History of Sexuality*, he turns to a criticism of the doctrine of internalization for separate purposes in the context of his history of criminology. In a sense, *Discipline and Punish* can be read as Foucault's effort to rewrite Nietzsche's doctrine of internalization in *On the Genealogy of Morals* on the model of *inscription*. In the context of prisoners, Foucault writes, the strategy has been not to enforce a repression of their desires, but to compel their bodies to signify the prohibitive law as their very essence, style, and necessity. That law is not literally internal-ized, but incorporated, with the consequence that bodies are produced which signify that law on and through the body; there the law is manifest as the essence of their selves, the meaning of their soul, their conscience, the law of their desire. In effect, the law is at once fully manifest and fully latent, for it never appears as external to the bodies it subjects and subjectivates. Foucault writes:

> It would be wrong to say that the soul is an illusion, or an ideological effect. On the contrary, it exists, it has a reality, it is produced permanently *around, on, within*, the body by the functioning of a power that is exercised on those that are punished. (my emphasis)[13]

The figure of the interior soul understood as "within" the body is signified through its inscription *on* the body, even though its primary mode of significa-tion is through its very absence, its potent invisibility. The effect of a structur-ing inner space is produced through the signification of a body as a vital and sacred enclosure. The soul is precisely what the body lacks; hence, the body presents itself as a signifying lack. That lack which *is* the body signifies the soul as that which cannot show. In this sense, then, the soul is a surface signification that contests and displaces the inner/outer distinction itself, a figure of interior psychic space inscribed *on* the body as a social signification that perpetually renounces itself as such. In Foucault's terms, the soul is not imprisoned by or within the body, as some Christian imagery would suggest, but "the soul is the prison of the body."[14]

The redescription of intrapsychic processes in terms of the surface politics of the body implies a corollary redescription of gender as the disciplinary production of the figures of fantasy through the play of presence and absence on the body's surface, the construction of the gendered body through a series of exclusions and denials, signifying absences. But what determines the manifest and latent text of the body politic? What is the prohibitive law that generates the corporeal stylization of gender, the fantasied and fantastic figuration of the body? We have already considered the incest taboo and the prior taboo against homosexuality as the generative moments of gender identity, the prohibitions that produce identity along the culturally intelligible grids of an idealized and compulsory heterosexuality. That disciplinary production of gender effects a false stabilization of gender in the interests of the heterosexual construction and regulation of sexuality within the reproductive domain. The construction of coherence conceals the gender discontinuities that run rampant within heterosexual, bisexual, and gay and lesbian contexts in which gender does not necessarily follow from sex, and desire, or sexuality generally, does not seem to follow from gender – indeed, where none of these dimensions of significant corporeality express or reflect one another. When the disorganization and disaggregation of the field of bodies disrupt the regulatory fiction of heterosexual coherence, it seems that the expressive model loses its descriptive force. That regulatory ideal is then exposed as a norm and a fiction that disguises itself as a developmental law regulating the sexual field that it purports to describe.

According to the understanding of identification as an enacted fantasy or incorporation, however, it is clear that coherence is desired, wished for, idealized, and that this idealization is an effect of a corporeal signification. In other words, acts, gestures, and desire produce the effect of an internal core or substance, but produce this *on the surface* of the body, through the play of signifying absences that suggest, but never reveal, the organizing principle of identity as a cause. Such acts, gestures, enactments, generally construed, are *performative* in the sense that the essence or identity that they otherwise purport to express are *fabrications* manufactured and sustained through corporeal signs and other discursive means. That the gendered body is performative suggests that it has no ontological status apart from the various acts which constitute its reality. This also suggests that if that reality is fabricated as an interior essence, that very interiority is an effect and function of a decidedly public and social discourse, the public regulation of fantasy through the surface politics of the body, the gender border control that differentiates inner from outer, and so institutes the "integrity" of the subject. In other words, acts and gestures, articulated and enacted desires create the illusion of an interior and organizing gender core, an illusion discursively maintained for the purposes of the regulation of sexuality within the obligatory frame of reproductive heterosexuality. If the "cause" of desire, gesture, and act can be localized within the "self" of the actor, then the political regulations and disciplinary practices which produce that ostensibly coherent gender are effectively displaced from view. The displacement of a political and discursive origin of gender identity onto a psychological "core" precludes an analysis of the political constitution of the gendered subject and its fabricated notions about the ineffable interiority of its sex or of its true identity.

If the inner truth of gender is a fabrication and if a true gender is a fantasy instituted and inscribed on the surface of bodies, then it seems that genders can be neither true nor false, but are only produced as the truth effects of a discourse of primary and stable identity. In *Mother Camp: Female Impersonators in America*, anthropologist Esther Newton suggests that the structure of impersonation reveals one of the key fabricating mechanisms through which the social construction of gender takes place.[15] I would suggest as well that drag fully subverts the distinction between inner and outer psychic space and effectively mocks both the expressive model of gender and the notion of a true gender identity. Newton writes:

> At its most complex, [drag] is a double inversion that says, "appearance is an illusion." Drag says [Newton's curious personification] "my 'outside' appearance is feminine, but my essence 'inside' [the body] is masculine." At the same time it symbolizes the opposite inversion; "my appearance 'outside' [my body, my gender] is masculine but my essence 'inside' [myself] is feminine."[16]

Both claims to truth contradict one another and so displace the entire enactment of gender significations from the discourse of truth and falsity.

The notion of an original or primary gender identity is often parodied within the cultural practices of drag, cross-dressing, and the sexual stylization of butch/femme identities. Within feminist theory, such parodic identities have been understood to be either degrading to women, in the case of drag and cross-dressing, or an uncritical appropriation of sex-role stereotyping from within the practice of heterosexuality, especially in the case of butch/femme lesbian identities. But the relation between the "imitation" and the "original" is, I think, more complicated than that critique generally allows. Moreover, it gives us a clue to the way in which the relationship between primary identification — that is, the original meanings accorded to gender — and subsequent gender experience might be reframed. The performance of drag plays upon the distinction between the anatomy of the performer and the gender that is being performed. But we are actually in the presence of three contingent dimensions of significant corporeality: anatomical sex, gender identity, and gender performance. If the anatomy of the performer is already distinct from the gender of the performer, and both of those are distinct from the gender of the performance, then the performance suggests a dissonance not only between sex and performance, but sex and gender, and gender and performance. As much as drag creates a unified picture of "woman" (what its critics often oppose), it also reveals the distinctness of those aspects of gendered experience which are falsely naturalized as a unity through the regulatory fiction of heterosexual coherence. *In imitating gender, drag implicitly reveals the imitative structure of gender itself – as well as its contingency.* Indeed, part of the pleasure, the giddiness of the performance is in the recognition of a radical contingency in the relation between sex and gender in the face of cultural configurations of causal unities that are regularly assumed to be natural and necessary. In the place of the law of heterosexual coherence, we see sex and gender denaturalized by means of a performance which avows their distinctness and dramatizes the cultural mechanism of their fabricated unity.

The notion of gender parody defended here does not assume that there is an original which such parodic identities imitate. Indeed, the parody is *of* the very notion of an original; just as the psychoanalytic notion of gender identification is constituted by a fantasy of a fantasy, the transfiguration of an Other who is always already a "figure" in that double sense, so gender parody reveals that the original identity after which gender fashions itself is an imitation without an origin. To be more precise, it is a production which, in effect – that is, in its effect – postures as an imitation. This perpetual displacement constitutes a fluidity of identities that suggests an openness to resignification and recontextualization; parodic proliferation deprives hegemonic culture and its critics of the claim to naturalized or essentialist gender identities. Although the gender meanings taken up in these parodic styles are clearly part of hegemonic, misogynist culture, they are nevertheless denaturalized and mobilized through their parodic recontextualization. As imitations which effectively displace the meaning of the original, they imitate the myth of originality itself. In the place of an original identification which serves as a determining cause, gender identity might be reconceived as a personal/cultural history of received meanings subject to a set of imitative practices which refer laterally to other imitations and which, jointly, construct the illusion of a primary and interior gendered self or parody the mechanism of that construction.

According to Fredric Jameson's "Postmodernism and Consumer Society," the imitation that mocks the notion of an original is characteristic of pastiche rather than parody:

> Pastiche is, like parody, the imitation of a peculiar or unique style, the wearing of a stylistic mask, speech in a dead language: but it is a neutral practice of mimicry, without parody's ulterior motive, without the satirical impulse, without laughter, without that still latent feeling that there exists something *normal* compared to

which what is being imitated is rather comic. Pastiche is blank parody, parody that has lost it humor.[17]

The loss of the sense of "the normal," however, can be its own occasion for laughter, especially when "the normal," "the original" is revealed to be a copy, and an inevitably failed one, an ideal that no one *can* embody. In this sense, laughter emerges in the realization that all along the original was derived.

Parody by itself is not subversive, and there must be a way to understand what makes certain kinds of parodic repetitions effectively disruptive, truly troubling, and which repetitions become domesticated and recirculated as instruments of cultural hegemony. A typology of actions would clearly not suffice, for parodic displacement, indeed, parodic laughter, depends on a context and reception in which subversive confusions can be fostered. What performance where will invert the inner/outer distinction and compel a radical rethinking of the psychological presuppositions of gender identity and sexuality? What performance where will compel a reconsideration of the *place* and stability of the masculine and the feminine? And what kind of gender performance will enact and reveal the performativity of gender itself in a way that destabilizes the naturalized categories of identity and desire.

If the body is not a "being," but a variable boundary, a surface whose permeability is politically regulated, a signifying practice within a cultural field of gender hierarchy and compulsory heterosexuality, then what language is left for understanding this corporeal enactment, gender, that constitutes its "interior" signification on its surface? Sartre would perhaps have called this act "a style of being," Foucault, "a stylistics of existence." And in my earlier reading of Beauvoir, I suggest that gendered bodies are so many "styles of the flesh." These styles all never fully self-styled, for styles have a history, and those histories condition and limit the possibilities. Consider gender, for instance, as *a corporeal style*, an "act," as it were, which is both intentional and performative, where *"performative"* suggests a dramatic and contingent construction of meaning.

Wittig understands gender as the workings of "sex," where "sex" is an obligatory injunction for the body to become a cultural sign, to materialize itself in obedience to a historically delimited possibility, and to do this, not once or twice, but as a sustained and repeated corporeal project. The notion of a "project," however, suggests the originating force of a radical will, and because gender is a project which has cultural survival as its end, the term *strategy* better suggests the situation of duress under which gender performance always and variously occurs. Hence, as a strategy of survival within compulsory systems, gender is a performance with clearly punitive consequences. Discrete genders are part of what "humanizes" individuals within contemporary culture; indeed, we regularly punish those who fail to do their gender right. Because there is neither an "essence" that gender expresses or externalizes nor an objective ideal to which gender aspires, and because gender is not a fact, the various acts of gender create the idea of gender, and without those acts, there would be no gender at all. Gender is, thus, a construction that regularly conceals its genesis; the tacit collective agreement to perform, produce, and sustain discrete and polar genders as cultural fictions is obscured by the credibility of those productions – and the punishments that attend not agreeing to believe in them; the construction "compels" our belief in its necessity and naturalness. The historical possibilities materialized through various corporeal styles are nothing other than those punitively regulated cultural fictions alternately embodied and deflected under duress.

Consider that a sedimentation of gender norms produces the peculiar phenomenon of a "natural sex" or a "real woman" or any number of prevalent and compelling social fictions, and that this is a sedimentation that over time has produced a set of corporeal styles which, in reified form, appear as the natural configuration of bodies into sexes existing in a binary relation to one another. If these styles are enacted, and if they produce the coherent gendered subjects who pose as their originators, what kind of performance might reveal this ostensible "cause" to be an "effect"?

In what senses, then, is gender an act? As in other ritual social dramas, the action of gender requires a performance that is *repeated*. This repetition is at once a reenactment and reexperiencing of a set of meanings already socially established; and it is the mundane and ritualized form of their legitimation.[18] Although there are individual bodies that enact these significations by becoming stylized into gendered modes, this "action" is a public action. There are temporal and collective dimensions to these actions, and their public character is not inconsequential; indeed, the performance is effected with the strategic aim of maintaining gender within its binary frame – an aim that cannot be attributed to a subject, but, rather, must be understood to found and consolidate the subject.

Gender ought not to be construed as a stable identity or locus of agency from which various acts follow; rather, gender is an identity tenuously constituted in time, instituted in an exterior space through a *stylized repetition of acts*. The effect of gender is produced through the stylization of the body and, hence, must be understood as the mundane way in which bodily gestures, movements, and styles of various kinds constitute the illusion of an abiding gendered self. This formulation moves the conception of gender off the ground of a substantial model of identity to one that requires a conception of gender as a constituted *social temporality*. Significantly, if gender is instituted through acts which are internally discontinuous, then the *appearance of substance* is precisely that, a constructed identity, a performative accomplishment which the mundane social audience, including the actors themselves, come to believe and to perform in the mode of belief. Gender is also a norm that can never be fully internalized; "the internal" is a surface signification, and gender norms are finally phantasmatic, impossible to embody. If the ground of gender identity is the stylized repetition of acts through time and not a seemingly seamless identity, then the spatial metaphor of a "ground" will be displaced and revealed as a stylized configuration, indeed, a gendered corporealization of time. The abiding gendered self will then be shown to be structured by repeated acts that seek to approximate the ideal of a substantial ground of identity, but which, in their occasional *dis*continuity, reveal the temporal and contingent groundlessness of this "ground." The possibilities of gender transformation are to be found precisely in the arbitrary relation between such acts, in the possibility of a failure to repeat, a de-formity, or a parodic repetition that exposes the phantasmatic effect of abiding identity as a politically tenuous construction.

If gender attributes, however, are not expressive but performative, then these attributes effectively constitute the identity they are said to express or reveal. The distinction between expression and performativeness is crucial. If gender attributes and acts, the various ways in which a body shows or produces its cultural signification, are performative, then there is no preexisting identity by which an act or attribute might be measured; there would be no true or false, real or distorted acts of gender, and the postulation of a true gender identity would be revealed as a regulatory fiction. That gender reality is created through sustained social performances means that the very notions of an essential sex and a true or abiding masculinity or femininity are also constituted as part of the strategy that conceals gender's performative character and the performative possibilities for proliferating gender configurations outside the restricting frames of masculinist domination and compulsory heterosexuality.

Genders can be neither true nor false, neither real nor apparent, neither original nor derived. As credible bearers of those attributes, however, genders can also be rendered thoroughly and radically *incredible*.

Notes

Introduction

1   See 1999 preface *to Subjects of Desire*, xiv.
2   Preface to anniversary edition of *Gender Trouble*: see pp. 98–9, 103.
3   Eve Kosofsky Sedgwick, *Tendencies* (London: Routledge, 1994), 11.

4   *On the Genealogy of Morals*, 29.
5   *The Ego and the Id*, volume XIX of *the Standard Edition of the Complete Psychological Works of Sigmund Freud*, ed. and trans. James Strachey (London: Hogarth Press, 1973–4), 367.
6   Ibid., 372.
7   *Gender Trouble*, 61.
8   See G. W. F. Hegel, *Phenomenology of Spirit*, 111–19.
9   Preface to anniversary edition of *Gender Trouble*; see p. 103.
10 Ibid., p. 99.
11 Preface to anniversary edition of *Gender Trouble*; see p. 100.
12 Ibid., p. 94.

Preface (1999)

1   For a more or less complete bibliography of my publications and citations of my work, see the excellent work of Eddie Yeghiayan at the University of California at Irvine Library: http://sun3.lib.uci.edu/~scctr/Wellek/index.html.
2   I am especially indebted to Biddy Martin, Eve Sedgwick, Slavoj Žižek, Wendy Brown, Saidiya Hartman, Mandy Merck, Lynne Layton, Timothy Kaufmann-Osborne, Jessica Benjamin, Seyla Benhabib, Nancy Fraser, Diana Fuss, Jay Presser, Lisa Duggan, and Elizabeth Grosz for their insightful criticisms of the theory of performativity.
3   This notion of the ritual dimension of performativity is allied with the notion of the habitus in Pierre Bourdieu's work, something which I only came to realize after the fact of writing this text. For my belated effort to account for this resonance, see the final chapter of *Excitable Speech: A Politics of the Performative* (New York: Routledge, 1997).
4   Jacqueline Rose usefully pointed out to me the disjunction between the earlier and later parts of this text. The earlier parts interrogate the melancholy construction of gender, but the later seem to forget the psychoanalytic beginnings. Perhaps this accounts for some of the "mania" of the final chapter, a state defined by Freud as part of the disavowal of loss that is melancholia. *Gender Trouble* in its closing pages seems to forget or disavow the loss it has just articulated.
5   See *Bodies that Matter* (New York: Routledge, 1993) as well as an able and interesting critique that relates some of the questions raised there to contemporary science studies by Karen Barad, "Getting Real: Technoscientific Practices and the Materialization of Reality," *differences*, 5, no. 2, pp. 87–126.
6   Saidiya Hartman, Lisa Lowe, and Dorinne Kondo are scholars whose work has influenced my own. Much of the current scholarship on "passing" has also taken up this question. My own essay on Nella Larsen's "Passing" in *Bodies That Matter* sought to address the question in a preliminary way. Of course, Homi Bhabha's work on the mimetic splitting of the postcolonial subject is close to my own in several ways: not only the appropriation of the colonial "voice" by the colonized, but the split condition of identification are crucial to a notion of performativity

that emphasizes the way minority identities are produced and riven at the same time under conditions of domination.

7   The work of Kobena Mercer, Kendall Thomas, and Hortense Spillers has been extremely useful to my post-*Gender Trouble* thinking on this subject. I also hope to publish an essay on Frantz Fanon soon engaging questions of mimesis and hyperbole in his *Black Skins, White Masks*. I am grateful to Greg Thomas, who has recently completed his dissertation in rhetoric at Berkeley, on racialized sexualities in the US, for provoking and enriching my understanding of this crucial intersection.

8   I have offered reflections on universality in subsequent writings, most prominently in chapter 2 of *Excitable Speech*.

9   See the important publications of the Intersex Society of North America (including the publications of Cheryl Chase) which has, more than any other organization, brought to public attention the severe and violent gender policing done to infants and children born with gender anomalous bodies. For more information, contact them at http://www.isna.org.

10 I thank Wendy Brown, Joan W. Scott, Alexandra Chasin, Frances Bartkowski, Janet Halley, Michel Feher, Homi Bhabha, Drucilla Cornell, Denise Riley, Elizabeth Weed, Kaja Silverman, Ann Pellegrini, William Connolly, Gayatri Chakravorty Spivak, Ernesto Laclau, Eduardo Cadava, Florence Dore, David Kazanjian, David Eng, and Dina Al-kassim for their support and friendship during the Spring of 1999 when this preface was written.

Bodily Inscriptions, Performative Subversions

1   Michel Foucault, "Nietzsche, Genealogy, History," in *Language, Counter-Memory, Practice: Selected Essays and Interviews*, trans. Donald F. Bouchard and Sherry Simon, ed. Donald F. Bouchard (Ithaca, NY: Cornell University Press, 1977), p. 148. References in the text are to this essay.

2   Mary Douglas, *Purity and Danger* (London, Boston, and Henley: Routledge and Kegan Paul, 1969), p. 4.

3   Ibid., p. 113.

4   Simon Watney, *Policing Desire: AIDS, Pornography, and the Media* (Minneapolis: University of Minnesota Press, 1988).

5   Douglas, *Purity and Danger*, p. 115.

6   Ibid., p. 121.

7   Ibid., p. 140.

8   Foucault's essay "A Preface to Transgression" (in *Language, Counter-Memory, Practice*) does provide an interesting juxtaposition with Douglas's notion of body boundaries constituted by incest taboos. Originally written in honor of Georges Bataille, this essay explores in part the metaphorical "dirt" of transgressive pleasures and the association of the forbidden orifice with the dirt-covered tomb. See pp. 46–8.

9   Kristeva discusses Mary Douglas's work in a short section of *Powers of Horror: An Essay on Abjection*, trans. Leon Roudiez (New York: Columbia University Press,

1982), originally published as *Pouvoirs de l'horreur* (Paris: Éditions de Seuil, 1980). Assimilating Douglas's insights to her own reformulation of Lacan, Kristeva writes, "Defilement is what is jettisoned from the *symbolic system*. It is what escapes that social rationality, that logical order on which a social aggregate is based, which then becomes differentiated from a temporary agglomeration of individuals and, in short, constitutes a *classification system* or a *structure*" (p. 65).

10   Ibid., p. 3.

11   Iris Marion Young, "Abjection and Oppression: Dynamics of Unconscious Racism, Sexism, and Homophobia," paper presented at the Society of Phenomenology and Existential Philosophy Meetings, Northwestern University, 1988. In *Crises in Continental Philosophy*, ed. Arleen B. Dallery and Charles E. Scott with Holley Roberts (Albany: SUNY Press, 1990), pp. 201–14.

12   Parts of the following discussion were published in two different contexts, in my "Gender Trouble, Feminist Theory, and Psychoanalytic Discourse," in *Feminism/ Postmodernism*, ed. Linda J. Nicholson (New York: Routledge, 1989) and "Performative Acts and Gender Constitution: An Essay in Phenomenology and Feminist Theory," *Theatre Journal*, 20, no. 3, Winter 1988.

13   Michel Foucault, *Discipline and Punish: the Birth of the Prison*, trans. Alan Sheridan (New York: Vintage, 1979), p. 29.

14   Ibid., p. 30.

15   See the chapter "Role Models" in Esther Newton, *Mother Camp: Female Impersonators in America* (Chicago: University of Chicago Press, 1972).

16   Ibid., p. 103.

17   Fredric Jameson, "Postmodernism and Consumer Society," in *The Anti-Aesthetic: Essays on Postmodern Culture*, ed. Hal Foster (Port Townsend, WA.: Bay Press, 1983), p. 114.

18   See Victor Turner, *Dramas, Fields and Metaphors* (Ithaca: Cornell University Press, 1974). See also Clifford Geertz, "Blurred Genres: The Refiguration of Thought," in *Local Knowledge, Further Essays in Interpretive Anthropology* (New York: Basic Books, 1983).

4

Imitation and Gender Insubordination (1990)[1]

Introduction

Although parts of this article were presented at the Conference on Homosexuality at Yale University in 1989, "Imitation and Gender Insubordination" appeared in print after the publication of *Gender Trouble*, and it addresses and extends a number of the issues Butler dealt with there. Expressing her concern at the inclusion of her article in a volume of "lesbian theories, gay theories," Butler explains that she understands herself neither as a defender of theory, nor as a "lesbian" in any strictly defined sense. Indeed, her work to date has questioned both the stability and the value of identity categories, since they invariably operate in the service of oppressive, exclusionary, regulatory regimes. Accordingly, Butler announces her willingness to appear under the sign of "lesbian" only in order to contest it, and here as elsewhere, she sees such disclaimers of identity categories as a more effective political practice than the strategic essentialism favored by other theorists. Summarizing the position she adopted in this essay, Butler has stated that at the time she thought that saying one is a lesbian may not overcome the opacity that is associated with sexuality and identity. On the other hand, Butler does come out in this essay, which is a coming-out act, the moment in which she claims the term "lesbian" as the field of theoretical operation. The essay is also the arena in which "Butler" plays at being a lesbian in a deep-seated way, since she couldn't play at being anything else. Thus the undeniability of her lesbianism is as important as her assertion that claiming it is insufficient to describe or explain who she is.

There is political potential in such insufficiency, as well as in the catachrestic deployment of an "I" that cannot be said to precede the act of revelation. If coming out is always an incomplete act, then "lesbian" itself is an open-ended, non-discrete category constituted in part by its cross-identifications with heterosexuality. Reinscribing lesbian sexuality within a heterosexual matrix calls the heterosexual presumption of priority into question, reworking the notion that lesbianism is an imitation of "original" heterosexuality. Lesbian identities do not imitate heterosexual identities; rather, they panic them by confounding the origin-to-copy/heterosexual-to-lesbian line of causation, thereby exposing heterosexual claims to originality as illusory. Parodic practices such as drag spotlight

From Diana Fuss (ed.), *Inside Out: Lesbian Theories, Gay Theories*, pp. 13–31. New York: Routledge, 1991. Reproduced by permission of Routledge, an imprint of Taylor & Francis Books, Inc.

the imitative nature of *all* gender identities which are copies of copies without an original; in particular, they expose the panicked, imitative nature of heterosexuality even as it attempts to set itself up as "natural."

Here, as in *Gender Trouble*, Butler rejects the notion that a volitional subject precedes its acts of parodic repetition, and she continues to insist that gender performativity is constitutive of the subject-effect it is said to express. Denying the priority of the subject is not the same as denying the subject itself, and Butler is careful to distinguish between subject and psyche, asserting that the latter always exceeds the former. In "Imitation and Gender Insubordination" Butler once again deploys psychoanalytic insights and paradigms, drawing on Freud in her characterization of gender as a form of psychic mime that is the subject's melancholic response to the lost identifications it mimetically incorporates. The subversive deployment of "troublesome" identifications deinstates those gender identities that currently present themselves as singular and stable, and gender may be fabricated in ways that confound the notion of "original," "true," "inner" gender cores by revealing them to be no more than parodic effects. It is here that Butler continues to see political promise in what she calls the disruptive play of performances that in no way presuppose the existence of self-identical actors.

So what is this divided being introduced into language through gender? It is an impossible being, it is a being that does not exist, an ontological joke.   Monique Wittig[2]

Beyond physical repetition and the psychical or metaphysical repetition, is there an ontological repetition? . . . This ultimate repetition, this ultimate theatre, gathers everything in a certain way; and in another way, it destroys everything; and in yet another way, it selects from everything.   Gilles Deleuze[3]

To Theorize as a Lesbian?

At first I considered writing a different sort of essay, one with a philosophical tone: the "being" of being homosexual. The prospect of *being* anything, even for pay, has always produced in me a certain anxiety, for "to be" gay, "to be" lesbian seems to be more than a simple injunction to become who or what I already am. And in no way does it settle the anxiety for me to say that this is "part" of what I am. To write or speak *as a lesbian* appears a paradoxical appearance of this "I," one which feels neither true nor false. For it is a production, usually in response to a request, to come out or write in the name of an identity which, once produced, sometimes functions as a politically efficacious phantasm. I'm not at ease with "lesbian theories, gay theories," for as I've argued elsewhere,[4] identity categories tend to be instruments of regulatory regimes, whether as the normalizing categories of oppressive structures or as the rallying points for a liberatory contestation of that very oppression. This is not to say that I will not appear at political occasions under the sign of lesbian, but that I would like to have it permanently unclear what precisely that sign signifies. So it is unclear how it is that I can contribute to this book and appear under its title, for it announces a set of terms that I propose to contest. One risk I take is to be recolonized by the sign under which I write, and so it is this risk that I seek to thematize. To propose that the invocation of identity is always a risk does not imply that resistance to it is always or only symptomatic of a self-inflicted homophobia. Indeed, a Foucaultian perspective might argue that the affirmation of "homosexuality" is itself an extension of a homophobic discourse. And yet "discourse," he writes on the same page, "can be both an instrument and an effect of power, but also a hindrance, a stumbling-block, a point of resistance and a starting point for an opposing strategy."[5]

So I am skeptical about how the "I" is determined as it operates under the title of the lesbian sign, and I am no more comfortable with its homophobic determination than with those normative definitions offered by other members of the "gay or lesbian community." I'm permanently troubled by identity categories, consider them to be invariable stumbling-blocks, and understand them, even promote them, as sites of necessary trouble. In fact, if the category were to offer no trouble, it would cease to be interesting to me: it is precisely the *pleasure* produced by the instability of those categories which sustains the various erotic practices that make me a candidate for the category to begin with. To install myself within the terms of an identity category would be to turn against the sexuality that the category purports to describe; and this might be true for any identity category which seeks to control the very eroticism that it claims to describe and authorize, much less "liberate."

And what's worse, I do not understand the notion of "theory," and am hardly interested in being cast as its defender, much less in being signified as part of an elite gay/lesbian theory crowd that seeks to establish the legitimacy and domestication of gay/lesbian studies within the academy. Is there a pregiven distinction between theory, politics, culture, media? How do those divisions operate to quell a certain intertextual writing that might well generate wholly different epistemic maps? But I am writing here now: is it too late? Can this writing, can any writing, refuse the terms by which it is appropriated even as, to some extent, that very colonizing discourse enables or produces this stumbling block, this resistance? How do I relate the paradoxical situation of this dependency and refusal?

If the political task is to show that theory is never merely *theoria*, in the sense of disengaged contemplation, and to insist that it is fully political (*phronesis* or even *praxis*), then why not simply call this operation *politics*, or some necessary permutation of it?

I have begun with confessions of trepidation and a series of disclaimers, but perhaps it will become clear that *disclaiming*, which is no simple activity, will be what I have to offer as a form of affirmative resistance to a certain regulatory operation of homophobia. The discourse of "coming out" has clearly served its purposes, but what are its risks? And here I am not speaking of unemployment or public attack or violence, which are quite clearly and widely on the increase against those who are perceived as "out" whether or not of their own design. Is the "subject" who is "out" free of its subjection and finally in the clear? Or could it be that the subjection that subjectivates the gay or lesbian subject in some ways continues to oppress, or oppresses most insidiously, once "outness" is claimed? What or who is it that is "out," made manifest and fully disclosed, when and if I reveal myself as lesbian? What is it that is now known, anything? What remains permanently concealed by the very linguistic act that offers up the promise of a transparent revelation of sexuality? Can sexuality even remain sexuality once it submits to a criterion of transparency and disclosure, or does it perhaps cease to be sexuality precisely when the semblance of full explicitness is achieved?[6] Is sexuality of any kind even possible without that opacity designated by the unconscious, which means simply that the conscious "I" who would reveal its sexuality is perhaps the last to know the meaning of what it says?

To claim that this is what I *am* is to suggest a provisional totalization of this "I." But if the I can so determine itself, then that which it excludes in order to make that determination remains constitutive of the determination itself. In other words, such a statement presupposes that the "I" exceeds its determination, and even produces that very excess in and by the act which seeks to exhaust the semantic field of that "I." In the act which would disclose the true and full content of that "I," a certain radical *concealment* is thereby produced. For it is always finally unclear what is meant by invoking the lesbian-signifier, since its signification is always to some degree out of one's control, but also because its *specificity* can only be demarcated by exclusions that return to disrupt its claim to coherence. What, if anything, can lesbians be said to share? And who will decide this question, and in the name of whom? If I claim to be a lesbian, I "come out" only to produce a new and different "closet." The "you" to whom I come out now has access to a different region of opacity. Indeed, the locus of opacity has simply shifted: before, you did not know whether I "am," but now you do not know what that means, which is to say that the copula is empty, that it cannot be substituted for with a set of descriptions.[7] And perhaps that is a situation to be valued. Conventionally, one comes out *of* the closet (and yet, how often is it the case that we are "outed" when we are young and without resources?); so we are out of the closet, but into what? what new unbounded spatiality? the room, the den, the attic, the basement, the house, the bar, the university, some new enclosure whose door, like Kafka's door, produces the expectation of a fresh air and a light of illumination that never arrives? Curiously, it is the figure of the closet that produces this expectation, and which guarantees its dissatisfaction. For being "out" always depends to some extent on being "in"; it gains its meaning only within that polarity. Hence, being "out" must produce the closet again and again in order to maintain itself as "out." In this sense, *outness* can only produce a new opacity; and *the closet* produces the promise of a disclosure that can, by definition, never come. Is this infinite postponement of the disclosure of "gayness," produced by the very act of "coming out," to be lamented? Or is this very deferral of the signified *to be valued*, a site for the production of values, precisely because the term now takes on a life that cannot be, can never be, permanently controlled?

It is possible to argue that whereas no transparent or full revelation is afforded by "lesbian" and "gay," there remains a political imperative to use these necessary errors or category mistakes, as it were (what Gayatri Spivak might call "catachrestic" operations: to use a proper name improperly[8]), to rally and represent an oppressed political constituency. Clearly, I am not legislating against the use of the term. My question is simply: which use will be legislated, and what play will there be between legislation and use such that the instrumental uses of "identity" do not become regulatory imperatives? If it is already true that "lesbians" and "gay men" have been traditionally designated as impossible identities, errors of classification, unnatural disasters within jur- idico-medical discourses, or, what perhaps amounts to the same, the very paradigm of what calls to be classified, regulated, and controlled, then perhaps these sites of disruption, error, confusion, and trouble can be the very rallying points for a certain resistance to classification and to identity as such.

The question is not one of *avowing* or *disavowing* the category of lesbian or gay, but, rather, why it is that the category becomes the site of this "ethical" choice? What does it mean to *avow* a category that can only maintain its specificity and coherence by performing a prior set of *disavowals?* Does this make "coming out" into the avowal of disavowal, that is, a return to the closet under the guise of an escape? And it is not something like heterosexuality or bisexuality that is disavowed by the category, but a set of identificatory and practical crossings between these categories that renders the discreteness of each equally suspect. Is it not possible to maintain and pursue heterosexual identifi- cations and aims within homosexual practice, and homosexual identifications and aims within heterosexual practices? If a sexuality is to be disclosed, what will be taken as the true determinant of its meaning: the phantasy structure, the act, the orifice, the gender, the anatomy? And if the practice engages a complex interplay of all of those, which one of this erotic dimensions will come to stand for the sexuality that requires them all? Is it the *specificity* of a lesbian experience or lesbian desire or lesbian sexuality that lesbian theory needs to elucidate? Those efforts have only and always produced a set of contests and refusals which should by now make it clear that there is no necessarily common element among lesbians, except perhaps that we all know something about how homophobia works against women – although, even then, the language and the analysis we use will differ.

To argue that there might be a *specificity* to lesbian sexuality has seemed a necessary counterpoint to the claim that lesbian sexuality is just heterosexuality once removed, or that it is derived, or that it does not exist. But perhaps the claim of specificity, on the one hand, and the claim of derivativeness or non-existence, on the other, are not as contradictory as they seem. Is it not possible that lesbian sexuality is a process that reinscribes the power domains that it resists, that it is constituted in part from the very heterosexual matrix that it seeks to displace, and that its specificity is to be established, not *outside* or *beyond* that reinscription or reiteration, but in the very modality and effects of that reinscription? In other words, the negative constructions of lesbianism as a fake or a bad copy can be occupied and reworked to call into question the claims of heterosexual priority. In a sense I hope to make clear in what follows, lesbian sexuality can be understood to redeploy its "derivativeness" in the service of displacing hegemonic heterosexual norms. Understood in this way, the political problem is not to establish the specificity of lesbian sexuality over and against its derivativeness, but to turn the homophobic construction of the bad copy against the framework that privileges heterosexuality as origin, and so "derive" the former from the latter. This description requires a reconsideration of imitation, drag, and other forms of sexual crossing that affirm the internal complexity of a lesbian sexuality constituted in part within the very matrix of power that it is compelled both to reiterate and to oppose.

On the Being of Gayness as Necessary Drag

The professionalization of gayness requires a certain performance and production of a "self" which is the *constituted effect* of a discourse that nevertheless claims to "represent" that self as a prior truth. When I spoke at the conference on homosexuality in 1989,[9] I found myself telling my friends beforehand that I was off to Yale to be a lesbian, which of course didn't mean that I wasn't one before, but that somehow then, as I spoke in that context, I *was* one in some more thorough and totalizing way, at least for the time being. So I *am* one, and my qualifications are even fairly unambiguous. Since I was sixteen, being a lesbian is what I've been. So what's the anxiety, the discomfort? Well, it has something to do with that redoubling, the way I can say, I'm going to Yale to be a lesbian; a lesbian is what I've been being for so long. How is it that I can both "be" one, and yet endeavor to be one at the same time? When and where does my being a lesbian come into play, when and where does this playing a lesbian constitute something like what I am? To say that I "play" at being one is not to say that I am not one "really"; rather, how and where I play at being one is the way in which that "being" gets established, instituted, circulated, and confirmed. This is not a performance from which I can take radical distance, for this is deep-seated play, psychically entrenched play, *and this "I" does not play its lesbianism as a role.* Rather, it is through the repeated play of this sexuality that the "I" is insistently reconstituted as a lesbian "I"; paradoxically, it is precisely the *repetition* of that play that establishes as well the *instability* of the very category that it constitutes. For if the "I" is a site of repetition, that is, if the "I" only achieves the semblance of identity through a certain repetition of itself, then the "I" is always displaced by the very repetition that sustains it. In other words, does or can the "I" ever repeat itself, cite itself, faithfully, or is there always a displacement from its former moment that establishes the permanently non-self-identical status of that "I" or its "being lesbian"? What "performs" does not exhaust the "I"; it does not lay out in visible terms the comprehensive content of that "I," for if the performance is "repeated," there is always the question of what differentiates from each other the moments of identity that are repeated. And if the "I" is the effect of a certain repetition, one which produces the semblance of a continuity or coherence, then there is no "I" that precedes the gender that it is said to perform; the repetition, and the failure to repeat, produce a string of performances that constitute and contest the coherence of that "I."

But *politically*, we might argue, isn't it quite crucial to insist on lesbian and gay identities precisely because they are being threatened with erasure and obliteration from homophobic quarters? Isn't the above theory *complicitous* with those political forces that would obliterate the possibility of gay and lesbian identity? Isn't it "no accident" that such theoretical contestations of identity emerge within a political climate that is performing a set of similar obliterations of homosexual identities through legal and political means?

The question I want to raise in return is this: ought such threats of obliteration dictate the terms of the political resistance to them, and if they do, do such homophobic efforts to that extent win the battle from the start? There is no question that gays and lesbians are threatened by the violence of public erasure, but the decision to counter that violence must be careful not to reinstall another in its place. Which version of lesbian or gay ought to be rendered visible, and which internal exclusions will that rendering visible institute? Can the visibility of identity *suffice* as a political strategy, or can it only be the starting point for a strategic intervention which calls for a trans-formation of policy? Is it not a sign of despair over public politics when identity becomes its own policy, bringing with it those who would "police" it from various sides? And this is not a call to return to silence or invisibility, but, rather, to make use of a category that can be called into question, made to account for what it excludes. That any consolidation of identity requires some set of differentiations and exclusions seems clear. But which ones ought to be valorized? That the identity-sign I use now has its purposes seems right, but there is no way to predict or control the political uses to which that sign will be put in the future. And perhaps this is a kind of openness, regardless of its risks, that ought to be safeguarded for political reasons. If the rendering visible of lesbian/gay identity now presupposes a set of exclusions, then perhaps part of what is necessarily excluded is *the future uses of the sign*. There is a political necessity to use some sign now, and we do, but how to use it in such a way that its futural significations are not *foreclosed*? How to use the sign and avow its temporal contingency at once?

In avowing the sign's strategic provisionality (rather than its strategic essentialism), that identity can become a site of contest and revision, indeed, take on a future set of significations that those of us who use it now may not be able to foresee. It is in the safeguarding of the future of the political signifiers – preserving the signifier as a site of rearticulation – that Laclau and Mouffe discern its democratic promise.

Within contemporary US politics, there are a vast number of ways in which lesbianism in particular is understood as precisely that which cannot or dare not *be*. In a sense, Jesse Helms's attack on the NEA for sanctioning representations of "homoeroticism" focuses various homophobic fantasies of what gay men are and do on the work of Robert Mapplethorpe.[10] In a sense, for Helms, gay men exist as objects of prohibition; they are, in his twisted fantasy, sadomasochistic exploiters of children, the paradigmatic exemplars of "obscenity"; in a sense, the lesbian is not even produced within this discourse as a prohibited object. Here it becomes important to recognize that oppression works not merely through acts of overt prohibition, but covertly, through the constitution of viable subjects and through the corollary constitution of a domain of unviable (un)subjects – *abjects*, we might call them – who are neither named nor prohibited within the economy of the law. Here oppression works through the production of a domain of unthinkability and unnameability. Lesbianism is not explicitly prohibited in part because it has not even made its way into the thinkable, the imaginable, that grid of cultural intelligibility that regulates the real and the nameable. How, then, to "be" a lesbian in a political context in which the lesbian does not exist? That is, in a political discourse that wages its violence against lesbianism in part by excluding lesbianism from discourse itself? To be prohibited explicitly is to occupy a discursive site from which something like a reverse-discourse can be articulated; to be implicitly proscribed is not even to qualify as an object of prohibition.[11] And though homosexualities of all kinds in this present climate are being erased, reduced, and (then) reconstituted as sites of radical homophobic fantasy, it is important to retrace the different routes by which the unthinkability of homosexuality is being constituted time and again.

It is one thing to be erased from discourse, and yet another to be present within discourse as an abiding falsehood. Hence, there is a political imperative to render lesbianism visible, but how is that to be done outside or through existing regulatory regimes? Can the exclusion from ontology itself become a rallying point for resistance?

Here is something like a confession which is meant merely to thematize the impossibility of confession: As a young person, I suffered for a long time, and I suspect many people have, from being told, explicitly or implicitly, that what I "am" is a copy, an imitation, a derivative example, a shadow of the real. Compulsory heterosexuality sets itself up as the original, the true, the authentic; the norm that determines the real implies that "being" lesbian is always a kind of miming, a vain effort to participate in the phantasmatic plenitude of naturalized heterosexuality which will always and only fail.[12] And yet, I remember quite distinctly when I first read in Esther Newton's *Mother Camp: Female Impersonators in America*[13] that drag is not an imitation or a copy of some prior and true gender; according to Newton, drag enacts the very structure of impersonation by which *any* gender is assumed. Drag is not the putting on of a gender that belongs properly to some other group, i.e. an act of *expropriation* or *appropriation* that assumes that gender is the rightful property of sex, that "masculine" belongs to "male" and "feminine" belongs to "female." There is no "proper" gender, a gender proper to one sex rather than another, which is in some sense that sex's cultural property. Where that notion of the "proper" operates, it is always and only *improperly* installed as the effect of a compulsory system. Drag constitutes the mundane way in which genders are appropriated, theatricalized, worn, and done; it implies that all gendering is a kind of impersonation and approximation. If this is true, it seems, there is no original or primary gender that drag imitates, but *gender is a kind of imitation for which there is no original;* in fact, it is a kind of imitation that produces the very notion of the original as an *effect* and consequence of the imitation itself. In other words, the naturalistic effects of heterosexualized genders are produced through imitative strategies; what they imitate is a phantasmatic ideal of heterosexual identity, one that is produced by the imitation as its effect. In this sense, the "reality" of heterosexual identities is performatively constituted through an imitation that sets itself up as the origin and the ground of all imitations. In other words, heterosexuality is always in the process of imitating and approximating its own phantasmatic idealization of itself – *and failing*. Precisely because it is bound to fail, and yet endeavors to succeed, the project of heterosexual identity is propelled into an endless repetition of itself. Indeed, in its efforts to naturalize itself as the original, heterosexuality must be understood as a compulsive and compulsory repetition that can only produce the *effect* of its own originality; in other words, compulsory heterosexual identities, those ontologically consolidated phantasms of "man" and "woman," are theatrically produced effects that posture as grounds, origins, the normative measure of the real.[14]

Reconsider then the homophobic charge that queens and butches and femmes are imitations of the heterosexual real. Here "imitation" carries the meaning of "derivative" or "secondary," a copy of an origin which is itself the ground of all copies, but which is itself a copy of nothing. Logically, this notion of an "origin" is suspect, for how can something operate as an origin if there are no secondary consequences which retrospectively confirm the originality of that origin? The origin requires its derivations in order to affirm itself as an origin, for origins only make sense to the extent that they are differentiated from that which they produce as derivatives. Hence, if it were not for the notion of the homosexual *as* copy, there would be no construct of heterosexuality *as* origin. Heterosexuality here presupposes homosexuality. And if the homosexual *as* copy *precedes* the heterosexual as *origin*, then it seems only fair to concede that the copy comes before the origin, and that homosexuality is thus the origin, and heterosexuality the copy.

But simple inversions are not really possible. For it is only *as* a copy that homosexuality can be argued to *precede* heterosexuality as the origin. In other words, the entire framework of copy and origin proves radically unstable as each position inverts into the other and confounds the possibility of any stable way to locate the temporal or logical priority of either term.

But let us then consider this problematic inversion from a psychic/political perspective. If the structure of gender imitation is such that the imita*ted* is to some degree produced – or, rather, re*produced* – by imitation (see again Derrida's inversion and displacement of mimesis in "The Double Session"), then to claim that gay and lesbian identities are implicated in heterosexual norms or in hegemonic culture generally is not to *derive* gayness from straightness. On the contrary, *imitation* does not copy that which is prior, but produces and *inverts* the very terms of priority and derivativeness. Hence, if gay identities are implicated in heterosexuality, that is not the same as claiming that they are determined or derived from heterosexuality, and it is not the same as claiming that that heterosexuality is the only cultural network in which they are implicated. These are, quite literally, *inverted* imitations, ones which invert the order of imitated and imitation, and which, in the process, expose the fundamental dependency of "the origin" on that which it claims to produce as its secondary effect.

What follows if we concede from the start that gay identities as derivative inversions are in part defined in terms of the very heterosexual identities from which they are differentiated? If heterosexuality is an impossible imitation of itself, an imitation that performatively constitutes itself as the original, then the imitative parody of "heterosexuality" – when and where it exists in gay cultures – is always and only an imitation of an imitation, a copy of a copy, for which there is no original. Put in yet a different way, the parodic or imitative effect of gay identities works neither to copy nor to emulate hetero-sexuality, but rather, to expose heterosexuality as an incessant and *panicked* imitation of its own naturalized idealization. That heterosexuality is always in the act of elaborating itself is evidence that it is perpetually at risk, that is, that it "knows" its own possibility of becoming undone: hence, its compulsion to repeat which is at once a foreclosure of that which threatens its coherence. That it can never eradicate that risk attests to its profound dependency upon the homosexuality that it seeks fully to eradicate and never can or that it seeks to make second, but which is always already there as a prior possibility.[15] Although this failure of naturalized heterosexuality might constitute a source of pathos for heterosexuality itself – what its theorists often refer to as its constitutive malaise – it can become an occasion for a subversive and prolifer-ating parody of gender norms in which the very claim to originality and to the real is shown to be the effect of a certain kind of naturalized gender mime.

It is important to recognize the ways in which heterosexual norms reappear within gay identities, to affirm that gay and lesbian identities are not only structured in part by dominant heterosexual frames, but that they are *not* for that reason *determined* by them. They are running commentaries on those naturalized positions as well, parodic replays and resignifications of precisely those heterosexual structures that would consign gay life to discursive domains of unreality and unthinkability. But to be constituted or structured in part by the very heterosexual norms by which gay people are oppressed is not, I repeat, to be claimed or determined by those structures. And it is not necessary to think of such heterosexual constructs as the pernicious intrusion of "the straight mind," one that must be rooted out in its entirety. In a way, the presence of heterosexual constructs and positionalities in whatever form in gay and lesbian identities presupposes that there is a gay and lesbian repetition of straightness, a recapitulation of straightness – which is itself a repetition and recapitulation of its own ideality – within its own terms, a site in which all sorts of resignifying and parodic repetitions become possible. The parodic replication and resignification of heterosexual constructs within non-heterosexual frames brings into relief the utterly constructed status of the so-called original, but it shows that heterosexuality only constitutes itself as the original through a convincing act of repetition. The more that "act" is expropriated, the more the heterosexual claim to originality is exposed as illusory.

Although I have concentrated in the above on the reality-effects of gender practices, performances, repetitions, and mimes, I do not mean to suggest that drag is a "role" that can be taken on or taken off at will. There is no volitional subject behind the mime who decides, as it were, which gender it will be today. On the contrary, the very possibility of becoming a viable subject requires that a certain gender mime be already underway. The "being" of the subject is no more self-identical than the "being" of any gender; in fact, coherent gender, achieved through an apparent repetition of the same, produces as its *effect* the illusion of a prior and volitional subject. In this sense, gender is not a performance that a prior subject elects to do, but gender is *performative* in the sense that it constitutes as an effect the very subject it appears to express. It is a *compulsory* performance in the sense that acting out of line with heterosexual norms brings with it ostracism, punishment, and violence, not to mention the transgressive pleasures produced by those very prohibitions.

To claim that there is no performer prior to the performed, that the performance is performative, that the performance constitutes the appearance of a "subject" as its effect is difficult to accept. This difficulty is the result of a predisposition to think of sexuality and gender as "expressing" in some indirect or direct way a psychic reality that precedes it. The denial of the *priority* of the subject, however, is not the denial of the subject; in fact, the refusal to conflate the subject with the psyche marks the psychic as that which exceeds the domain of the conscious subject. This psychic excess is precisely what is being systematically denied by the notion of a volitional "subject" who elects at will which gender and/or sexuality to be at any given time and place. It is this excess which erupts within the intervals of those repeated gestures and acts that construct the apparent uniformity of heterosexual positionalities, indeed which compels the repetition itself, and which guarantees its perpetual failure. In this sense, it is this excess which, within the heterosexual economy, implicitly includes homosexuality, that perpetual threat of a disruption which is quelled through a reenforced repetition of the same. And yet, if repetition is the way in which power works to construct the illusion of a seamless heterosexual identity, if heterosexuality is compelled to *repeat itself* in order to establish the illusion of its own uniformity and identity, then this is an identity permanently at risk, for what if it fails to repeat, or if the very exercise of repetition is redeployed for a very different performative purpose? If there is, as it were, always a compulsion to repeat, repetition never fully accomplishes identity. That there is a need for a repetition at all is a sign that identity is not self-identical. It requires to be instituted again and again, which is to say that it runs the risk of becoming *de*-instituted at every interval.

So what is this psychic excess, and what will constitute a subversive or *de*-instituting repetition? First, it is necessary to consider that sexuality always exceeds any given performance, presentation, or narrative which is why it is not possible to derive or read off a sexuality from any given gender presentation. And sexuality may be said to exceed any definitive narrativization. Sexuality is never fully "expressed" in a performance or practice; there will be passive and butchy femmes, femmy and aggressive butches, and both of those, and more, will turn out to describe more or less anatomically stable "males" and "females." There are no direct expressive or causal lines between sex, gender, gender presentation, sexual practice, fantasy and sexuality. None of those terms captures or determines the rest. Part of what constitutes sexuality is precisely that which does not appear and that which, to some degree, can never appear. This is perhaps the most fundamental reason why sexuality is to some degree always closeted, especially to the one who would express it through acts of self-disclosure. That which is excluded for a given gender presentation to "succeed" may be precisely what is played out sexually, that is, an "inverted" relation, as it were, between gender and gender presentation, and gender presentation and sexuality. On the other hand, both gender presentation and sexual practices may corollate such that it appears that the former "expresses" the latter, and yet both are jointly constituted by the very sexual possibilities that they exclude.

This logic of inversion gets played out interestingly in versions of lesbian butch and femme gender stylization. For a butch can present herself as capable, forceful, and all-providing, and a stone butch may well seek to constitute her lover as the exclusive site of erotic attention and pleasure. And yet, this "providing" butch who seems *at first* to replicate a certain husband-like role, can find herself caught in a logic of inversion whereby that "providingness" turns to a self-sacrifice, which implicates her in the most ancient trap of feminine self-abnegation. She may well find herself in a situation of radical need, which is precisely what she sought to locate, find, and fulfill in her femme lover. In effect, the butch inverts into the femme or remains caught up in the specter of that inversion, or takes pleasure in it. On the other hand, the femme who, as Amber Hollibaugh has argued, "orchestrates" sexual exchange,[16] may well eroticize a certain dependency only to learn that the very power to orchestrate that dependency exposes her own incontrovertible power, at which point she inverts into a butch or becomes caught up in the specter of that inversion, or perhaps delights in it.

Psychic Mimesis

What stylizes or forms an erotic style and/or a gender presentation – and that which makes such categories inherently unstable – is a set of *psychic identifications* that are not simple to describe. Some psychoanalytic theories tend to construe identification and desire as two mutually exclusive relations to love objects that have been lost through prohibition and/or separation. Any intense emotional attachment thus divides into either wanting to have someone or wanting to be that someone, but never both at once. It is important to consider that identification and desire can coexist, and that their formulation in terms of mutually exclusive oppositions serves a heterosexual matrix. But I would like to focus attention on yet a different construal of that scenario, namely, that "wanting to be" and "wanting to have" can operate to differentiate mutually exclusive positionalities internal to lesbian erotic exchange. Consider that identifications are always made in response to loss of some kind, and that they involve a certain *mimetic practice* that seeks to incorporate the lost love within the very "identity" of the one who remains. This was Freud's thesis in "Mourning and Melancholia" in 1917 and continues to inform contemporary psychoanalytic discussions of identification.[17]

For psychoanalytic theorists Mikkel Borch-Jacobsen and Ruth Leys, however, identification and, in particular, identificatory mimetism, *precedes* "identity" and constitutes identity as that which is fundamentally "other to itself." The notion of this Other *in* the self, as it were, implies that the self/Other distinction is *not* primarily external (a powerful critique of ego psychology follows from this); the self is from the start radically implicated in the "Other." This theory of primary mimetism differs from Freud's account of melancholic incorporation. In Freud's view, which I continue to find useful, incorporation – a kind of psychic miming – is a response to, and refusal of, *loss*. Gender as the site of such psychic mimes is thus constituted by the variously gendered Others who have been loved and lost, where the loss is suspended through a melancholic and imaginary incorporation (and preservation) of those Others into the psyche. Over and against this account of psychic mimesis by way of incorporation and melancholy, the theory of primary mimetism argues an even stronger position in favor of the non-self-identity of the psychic subject. Mimetism is not motivated by a drama of loss and wishful recovery, but appears to precede and constitute desire (and motivation) itself; in this sense, mimetism would be prior to the possibility of loss and the disappointments of love.

Whether loss or mimetism is primary (perhaps an undecidable problem), the psychic subject is nevertheless constituted internally by differentially gendered Others and is, therefore, never, as a gender, self-identical.

In my view, the self only becomes a self on the condition that it has suffered a separation (grammar fails us here, for the "it" only becomes differentiated through that separation), a loss which is suspended and provisionally resolved through a melancholic incorporation of some "Other." That "Other" installed in the self thus establishes the permanent incapacity of that "self" to achieve self-identity; it is as it were always already disrupted by that Other; the disruption of the Other at the heart of the self is the very condition of that self's possibility.[18]

Such a consideration of psychic identification would vitiate the possibility of any stable set of typologies that explain or describe something like gay or lesbian identities. And any effort to supply one – as evidenced in Kaja Silverman's recent inquiries into male homosexuality – suffers from simplification, and conforms, with alarming ease, to the regulatory requirements of diagnostic epistemic regimes. If incorporation in Freud's sense in 1914 is an effort to *preserve* a lost and loved object and to refuse or postpone the recognition of loss and, hence, of grief, then to become *like* one's mother or father or sibling or other early "lovers" may be an act of love and/or a hateful effort to replace or displace. How would we "typologize" the ambivalence at the heart of mimetic incorporations such as these?[19]

How does this consideration of psychic identification return us to the question, what constitutes a subversive repetition? How are troublesome identifications apparent in cultural practices? Well, consider the way in which heterosexuality naturalizes itself through setting up certain illusions of continuity between sex, gender, and desire. When Aretha Franklin sings, "you make me feel like a natural woman," she seems at first to suggest that some natural potential of her biological sex is actualized by her participation in the cultural position of "woman" as object of heterosexual recognition. Something in her "sex" is thus expressed by her "gender" which is then fully known and consecrated within the heterosexual scene. There is no breakage, no discontinuity between "sex" as biological facticity and essence, or between gender and sexuality. Although Aretha appears to be all too glad to have her naturalness confirmed, she also seems fully and paradoxically mindful that that confirmation is never guaranteed, that the effect of naturalness is only achieved as a consequence of that moment of heterosexual recognition. After all, Aretha sings, you make me feel *like* a natural woman, suggesting that this is a kind of metaphorical substitution, an act of imposture, a kind of sublime and momentary participation in an ontological illusion produced by the mundane operation of heterosexual drag.

But what if Aretha were singing to me? Or what if she were singing to a drag queen whose performance somehow confirmed her own?

How do we take account of these kinds of identifications? It's not that there is some kind of *sex* that exists in hazy biological form that is somehow *expressed* in the gait, the posture, the gesture; and that some sexuality then expresses both that apparent gender or that more or less magical sex. If gender is drag, and if it is an imitation that regularly produces the ideal it attempts to approximate, then gender is a performance that *produces* the illusion of an inner sex or essence or psychic gender core; it *produces* on the skin, through the gesture, the move, the gait (that array of corporeal theatrics understood as gender presentation), the illusion of an inner depth. In effect, one way that genders gets naturalized is through being constructed as an inner psychic or physical *necessity*. And yet, it is always a surface sign, a signification on and with the public body that produces this illusion of an inner depth, necessity or essence that is somehow magically, causally expressed.

To dispute the psyche as *inner depth*, however, is not to refuse the psyche altogether. On the contrary, the psyche calls to be rethought precisely as a compulsive repetition, as that which conditions and disables the repetitive performance of identity. If every performance repeats itself to institute the effect of identity, then every repetition requires an interval between the acts, as it were, in which risk and excess threaten to disrupt the identity being constituted. The unconscious is this excess that enables and contests every performance, and which never fully appears within the performance itself. The psyche is not "in" the body, but in the very signifying process through which that body comes to appear; it is the lapse in repetition as well as its compulsion, precisely what the performance seeks to deny, and that which compels it from the start.

To locate the psyche within this signifying chain as the instability of all iterability is not the same as claiming that it is inner core that is awaiting its full and liberatory expression. On the contrary, the psyche is the permanent failure of expression, a failure that has its values, for it impels repetition and so reinstates the possibility of disruption. What then does it mean to pursue disruptive repetition within compulsory heterosexuality?

Although compulsory heterosexuality often presumes that there is first a sex that is expressed through a gender and then through a sexuality, it may now be necessary fully to invert and displace that operation of thought. If a regime of sexuality mandates a compulsory performance of sex, then it may be only through that performance that the binary system of gender and the binary system of sex come to have intelligibility at all. It may be that the very categories of sex, of sexual identity, of gender are produced or maintained in the *effects* of this compulsory performance, effects which are disingenuously renamed as causes, origins, disingenuously lined up within a causal or expressive sequence that the heterosexual norm produces to legitimate itself as the origin of all sex. How then to expose the causal lines as retrospectively and performatively produced fabrications, and to engage gender itself as an inevitable fabrication, to fabricate gender in terms which reveal every claim to the origin, the inner, the true, and the real as nothing other than the effects of *drag*, whose subversive possibilities ought to be played and replayed to make the "sex" of gender into a site of insistent political play? Perhaps this will be a matter of working sexuality *against* identity, even against gender, and of letting that which cannot fully appear in any performance persist in its disruptive promise.

Notes

1   Parts of this essay were given as a presentation at the Conference on Homosexuality at Yale University in October, 1989.
2   "The Mark of Gender," *Feminist Issues* 5 no. 2 (1985): 6.
3   *Différence et répétition* (Paris: PUF, 1968), 374; my translation.
4   *Gender Trouble: Feminism and the Subversion of Identity* (New York and London: Routledge, 1990).
5   Michel Foucault, *The History of Sexuality, Vol. I*, trans. John Hurley (New York: Random House, 1980), 101.
6   Here I would doubtless differ from the very fine analysis of Hitchcock's *Rope* offered by D. A. Miller in *Inside Out: Lesbian Theories, Gay Theories*, ed. Diane Fuss (New York: Routledge, 1991).
7   For an example of "coming out" that is strictly unconfessional and which, finally, offers no content for the category of lesbian, see Barbara Johnson's deftly constructed "Sula Passing: No Passing" presentation at UCLA, May 1990.
8   Gayatri Chakravorty Spivak, "Displacement and the Discourse of Woman," in *Displacement: Derrida and After*, ed. Mark Krupnick (Bloomington: Indiana University Press, 1983).
9   Let me take this occasion to apologize to the social worker at that conference who asked a question about how to deal with those clients with AIDS who turn to Bernie Segal and others for the purposes of psychic healing. At the time, I understood this questioner to be suggesting that such clients were full of self-hatred because they were trying to find the causes of AIDS in their own selves. The questioner and I appear to agree that any effort to locate the responsibility for AIDS in those who suffer from it is politically and ethically wrong. I thought, however, the questioner was prepared to tell his clients that they were self-hating, and I reacted strongly (too strongly) to the paternalistic prospect that this person was going to pass judgment on someone who was clearly not only suffering, but already passing judgment on him or herself. To call another person self-hating is itself an act

of power that calls for some kind of scrutiny, and I think in response to someone who is already dealing with AIDS, that is perhaps the last thing one needs to hear. I also happened to have a friend who sought out advice from Bernie Segal, not with the belief that there is an exclusive or even primary psychic cause or solution for AIDS, but that there might be a psychic contribution to be made to surviving with AIDS. Unfortunately, I reacted quickly to this questioner, and with some anger. And I regret now that I didn't have my wits about me to discuss the distinctions with him that I have just laid out.

Curiously, this incident was invoked at a CLAGS (Center for Lesbian and Gay Studies) meeting at CUNY sometime in December of 1989 and, according to those who told me about it, my angry denunciation of the social worker was taken to be symptomatic of the political insensitivity of a "theorist" in dealing with someone who is actively engaged in AIDS work. That attribution implies that I do not do AIDS work, that I am not politically engaged, and that the social worker in question does not read theory. Needless to say, I was reacting angrily on behalf of an absent friend with AIDS who sought out Bernie Segal and company. So as I offer this apology to the social worker, I wait expectantly for the CLAGS member who misunderstood me to offer me one in turn.

10   See my essay "The Force of Fantasy: Feminism, Mapplethorpe, and Discursive Excess," *differences* 2, no. 2 (Summer 1990, reprinted below, pp. 183–203). Since the writing of this essay, lesbian artists and representations have also come under attack.

11   It is this particular ruse of erasure which Foucault for the most part fails to take account of in his analysis of power. He almost always presumes that power takes place through discourse as its instrument, and that oppression is linked with subjection and subjectivation, that is, that it is installed as the formative principle of the identity of subjects.

12   Although miming suggests that there is a prior model which is being copied, it can have the effect of exposing that prior model as purely phantasmatic. In Jacques Derrida's "The Double Session" in *Dissemination*, trans. Barbara Johnson (Chicago: University of Chicago Press, 1981), he considers the textual effect of the mime in Mallarmé's "Mimique." There Derrida argues that the mime does not imitate or copy some prior phenomenon, idea, or figure, but constitutes – some might say *performatively* – the phantasm of the original in and through the mime:

> He represents nothing, imitates nothing, does not have to conform to any prior referent with the aim of achieving adequation or verisimilitude. One can here foresee an objection: since the mime imitates nothing, reproduces nothing, opens up in its origin the very thing he is tracing out, presenting, or producing, he must be the very movement of truth. Not, of course, truth in the form of adequation between the representation and the present of the thing itself, or between the imitator and the imitated, but truth as the present unveiling of the present.... But such is not the case.... We are faced then with mimicry imitating nothing; faced, so to speak, with a double that doubles no simple, a double that nothing anticipates, nothing

at least that is not itself already double. There is no simple reference. . . . This speculum reflects no reality: it produces mere "reality-effects." . . . In this speculum with no reality, in this mirror of a mirror, a difference or dyad does exist, since there are mimes and phantoms. But it is a difference without reference, or rather a reference without a referent, without any first or last unit, a ghost that is the phantom of no flesh . . . (205–6)

13   Esther Newton, *Mother Camp: Female Impersonators in America* (Chicago: University of Chicago Press, 1972).

14   In a sense, one might offer a redescription of the above in Lacanian terms. The sexual "positions" of heterosexually differentiated "man" and "woman" are part of the *Symbolic*, that is, an ideal embodiment of the Law of sexual difference which constitutes the object of imaginary pursuits, but which is always thwarted by the "real." These symbolic positions for Lacan are by definition impossible to occupy even as they are impossible to resist as the structuring telos of desire. I accept the former point, and reject the latter one. The imputation of universal necessity to such positions simply encodes compulsory heterosexuality at the level of the Symbolic, and the "failure" to achieve it is implicitly lamented as a source of heterosexual pathos.

15   Of course, it is Eve Kosofsky Sedgwick's *Epistemology of the Closet* (Berkeley: University of California Press, 1990) which traces the subtleties of this kind of panic in Western heterosexual epistemes.

16   Amber Hollibaugh and Cherríe Moraga, "What We're Rollin Around in Bed With: Sexual Silences in Feminism," in *Powers of Desire: The Politics of Sexuality*, ed. Ann Snitow, Christine Stansell, and Sharon Thompson (New York: Monthly Review Press, 1983), 394–405.

17   Mikkel Borch-Jacobsen, *The Freudian Subject* (Stanford: Stanford University Press, 1988); for citations of Ruth Leys's work, see the following two endnotes.

18   For a very fine analysis of primary mimetism with direct implications for gender formation, see Ruth Leys, "The Real Miss Beauchamp: The History and Sexual Politics of the Multiple Personality Concept," in *Feminists Theorize the Political*, ed. Judith Butler and Joan W. Scott (New York and London: Routledge, 1991). For Leys, a primary mimetism or suggestibility requires that the "self" from the start is constituted by its incorporations; the effort to differentiate oneself from that by which one is constituted is, of course, impossible, but it does entail a certain "incorporative violence," to use her term. The violence of identification is in this way in the service of an effort at differentiation, to take the place of the Other who is, as it were, installed at the foundation of the self. That this replacement, which seeks to be a displacement, fails, and must repeat itself endlessly, becomes the trajectory of one's psychic career.

19   Here again, I think it is the work of Ruth Leys which will clarify some of the complex questions of gender constitution that emerge from a close psychoanalytic consideration of imitation and identification. Her forthcoming book manuscript will doubtless galvanize this field: *The Subject of Imitation*.

The Lesbian Phallus and the
Morphological Imaginary (1993)

Introduction

"What about the materiality of the body, *Judy?*" This was the question with which Butler was frequently accosted after the publication of *Gender Trouble*, the familiar, diminutive appellation intended, she suspects, to bring her back to a sense of her bodily belonging. Perhaps one can sympathize with Butler's interlocutors' mild sense of outrage: after all, it is one thing to argue that one is not born but rather becomes a woman, but surely by "woman" Beauvoir and Butler mean "feminine" rather than "female"? Wouldn't both theorists accept that one is born with a sexed body, i.e. with recognizably male or female genitalia, and that one's sex is determined before one is born? In *Gender Trouble*, Butler described gender as a "corporeal style" and she gave extensive analyses of how foreclosed sexual desire is incorporated on the surface of the body. However, wouldn't it be rather far-fetched to argue that there is no body preceding that melancholic incorporation? How could sex be a performative construct, a "repeated stylization" which only *appears* to be the basis or "ground" for sex and gender but turns out in the end to be no ground at all? Surely Butler can't argue away physical experiences such as pleasure and pain, experiences which lie outside of and have nothing to do with language? Or can she?

These are some of the questions posed in *Bodies That Matter* where, at least in part as a response to criticisms and queries arising from *Gender Trouble*, Butler sets out to demonstrate how the materiality of sex is forcibly produced within highly gendered regulatory schemas. That Butler should write a book deconstructing the "matter" of the body will come as no surprise, since she formulates the idea that sex is gendered in the early article "Variations on Sex and Gender" (see pp. 21–38) where Butler rejects and collapses the Cartesian mind/body dualism. Similarly, *Gender Trouble* continues the discursive analysis of concrete bodies in complex historical situations for which Butler calls at the end of *Subjects of Desire*.

Bodies That Matter is divided into two parts consisting of four chapters each: the first three chapters theorize the "matter" of the body through philosophers ranging from Plato

Chapter 2, pp. 57–91, 257–65 (notes) from *Bodies That Matter: On the Discursive Limits of "Sex."* New York: Routledge, 1993. Reproduced by permission of Routledge, an imprint of Taylor & Francis Books, Inc.

and Aristotle to Foucault, Lacan, and Irigaray, while chapters 4, 5, and 6 give analyses of matter in "literary" texts (prose fiction and a film). Chapter 7, "Arguing with the Real" takes issue with a number of the theories formulated by the Slovenian Lacanian theorist, Slavoj Žižek, while the final essay, "Critically Queer," discusses how "queer" practices rework abjection into political agency by enacting performativity as citationality. In all these analyses, and particularly in her readings of Jenny Livingstone's film *Paris is Burning* and Nella Larsen's novella *Passing*, Butler pays close attention to what she calls "the racializing of gender norms." Although sex, sexuality, and gender are given prominence in some psychoanalytic and feminist accounts, Butler insists that they do not precede race and that normative heterosexuality is not the only regulatory regime operating in the production of the body. "The symbolic – that register of regulatory ideality – is also and always a racial industry, indeed, [it is] the reiterated practice of *racializing* interpellations," she asserts. Since Butler's discussions of race do not make sense outside the context of her other theorizations of matter, I will deal with interpellation, performativity, and citationality before returning to the "matter of race."[1]

If sex turns out to have been gendered all along as Butler asserts, then clearly sex, gender, and race cannot be theorized separately. In *Bodies That Matter* Butler shows how sex, like gender, is performative, not an act but a reiterative and citational practice taking place repeatedly over time. Butler's poststructuralist rewriting of discursive performativity starts out from the following premise: one is not born, but rather one is *called* a woman and it is discourse that does the metaphorical "calling." Here Butler draws from "Ideology and Ideological State Apparatuses" (translated in 1969) in which Althusser describes how individuals are interpellated or "called" into subjectivity by ideology. Althusser gives the example of a policeman calling out "Hey, you there!" to a man in the street who turns around and acknowledges that he is being addressed. "By this mere one-hundred-and-eighty-degree physical conversion [i.e. turning around] he becomes a subject," Althusser writes. "Why? Because he has recognized that the hail was 'really' addressed to him, that 'it was *really* him who was hailed' (and not someone else)...The existence of ideology and the hailing or interpellation of individuals as subjects are one and the same thing."[2]

How is it possible to be "hailed" into sex? Who or what is doing the hailing and who or what is turning around? In her introduction to *Bodies That Matter*, Butler asks us to consider the medical interpellation whereby an infant is shifted from an "it" to a "she" or a "he." "[I]n that naming the girl is 'girled,' brought into the domain of language and kinship through the interpellation of gender," Butler writes. "But that 'girling' of the girl does not end there; on the contrary, that founding interpellation is reiterated by various authorities and throughout the various intervals of time to reinforce or contest this naturalized effect. The naming is at once the setting of a boundary, and also the repeated inculcation of a norm."[3] The exclamation "It's a girl!" is not a descriptive (or constative) utterance, since in uttering these words, the doctor or nurse interpellates the girl's (or boy's) gender, "girling" or "boying" the individual into subject-hood. Thus, as Butler asserts, "the constative (i.e. the descriptive) claim is always to some degree performative," a claim that will be discussed in more detail below.[4]

In *Gender Trouble*, Butler described parody and drag as examples of "performative gender," and many readers mistakenly assumed that performativity was synonymous with "performance" or "theater." Butler clears up this misapprehension in the preface to *Bodies That Matter*, where she rejects the notion that performative gender describes a preexisting subject who willfully dons and discards gender "costumes" from a preexisting wardrobe. Clearly, if one is "girled" or "boyed" (i.e. interpellated) from the start then there is no instrumental subject who chooses her or his gender style.[5] If we wanted to retain the rejected wardrobe analogy, we might say that the subject who "peruse[s] the closet or some more open space for the gender of choice" has already been "girled" or "boyed" by the time s/he gets to the wardrobe, so that his or her choosing is inevitably and already circumscribed. Moreover, far from an "open space," the wardrobe itself exists within the bounds of gendered and sexed discourses which will delimit in advance which gender/sex "styles" are hanging in the closet, so to speak.

This still does not quite answer the question as to exactly how "sex" is performative. As in *Gender Trouble*, Butler reads sex through a Foucauldian lens in order to show how an apparently "natural" body turns out to be a "naturalized effect" of discourse. This is the body as signified and as signification, a body that is linguistically and discursively constructed through performative utterances such as "It's a girl!" It is in this sense that, as Butler claims in the phrase I quoted above, the constative claim is always to some degree performative. She derives this assertion from the speech act theories formulated by J. L. Austin in *How To Do Things With Words* (1955), along with Jacques Derrida's response to Austin in his essay "Signature, Event, Context" (1972). Austin attempts to distinguish between constative and performative utterances, asserting that while the latter are statements of fact ("It's raining"; "I went shopping"), performative utterances actually perform the act in the utterance of it. To illustrate the nature of performative utterances, Austin gives the examples of a dignitary naming a ship or a registrar pronouncing a heterosexual couple man and wife. "None of the utterances is true or false," claims Austin. "To name the ship *is* to say (in the appropriate circumstances) the words 'I name &c.' When I say, before the registrar or altar &c., 'I do,' I am not reporting on a marriage, I am indulging in it."[6]

It is difficult for Austin to maintain the somewhat blurred distinction between performative and constative utterances, and this is an instability that Butler, following Derrida, exploits. "It's a girl!" is not a constative utterance but a performative one in which the girl, rather than being described in "neutral" terms, is interpellated as and thereby "becomes" a sexed and gendered subject, just as the heterosexual couple "become" man and wife when the Registrar pronounces them so. Butler returns to the birth scene in "Critically Queer" where she claims that "the naming of the 'girl' is transitive, that is, initiates the process by which a certain 'girling' is compelled." According to Butler, it follows that sex and gender are not choices but what she calls "forcible citation[s] of a norm," where citing the norm is necessary in order to qualify as a subject. However, there are "disobedient" ways of responding to the performative, interpellative call of the law, thus subverting existing norms (Butler discusses subversion and the law in *The Psychic Life of Power*).

Like the feminist social anthropologist Gayle Rubin, Butler argues that sexual differences are instituted and compelled by a "sex-gender system" (to use Rubin's term) which has a vested interest in instituting and maintaining strict distinctions between "man" and "woman," "gay" and "straight," "black" and "white" and so forth. In "The Lesbian Phallus and the Morphological Imaginary" (chapter 2 of *Bodies That Matter*, reprinted here) Butler gives a psychoanalytic reading of the construction of sexual differences through the significatory investment of body parts. Within a Lacanian bodily schema, the phallus is installed as the primary bodily signifier, and in spite of the masculinism of such a privileging, Butler concurs with Lacan's insight that phallus and penis are not synonymous.[7] Rather, the phallus is no more than the *symbol* of a body part, "the effect of a signifying chain summarily suppressed" as Butler puts it, a "dissimulated citationality." If phallus and penis are unstable signifiers which are not intrinsically or necessarily connected, then the phallus could just as well symbolize any other part, and this means that people who don't have penises will be able to symbolize them by "recirculating" the phallus: "The viability of the lesbian phallus depends on this displacement," Butler asserts. "[T]he displaceability of the phallus, its capacity to symbolize in relation to other body parts or other body-like things, opens the way for the lesbian phallus, an otherwise contradictory formulation."[8] Women can both "have" and "be" the phallus (an important distinction for Lacan and Butler), which means that women may suffer from castration anxiety as well as penis envy, while a man's castration complex may well be accompanied by "phallus envy." What Butler calls the "aggressive reterritorialization" of this re-citable body part is made possible by the disjunction of sign (phallus) and referent (penis), a deconstructive insight which dovetails with Butler's insistence on the "expropriability" and citationality of heterosexual norms (gendered or sexed) which may be performatively "reworked" as citationality. Butler continues her argument with the Lacanian symbolic in *Antigone's Claim* (see below, pp. 280–301).

"Citation," which here refers to the deployment of ontological norms in discourse, is the term Derrida uses in "Signature Event Context," his response to J. L. Austin's *How To Do Things With Words*. Unlike Austin, who insists that performative utterances are (or should be) bound by context and convention, Derrida argues that any statement may be taken out of its prior context and "grafted" onto another one. What Derrida calls "the essential iterability of the sign" means that signs and their meanings can never be delimited or enclosed by context, convention, or authorial intention, and that every sign can be "*cited*, put between quotation marks" (as Derrida expresses it) and made to signify in unintended, unexpected ways. The lesbian phallus is one such citing of sexual and sexed norms, and in "Critically Queer" Butler gives other examples of how "queer trouble" can take place through subversive theatrical practices such as parody and drag.

Now the question arises as to whether race, like sex, sexuality, and gender can be "aggressively reterritorialized," cited and re-cited in ways which reveal the vulnerability of racial discourses to appropriation and subversion. Looking ahead to *Excitable Speech* and the article on Rodney King, it would seem that the subversive appropriation of "words that wound" such as "nigger" is not absolutely identical to the radical appropriation of terms such as "queer." All the same, Butler insists that those practices which inculcate a heterosexual imperative are also at work in securing the boundaries of racial differentiation. It has not been Butler's aim to refute the existence of "matter" in *Bodies That Matter*, and she would clearly not deny that certain bodies are "raced" as black while others are "raced" as white (to choose only two examples). While no one usually declares "It's black/white!" when a child is born, presumably Butler would argue that this particular performative utterance could just as well operate in the context of race. In chapter 8 of *Bodies That Matter*, "Critically Queer," Butler describes a cartoon strip in which a new-born infant is announced with the words "It's a lesbian!" "Far from an essentialist joke, the queer appropriation of the performative mimes and exposes both the binding power of the heterosexualizing law *and its expropriability*," Butler argues (emphasis in text).[9] Obviously, the proclamation "It's black/white!" would not have the same kind of subversive irony as the joke Butler cites, but her point has not been that race, gender, sex, and sexuality are "the same." Rather, Butler asserts that no one of these terms is foundational or primary, and that theorizations of them must take into account the imbricated, implicated nature of the nexus they form. At the same time, to talk in terms of "racializing norms" is to suggest that race, like gender, sex, and sexuality, is constructed rather than natural, the effect of discourses and interpellations which performatively constitute subjects as "raced."[10]

If this is indeed the case, then it will be possible to destabilize, appropriate, and reterritorialize racializing and sexualizing norms. In "Critically Queer," Butler focuses on queer practices such as parody and drag, and she acknowledges that if *all* signs are vulnerable to re-citation and recontextualization, such practices will not in themselves be subversive. For this reason it is sometimes difficult to distinguish queer subversion from those drag performances which merely consolidate heterosexual hegemony, and yet Butler remains sanguine about the political potential of theatrical performances such as drag, along with other practices which allegorize heterosexual melancholy. What Butler calls "queer trouble" might best be exemplified by the appropriation of the word "queer," once a term of abuse but now an affirmative political signifier which (like the phallus) has been reclaimed and positively reterritorialized. Indeed, "queer" crystallizes the way in which subversive practices are necessarily implicated in what they oppose: existing modalities of power are turned against themselves in order to produce alternative power structures in what Butler calls "a difficult labor of forging a future from resources inevitably impure."

For this reason, subversive re-citation always involves an element of risk, since it is impossible to distinguish in advance the power we promote from the power we oppose. Butler returns to the question of risk in her essay 'What Is Critique?' (see below, pp. 302–22), but in the closing sentences of *Bodies That Matter* she acknowledges that signifiers are both productively and dangerously unstable. Anticipating potential expropriations of her *own* writing, she claims that the inevitable "yielding of ownership" and the "not owning of one's words" may have unforeseen political consequences. Butler returns to these important issues of linguistic responsibility and words that wound in her discussions of hate speech, "obscenity," and censorship in her next book, *Excitable Speech.*

The whole of chapter 2, "The Lesbian Phallus and the Morphological Imaginary," where Butler engages with psychoanalytic theorizations of the body in order to dispute Lacan's masculinist privileging of the phallus as the "original" bodily signifier, is included below.

The Lacanian's desire clearly to separate phallus *from* penis, *to control the meaning of the signifier* phallus, *is precisely symptomatic of their desire to have the phallus, that is, their desire to be at the center of language, at its origin. And their inability to control the meaning of the word* phallus *is evidence of what Lacan calls symbolic castration.*

—Jane Gallop, "Beyond the Phallus"

All sorts of things in the world behave like mirrors.

—Jacques Lacan, *Seminar II*

After such a promising title, I knew that I could not possibly offer a satisfying essay; but perhaps the promise of the phallus is always dissatisfying in some way. I would like, then, to acknowledge that failure from the start and to work that failure for its uses and to suggest that something more interesting than satisfying the phallic ideal may come of the analysis that I propose. Indeed, perhaps a certain wariness with respect to that allure is a good thing. What I would like to do instead is make a critical return to Freud, to his essay "On Narcissism: An Introduction," and consider the textual contradictions he produces as he tries to define the boundaries of erotogenic body parts. It may not seem that the lesbian phallus has much to do with what you are about to read, but I assure you (promise you?) that it couldn't have been done without it.

The essay "On Narcissism: An Introduction" $(1914)^1$ is an effort to explain the theory of libido in terms of those experiences which seem at first to be most improbably conducive to its terms. Freud begins by considering bodily pain, and he asks whether we might understand the obsessive self-preoccupations of those who suffer physical illness or injury to be a kind of libidinal investment in pain. And he asks further whether this negative investment in one's own bodily discomfort can be understood as a kind of narcissism. For the moment I want to suspend the question of why it is that Freud chooses illness and then hypochondria as the examples of bodily experience that narcissism describes and, indeed, why it seems that narcissism seems to be negative narcissism from the start; I will, however, return to this question once the relationship between illness and erotogenicity is established. In the essay on narcissism, then, Freud first considers organic disease as that which "withdraws libido from love objects, [and] lavishes libido on itself" (82). As the first in what will become a string of examples, he cites a line of poetry from Wilhelm Busch's *Balduin Bahlamin* on the erotics of the toothache: "concentrated is his soul . . . in his molar's [jaw-tooth's] aching hole" (82).[2]

According to the theory of libido, the concentration eroticizes that hole in the mouth, that cavity within a cavity, redoubling the pain of the physical as and through a psychically invested pain – a pain of or from the soul, the psyche. From this example of libidinal self-investment, Freud extrapolates to other examples: sleep and then dreams, both considered as exercises in sustained self-preoccupation, and then to hypochondria. The example of physical pain thus gives way, through a textual detour through sleep, dreams, and the imaginary, to an analogy with hypochondria and finally to an argument that establishes the theoretical indissolubility of physical and imaginary injury. This position has consequences for determining what constitutes a body part at all, and, as we shall see, what constitutes an erotogenic body part in particular. In the essay on narcissism, hypochondria lavishes libido on a body part, but in a significant sense, that body part does not exist for consciousness prior to that investiture; indeed, that body part is delineated and becomes knowable for Freud only on the condition of that investiture.

Nine years later, in *The Ego and the Id* (1923)[3] Freud will state quite clearly that bodily pain is the precondition of bodily self-discovery. In this text he asks how one can account for the *formation* of the ego, that bounded sense of self, and concludes that it is differentiated from the id partially through pain:

> Pain seems to play a part in the process, and the way in which we gain new knowledge of our organs during painful illnesses is perhaps a model of the way by which in general we arrive at the idea of our own body (25–6).

In a move that prefigures Lacan's argument in "The Mirror Stage," Freud connects the formation of one's ego with the externalized idea one forms of one's own body. Hence, Freud's claim, "The ego is first and foremost a bodily ego; it is not merely a surface entity, but is itself the projection of a surface" (26).[4]

What is meant by the imaginary construction of body parts? Is this an idealist thesis or one which asserts the indissolubility of the psychic and physical body?[5] Curiously, Freud associates the process of erotogenicity with the consciousness of bodily pain: "Let us now, taking any part of the body, describe its activity of sending sexually exciting stimuli to the mind as its 'erotogenicity'" (Freud 1914, 84). Here, however, it is fundamentally unclear, even undecidable, whether this is a consciousness that imputes pain to the object, thereby delineating it – as is the case in hypochondria – or whether it is a pain caused by organic disease which is retrospectively registered by an attending consciousness. This ambiguity between a real and conjured pain, however, is sustained in the analogy with erotogenicity, which seems defined as the very vacillation between real and imagined body parts. If erotogenicity is produced through the conveying of a bodily activity through an idea, then the idea and the conveying are phenomenologically coincident. As a result, it would not be possible to speak about a body part that precedes and gives rise to an idea, for it is the idea that emerges simultaneously with the phenomenologically accessible body, indeed, that guarantees its accessibility. Although Freud's language engages a causal temporality that has the body part precede its "idea," he nevertheless confirms here the indissolubility of a body part and the phantasmatic partitioning that brings it into psychic experience. Later, in the first *Seminar*, Lacan will read Freud along these latter lines, arguing in his discussion on "The Two Narcissisms" that "the libidinal drive is centred on the function of the imaginary."[6]

Already in the essay on narcissism, however, we find the beginnings of this latter formulation in the discussion of the erotogenicity of body parts. Directly following his argument in favor of hypochondria as anxiety-neurosis, Freud argues that libidinal self-attention is precisely what delineates a body part as a part: "Now the familiar prototype [*Vorbild*] of an organ sensitive to pain, in some way changed and yet not diseased in the ordinary sense, is that of the genital organ in a state of excitation . . . " (Freud 1914, 84).

Clearly there is an assumption here of a singular genital organ, the sex which is one, but as Freud continues to write about it, it appears to lose its proper place and proliferate in unexpected locations. This example at first provides the occasion for the definition of erotogenicity I already cited, "that activity of a given bodily area which consists in conveying sexually exciting stimuli to the mind." Freud then proceeds to communicate as already accepted knowledge "that certain other areas of the body – the *erotogenic* zones – may act as substitutes for the genitals and behave analogously to them" (Freud 1914, 84). Here it seems that "the genitals," presumed to be male genitals, are at first an example of body parts delineated through anxiety-neurosis, but, as a "prototype," they are the example of examples of that process whereby body parts become epistemologically accessible through an imaginary investiture. As an exemplar or prototype, these genitals have already within Freud's text substituted not only *for* a variety of other body parts or types, but for the effects of other hypochondriacal processes as well. The gaping hole in the mouth, the panoply of organic and hypochondriacal ailments are synthesized in and summarized by the prototypical male genitals.

This collapse of substitutions performed by these genitals is, however, reversed and erased in the sentence that follows in which the erotogenic zones are said to act as substitutes *for* the genitals. In the latter case, it seems that these self-same genitals – the result or effect of a set of substitutions – are that *for which* other body parts act as substitutes. Indeed, the male genitals are suddenly themselves an originary site of erotogenization which then subsequently becomes the occasion for a set of substitutions or displacements. At first, it seems logically incompatible to assert that these genitals are at once a cumulative example *and* a prototype or originary site which occasions a process of secondary exemplifications. In the first case, they are the effect and sum of a set of substitutions, and in the second, they are an origin for which substitutions exist. But perhaps this logical problem only symptomizes a wish to understand these genitals as an originating idealization, that is, as the symbolically encoded phallus.

The phallus, which Freud invokes in *The Interpretation of Dreams*, is considered the privileged signifier by Lacan, that which originates or generates significations, but is not itself the signifying effect of a prior signifying chain. To offer a definition of the phallus – indeed, to attempt denotatively to fix its meaning – is to posture as if one *has* the phallus and, hence, to presume and enact precisely what remains to be explained.[7] In a sense, Freud's essay enacts the paradoxical process by which the phallus as the privileged and generative signifier is itself generated *by* a string of examples of erotogenic body parts. The phallus is then set up as that which confers erotogenicity and signification on these body parts, although we have seen through the metonymic slide of Freud's text the way in which the phallus is installed as an "origin" precisely to suppress the ambivalence produced in the course of that slide.

If Freud is here endeavoring to circumscribe the phallic function and proposing a conflation of the penis and the phallus, then the genitals would necessarily function in a double way: as the (symbolic) ideal that offers an impossible and originary measure for the genitals to approximate, and as the (imaginary) anatomy which is marked by the failure to accomplish that return to that symbolic ideal. Insofar as the male genitals become the site of a textual vacillation, they enact the impossibility of collapsing the distinction between penis and phallus. (Note that I have consigned the penis, conventionally described as "real anatomy" to the domain of the imaginary.[8] I will pursue the consequences of this consignment [or liberation] toward the end of this essay.)

As if foundering amid a set of constitutive ambivalences out of his control, Freud follows his paradoxical articulation of the male genitals as prototype and origin by adding yet another inconsistent claim to the list: "We can decide to regard," he claims, "erotogenicity as a general characteristic of all organs and may then speak of an increase or decrease of it in a particular part of the body" (Freud 1914, 84).

In this last remark, which, it seems, Freud must force himself to make – as if pure conviction will issue forth its own truth – reference to the temporal or ontological primacy of any given body part is suspended. To be a property of all organs is to be a property necessary to *no* organ, a property defined by its very *plasticity, transferability,* and *expropriability.* In a sense, we have been following the metonymic chain of this roving property from the start. Freud's discussion began with the line from Wilhelm Busch, "the jaw-tooth's aching hole," a figure that stages a certain collision of figures, a punctured instrument of penetration, an inverted vagina dentata, anus, mouth, orifice in general, the spectre of the penetrating instrument penetrated.[9] Insofar as the tooth, as that which bites, cuts, breaks through, and enters is that which is itself already entered, broken into, it figures an ambivalence that, it seems, becomes the source of pain analogized with the male genitals a few pages later. This figure is immediately likened to other body parts in real or imagined pain, and is then replaced and erased by the prototypical genitals. This wounded instrument of penetration can only suffer under the ideal of its own invulnerability, and Freud attempts to restore its imaginary power by installing it first as prototype and then as originary site of erotogenization.

In the course of restoring this phallic property to the penis, however, Freud enumerates a set of analogies and substitutions that rhetorically affirm the fundamental transferability of that property. Indeed, the phallus is neither the imaginary construction of the penis nor the symbolic valence for which the penis is a partial approximation. For that formulation is still to affirm the phallus as the prototype or idealized property of the penis. And yet it is clear from the metonymic trajectory of Freud's own text, the ambivalence at the center of any construction of the phallus belongs to no body part, but is fundamentally transferable and is, at least within his text, the very principle of erotogenic transferability. Moreover, it is through this transfer, understood as a substitution of the psychical for the physical or the metaphorizing logic of hypochondria, that body parts become phenomenologically accessible at all. Here we might understand the pain/pleasure nexus that conditions erotogenicity as partially constituted by the very idealization of anatomy designated by the phallus.

On this reading, then, Freud's textualized effort to resolve the figure of the jaw-tooth's aching hole into the penis as prototype and then as phallus rhetorically enacts the very process of narcissistic investment and idealization that he seeks to document, overcoming that ambivalence through the conjuring of an ideal. One might want to read the psychic idealization of body parts as an effort to resolve a prior, physical pain. It may be, however, that the idealization produces erotogenicity as a scene of necessary failure and ambivalence, one that then prompts a return to that idealization in a vain effort to escape that conflicted condition. To what extent is this conflicted condition precisely the repetitive propulsionality of sexuality? And what does "failure to approximate" mean in the context in which every body does precisely that?

One might also argue that to continue to use the term "phallus" for this symbolic or idealizing function is to prefigure and valorize which body part will be the site of erotogenization; this is an argument that deserves a serious response. To insist, on the contrary, on the transferability of the phallus, the phallus as transferable or plastic property, is to destabilize the distinction between *being* and *having* the phallus, and to suggest that a logic of non-contradiction does not necessarily hold between those two positions. In effect, the "having" is a symbolic position which, for Lacan, institutes the masculine position within a heterosexual matrix, and which presumes an idealized relation of property which is then only partially and vainly approximated by those marked masculine beings who vainly and partially occupy that position within language. But if this attribution of property is itself improperly attributed, if it rests on a denial of that property's transferability (i.e., if this is a transfer into a non-transferable site or a site which occasions other transfers, but which is itself not transferred from anywhere), then the repression of that denial will constitute that system internally and, therefore, pose as the promising spectre of its destabilization.

Insofar as any reference to a lesbian phallus appears to be a spectral representation of a masculine original, we might well question the spectral production of the putative "originality" of the masculine. In this sense, Freud's text might be read as the forcible production of a masculinist "original" in much the same way as Plato's *Timaeus* was read. In Freud's text, this claim to originality is constituted through a reversal and erasure of a set of substitutions produced in ambivalence.

It seems that this imaginary valorization of body parts is to be derived from a kind of eroticized hypochondria. Hypochondria is an imaginary investment which, according to the early theory, constitutes a libidinal projection of the body-surface which in turn establishes its epistemological accessibility. Hypochondria here denotes something like a *theatrical* delineation or production of the body, one which gives imaginary contours to the ego itself, projecting a body which becomes the occasion of an identification which in its imaginary or projected status is fully tenuous.

But something is clearly awry in Freud's analysis from the start. For how is it that the self-preoccupation with bodily suffering or illness becomes the analogy for the erotogenic discovery and conjuring of body parts? In *The Ego and the Id*, Freud himself suggests that to figure sexuality *as* illness is symptomatic of the structuring presence of a moralistic framework of guilt. In this text, Freud argues that narcissism must give way to objects, and that one must finally love in order not to fall ill. Insofar as there is a *prohibition on love* accompanied by threats of imagined death, there is a great temptation to refuse to love, and so to be taken in by that prohibition and contract neurotic illness. Once this prohibition is installed, then, body parts emerge as sites of punishable pleasure and, hence, of pleasure and pain. In this kind of neurotic illness, then, guilt is manifest as pain that suffuses the bodily surface, and can appear as physical illness. What follows, then, if it is *this* kind of guilt-induced bodily suffering which is, as Freud claimed of other kinds of pain, analogous to the way in which we achieve an "idea" of our own body?

If prohibitions in some sense constitute projected morphologies, then reworking the terms of those prohibitions suggests the possibility of variable projections, variable modes of delineating and theatricalizing body surfaces. These would be "ideas" of the body without which there could be no ego, no temporary centering of experience. To the extent that such supporting "ideas" are regulated by prohibition and pain, they can be understood as the forcible and materialized effects of regulatory power. But precisely because prohibitions do not always "work," that is, do not always produce the docile body that fully conforms to the social ideal, they may delineate body surfaces that do not signify conventional heterosexual polarities. These variable body surfaces or bodily egos may thus become sites of transfer for properties that no longer belong properly to any anatomy. I'll make almost clear what this means for thinking through alternative imaginaries and the lesbian phallus, but first a cautionary note on Freud.

The pathologization of erotogenic parts in Freud calls to be read as a discourse produced in guilt, and although the imaginary and projective possibilities of hypochondria are useful, they call to be dissociated from the meta-phorics of illness that pervade the description of sexuality. This is especially urgent now that the pathologization of sexuality generally, and the specific description of homosexuality as the paradigm for the pathological as such, are symptomatic of homophobic discourse on AIDS.

Insofar as Freud accepts the analogy between erotogenicity and illness, he produces a pathological discourse on sexuality that allows figures for organic disease to construct figures for erotogenic body parts. This conflation has a long history, no doubt, but it finds one of its contemporary permutations in the homophobic construction of male homosexuality as always already pathological – an argument recently made by Jeff Nunokawa[10] – such that AIDS is phantasmatically construed as the pathology of homosexuality itself. Clearly, the point is to read Freud not for the moments in which illness and sexuality are conflated, but, rather, for the moments in which that conflation fails to sustain itself, and where he fails to read himself in precisely the ways he teaches us to read ("Commenting on a text is like doing an analysis" [Lacan, *I*, 73]).

Prohibitions, which include the prohibition on homosexuality, work through the pain of guilt. Freud offers this link at the end of his essay when he accounts for the genesis of conscience, and its self-policing possibilities, as the introjection of the homosexual cathexis. In other words, the ego-ideal which governs what Freud calls the ego's "self-respect" requires the prohibition on homosexuality. This prohibition against homosexuality *is* homosexual desire turned back upon itself; the self-beratement of conscience *is* the reflexive rerouting of homosexual desire. If, then, as Freud contends, pain has a delineating effect, i.e., may be one way in which we come to have an idea of our body at all, it may also be that gender-instituting prohibitions work through suffusing the body with a pain that culminates in the projection of a surface, that is, a sexed morphology which is at once a compensatory fantasy and a fetishistic mask. And if one must either love or fall ill, then perhaps the sexuality that appears as illness is the insidious effect of a such a censoring of love. Can the very production of the *morphe* be read as an allegory of prohibited love, the *incorporation* of loss?

The relation between incorporation and melancholy is a complicated one to which we will return in the final chapter. Suffice it to say that the boundaries of the body are the lived experience of differentiation, where that differentiation is never neutral to the question of gender difference or the heterosexual matrix. What is excluded from the body for the body's boundary to form? And how does that exclusion haunt that boundary as an internal ghost of sorts, the incorporation of loss as melancholia? To what extent is the body surface the dissimulated effect of that loss? Freud offers something like a map of this problematic without following through on the analysis that it requires.

If this effort to rethink the physical and the psychical works well, then it is no longer possible to take anatomy as a stable referent that is somehow valorized or signified through being subjected to an imaginary schema. On the contrary, the very accessibility of anatomy is in some sense dependent on this schema and coincident with it. As a result of this coincidence, it is unclear to me that lesbians can be said to be "of" the same sex or that homosexuality in general ought to be construed as love of the same. If sex is always schematized in this sense, then there is no necessary reason for it to remain the same for all women. The indissolubility of the psychic and the corporeal suggests that any description of the body, including those that are deemed conventional within scientific discourse, takes place through the circulation and validation of such an imaginary schema.

But if the descriptions of the body take place in and through an imaginary schema, that is, if these descriptions are psychically and phantasmatically invested, is there still something we might call the body itself which escapes this schematization? At least two responses can be offered to this question. First, psychic projection confers boundaries and, hence, unity on the body, so that the very contours of the body are sites that vacillate between the psychic and the material. Bodily contours and morphology are not merely implicated in an irreducible tension between the psychic and the material but *are* that tension. Hence, the psyche is not a grid through which a pregiven body appears. That formulation would figure the body as an ontological in-itself which only becomes available through a psyche which establishes its mode of appearance as an epistemological object. In other words, the psyche would be an epistemic grid through which the body is known, but the sense in which the psyche is formative of morphology, that is, is somaticizing, would be lost.[11]

That Kantian formulation of the body requires to be reworked, first, in a more phenomenological register as an imaginary formation and, second, through a theory of signification as an effect and token of sexual difference. As for the phenomenological sense, which is sustained in the second, we might understand the psyche in this context as that which constitutes the mode by which that body is given, the condition and contour of that givenness. Here the materiality of the body ought not to be conceptualized as a unilateral or causal *effect* of the psyche in any sense that would reduce that materiality to the psyche or make of the psyche the monistic stuff out of which that materiality is produced and/or derived. This latter alternative would constitute a clearly untenable form of idealism. It must be possible to concede and affirm an array of "materialities" that pertain to the body, that which is signified by the domains of biology, anatomy, physiology, hormonal and chemical composition, illness, age, weight, metabolism, life and death. None of this can be denied. But the undeniability of these "materialities" in no way implies what it means to affirm them, indeed, what interpretive matrices condition, enable and limit that necessary affirmation. That each of those categories have a history and a historicity, that each of them is constituted through the boundary lines that distinguish them and, hence, by what they exclude, that relations of discourse and power produce hierarchies and overlappings among them and challenge those boundaries, implies that these are *both* persistent and contested regions.

We might want to claim that what persists within these contested domains is the "materiality" of the body. But perhaps we will have fulfilled the same function, and opened up some others, if we claim that what persists here is *a demand in and for language*, a "that which" which prompts and occasions, say, within the domain of science, calls to be explained, described, diagnosed, altered or within the cultural fabric of lived experience, fed, exercised, mobilized, put to sleep, a site of enactments and passions of various kinds. To insist upon this demand, this site, as the "that without which" no psychic operation can proceed, but also as that on which and through which the psyche also operates, is to begin to circumscribe that which is invariably and persistently the psyche's site of operation; not the blank slate or passive medium upon which the psyche acts, but, rather, the constitutive demand that mobilizes psychic action from the start, that is that very mobilization, and, in its transmuted and projected bodily form, remains that psyche.

How, then, to answer the second requirement to cast the notion of "bodies" as a matter of signification?

"Are Bodies Purely Discursive?"

The linguistic categories that are understood to "denote" the materiality of the body are themselves troubled by a referent that is never fully or permanently resolved or contained by any given signified. Indeed, that referent persists only as a kind of absence or loss, that which language does not capture, but, instead, that which impels language repeatedly to attempt that capture, that circumscription – and to fail. This loss takes its place in language as an insistent call or demand that, while *in* language, is never fully *of* language. To posit a materiality outside of language is still to posit that materiality, and the materiality so posited will retain that positing as its constitutive condition. To posit a materiality outside of language, where that materiality is considered ontologically distinct from language, is to undermine the possibility that language might be able to indicate or correspond to that domain of radical alterity. Hence, the absolute distinction between language and materiality which was to secure the referential function of language undermines that function radically.

This is not to say that, on the one hand, the body is simply linguistic stuff or, on the other, that it has no bearing on language. It bears on language all the time. The materiality of language, indeed, of the very sign that attempts to denote "materiality," suggests that it is not the case that everything, including materiality, is always already language. On the contrary, the materiality of the signifier (a "materiality" that comprises both signs and their significatory efficacy) implies that there can be no reference to a pure materiality except via materiality. Hence, it is not that one cannot get outside of language in order to grasp materiality in and of itself; rather, every effort to refer to materiality takes place through a signifying process which, in its phenomenality, is always already material. In this sense, then, language and materiality are not opposed, for language both is and refers to that which is material, and what is material never fully escapes from the process by which it is signified.

But if language is not opposed to materiality, neither can materiality be summarily collapsed into an identity with language. On the one hand, the process of signification is always material; signs work *by appearing* (visibly, aurally), and appearing through material means, although what appears only signifies by virtue of those non-phenomenal relations, i.e., relations of differentiation, that tacitly structure and propel signification itself. Relations, even the notion of différance, institute and require relata, terms, phenomenal signifiers. And yet what allows for a signifier to signify will never be its materiality alone; that materiality will be at once an instrumentality and deployment of a set of larger linguistic relations.

The materiality of the signifier will signify only to the extent that it is impure, contaminated by the ideality of differentiating relations, the tacit structurings of a linguistic context that is illimitable in principle. Conversely, the signifier will work to the extent that it is also contaminated constitutively by the very materiality that the ideality of sense purports to overcome. Apart from and yet related to the materiality of the signifier is the materiality of the signified as well as the referent approached through the signified, but which remains irreducible to the signified. This radical difference between *referent* and *signified* is the site where the materiality of language and that of the world which it seeks to signify are perpetually negotiated. This might usefully be compared with Merleau-Ponty's notion of the flesh of the world.[12] Although the referent cannot be said to exist apart from the signified, it nevertheless cannot be reduced to it. That referent, that abiding function of the world, is to persist as the horizon and the "that which" which makes its demand in and to language. Language and materiality are fully embedded in each other, chiasmic in their interdependency, but never fully collapsed into one another, i.e., reduced to one another, and yet neither fully ever exceeds the other. Always already implicated in each other, always already exceeding one another, language and materiality are never fully identical nor fully different.

But what then do we make of the kind of materiality that is associated with the body, its physicality as well as its location, including its social and political locatedness, and that materiality that characterizes language? Do we mean "materiality" in a common sense, or are these usages examples of what Althusser refers to as modalities of matter?[13]

To answer the question of the relation between the materiality of bodies and that of language requires first that we offer an account of how it is that bodies materialize, that is, how they come to assume the *morphe*, the shape by which their material discreteness is marked. The materiality of the body is not to be taken for granted, for in some sense it is acquired, constituted, through the development of morphology. And within the Lacanian view, language, understood as rules of differentiation based on idealized kinship relations, is essential to the development of morphology. Before we consider one account of the development of linguistic and corporeal morphology, let us turn briefly to Kristeva, to provide a contrast with Lacan, and a critical introduction.

Insofar as language might be understood to emerge from the materiality of bodily life, that is, as the reiteration and extension of a material set of relations, language is a substitute satisfaction, a primary act of displacement and condensation. Kristeva argues that the materiality of the spoken signifier, the vocalization of sound, is already a psychic effort to reinstall and recapture a lost maternal body; hence, these vocalizations are temporarily recaptured in sonorous poetry which works language for its most material possibilities.[14] Even here, however, those material sputterings are already psychically invested, deployed in the service of a fantasy of mastery and restoration. Here the materiality of bodily relations, prior to any individuation into a separable body or, rather, simultaneous with it, is displaced onto the materiality of linguistic relations. The language that is the effect of this displacement nevertheless carries the trace of that loss precisely in the phantasmatic aim of recovery that mobilizes vocalization itself. Here, then, it is the materiality of that (other) body which is phantasmatically reinvoked in the materiality of signifying sounds. Indeed, what gives those sounds the power to signify is that phantasmatic structure. The materiality of the signifier is thus the displaced repetition of the materiality of the lost maternal body. In this sense, materiality is constituted in and through iterability. And to the extent that the referential impulse of language is to return to that lost originary presence, the maternal body becomes, as it were, the paradigm or figure for any subsequent referent. This is in part the function of the Real in its convergence with the unthematizable maternal body in Lacanian discourse. The Real is that which resists and compels symbolization. Whereas the "real" remains unrepresentable within Lacanian doctrine, and the spectre of its representability is the spectre of psychosis, Kristeva redescribes and reinterprets what is "outside" the symbolic as the semiotic, that is, as a poetic mode of signifying that, although dependent on the symbolic, can neither be reduced to it nor figured as its unthematizable Other.

For Kristeva, the materiality of language is in some sense derived from the materiality of infantile bodily relations; language becomes something like the infinite displacement of that *jouissance* that is phantasmatically identified with the maternal body. Every effort to signify encodes and repeats this loss. Moreover, it is only on the condition of this primary loss of the referent, the Real, understood as the maternal presence, that signification – and the materialization of language – can take place. The materiality of the maternal body is only figurable within language (a set of already differentiated relations) as the phantasmatic site of a deindividuated fusion, a *jouissance* prior to the differentiation and emergence of the subject.[15] But insofar as this loss is figured *within language* (i.e., appears as a figure in language), that loss is also denied, for language both performs and defends against the separation that it figures; as a result, any figuration of that loss will both repeat and refuse the loss itself. The relations of differentiation between parts of speech which produce signification are themselves the *reiteration* and extension of the primary acts of differentiation and separation from the maternal body by which a speaking subject comes into being. Insofar as language appears to be motivated by a loss it cannot grieve, and to repeat the very loss that it refuses to recognize, we might regard this ambivalence at the heart of linguistic iterability as the melancholy recesses of signification.

The postulation of the primacy of the maternal body in the genesis of signification is clearly questionable, for it cannot be shown that a differentiation from such a body is that which primarily or exclusively inaugurates the relation to speech. The maternal body prior to the formation of the subject is always and only known by a subject who by definition postdates that hypothetical scene. Lacan's effort to offer an account of the genesis of bodily boundaries in "The Mirror Stage" (1949) takes the narcissistic relation as primary, and so displaces the maternal body as a site of primary identification. This happens within the essay itself when the infant is understood to overcome with jubilation the obstruction of the support which presumably holds the infant in place before the mirror. The reification of maternal dependency as a "support" and an "obstruction" signified primarily as that which, in the overcoming, occasions jubilation, suggests that there is a discourse on the differentiation from the maternal in the mirror stage. The maternal is, as it were, already put under erasure by the theoretical language which reifies her function and enacts the very overcoming that it seeks to document.

Insofar as the mirror stage involves an *imaginary* relation, it is that of psychic projection, but not, strictly speaking, in the register of the Symbolic, i.e., in language, the differentiated/ing use of speech. The mirror stage is not a *developmental* account of how the idea of one's own body comes into being. It does suggest, however, that the capacity to project a *morphe*, a shape, onto a surface is part of the psychic (and phantasmatic) elaboration, centering, and containment of one's own bodily contours. This process of psychic projection or elaboration implies as well that the sense of one's own body is not (only) achieved through differentiating from another (the maternal body), but that any sense of bodily contour, as projected, is articulated through a necessary self-division and self-estrangement. In this sense, Lacan's mirror stage can be read as a rewriting of Freud's introduction of the bodily ego in *The Ego and the Id*, as well as the theory of narcissism. Here it is not a question of whether the mother or the imago comes first or whether they are fully distinct from one another, but, rather, how to account for individuation through the unstable dynamics of sexual differentiation and identification that take place through the elaboration of imaginary bodily contours.

For Lacan, the body or, rather, morphology is an imaginary formation,[16] but we learn in the second seminar that this percipi or visual production, the body, can be sustained in its phantasmatic integrity only through submitting to language and to a marking by sexual difference: "the percipi of man (sic) can only be sustained within a zone of nomination (*C'est par la nomination que l'homme fait subsister les objets dans une certaine consistance*)" (Lacan, *II*, 177/202). Bodies only become whole, i.e., totalities, by the idealizing and totalizing specular image which is sustained through time by the sexually marked name. To have a name is to be positioned within the Symbolic, the idealized domain of kinship, a set of relationships structured through sanction and taboo which is governed by the law of the father and the prohibition against incest. For Lacan, names, which emblematize and institute this paternal law, *sustain* the integrity of the body. What constitutes the integral body is not a natural boundary or organic telos, but the law of kinship that works through the name. In this sense, the paternal law produces versions of bodily integrity; the name, which installs gender and kinship, works as a politically invested and investing performative. To be named is thus to be inculcated into that law and to be formed, bodily, in accordance with that law.[17]

Rewriting the Morphological Imaginary

Consciousness occurs each time there is a surface such that it can produce what is called an image. That is a materialist definition. (Lacan, *II*, 49/65)

There is something originally, inaugurally, profoundly wounded in the human relation to the world . . . that is what comes out of the theory of narcissism Freud gave us, insofar as this framework introduces an indefinable, a *no exit*, marking all relations, and especially the libidinal relations of the subject. (Lacan, *II*, 167/199)

The following selective reading of Lacan will explore the consequences of the theory of narcissism for the formation of the bodily ego and its marking by sex. Insofar as the ego is formed from the psyche through projecting the body, and the ego *is* that projection, the condition of reflexive (mis)knowing, it is invariably a bodily ego. This projection of the body, which Lacan narrates as the mirror stage, rewrites Freud's theory of narcissism through the dynamics of projection and misrecognition (*méconnaissance*). In the course of that rewriting, Lacan establishes the morphology of the body as a psychically invested projection, an idealization or "fiction" of the body as a totality and locus of control. Moreover, he suggests that this narcissistic and idealizing projection that establishes morphology constitutes the condition for the generation of objects and the cognition of other bodies. The morphological scheme established through the mirror stage constitutes precisely that reserve of morphe from which the contours of objects are produced; both objects and others come to appear only through the mediating grid of this projected or imaginary morphology.

This Lacanian trajectory will be shown to become problematic on (at least) two counts: (1) the morphological scheme which becomes the epistemic condition for the world of objects and others to appear is marked as masculine, and, hence, becomes the basis for an anthropocentric and androcentric epistemological imperialism (this is one criticism of Lacan offered by Luce Irigaray and supplies the compelling reason for her project to articulate a feminine imaginary[18]); and (2) the idealization of the body as a center of control sketched in "The Mirror Stage" is rearticulated in Lacan's notion of the phallus as that which controls significations in discourse, in "The Signification of the Phallus" (1958). Although Lacan explicitly denounces the possibility that the phallus is a body part or an imaginary effect, that repudiation will be read as constitutive of the very symbolic status he confers on the phallus in the course of the later essay. As an idealization of a body part, the phantasmatic figure of the phallus within Lacan's essay undergoes a set of contradictions similar to those which unsettled Freud's analysis of erotogenic body parts. The lesbian phallus may be said to intervene as an unexpected consequence of the Lacanian scheme, an apparently contradictory signifier which, through a critical mimesis,[19] calls into question the ostensibly originating and controlling power of the Lacanian phallus, indeed, its installation as the privileged signifier of the symbolic order. The move emblematized by the lesbian phallus contests the relationship between the logic of non-contradiction and the legislation of compulsory heterosexuality at the level of the symbolic and bodily morphogenesis. Consequently, it seeks to open up a discursive site for reconsidering the tacitly political relations that constitute and persist in the divisions between body parts and wholes, anatomy and the imaginary, corporeality and the psyche.

In his seminar of 1953, Lacan argued that "the mirror stage is not simply a moment in development. It also has an exemplary function, because it reveals some of the subject's relations to his image, in so far as it is the *Urbild* of the ego" (Lacan, *I*, 74/88). In "The Mirror Stage," published four years earlier, Lacan argues that "we have ... to understand the mirror stage *as an identification...*," and then slightly later in the essay suggests that the ego is the cumulative effect of its formative identifications.[20] Within the American reception of Freud, especially in ego psychology and certain versions of object relations, it is perhaps customary to suggest that the ego preexists its identifications, a notion confirmed by the grammar that insists that "an ego identifies with an object outside itself." The Lacanian position suggests not only that identifications *precede* the ego, but that the identificatory relation to the image establishes the ego. Moreover, the ego established through this identificatory relation is itself a relation, indeed, the cumulative history of such relations. As a result, the ego is not a self-identical substance, but a sedimented history of imaginary relations which locate the center of the ego outside itself, in the externalized *imago* which confers and produces bodily contours. In this sense, Lacan's mirror does not reflect or represent a preexisting ego, but, rather, provides the frame, the boundary, the spatial delineation for the projective elaboration of the ego itself. Hence, Lacan claims, "the image of the body gives the subject the first form which allows him to locate what pertains to the ego ["ce qui est du moi"] and what does not" (Lacan, *I*, 79/94).

Strictly speaking, then, the ego cannot be said to identify with an object outside itself; rather, it is through an identification with an imago, which is itself a relation, that the "outside" of the ego is first ambiguously demarcated, indeed, that a spatial boundary that negotiates "outside" and "inside" is established in and as the imaginary: "the function of the mirror stage [is] a particular case of the function of the *imago*, which is to establish a relation between the organism and its reality – or, as they say, between the *Innenwelt* and the *Umwelt*."[21] The specular image that the child sees, that is, the imagining that the child produces, confers a visual integrity and coherence on his own body (appearing as other) which compensates for his limited and pre-specular sense of motility and undeveloped motor control. Lacan goes on to identify this specular image with the ego-ideal (*je-idéal*) and with the subject, although these terms will in his later lectures be distinguished from one another on other grounds.[22]

Significantly, this idealized totality that the child sees is a mirror image. One might say that it confers an ideality and integrity on his body, but it is perhaps more accurate to claim that the very sense of the body is generated through this projection of ideality and integrity. Indeed, this mirroring transforms a lived sense of disunity and loss of control into an ideal of integrity and control ("la puissance") through that event of specularization. Shortly, we will argue that this idealization of the body articulated in "The Mirror Stage" reemerges unwittingly in the context of Lacan's discussion of the phallus as the idealization and symbolization of anatomy. At this point, it is perhaps enough to note that the *imago* of the body is purchased through a certain loss; libidinal dependency and powerlessness is phantasmatically overcome by the installation of a boundary and, hence, a hypostasized center which produces an idealized bodily ego; that integrity and unity is achieved through the ordering of a wayward motility or disaggregated sexuality not yet restrained by the boundaries of individuation: "the human object [*l'objet humain*] always constitutes itself through the intermediary of a first loss — nothing fruitful takes place in man [*rien de fécond n'a lieu pour l'homme*] save through the intermediary of a loss of an object" (Lacan, *II*, 136/F165).[23]

Lacan remarks in the second seminar that "the body in pieces [*le corps morcelé*] finds its unity in the image of the Other, which is its own anticipated image — a dual situation in which a polar, but non-symmetrical relation, is sketched out" (Lacan, *II*, 54/72). The ego is formed around the specular image of the body itself, but this specular image is itself an *anticipation*, a subjunctive delineation. The ego is first and foremost an object which cannot coincide temporally with the subject, a temporal *ek-stasis*; the ego's temporal futurity, and its exteriority as a *percipi*, establish its alterity to the subject. But this alterity is ambiguously located: first, within the circuit of a psyche which constitutes/finds the ego as a mistaken and decentering token of itself (hence, an interior alterity); second, as an object of perception, like other objects, and so at a radical epistemic distance from the subject: "The ego ... is a particular object within the experience of the subject. Literally, the ego is an object — an object which fills a certain function which we here call the imaginary function" (Lacan, *II*, 44/60).[24] As imaginary, the ego as object is neither interior nor exterior to the subject, but the permanently unstable site where that spatialized distinction is perpetually negotiated; it is this ambiguity that marks the ego as *imago*, that is, as an identificatory relation. Hence, identifications are never simply or definitively *made* or *achieved*; they are insistently constituted, contested, and negotiated.

The specular image of the body itself is in some sense the image of the Other. But it is only on the condition that the anticipated, ambiguously located body furnishes an *imago* and a boundary for the ego that objects come into perception. "The object is always more or less structured as the image of the body of the subject. The reflection of the subject, its mirror stage [*image spéculaire*], is always found somewhere in every perceptual picture [*tableau perceptif*], and that is what gives it a quality, a special inertia" (Lacan, *II*, 167/199). Here we not only have an account of the social constitution of the ego, but the modes by which the ego is differentiated from its Other, and how that *imago* that sustains and troubles that differentiation *at the same time* generates objects of perception. "On the libidinal level, the object is only even apprehended through the grid of the narcissistic relation" (Lacan, *II*, 167). And this is made all the more complex when we see that the reflexive relation to/of the ego is always ambiguously related to a relation to the "Other." Far from being a merely narcissistic precondition of object genesis, this claim offers instead an irreducible equivocation of narcissism and sociality which becomes the condition of the epistemological generation of and access to objects.

The idealization of the body as a spatially bounded totality, characterized by a control exercized by the gaze, is lent out to the body as its own self-control. This will become crucial to the understanding of the phallus as a privileged signifier that appears to control the significations that it produces. Lacan suggests as much in the second seminar: "The issue is knowing which organs come into play in [*entrent en jeu dans*] the narcissistic imaginary relation to the other whereby the ego is formed, *bildet*. The imaginary structuration of the ego forms around the specular image of the body itself, of the image of the Other" (Lacan, *II*, 94–95/119).

But some parts of the body become the tokens for the centering and controlling function of the bodily *imago*: "certain organs are caught up in [*sont intéressés dans*] the narcissistic relation, insofar as it structures both the relation of the ego to the other and the constitution of the world of objects" (Lacan, *II*, 95/119). Although these organs are not named, it seems that they are, first of all, organs [*les organes*] and that they enter into play in the narcissistic relation; they are that which act as the token or conjectured basis for narcissism. If these organs are the male genitals, they function as both the site and token of a specifically masculine narcissism. Moreover, insofar as these organs are set into play by a narcissism which is said to provide the structure of relations to the Other and to the world of objects, then these organs become part of the imaginary elaboration of the ego's bodily boundary, token and "proof" of its integrity and control, and the imaginary epistemic condition of its access to the world. By entering into that narcissistic relation, the organs cease to be organs and become imaginary effects. One might be tempted to argue that in the course of being set into play by the narcissistic imaginary, the penis becomes the phallus. And yet, curiously and significantly, in Lacan's essay on "The Signification of the Phallus," he will deny that the phallus is either an organ or an imaginary effect; it is instead a "privileged signifier."[25] We will turn to the textual knots that those series of denials produce in Lacan's essay, but here it is perhaps important to note that these narcissistically engaged organs become part of the condition and structure of every object and Other that can be perceived.

"What did I try to get across with the mirror stage? . . . The image of [man's] body is the principle of every unity he perceives in objects . . . all the objects of his world are always structured around the wandering shadow of his own ego [*c'est toujours autour de l'ombre errante de son propre moi que se structureront tous les objets de son monde*]" (Lacan, *II*, 166/198). This extrapolating function of narcissism becomes phallogocentrism at the moment in which the aforementioned organs, engaged by the narcissistic relation, become the model or principle by which any other object or Other is known. At this point, the organs are installed as a "privileged signifier." Within the orbit of this emerging phallogocentrism, "*Verliebtheit* [being in love] is fundamentally narcissistic. On the libidinal level, the object is only even apprehended through the grid of the narcissistic relation [*la grille du rapport narcissique*]" (Lacan, *II*, 167/199).

Lacan claims that the organs are "taken up" by a narcissistic relation, and that this narcissistically invested anatomy becomes the structure, the principle, the grid of all epistemic relations. In other words, it is the narcissistically imbued organ which is then elevated to a structuring principle which forms and gives access to all knowable objects. In the first place, this account of the genesis of epistemological relations implies that all knowable objects will have an anthropomorphic and androcentric character.[26] Secondly, this androcentric character will be phallic.

At this juncture it makes sense to consider the relation between the account of specular relations in "The Mirror Stage," the argument that morphology preconditions epistemological relations, and the later move in "The Signification of the Phallus" which asserts that the phallus is a privileged signifier. The differences between the language and aims of the two essays are marked: the earlier essay concerns epistemological relations which are not yet theorized in terms of signification; the latter appears to have emerged after a shift from epistemological to significatory models (or, rather, an embedding of the epistemological within the symbolic domain of signification). And yet, there is another difference here, one which might be understood as a reversal. In the earlier essay, the "organs" are taken up by the narcissistic relation and become the phantasmatic morphology which generates, through a specular extrapolation, the structure of knowable objects. In the later essay, Lacan introduces the phallus which functions as a privileged signifier and delimits the domain of the signifiable.

In a limited sense, the narcissistically invested organs in "The Mirror Stage" serve a function parallel to that of the phallus in "The Signification of the Phallus": the former establish the conditions for knowability; the latter establish the conditions for signifiability. Further, the theoretical context in which "The Signification of the Phallus" occurs is one in which signification is the condition of all knowability, and the image can be sustained only by the sign (the imaginary within the terms of the symbolic); it appears to follow that the narcissistically invested organs in the former essay are in some way maintained in and by the notion of the phallus. Even if we were to argue that "The Mirror Stage" documents an imaginary relation, whereas "The Signification of the Phallus" is concerned with signification at the level of the symbolic, it is unclear whether the former can be sustained without the latter and, perhaps more significantly, the latter (i.e., the Symbolic), without the former. And yet this logical conclusion is thwarted by Lacan himself in his insistence that the phallus is neither an anatomical part nor an imaginary relation. Is this repudiation of the anatomical and imaginary origins of the phallus to be read as a refusal to account for the very genealogical process of idealizing the body that Lacan himself provided in "The Mirror Stage"? Are we to accept the priority of the phallus without questioning the narcissistic investment by which an organ, a body part, has been elevated/erected to the structuring and centering principle of the world? If "The Mirror Stage" reveals how, through the synecdochal function of the imaginary, parts come to stand for wholes and a decentered body is transfigured into a totality with a center, then we might be led to ask which organs perform this centering and synecdochal function. "The Signification of the Phallus" effectively refuses the question that the former essay implicitly raised. For if the phallus in its symbolic function is neither an organ nor an imaginary effect, then it is not constructed through the imaginary, and maintains a status and integrity independent of it. This corresponds, of course, to the distinction that Lacan makes throughout his work between the imaginary and the symbolic. But if the phallus can be shown to be a synecdochal effect, if it both stands for the part, the organ, and is the imaginary transfiguration of that part into the centering and totalizing function of the body, then the phallus appears *as symbolic only to the extent that its construction through the transfigurative and specular mechanisms of the imaginary is denied*. Indeed, if the phallus is an imaginary effect, a wishful transfiguration, then it is not merely the *symbolic* status of the phallus that is called into question, but the very distinction between the symbolic and the imaginary. If the phallus is the privileged signifier of the symbolic, the delimiting and ordering principle of what can be signified, then this signifier gains its privilege through becoming an imaginary effect that pervasively denies its own status as both imaginary and an effect. If this is true of the signifier that delimits the domain of the signifiable within the symbolic, then it is true of all that is signified as the symbolic. In other words, what operates under the sign of the symbolic may be nothing other than precisely that set of imaginary effects which have become naturalized and reified as the law of signification.

"The Mirror Stage" and "The Signification of the Phallus" follow (at least) two very different narrative trajectories: the first follows the premature and imaginary transformation of a decentered body − a body in pieces [*le corps morcelé*] − into the specular body, a morphological totality invested with a center of motor control; the second follows the differential "accession" of bodies to sexed positions within the symbolic. In the one instance, there is narrative recourse to a body before the mirror; in the other, a body before the law. Such a discursive reference is one which, within Lacan's own terms, is to be construed less as a developmental explanation than as a necessary heuristic fiction.

In "The Mirror Stage," that body is figured "in pieces" [*une image morcelée du corps*];[27] in Lacan's discussion of the phallus, the body, and anatomy are described only through negation: anatomy and, in particular, anatomical parts, are *not the phallus, but only that which the phallus symbolizes* (*Il est encore bien moins l'organe, pénis ou clitoris, qu'il symbolise* [690]). In the former essay, then (shall we call it a "piece"?), Lacan narrates the overcoming of the partitioned body through the specular and phantasmatic production of a morphological whole. In the latter essay, that drama is enacted – or symptomatized – by the narrative movement of the theoretical performance itself, what we will consider briefly as the performativity of the phallus. But if it is possible to read "The Signification of the Phallus" as symptomatizing the specular phantasm described in "The Mirror Stage," it is also possible, and useful, to reread "The Mirror Stage" as offering an implicit theory of "mirroring" as a signifying practice.

If the body is "in pieces" before the mirror, it follows that the mirroring works as a kind of synecdochal extrapolation by which those pieces or parts come to stand (in and by the mirror) for the whole; or, put differently, the part substitutes for the whole and thereby becomes a token for the whole. If this is right, then perhaps "The Mirror Stage" proceeds through a synecdochal logic that institutes and maintains a phantasm of control. It makes sense to ask, then, whether the theoretical construction of the phallus is such a synecdochal extrapolation. By changing the name of the penis to "the phallus," is the part status of the former phantasmatically and synecdochally overcome through the inauguration of the latter as "the privileged signifier"? And does this name, like proper names, secure and sustain the morphological distinctness of the masculine body, sustaining the *percipi* through nomination?

In Lacan's discussion of what the phallus is, to be distinguished from his discussion of who "is" the phallus, he quarrels with various psychoanalytic practitioners about who is entitled to name the phallus, who knows where and how the name applies, who is in the position to name the name. He objects to the relegation of the phallus to a "phallic stage" or to the conflation and diminution of the phallus to a "partial object." Lacan faults Karl Abraham in particular for introducing the notion of the partial object, but it is clear that he is most strongly opposed to Melanie Klein's theory of introjected body parts and with Ernest Jones's influential acceptance of these positions. Lacan associates the normalization of the phallus as partial object with the degradation of psychoanalysis on American soil, "*la dégradation de la psychanalyse, consécutive à sa transplantation américaine*" (Lacan, *Écrits*, 77/687). Other theoretical tendencies associated with this degradation are termed "culturalist" and "feminist." In particular, he is opposed to those psychoanalytic positions which consider the phallic phase to be an effect of repression, and the phallic object as a symptom.

Here the phallus is negatively defined through a string of attributes: not partial, not an object, not a symptom. Moreover, the "not" which precedes each of these attributes is "not" to be read as a "*refoulement*" (repression); in other words, negation *in these textual instances* is not to be read psychoanalytically (Lacan, *Écrits*, 79/687).

How, then, can we read the symptomatic dimension of Lacan's text here? Does the rejection of the phallic phase and, in particular, of the figuration of the phallus as a partial or approximative object, seek to overcome a degradation in favor of an idealization, a specular one? Do these psychoanalytic texts fail to mirror the phallus as specular center, and do they threaten to expose the synecdochal logic by which the phallus is installed as privileged signifier? If the position for the phallus erected by Lacan symptomatizes the specular and idealizing mirroring of a decentered body in pieces before the mirror, then we can read here the phantasmatic rewriting of an organ or body part, the penis, as the phallus, a move effected by a transvaluative denial of its substitutability, dependency, diminuitive size, limited control, partiality. The phallus would then emerge as a symptom, and its authority could be established only through a metaleptic reversal of cause and effect. Rather than the postulated origin of signification or the signifiable, the phallus would be the effect of a signifying chain summarily suppressed.

But this analysis still needs to take into account why it is that the body is in pieces before the mirror and before the law. Why should the body be given in parts before it is specularized as a totality and center of control? How did this body come to be in pieces and parts? To have a sense of a piece or a part is to have in advance a sense for the whole to which they belong. Although "The Mirror Stage" attempts to narrate how a body comes to have a sense of its own totality for the first time, the very description of a body before the mirror as being in parts or pieces takes as its own precondition an *already* established sense of a whole or integral morphology. If to be in pieces is to be without control, then the body before the mirror is without the phallus, symbolically castrated; and by gaining specularized control through the ego constituted in the mirror, that body "assumes" or "comes to have" the phallus. But the phallus is, as it were, already in play in the very description of the body in pieces before the mirror; as a result, the phallus governs the description of its own genesis and, accordingly, wards off a genealogy that might confer on it a derivative or projected character.

Although Lacan claims quite explicitly that the phallus "is not an imaginary effect,"[28] that denial might be read as constitutive of the very formation of the phallus as privileged signifier; that denial appears to facilitate that privileging. As an imaginary effect, the phallus would be as decentered and tenuous as the ego. In an effort to recenter and ground the phallus, the phallus is elevated to the status of the privileged signifier, and it is offered at the end of a long list of improper usages for the term, ways in which the term has gotten out of hand, signified where it ought not to have and in ways that are wrong:

> ...the phallus is not a fantasy, if what is understood by that is an imaginary effect. Nor is it an object (part, internal, good, bad, etc....) in so far as this term tends to accentuate the reality involved in a relationship. It is even less the organ, penis or clitoris, which it symbolizes. And it is not by accident that Freud took his reference for it from the simulacrum which it represented for the Ancients.
> For the phallus is a signifier... [Rose, 79][29]

In this last pronouncement, Lacan seeks to relieve the term of its catachrestic wanderings, to reestablish the phallus as a site of control (as that which is "to designate as a whole the effect of there being a signified") and hence to position Lacan himself as the one to control the meaning of the phallus. As Jane Gallop has argued (to cite her is perhaps to transfer the phallus from him to her, but also then affirms my point that the phallus is fundamentally transferable): "And their inability to control the meaning of the word *phallus* is evidence of what Lacan calls symbolic castration" (126).

If not being able to control the significations that follow from the signifier phallus is evidence of symbolic castration, then the body "in pieces" and out of control before the mirror may be understood as symbolically castrated, and the specular and synecdochal idealization of the (phallic) body may be read as a compensatory mechanism by which this phantasmatic castration is overcome. Not unlike Freud's efforts to put a stop to the proliferation of erotogenic body parts in his text, parts which were also sites of pain, Lacan stalls the sliding of the signifier into a proliferative catachresis through a preemptive assertion of the phallus as privileged signifier. To claim for the phallus the status of a privileged signifier performatively produces and effects this privilege. The announcement of that privileged signifier is its performance. That performative assertion produces and enacts the very process of privileged signification, one whose privilege is potentially contested by the very list of alternatives it discounts, and the negation of which constitutes and precipitates that phallus. Indeed, the phallus is *not* a body part (but the whole), is *not* an imaginary effect (but the origin of all imaginary effects). These negations are constitutive; they function as disavowals that precipitate – and are then erased by – the idealization of the phallus.

The paradoxical status of the negation that introduces and institutes the phallus becomes clear in the grammar itself: "*Il est encore moins l'organe, pénis ou clitoris, qu'il symbolise.*" Here the sentence suggests that the phallus, "even less" than an imaginary effect, is not an organ. Here Lacan thus suggests gradations of negation: the phallus is more likely to be an imaginary effect than an organ; if it is either one, it is more of an imaginary effect than an organ. This is not to say that it is not at all an organ, but that the "copula" – that which asserts a linguistic and ontological identity – is the least adequate way of expressing the relation between them. In the very sentence in which the minimization of any possible identity between penis and phallus is asserted, an alternative relation between them is offered, namely, the relation of *symbolization*. The phallus *symbolizes* the penis; and insofar as it symbolizes the penis, retains the penis as that which it symbolizes; it *is* not the penis. To be the object of symbolization is precisely not to be that which symbolizes. To the extent that the phallus symbolizes the penis, it is not that which it symbolizes. The more symbolization occurs, the less ontological connection there is between symbol and symbolized. Symbolization presumes and produces the ontological difference between that which symbolizes – or signifies – and that which is symbolized – or signified. Symbolization depletes that which is symbolized of its ontological connection with the symbol itself.

But what is the status of this particular assertion of ontological difference if it turns out that this symbol, the phallus, always takes the penis as that which it symbolizes?[30] What is the character of this bind whereby the phallus symbolizes the penis to the extent that it differentiates itself from the penis, where the penis becomes the privileged referent to be negated? If the phallus *must* negate the penis in order to symbolize and signify in its privileged way, then the phallus is bound to the penis, not through simple identity, but through determinate negation. If the phallus only signifies to the extent that it is *not* the penis, and the penis is qualified as that body part that it must *not be*, then the phallus is fundamentally dependent upon the penis in order to symbolize at all. Indeed, the phallus would be nothing without the penis. And in that sense in which the phallus requires the penis for its own constitution, the identity of the phallus includes the penis, that is, a relation of identity holds between them. And this is, of course, not only a logical point, for we have seen that the phallus not only opposes the penis in a logical sense, but is itself instituted through the repudiation of its partial, decentered, and substitutable character.

The question, of course, is why it is assumed that the phallus requires that particular body part to symbolize, and why it could not operate through symbolizing other body parts. The viability of the lesbian phallus depends on this displacement. Or, to put it more accurately, the displaceability of the phallus, its capacity to symbolize in relation to other body parts or other body-like things, opens the way for the lesbian phallus, an otherwise contradictory formulation. And here it should be clear that the lesbian phallus crosses the orders of *having* and *being*, it both wields the threat of castration (which is in that sense a mode of "being" the phallus, as women "are") and suffers from castration anxiety (and so is said "to have" the phallus, and to fear its loss).

To suggest that the phallus might symbolize body parts other than the penis is compatible with the Lacanian scheme. But to argue that certain body parts or body-like things other than the penis are symbolized as "having" the phallus is to call into question the mutually exclusive trajectories of castration anxiety and penis envy.[31] Indeed, if men are said to "have" the phallus symbolically, their anatomy is also a site marked by having lost it; the anatomical part is never commensurable with the phallus itself. In this sense, men might be understood to be both castrated (already) and driven by penis envy (more properly understood as phallus envy).[32] Conversely, insofar as women might be said to "have" the phallus and fear its loss (and there is no reason why that could not be true in both lesbian and heterosexual exchange, raising the question of an implicit heterosexuality in the former, and homosexuality in the latter), they may be driven by castration anxiety.[33]

Although a number of theorists have suggested that lesbian sexuality is outside the economy of phallogocentrism, that position has been critically countered by the notion that lesbian sexuality is *as* constructed as any other form of sexuality within contemporary sexual regimes. Of interest here is not whether the phallus persists in lesbian sexuality as a structuring principle, but *how* it persists, how it is constructed, and what happens to the "privileged" status of that signifier within this form of constructed exchange. I am not arguing that lesbian sexuality is only or even primarily structured by the phallus, or even that such an impossible monolith as "lesbian sexuality" exists. But I do want to suggest that the phallus constitutes an ambivalent site of identification and desire that is significantly different from the scene of normative heterosexuality to which it is related. If Lacan claimed that the phallus only operates as "veiled," we might ask in return what kind of "veiling" the phallus invariably performs. And what is the logic of "veiling" and, hence, of "exposure" that emerges within lesbian sexual exchange in relation to the question of the phallus?

Clearly, there is no single answer, and the kind of culturally textured work that might approximate an answer to this question will doubtless need to take place elsewhere; indeed, "the" lesbian phallus is a fiction, but perhaps a theoretically useful one, for there are questions of imitation, subversion, and the recirculation of phantasmatic privilege that a psychoanalytically informed reading might attend.

If the phallus is that which is excommunicated from the feminist orthodoxy on lesbian sexuality as well as the "missing part," the sign of an inevitable dissatisfaction that is lesbianism in homophobic and misogynist constructions, then the admission of the phallus into that exchange faces two convergent prohibitions: first, the phallus signifies the persistence of the "straight mind," a masculine or heterosexist identification and, hence, the defilement or betrayal of lesbian specificity; secondly, the phallus signifies the insuperability of heterosexuality and constitutes lesbianism as a vain and/or pathetic effort to mime the real thing. Thus, the phallus enters lesbian sexual discourse in the mode of a transgressive "confession" conditioned and confronted by both the feminist and misogynist forms of repudiation: it's not the real thing (the lesbian thing) or it's not the real thing (the straight thing). What is "unveiled" is precisely the repudiated desire, that which is abjected by heterosexist logic and that which is defensively foreclosed through the effort to circumscribe a specifically feminine morphology for lesbianism. In a sense, what is unveiled or exposed is a desire that is produced through a prohibition.

And yet, the phantasmatic structure of this desire will operate as a "veil" precisely at the moment in which it is "revealed." That phantasmatic transfiguration of bodily boundaries will not only expose its own tenuousness, but will turn out to *depend on* that tenuousness and transience in order to signify at all. The phallus as signifier within lesbian sexuality will engage the spectre of shame and repudiation delivered by that feminist theory which would secure a feminine morphology in its radical distinctness from the masculine (a binarism that is secured through heterosexual presumption), a spectre delivered in a more pervasive way by the masculinist theory which would insist on the male morphology as the only possible figure for the human body. Traversing those divisions, the lesbian phallus signifies a desire that is produced historically at the crossroads of these prohibitions, and is never fully free of the normative demands that condition its possibility and that it nevertheless seeks to subvert. Insofar as the phallus is an idealization of morphology, it produces a necessary effect of inadequation, one which, in the cultural context of lesbian relations, can be quickly assimilated to the sense of an inadequate derivation from the supposedly real thing, and, hence, a source of shame.

But precisely *because* it is an idealization, one which no body can adequately approximate, the phallus is a transferable phantasm, and its naturalized link to masculine morphology can be called into question through an aggressive reterritorialization. That complex identificatory fantasies inform morphogenesis, and that they cannot be fully predicted, suggests that morphological idealization is both a necessary and unpredictable ingredient in the constitution of both the bodily ego and the dispositions of desire. It also means that there is not necessarily one imaginary schema for the bodily ego, and that cultural conflicts over the idealization and degradation of specific masculine and feminine morphologies will be played out at the site of the morphological imaginary in complex and conflicted ways. It may well be through a degradation of a feminine morphology, an imaginary and cathected degrading of the feminine, that the lesbian phallus comes into play, or it may be through a castrating occupation of that central masculine trope, fueled by the kind of defiance which seeks to overturn that very degradation of the feminine.

It is important to underscore, however, the way in which the stability of both "masculine" and "feminine" morphologies is called into question by a lesbian resignification of the phallus which depends on the crossings of phantasmatic identification. If the morphological distinctness of "the feminine" depends on its purification of all masculinity, and if this bodily boundary and distinctness is instituted in the service of the laws of a heterosexual symbolic, then that repudiated masculinity is *presumed* by the feminized morphology, and will emerge either as an impossible ideal that shadows and thwarts the feminine or as a disparaged signifier of a patriarchal order against which a specific lesbian-feminism defines itself. In either case, the relation to the phallus is constitutive; an identification is made which is at once disavowed.

Indeed, it is this disavowed identification that enables and informs the production of a "distinct" feminine morphology from the start. It is doubtless possible to take account of the structuring presence of cross-identifications in the elaboration of the bodily ego, and to frame these identifications in a direction beyond a logic of repudiation by which one identification is always and only worked at the expense of another. For the "shame" of the lesbian phallus presumes that it will come to represent the "truth" of lesbian desire, a truth which will be figured as a falsehood, a vain imitation or derivation from the heterosexual norm. And the counterstrategy of confessional defiance presumes as well that what has been excluded from dominant sexual discourses on lesbianism thereby constitutes its "truth." But if the "truth" is, as Nietzsche suggests, only a series of mistakes configured in relation to one another or, in Lacanian terms, a set of constituting *méconnaissances*, then the phallus is but one signifier among others in the course of lesbian exchange, neither the originating signifier nor the unspeakable outside. The phallus will thus always operate as both veil and confession, a deflection from an erotogenicity that includes and exceeds the phallus, an exposure of a desire which attests to a morphological transgression and, hence, to the instability of the imaginary boundaries of sex.

Conclusion

If the phallus is an imaginary effect (which is reified as the privileged signifier of the symbolic order), then its structural place is no longer determined by the logical relation of mutual exclusion entailed by a heterosexist version of sexual difference in which men are said to "have" and women to "be" the phallus. This logical and structural place is secured through the move that claims that by virtue of the penis, one is symbolized as "having"; that structural bond (or bind) secures a relation of identity between the phallus and the penis that is explicitly denied (it also performs a synecdochal collapse of the penis and the one who has it). If the phallus only symbolizes to the extent that there is a penis there to be symbolized, then the phallus is not only fundamentally dependent upon the penis, but cannot exist without it. But is this true?

If the phallus operates as a signifier whose privilege is under contest, if its privilege is shown to be secured precisely through the reification of logical and structural relations within the symbolic, then the structures within which it is put into play are more various and revisable than the Lacanian scheme can affirm. Consider that "having" the phallus can be symbolized by an arm, a tongue, a hand (or two), a knee, a thigh, a pelvic bone, an array of purposefully instrumentalized body-like things. And that this "having" exists in relation to a "being the phallus" which is both part of its own signifying effect (the phallic lesbian as potentially castrating) and that which it encounters in the woman who is desired (as the one who, offering or withdrawing the specular guarantee, wields the power to castrate). That this scene can reverse, that being and having can be confounded, upsets the logic of non-contradiction that serves the either-or of normative heterosexual exchange. In a sense, the simultaneous acts of deprivileging the phallus and removing it from the normative heterosexual form of exchange, and recirculating and reprivileging it between women deploys the phallus to break the signifying chain in which it conventionally operates. If a lesbian "has" it, it is also clear that she does not "have" it in the traditional sense; her activity furthers a crisis in the sense of what it means to "have" one at all. The phantasmatic status of "having" is redelineated, rendered transferable, substitutable, plastic; and the eroticism produced within such an exchange depends on the displacement from traditional masculinist contexts as well as the critical redeployment of its central figures of power.

Clearly, the phallus operates in a privileged way in contemporary sexual cultures, but that operation is secured by a linguistic structure or position that is not independent of its perpetual reconstitution. Inasmuch as the phallus signifies, it is also always in the process of being signified and resignified. In this sense, it is not the incipient moment or origin of a signifying chain, as Lacan would insist, but part of a reiterable signifying practice and, hence, open to resignification: signifying in ways and in places that exceed its proper structural place within the Lacanian symbolic and contest the necessity of that place. If the phallus is a privileged signifier, it gains that privilege through being reiterated. And if the cultural construction of sexuality compels a repetition of that signifier, there is nevertheless in the very force of repetition, understood as resignification or recirculation, the possibility of deprivileging that signifier.

If what comes to signify under the sign of the phallus are a number of body parts, discursive performatives, alternative fetishes, to name a few, then the symbolic position of "having" has been dislodged from the penis as its privileged anatomical (or non-anatomical) occasion. The phantasmatic moment in which a part suddenly stands for and produces a sense of the whole or is figured as the center of control, in which a certain kind of "phallic" determination is made by virtue of which meaning appears radically generated, underscores the very plasticity of the phallus, the way in which it exceeds the structural place to which it has been consigned by the Lacanian scheme, the way in which that structure, to remain a structure, has to be *reiterated* and, as reiterable, becomes open to variation and plasticity.[34] When the phallus is lesbian, then it is and is not a masculinist figure of power; the signifier is significantly split, for it both recalls and displaces the masculinism by which it is impelled. And insofar as it operates at the site of anatomy, the phallus (re)produces the spectre of the penis only to enact its vanishing, to reiterate and exploit its perpetual vanishing as the very occasion of the phallus. This opens up anatomy – and sexual difference itself – as a site of proliferative resignifications.

In a sense, the phallus as I offer it here is both occasioned by Lacan and exceeds the purview of that form of heterosexist structuralism. It is not enough to claim that the signifier is not the same as the signified (phallus/penis), if both terms are nevertheless bound to each other by an essential relation in which that difference is contained. The offering of the lesbian phallus suggests that the signifier can come to signifier *in excess* of its structurally mandated position; indeed, the signifier can be repeated in contexts and relations that come to *displace* the privileged status of that signifier. The "structure" by which the phallus signifies the penis as its privileged occasion exists only through being instituted and reiterated, and, by virtue of that temporalization, is unstable and open to subversive repetition. Moreover, if the phallus symbolizes only through taking anatomy as its occasion, then the more various and unanticipated the anatomical (and non-anatomical) occasions for its symbolization, the more unstable that signifier becomes. In other words, the phallus has no existence separable from the occasions of its symbolization; it cannot symbolize without its occasion. Hence, the lesbian phallus offers the occasion (a set of occasions) for the phallus to signify differently, and in so signifying, to resignify, unwittingly, its own masculinist and heterosexist privilege.

The notion of the bodily ego in Freud and that of the projective idealization of the body in Lacan suggest that the very contours of the body, the delimitations of anatomy, are in part the consequence of an externalized identification. That identificatory process is itself motivated by a transfigurative wish. And that wishfulness proper to all morphogenesis is itself prepared and structured by a culturally complex signifying chain that not only constitutes sexuality, but establishes sexuality as a site where bodies and anatomies are perpetually reconstituted. If these central identifications cannot be strictly regulated, then the domain of the imaginary in which the body is partially constituted is marked by a constitutive vacillation. The anatomical is only "given" through its signification, and yet it appears to exceed that signification, to provide the elusive referent in relation to which the variability of significa-tion performs. Always already caught up in the signifying chain by which sexual difference is negotiated, the anatomical is never given outside its terms, and yet it is also that which exceeds and compels that signifying chain, that reiteration of difference, an insistent and inexhaustible demand.

If the heterosexualization of identification and morphogenesis is historically contingent, however hegemonic, then identifications, which are always al-ready imaginary, as they cross gender boundaries, reinstitute sexed bodies in variable ways. In crossing these boundaries, such morphogenetic identifications reconfigure the mapping of sexual difference itself. The bodily ego produced through identification is not *mimetically* related to a preexisting biological or anatomical body (that former body could only become available through the imaginary schema I am proposing here, so that we would be immediately caught up in an infinite regress or vicious circle). The body in the mirror does not represent a body that is, as it were, before the mirror: the mirror, even as it is instigated by that unrepresentable body "before" the mirror, produces that body as its delirious effect – a delirium, by the way, which we are compelled to live.

In this sense, to speak of the lesbian phallus as a possible site of desire is not to refer to an *imaginary* identification and/or desire that can be measured against a *real* one; on the contrary, it is simply to promote an alternative *imaginary* to a hegemonic imaginary and to show, through that assertion, the ways in which the hegemonic imaginary constitutes itself through the naturalization of an exclusionary heterosexual morphology. In this sense, it is important to note that it is the lesbian *phallus* and not the *penis* that is considered here. For what is needed is not a new body part, as it were, but a displacement of the hegemonic symbolic of (heterosexist) sexual difference and the critical release of alternative imaginary schemas for constituting sites of erotogenic pleasure.

Notes

Introduction

1   Like "sex," "race" is always contained within invisible inverted commas here in order to signal the problematic nature of this term.

2   "Ideology and Ideological State Apparatuses," 163.

3   *Bodies That Matter*, 8.

4   *Bodies That Matter*, 11.

5   *Bodies That Matter*, x.

6   *How To Do Things With Words*, 6.

7   See Lacan's two essays, "The Mirror Stage as Formative of the Function of the I as Revealed in Psychoanalytic Experience" (1949) and "The Signification of the Phallus" (1958).

8   *Bodies That Matter*, 84.

9   *Bodies That Matter*, 232.

10   For a discussion of "racialization" and race and/as melancholia, see Butler's interview with Vikki Bell, "On Speech, Race, and Melancholia," *Theory, Culture & Society*, 16:2 (1999), 163–74.

The Lesbian Phallus and the Morphological Imaginary

A version of the first part of this chapter was given as "The Lesbian Phallus: Does Heterosexuality Exist?" at the Modern Language Association Meetings in Chicago, December 1990. An earlier version of this chapter was published as "The Lesbian Phallus and the Morphological Imaginary" in *differences: A Journal of Feminist Cultural Studies*, 4, no. 1 (Spring, 1992), pp. 133–71.

1   Sigmund Freud, "On Narcissism: An Introduction" (1914), *The Standard Edition of the Complete Psychological Works of Sigmund Freud*, vol. 14, tr. and ed. James Strachey (London: Hogarth, 1961), pp. 67–104; original: "Zur Einführung des Narzissmus," *Gesammelte Werke*, vol. 10 (London: Imago, 1946), pp. 137–70. This reference will be given as "1914" in the text.

2   "Einzig in der engen Höhle, des Bachenzahnes weilt die Seele" quoted in Freud, "On Narcissism," p. 82. A better translation would be: "Alone in the narrow hole of the jaw-tooth dwells the soul."

3   Freud, "The Ego and the Id," *The Standard Edition, XIX*, pp. 1–66.

4   Freud then supplies a footnote: "i.e., the ego is ultimately derived from bodily sensations, chiefly from those springing from the surface of the body. It may thus be regarded as a mental projection of the surface of the body, besides...representing the superficies of the mental apparatus" (Freud, *XIX*, 26). Although Freud is offering an account of the development of the ego, and claiming that the ego is derived from the projected surface of the body, he is inadvertently establishing the conditions for the articulation of the body *as morphology*.

5   For an extended and informative discussion of this problem in psychological and philosophical literature that bears on psychoanalysis, see Elizabeth Grosz, *Volatile Bodies* (Bloomington: Indiana University Press, 1993).

6   Jacques Lacan, *The Seminar of Jacques Lacan, Book 1: Freud's Papers on Technique, 1953–54*, tr. Alan Sheridan (New York: Norton, 1985) p. 122; original: *Le Séminaire de Jacques Lacan, Livre I: Les écrits techniques de Freud* (Paris: Seuil, 1975), p. 141. Subsequent citations will appear in the text as (*I*), and citations to other seminars will appear in the text as roman numerals as well. A slash ("/") separates English and French pagination respectively.

7   Jane Gallop, *Thinking Through the Body* (New York: Columbia University Press, 1988), p. 126.
8   See Kaja Silverman, "The Lacanian Phallus," *differences: A Journal of Feminist Cultural Studies*, 4; no. 1 (1992), pp. 84–115.
9   This figure of the threatening mouth recalls Freud's description of Irma's mouth in *The Interpretation of Dreams*. Lacan refers to that mouth as "this something which properly speaking is unnameable, the back of this throat, the complex unlocatable form, which also makes it into the primitive object *par excellence*, the abyss of the feminine organ from which all life emerges, this gulf of the mouth, in which everything is swallowed up, and no less the image of death in which everything comes to its end" (*II*, 164).
10 Jeff Nunokawa, "In Memorium and the Extinction of the Homosexual," *ELH* 58 (Winter 1991): pp. 130–55.
11 Although somaticization is understood as part of symptom-formation, it may be that morphological development and the assumption of sex is the generalized form of the somatic symptom.

    Richard Wollheim offers an extended discussion of the bodily ego in which he maintains that incorporative fantasies are central to corporeal self-representation and to psychic development. Kleinian in approach, Wollheim argues that not only incorporative fantasy, but internalization as well casts doubt on the separability of the subject from its internalized objects. The thesis of the bodily ego is the thesis of this inseparability. See Richard Wollheim, "The Bodily Ego" in Richard Wollheim and James Hopkins (eds), *Philosophical Essays ou Freud* (New York and London: Cambridge University Press, 1982), pp. 124–38.
12 See Maurice Merleau-Ponty on "the flesh of the world" and the intertwining of touch, surface, and vision in "The Intertwining – The Chiasm," in *The Visible and the Invisible*, tr. Alphonso Lingis; ed. Claude Lefort (Evanston, Ill.: Northwestern University Press, 1968), pp. 130–55.
13 See Louis Althusser, "Ideology and Ideological State Apparatuses (Notes towards an Investigation)," p. 166.
14 Julia Kristeva, *Desire in Language: A Semiotic Approach to Literature and Art*, ed. Leon Roudiez; tr. Thomas Gorz, Alice Jardine, and Leon Roudiez (New York: Columbia University Press, 1980), pp. 134–6.
15 Irigaray prefers to formulate this primary material relation in terms of material contiguity or proximity. See her "The Power of Discourse and the Subordination of the Feminine" in *This Sex Which Is Not One*, tr. Catherine Porter with Carolyn Burke (Ithaca, NY: Cornell University Press, 1985), p. 75.
16 In "the mirror stage" the imaginary is not yet distinguished from the symbolic as it will be later for Lacan.
17 One might read Monique Wittig's strategy with respect to renaming in *The Lesbian Body* as a reworking of this Lacanian presumption. The name confers morphological distinctness, and names which explicitly disavow the patronymic lineage become the occasions for the disintegration of the (paternal) version of bodily integrity as well as the reintegration and reformation of other versions of bodily coherence.

18 See Margaret Whitford's recent excellent discussion on Luce Irigaray and the feminine imaginary in her *Luce Irigaray: Philosophy in the Feminine* (London: Routledge, 1991), pp. 53–74.

19 Naomi Schor, "This Essentialism Which Is Not One: Coming to Grips with Irigaray," *differences* 2:1 (1989), p. 48.

20 "Il y suffit de comprendre le stade du miroir comme une identification au sens plein que l'analyse donne à ce terme: à savoir la transformation produite chez le sujet quand il assume une image, – dont la prédestination à cet effet de phase est suffisamment indiquée par l'usage, dans la théorie, du terme antique d'*imago*" (Jacques Lacan, "Le stade du miroir," *Écrits*, p. 90). From the introduction of the *imago*, Lacan then moves to the jubilant assumption by the infant of his [sic] "image spéculaire," an exemplary situation of the symbolic matrix in which the "je" or the subject is said to be precipitated in a primordial form, prior to the dialectic of identification with an other. Failing to distinguish here between the formation of the "je" and the "moi," Lacan proceeds in the next paragraph, with a further elucidation of "cette forme" as that which might rather be designated as the "*je-idéal*," the ego-ideal, a translation which effects the confusing convergence of the *je* with the *moi*. To claim that this form could be termed the "*je-idéal*" is contingent upon the explanatory uses that such a term authorizes. In this case, that provisional translation will put in a known register, "un registre connu," that is, known from Freud, that phantasmatic and primary identification which Lacan describes as "la souche des identifications secondaires . . ." Here it seems that the social construction of the ego takes place through a dialectic of identifications between an already partially constituted ego and the Other. The mirror-stage is precisely the primary identification, presocial and determined "dans une ligne de fiction," along a line of fiction (imaginary, specular) which precipitates the secondary (social and dialectical) identifications. Later, this will become clear when Lacan argues that the narcissistic relation prefigures and shapes social relations as well as relations to objects (which are also social in the sense of linguistically mediated). In a sense, the mirror-stage *gives form* or *morphe* to the ego through the phantasmatic delineation of a body in control. That primary act of form-giving is then displaced or extrapolated onto the world of other bodies and objects, providing the condition ("la souche": the trunk of a tree which, it appears, has fallen or has been cut down but which serves as fertile ground) of their appearance. This wood fallen or chopped, ready for use, resonates with the meanings of matter as "hyle" considered in chapter 1. In this sense, for Lacan, primary identifications are indissociable from matter.

21 Jacques Lacan, "The Mirror Stage," *Écrits: A Selection*, tr. Alan Sheridan (New York: Norton, 1977), p. 4; original: "La fonction du stade du miroir s'avère pour nous dès lors comme un cas particulier de la fonction de l'*imago* qui est d'établir une relation de l'organisme à sa réalité – ou, comme on dit, de l'*Innenwelt* à l'*Umwelt*" (*Écrits Vol. I* [Paris: Seuil, 1971], p. 93).

22 Lacan later comes to disjoin the ego from the subject, linking the ego with the register of the imaginary, and the subject with the register of the symbolic. The

subject pertains to the symbolic order and that which constitutes the structure/ language of the unconscious. In *Seminar I* he writes, "The ego is an imaginary function, but it is not to be confused with the subject." "The unconscious completely eludes that circle of certainties by which man recognizes himself as ego. There is something outside this field which has every right to speak as I . . . It is precisely what is most misconstrued by the domain of the ego which, in analysis, comes to be formulated as properly speaking the I" (p. 193). In *Seminar II*, he continues: "The ego . . . is a particular object within the experience of the subject. Literally, the ego is an object – an object which fills a certain function which we here call the imaginary function" (p. 44). And later: "The subject is no one. It is decomposed, in pieces. And it is jammed, sucked in by the image, the deceiving and realised image, of the other, *or equally* [my emphasis], by its own specular image" (p. 54).

23   The identification with this imago is called "anticipatory," a term that Alexandre Kojève reserves for the structure of *desire*. See Alexandre Kojève, *Introduction to the Reading of Hegel*, tr. James Nichols; ed. Allan Bloom (Ithaca: Cornell University Press, 1980), p. 4. As anticipatory, the *imago* is a futural projection, a proleptic and phantasmatic idealization of bodily control that cannot yet exist and that in some sense can never exist: "this form situates the agency of the ego, before its social determination, in a fictional direction . . . " The identificatory production of that boundary – the effect of the bounded mirror – establishes the ego as and through a fictional, idealizing, and centering spatial unity. This is the inauguration of the *bodily* ego, the phenomenological access to morphology and to a bounded or discrete sense of the "I." Of course, this constitutes a *méconnaissance* precisely by virtue of the incommensurability that marks the relation between that fictional, projected body and the decentered, disunified bodily matrix from which that idealizing gaze emerges. To reparaphrase Freud along Lacanian lines, then, the ego first and foremost misrecognizes itself outside itself in the *imago* as a bodily ego.

This image not only *constitutes* the ego, but constitutes the ego as *imaginary* (Lacan refers time and again to the "imaginary origin of the ego's function," i.e., the ego *as* a consequence of primary and secondary identifications constituted in the imaginary). In other words, the ego is an imaginary production, one which takes place foremost through the projection/production of a bodily ego, and which is necessary for the functioning of the subject, but which is equally and significantly *tenuous* as well. The loss of control that in the infant characterizes undeveloped motor control persists within the adult as that excessive domain of sexuality that is stilled and deferred through the invocation of the "ego-ideal" as a center of control. Hence, every effort to inhabit fully an identification with the *imago* (where "identification with" converges ambiguously with "production of") fails because the sexuality temporarily harnessed and bounded by that ego (one might say "jammed" by that ego) cannot be fully or decisively constrained by it. What is left outside the mirror frame, as it were, is precisely the unconscious that comes to call into question the representational status of what is shown *in* the mirror. In this sense, the ego is produced through *exclusion*, as any boundary is, and what is excluded is nevertheless negatively and vitally constitutive of what "appears" bounded within the mirror.

24 Note the precedent for the formulation of the ego as estranged object in Jean-Paul Sartre, *The Transcendence of the Ego*, tr. and intro., Forest Williams and Robert Kirkpatrick (New York: Noonday, 1957).

25 Jacques Lacan, "The Meaning of the Phallus," *Feminine Sexuality: Jacques Lacan and the École Freudienne*, tr. Jacqueline Rose, ed. Juliet Mitchell (New York: Norton, 1985), p. 82. Further citations in the text will be to "Rose."

26 For a fine analysis of how phallomorphism works in Lacan, and for an elucidation of Irigaray's trenchant critique of that phallomorphism, see Whitford, *Luce Irigaray: Philosophy in the Feminine*, pp. 58–74 and 150–2. Whitford reads Lacan's essay on the mirror stage through Irigaray's critique, and argues not only that the mirror stage is itself dependent upon the prior presumption of the maternal as ground, but that the phallomorphism that the essay articulates authorizes a "male imaginary [in which] male narcissism is extrapolate[d] to the transcendental" (p. 152). Whitford also traces Irigaray's efforts to establish a female imaginary over and against the male imaginary in Lacan. Although I am clearly in some sympathy with the project of deauthorizing the male imaginary, my own strategy will be to show that the phallus can attach to a variety of organs, and that the efficacious disjoining of phallus from penis constitutes both a narcissistic wound to phallomorphism and the production of an anti-heterosexist sexual imaginary. The implications of my strategy would seem to call into question the integrity of either a masculine or a feminine imaginary.

27 "... le stade du miroir est un drame dont la poussée interne se précipite de l'insuffisance à l'anticipation – et qui pour le sujet, pris au leurre de l'identification spatiale, machine les fantasmes qui se succèdent d'une image morcelée du corps à une forme que nous appellerons orthopédique de sa totalité, – et à l'armure enfin assumée d'une identité aliénante, qui va marquer de sa structure rigide tout son développement mental" (Lacan, *Écrits I*, pp. 93–4). It is interesting that the piecemeal character of the body is phantasmatically overcome through the taking on of a kind of armor or orthopedic support, suggesting that the artificial extension of the body is integral to its maturation and enhanced sense of control. The protective and expansive figural possibilities of armor and orthopedics suggest that insofar as a certain phallic potency is the effect of the transfigured body in the mirror, this potency is purchased through artificial methods of phallic enhancement, a thesis with obvious consequences for the lesbian phallus.

28 "In Freudian doctrine, the phallus is not a fantasy, if what is understood by that is an imaginary effect...." (Rose, p. 79).

29 "Le phallus ici s'éclaire de sa fonction. Le phallus dans la doctrine freudienne n'est pas un fantasme, s'il faut entendre par là un effet imaginaire. Il n'est pas non plus comme tel un objet (partiel, interne, bon, mauvais etc...) pour autant que ce terme tend à apprécier la réalité intéressée dans une relation. Il est encore moins l'organe, pénis ou clitoris, qu'il symbolise. Et ce n'est pas sans raison que Freud en a pris la référence au simulacre qu'il était pour les Anciens."

"Car le phallus est un signifiant. . . . " (*Écrits*, p. 690).

30 Clearly, Lacan also repudiates the clitoris as an organ that might be identified with the phallus. But note that the penis and the clitoris are always symbolized differently; the clitoris is symbolized as penis envy (not having), whereas the penis is symbolized as the castration complex (having with the fear of losing) (Rose, p. 75). Hence, the phallus symbolizes the clitoris as not having the penis, whereas the phallus symbolizes the penis through the threat of castration, understood as a kind of dispossession. To have a penis is to have that which the phallus *is* not, but which, precisely by virtue of this not-being, constitutes the occasion for the phallus to signify (in this sense, the phallus requires and reproduces the diminution of the penis in order to signify – almost a kind of master-slave dialectic between them).

    Not to have the penis is already to have lost it and, hence, to be the occasion for the phallus to signify its power to castrate; the clitoris will signify as penis-envy, as a lack which, through its envy, will wield the power to dispossess. To "be" the phallus, as women are said to be, is to be both dispossessed and dispossessing. Women "are" the phallus in the sense that they absently reflect its power; this is the signifying function of the lack. And those female body parts which are not the penis fail, therefore, to have the phallus, and so are precisely a set of "lacks." Those body parts fail to phenomenalize precisely because they cannot properly wield the phallus. Hence, the very description of how the phallus symbolizes (i.e., as penis-envy *or* castration) makes implicit recourse to differentially marked body parts, which implies that the phallus does not symbolize penis and clitoris in the same way. The clitoris can never be said, within this view, to be an example of "having" the phallus.

31 In the following chapter, "Phantasmatic Identification and the Assumption of Sex," I attempt to argue that the assumption of sexed positions within the symbolic operates through the threat of castration, a threat addressed to a male body, a body marked as male prior to its "assumption" of masculinity, and that the female body must be understood as the embodiment of this threat and, obversely, the guarantee that the threat will not be realized. This oedipal scenario which Lacan understands as central to the assumption of binary sex is itself founded on the threatening power of the threat, the unbearability of demasculinized manhood and phallicized femininity. Implicit to these two figures, I argue, is the spectre of homosexual abjection, one which is clearly culturally produced, circulated, contested, and contingent.

32 See Maria Torok, "The Meaning of Penis-Envy in Women," tr. Nicholas Rand, in *differences: A Journal of Feminist Cultural Studies*, 4, no.1 (Spring, 1992): pp. 1–39. Torok argues that penis-envy in women is a "mask" which symptomatizes the prohibition on masturbation and effects a deflection from the orgasmic pleasures of masturbation. Inasmuch as penis-envy is a modality of desire for which no satisfaction can be gained, it masks the ostensibly more prior desire for auto-erotic pleasures. According to Torok's highly normative theory of female sexual development, the masturbatory orgasmic pleasures experienced and then prohibited (by the mother's intervention) produce first a penis-envy which cannot be satisfied

and then a renunciation of that desire in order to rediscover and reexperience masturbatory orgasm in the context of adult heterosexual relations. Torok thus reduces penis-envy to a mask and prohibition which presumes that female sexual pleasure is not only centered in auto-eroticism, but that this pleasure is primarily *unmediated* by sexual difference. She also reduces all possibilities of cross-gendered phantasmatic identification to a deflection from the masturbatory heterosexual nexus, such that the primary prohibition is against unmediated self-love. Freud's own theory of narcissism argues that auto-eroticism is always modeled on imaginary object-relations, and that the Other structures the masturbatory scene phantasmatically. In Torok, we witness the theoretical installation of the Bad Mother whose primary task is to prohibit masturbatory pleasures and who must be overcome (the mother figured, as in Lacan, as obstruction) in order to rediscover masturbatory sexual happiness with a man. The mother thus acts as a prohibition that must be overcome in order for heterosexuality to be achieved and the return to self and wholeness that that purportedly implies for a woman. This developmental celebration of heterosexuality thus works through the implicit foreclosure of homosexuality or the abbreviation and rerouting of female homosexuality as masturbatory pleasure. Penis-envy would characterize a lesbian sexuality that is, as it were, stalled between the irrecoverable memory of masturbatory bliss and the heterosexual recovery of that pleasure. In other words, if penis-envy is in part code for lesbian pleasure, or for other forms of female sexual pleasure that are, as it were, stopped along the heterosexual developmental trajectory, then lesbianism is "envy" and, hence, both a deflection from pleasure and infinitely unsatisfying. In short, there can be lesbian pleasure for Torok, for if the lesbian is "envious", she embodies and enacts the very prohibition on pleasure that, it seems, only heterosexual union can lift. That this essay is found useful by some feminists continues to surprise and alarm me.

33 For a very interesting account of castration anxiety in lesbian subjectivity, see Teresa de Lauretis's recent work on the mannish lesbian, especially her discussion of Radclyffe Hall "before the mirror" in her book, *The Practice of Love: Lesbian Sexuality and Perverse Desire* (Bloomington: Indiana University Press, 1994).

34 Here it will probably be clear that I am in agreement with Derrida's critique of Lévi-Strauss's atemporalized notion of structure. In "Structure, Sign, and Play," Derrida asks what gives structure its structurality, that is, the quality of being a structure, suggesting that that status is endowed or derived and, hence, nonoriginary. A structure "is" a structure to the extent that it persists as one. But how to understand how the manner of that persistence inheres in the structure itself? A structure does not remain self-identical through time, but "is" to the extent that it is reiterated. Its iterability is thus the condition of its identity, but because iterability presupposes an interval, a difference, between terms, identity, constituted through this discontinuous temporality, is conditioned and contested by this difference from itself. This is a difference constitutive of identity – as well as the principle of its impossibility. As such, it is difference as *différance*, a deferral of any resolution into self-identity.

Part II

Fantasy, Censorship, and Discursive Power

6

The Force of Fantasy: Feminism, Mapplethorpe, and Discursive Excess (1990)

Introduction

What is the relationship between fantasy, reality and the law? Are pornographic representations harmful in any "real" sense towards those they depict, and if so, should such
representations be prohibited and censored? Butler enters the pornography/censorship
debate with her article "The Force of Fantasy" which was published in *differences: A
Journal Of Feminist Cultural Studies* the year after the notorious legal amendment
presented by Jesse Helms, the right-wing Republican Senator from North Carolina. In
his amendment, Helms sought to prevent the National Endowment for the Arts from
funding artistic projects deemed to be "obscene," and he attacked the photographer
Robert Mapplethorpe's work in particular for what Helms claimed were pornographic and
obscene sexual depictions. Rather than debating whether or not Mapplethorpe's work is
"obscene," Butler cleverly focuses on Helms's own discourse which she asserts is *itself* a
sadomasochistic, necrophiliac fantasy, exactly the kind of pornographic exercise it seeks
to prohibit. Indeed, throughout this article Butler argues that in their calls for censorship,
would-be censors such as Helms effectively recirculate the very discourses they aim to
renounce, an argument that is also deployed in *Excitable Speech*. While Helms's legal
clauses may be regarded as the homosexual fantasies of a "straight" senator, Butler
similarly asserts that the pro-censorship, anti-pornography campaigner Andrea Dworkin
makes use of "pornographic" discursive structures in her aggressive and insistent attacks
on "obscene" representations.

By blurring the distinction between pornographic representations and the law which
produces and recycles such representations, Butler problematizes the distinction between
fantasy and the "real." The argument that the real is a phantasmatic construction will be
familiar from *Bodies That Matter* where Butler describes the body as a linguistically
constituted psychic projection. Similarly, in "The Force of Fantasy," Butler understands the
real as "a variable construction which is always and only determined in relation to its

From *differences: A Journal of Feminist Cultural Studies* 2:2 (1990), pp. 105–25. Bloomington:
Indiana University Press. © 1990 by Indiana University Press. All rights reserved. Used by permission
of the publisher.

constitutive outside"; in other words, fantasy is essential to a real which itself turns out to be a construction established on the basis of its differentiation from fantasy. Crucially, fantasy is no more than "suspended action," and here, as in *Excitable Speech*, Butler assumes that even if representations like Mapplethorpe's offend, they should not be subject to censorship (although she finds herself in paradoxical alliance with Dworkin in her doubtful attitude towards Mapplethorpe's depiction of naked black men). Representations do not inevitably have the power to injure their viewers in any "real" or metaphorical sense for the following reasons: (i) "obscene" representations are not effective performatives which have the power to enact what they name; (ii) these fantastic, allegorical texts do not have a single meaning; and (iii) they are not bound to a single interpretation. Dworkin's epistemologically overdetermined readings and others like them regard pornographic texts as actually violent, casting the woman as victim and implying that there is only one way of reading. On the other hand, Butler insists that fantasies exceed the strict gender binarisms which currently structure heterosexual hegemony, so that what she calls "the possibility of a cross-identification" will lead to the kind of radical re-citation she has already described in *Gender Trouble* and *Bodies That Matter*.

   As in those two works, it is precisely this kind of "trouble" which interests Butler as she searches out moments of discursive excess in pornographic representations and the identity categories they depict. Here as before she engages Foucault's notion of "reverse discourse," asserting the uncontrollability of signifiers that proliferate and produce the insurgent identity categories which will challenge and subvert existing discursive structures. This recognition prevents Butler from calling for the censorship of Mapplethorpe's depictions of black men, troubling though they may be, or indeed of Helms's Amendment, that pornographic sadomasochistic fantasy which, according to its own logic should prohibit *itself*. Rather, Butler advocates the open production of those identity categories that are threatened by the regulatory violence of the law. As in her previous work, the failure to control the terms of identity and the uncontrollability of signifier and signified will provide opportunities to counter the authoritarianism of censors such as Helms and Dworkin.

A contemporary feminist interrogation of representation is inevitably caught up in a set of persistently ambivalent ontological claims. Recent feminist criticisms of poststructuralism and poststructuralist feminism take issue with what appears to be a refusal to grant a pre-given, pre-linguistic or self-identical status to the real. The so-called deconstruction of the real, however, is not a simple negation or thorough dismissal of any ontological claim, but constitutes an interrogation of the construction and circulation of what counts as an ontological claim. The critical point is to examine the exclusionary means by which the circumscription of the real is effected. And in a sense, this particular move to problematize the real has been part of feminist practice prior to there being any question of its status as a poststructuralist intrusion.

One feminist site where this critical problematization of the real has taken place is in theories of fantasy which are either implicitly or explicitly formulated in discussions of representation, feminist fictions, and feminist utopias and dystopias. Fantasy has been crucial to the feminist task of (re)thinking futurity; to that end feminist theory relies on the capacity to postulate through fantasy a future that is not yet (Bartkowski, Haraway). In this formulation, fantasy is not equated with what is not real, but rather with what is not *yet* real, what is possible or futural, or what belongs to a different version of the real.

In those anti-pornography positions that favor censorship, there is an implicit theory of fantasy that runs counter to the position sketched above. This implicit theory, by which I mean this set of untheorized presumptions, relies upon a representational realism that conflates the signified of fantasy with its (impossible) referent and construes "depiction" as an injurious act and, in legal terms, a discriminatory action or "real" effect. This gliding from representation to the ontological claim moves in two directions at once: it establishes the referent first as that which the representation reflects and re-presents and, second, as that which is effectively performed and performatively effected by the representation. This formulation of representation as injurious action operates through an implicit understanding of *fantasy* as that which both produces and is produced by representations and which, then, makes possible and enacts precisely the referent of that representation. According to this implicit theory, the real is positioned both before and after its representation; and representation becomes a moment of the reproduction and consolidation of the real.

This hyperdetermination of the ontological claim in some ways runs precisely counter (although not dialectically opposed) to the poststructuralist effort to problematize the ways in which the ontological claim, whatever the foundational or mimetic place it assumes, is performed as an effect of signifying acts. This kind of problematizing suspension of the ontological has also had its place within feminist critical practice. For part of the task of many feminist critical practices has been to question the line according to which the distinction between the real and unreal is drawn; to ask: what is it that passes as the real, that qualifies the extent or domain of "reality"? are the parameters of the real acceptable, contestable? in whose name is a given version of the real articulated? is the "real" a contemporary configuration that precludes any transformation by positing the "not yet" as the impossible, the unreal, rather than the unrealizable? If what goes under the description of the real is contingent, contrived, and instituted for a set of purposes, then the real is not a ground on which we might easily rely; indeed, it is a postulate that requires a political interrogation.

Whereas anti-pornography feminists presume a mimetic relation between the real, fantasy, and representation that presumes the priority of the real, we can understand the "real" as a variable construction which is always and only determined in relation to its constitutive outside: fantasy, the unthinkable, the unreal. The positivist version of the real will consign all absence to the unreal, even as it relies on that absence to stabilize its own boundaries. In this sense, the phantasmatic, as precisely such a constitutive exclusion, becomes essential to the construction of the real. If this is so, in what sense, then, can we understand the real as an installation and foreclosure of fantasy, a phantasmatic construction which receives a certain legitimation after which it is called the real and disavowed as the phantasmatic? In what sense is the phantasmatic most successful precisely in that determination in which its own phantasmatic status is eclipsed and renamed as the real? Here the distinction between real and unreal contrives a boundary between the legitimate domain of the phantasmatic and the illegitimate.

When we point to something as real, and in political discourse it is very often imperative to wield the ontological indicator in precisely that way, that is not the end but the beginning of the political problematic; to prove that events are real, one must already have a notion of the real within which one operates, a set of exclusionary and constitutive principles which confer on a given indication the force of an ontological designator; and if it is that very notion of the real that one wants, for political reasons, to contest, then the simple act of pointing will not suffice to delimit the principles which constitute the force of the indexical. In fact, the effect of transparency produced by indexical pointing will effectively foreclose the interrogation that is called for. Such a restrictively generated discursive domain provides exclusionary rules which guarantee in advance that that kind of pointing performs or produces the signification "real" that it appears to find as the simple and exterior referent to which it points. When pointing appears sufficient to designate the real, it is only through implicit recourse to certain entrenched and exclusionary conventions that frame and sanction that version of the real, and the real that is thereby designated would also and at the same time be *restricted* to a pre-given version of itself. To change the real, that is, to change what qualifies as the real, would be to contest the syntax within which pointing occurs and on which it tacitly relies. If the production of the real takes place through a restriction of the phantasmatic – and we shall soon see one political ramification of this thesis – then the phantasmatic emerges necessarily as the variable boundary from which the real is insistently contested. In what follows, I will look at one kind of pointing (Helms's pointing at Mapplethorpe) which functions in both a referential and accusatory sense, that is, which restrains the signified (and the domain of the signifiable) precisely in the moment in which the signified is collapsed into the referent. In a sense, it is precisely the moment in which the phantasmatic assumes the status of the real, that is, when the two become compellingly conflated, that the phantasmatic exercises its power most effectively.

Now this might seem like an increasingly philosophical discussion for an essay which on the surface makes some gestures towards thinking about pornography, Mapplethorpe, and fantasy. Although a feminist inquiry – as I will insist – this paper seeks to criticize an alternative feminist theory of fantasy, one that is almost nowhere explicity theorized, but which is implicit, operative, and politically effective.

In particular, I am concerned then with a theory of fantasy that informs some feminist efforts to read and, on occasion, to call for legal sanctions against pornography. And secondly, I am concerned with a theory of fantasy that appears to inform New Right efforts to prohibit federal funding of artists like Robert Mapplethorpe. The first draft of the bill recently passed by the Congress (HR 2788) which sets restrictions on the kinds of representations fundable by the state virtually cites the MacKinnon/Dworkin bill, known as the Minnesota anti-pornography bill (Title 7), to make its own case against Mapplethorpe.[1] In a sense, it is this sorry discursive alliance that I seek to understand in exposing what I take to be a common theory of fantasy and the phantasmatic that informs both views. But more broadly, I want to suggest that certain kinds of efforts to restrict practices of representation in the hopes of reigning in the imaginary, controlling the phantasmatic, end up reproducing and proliferating the phantasmatic in inadvertent ways, indeed, in ways that contradict the intended purposes of the restriction itself. The effort to limit representations of homoeroticism within the federally funded art world – an effort to censor the phantasmatic – always and only leads to its production; and the effort to produce and regulate it in politically sanctioned forms ends up effecting certain forms of exclusion that return, like insistent ghosts, to undermine those very efforts.

So what is meant by "phantasmatic" here? To say that something is phantasmatic is not to say that it is "unreal" or artificial or dismissable as a consequence. Wielded within political discourse, the real is a syntactically regulated phantasm that has enormous power and efficacy. Fantasy postures *as* the real; it establishes the real through a repeated and persistent posturing, but it also contains the possibility of suspending and interrogating the ontological claim itself, of reviewing its own productions, as it were, and contesting their claim to the real.

According to psychoanalytic theorists Jean Laplanche and J.-B. Pontalis, *fantasy constitutes a dimension of the real*, what they refer to as "psychic reality." In a sense, psychic reality is here inclusive of the real; it is the semantic excess, the constant verging on idealization and absolutization that characterizes the referential function and, in particular, the ways in which the phantasmatic assumes the places of the real within an untheorized use of referential language. In Jacqueline Rose's terms, the phantasmatic is also precisely that which haunts and contests the borders which circumscribe the construction of stable identities (90). I propose to revise this theory along Foucaultian lines to question how fantasy informs political discourse in ways that often defeat the very purposes to which political discourse is put. At stake is not the phantasmatic construction of the identity of the pornographer and the identity of the pornographee, but the dissimulation of "identity" in fantasy (its distribution and concealment), a dissimulation which is I think regularly misunderstood by both the advocates of censorship on the political right and those feminist theorists who, in their critique of pornography, propose to establish a logical or causal continuum among fantasy, representation, and action. Does fantasy compel a phantasmatic identification with aggression or victimization? Does it provide a motivational link between representation and action? If both of these questions are based upon a misconstrual of fantasy, then the arguments in favor of censorship are seriously weakened.

The ordinary language in which the meaning of fantasy is constituted misconstrues the status of fantasy altogether. We say, "I have a fantasy" or "this is my fantasy" and what is presupposed is an I, a subject who has a fantasy as a kind of interior and visual projection and possession. "And in my fantasy," we say, "I was sitting in the cafeteria and you came up to me." Already the "I" who fantasizes is displaced, for the "I" occurs at least twice, as the one who "has" the fantasy, and the "I" who is *in* the fantasy, indeed, who is in a sense "had" by that prior I. What is the proper place of the "I" in its redoubling? It is not enough to say that the "I" who reports the fantasy, who "has" it, is somehow "real" and the "I" who is "in" it is phantasmatic, for the reporting "I" is revealing and constituting its own content in and through the fantasy that is elaborated. The narrator of the fantasy is always already "in" the fantasy. The "I" both contributes to and *is* the frame, the complex of perspectives, the temporal and grammatical sequencing, the particular dramatic tempo and conclusion that constitutes the very action of the fantasy. Hence, the "I" is dissimulated into the entire scene, even as it appears that the "I" merely watches on as an epistemological observer to the event.

According to Laplanche and Pontalis, fantasy does not entail an identification with a single position within the fantasy; the identification is distributed among the various elements of the scene: the identification is with the "you" who comes up, the "me" who is sitting, but further, with the verbs themselves, "sitting," "coming up," even variously "coming" and "up," even, abject as it may seem, the grim landscape of cafeteria life that bespeaks the longing for a sudden and decisive erotic interruption. In any case, or rather in all of these cases, identification is multiple and shifting, and cannot be confined to the "me" alone. Laplanche and Pontalis write:

Fantasy is not the object of desire, but its setting. In fantasy the subject does not pursue the object or its sign; one appears oneself caught up in the sequence of images. One forms no representation of the desired object, but is oneself represented as participating in the scene although, in the earliest forms of fantasy, one cannot be assigned any fixed place in it (hence the danger, in treatment [and in politics] of interpretations which claim to do so). As a result, the subject, although always present in the fantasy, may be so in a desubjectivized form, that is to say, in the very syntax of the sequence in question. (Formations 26–27)[2]

There is, then, strictly speaking, no subject who has a fantasy, but only fantasy as the scene of the subject's fragmentation and dissimulation; fantasy enacts a splitting or fragmentation or, perhaps better put, a multiplication or proliferation of identifications that puts the very locatability of identity into question. In other words, although we might wish to think, even fantasize, that there is an "I" who has or cultivates its fantasy with some measure of mastery and possession, that "I" is always already undone by precisely that which it claims to master.

Within psychoanalytic theory, fantasy is usually understood in terms of wish-fulfillment, where the wish and its fulfillment belong to the closed circuit of a polymorphous auto-eroticism. Hence, sexual fantasies may express a longing for a scene outside the fantasy, but the fantasy always figures that outside within its own terms, that is, as a moment inside the scene, effecting its fulfillment through a staging and distributing of the subject in every possible position. The consequence is that although it may well be some Other that I fantasize about, the fantasizing recasts that Other within the orbit of my scene, for fantasy is self-reflexive in its structure, no matter how much it enacts a longing for that which is outside its reach. And yet, the subject cannot be collapsed into the subject-position of that fantasy; all positions are the subject, even as this subject has proliferated beyond recognition. In a sense, despite its apparent referentiality, fantasy is always and only its own object of desire. And this is not to say that fantasy supplies its own thematic, but that the boundaries of the real against which it is determined are precisely what become problematized in fantasy. Fantasy suspends the ontological claim of that which passes as the real under the usual description.

How does the relationship between fantasy and autoeroticism suggested by the above account provide insight in to the signifying status of the pornographic text? The psychoanalytic account resonates with an article by Dierdre English in *Mother Jones* from the early 1980s. Contrary to the claim that pornographic representation somehow leads to the action of rape by fueling violent fantasies, her argument was that most men interested in pornography were just benign masturbators for whom the auto-erotic moment was the be all and end all of sex.

Whereas English argued that pornographic fantasy substituted for action and provided for a catharsis in fantasy that made action superfluous, a very different position on fantasy has been operative within the anti-pornography movement and recent New Right calls for censorship. Both of these efforts to restrict or prohibit pornographic fantasy end up inadvertently but inevitably producing and authorizing in their own discursive actions precisely the scenes of sexual violence and aggression that they seek to censor. The effort to enforce a limit on fantasy can only and always fail, in part because limits are, in a sense, what fantasy loves most, what it incessantly thematizes and subordinates to its own aims. They fail because the very rhetoric by which certain erotic acts or relations are prohibited invariably eroticizes that prohibition in the service of a fantasy. These prohibitions of the erotic are always at the same time, and despite themselves, the eroticization of prohibition.

It would be mistaken to understand fantasy as a site of psychic multiplicity subsequently reduced and refused by the onset of a prohibitive law, as if fantasy were unproblematically before the law. Laplanche and Pontalis argue that in the *mise en scène* of desire, prohibition is always present in the very position of desire (*Vocabulaire* 156). This posited simultaneity of prohibition and desire, however, is given a circular temporality in Foucault. For Foucault, prohibition depends upon transgressive fantasies, and reproduces them in order to have an object upon which to act and augment itself. Prohibition appears to *precede* fantasy and to structure it essentially; this is part of what is meant earlier by the claim that fantasy designates the constitutive outside of the real. The moment of exclusion or prohibition produces and sustains the domain of the phantasmatic. The multiple sites through which the subject is dissimulated are produced, then, by the regulatory discourse which would institute the subject as a coherent and singular positionality. The "syntax" and "sequencing" that stage the self-dissimulating subject might then be reread as the specific rule-governed discourses of a given regulatory regime. In what follows, I will attempt a Foucaultian rereading of Laplanche and Pontalis in terms of the phantasmatic production that is the Helms amendment.

The recent legislative efforts by Jesse Helms to put a juridical harness on the imaginary by forbidding federal art funds appear in two forms, the original proposal, formulated in July 1989, and the final proposal, claimed as a "compromise bill" which passed the Senate and became law in late September (Public Law 101–121). Although the bill forbids the National Endowment for the Arts from funding artistic projects that depict "obscenity," the National

Endowment for the Humanities, in the spirit of solidarity, quickly volunteered to adopt the bill as internal policy. In the original formulation of the bill, federal funds were prohibited from being used to "promote, disseminate [!] or produce obscene *or indecent* materials, including but not limited to depictions of sado-masochism, homoeroticism, the exploitation of children, or individuals engaged in sex acts; *or, material which denigrates the objects or beliefs of the adherents of a particular religion or non-religion*" (italicized portions were subsequently deleted). In the original proposal the following clause also appeared continuous with what I just cited: "or that denigrates, debases or reviles a person, group or class of citizens on the basis of race, creed, sex, handicap, age or national origin" ("Senate"). This added clause may seem logically and legally discontinuous with the former, for while the last clause appears to protect certain individuals against debasement, the former clause appears to enact the very debasement that the latter disallows. By adding the last clause originally, Helms effectively confounded feminist and conservative discourses, for the latter clause is meant to protect individuals and groups against discrimination. The legal move that would establish as discrimination the depiction or representation of certain groups in subordinate or debased positions finds its precedents in those legislative efforts inspired by some anti-pornography feminists to ban representations of women in sexually debased or subordinated positions. In effect, the feminist legal effort to include "representations" or "depictions" as instances and enactments of discrimination has been deployed by Jesse Helms to suggest a legal and discursive alliance with anti-pornography feminists. On the one hand, we can argue that legislative efforts to ban pornography never intended to sanction these other kinds of legal prohibitions, and we can even call for qualifications in those legislative efforts to make sure that representations of "homoeroticism" and "individuals engaged in sex acts" escape the censor, although clearly sadomasochists would fare less well – possibly because the action of the prohibitive law resembles or mobilizes that power/dynamic most proximately (interestingly, though, without the qualification of consent insisted upon by libertarian sadomasochists).[3]

I would like to consider this alliance briefly in the context of a shared conception of representation as debasing and discriminatory action. I would suggest that the legal equivalence between representation and action could not be established were it not for an implicit and shared conception of fantasy as the causal link between representation and action, or between a psychic act that remains within the orbit of a visual economy, and an enacted fantasy in which the body literally enters what was previously a purely visualized or fantasized scene. Here the phantasmatic construction of the real is confused with a temporal linkage between fantasy and the real, as if fantasy could suddenly transmute into action, as if the two were separable from the start. I would argue, however, that fantasy constitutes a psychic action, and what is conjured as "physical action" by the above causal formulation is precisely the condensation and foreclosure of fantasy, not that which follows from it. Accordingly, fantasy furnishes the psychic overdetermination of meaning which is designated by "the real." "Fantasy" and "the real" are always already linked. If the phantasmatic remains in tension with the "real" effects it produces – and there is good reason to understand pornography as the erotic exploitation of this tension – then the "real" remains permanently within quotations, i.e., "action" is suspended, or, better yet, pornographic action is always suspended action.

The anti-pornography effort to impute a causal or temporal relation between the phantasmatic and the real raises a set of problems. If representations of women in subordinate or debased positions – assuming for the moment that some agreement could be achieved on what that is – if such representations *are* discriminatory actions, one way to understand representation is as the incipient moment of an inexorable action, containing within itself a teleological principle whereby the transformation of picture into fantasy is followed by the transformation of fantasy into action. By establishing causal lines among representation, fantasy, and action, one can effectively argue that the representation *is* discriminatory action. Here the view that fantasy motivates action rules out the possibility that fantasy is the very scene which *suspends* action and which, in its suspension, provides for a critical investigation of what it is that constitutes action.

Of course, the other way to argue that representation is discriminatory action is to claim that to see a given representation constitutes an injury, that representations injure, and that viewers are the passive recipients of that visual assault. Here again there is no interpretive leeway between the representation, its meanings, and its effects; they are given together, in one stroke – as it were – as an instantaneous teleology for which there is no alternative. And yet, if this were true, there could be no analysis of pornography. Even from within the epistemological discourse that Dworkin uses, one which links masculinity with agency and aggression, and femininity with passivity and injury, her argument defeats itself: no interpretive possibilities could be opened up by the pornographic text, for no interpretive distance could be taken from its ostensibly injurious effects; and the muted, passive, and injured stance of the woman viewer would effectively preclude a critical analysis of its structure and place within the field of social power.

The shift from an epistemological framework to one which takes the pornographic text as a site of multiple significations allows us to read Dworkin's move differently. The claim that the text permits of a single interpretation is itself a construction of the pornographic text as a site of univocal meaning; if pornography is a textualized fantasy of dissimulated and unstable identifications, then *the claim* that pornography enforces a foreclosure of the text's possible readings is itself the forcible act by which that foreclosure is effected.

The reason why representations do not jump off the page to club us over the head, although sometimes we fantasize precisely that, is that even pornographic representations as textualized fantasy do not supply a single point of identification for their viewers, whether presumed to be stabilized in subject-positions of male or female. Indeed, the postulation of a single identificatory access to the representation is precisely what stabilizes gender identity; the possibility of a cross-identification spells a kind of gender trouble that the anti-pornography analysis fully suppresses. In point of fact, it may well be more frightening to acknowledge an identification with the one who debases than with the one who is debased or perhaps no longer to have a clear sense of the gender position of either; hence, the insistence that the picture enforces an identification with victimization might be understood not only as a refusal to identify – even in fantasy – with aggression, but, further, as a displacement of that refused aggression onto the picture which then – as a transferential object of sorts – takes on a personified status as an active agent that abuses its passive viewer (or which stands in for the phantasmatic figure of "patriarchy" itself). Indeed, if pornography is to be understood as fantasy, as anti-pornography activists almost invariably insist, then the effect of pornography is not to force women to identify with a subordinate or debased position, but to provide the opportunity to identify with the entire scene of debasement, agents and recipients alike, when and if those "positions" are clearly discernable in the actions and landscapes of masturbatory scenes of triumph and humiliation. A feminist critic like Dworkin has shown us the importance of pornographic material in its status as *social text* which facilitates certain kinds of readings of domination. And yet, the pornographic fantasy does not restrict identification to any one position, and Dworkin, in her elaborate textual exegesis, paradoxically shows us how her form of interpretive mastery can be derived from a viewing which, in her own view, is supposed to restrict her to a position of mute and passive injury. The logic of epistemological determinism that stabilizes "masculine" and "feminine" within a frame of unilateral oppression is subject to a logical reversal which calls that frame into question: if the pornographic representation is someone else's fantasy, that of "men" – broadly and ambiguously construed – and if "the woman viewer" is the injured object of that fantasy-turned-action, then women are by her definition never agents of pornographic fantasy. The very possibility of identifying in fantasy with a debased position requires an active and persistent foreclosure of other possible identifications. Hence, "passivity" becomes a privileged mode of identification which requires the collapse and consolidation of multiple sites of identification into one.

A question to raise here would be, is it even possible to do the kind of reading that Dworkin does, that involves a retelling and repetition of the pornographic scene without making use of precisely the variable identifications that the pornographic fantasy itself occasions? From what source does Dworkin's reading draw its own strength and mastery if not through an identification and redeployment of the very representation of aggression that she abhors? In other words, does the identificatory process that her own reading requires effectively refute the theory of identification that she explicitly holds?

Prohibitions work both to generate and to restrict the thematics of fantasy. In its production, fantasy is as much conditioned as constrained by the prohibitions that appear to arrive only after fantasy has started to play itself out in the field of "representations." In this sense, Mapplethorpe's production anticipates the prohibition that will be visited upon it; and that anticipation of disapprobation is in part what generates the representations themselves. If it will become clear that Helms requires Mapplethorpe, it seems only right to admit in advance that Mapplethorpe requires Helms as well. This is not to say that Mapplethorpe knew before he died that Helms would appear with amendment in hand, or that Mapplethorpe should have known better. On the contrary: Helms operates as the *pre*condition of Mapplethorpe's enterprise, and Mapplethorpe attempts to subvert that generative prohibition by, as it were, becoming the exemplary fulfillment of its constitutive sexual wish.

Dworkin's call for sanctions can be read similarly as a *re*emergence of precisely the prohibition which occasioned and produced the pornographic material itself. In this sense, the pornographic text mobilizes and produces both the positionality of victimization and that of the critical agency that attends to that victimization. The text encodes and presupposes precisely the prohibition which will later impose itself as if it were externally related to the text itself.

The ambiguous temporal exchange between fantasy and its prohibition – which comes first – can be read in those positions, like Dworkin's, which assert at the same time not only that certain fantasies are "of" force or violence, but are *forcibly imposed* by certain kinds of representations. In this sense, the ostensible content of the representation and its rhetorical force are conflated and exchanged.

Something similar happens I think within the very amendment that Helms formulates. The amendment prohibits three kinds of activities, "promoting, disseminating, and/or producing obscene or indecent materials," and then goes on to state some of what will be included under that category. Significantly, the language reads, "including, but not limited to . . ." and then offers its list. "Including, but not limited to" is a phrase that invites conservative judicial activism and presumes that the kinds of depictions to be deprived of federal funding have the possibility to spread, "to disseminate" like a disease perhaps? like AIDS, from which Mapplethorpe himself died? The presumption that the obscene and the pornographic have a way of getting out of hand is confirmed repeatedly in this fateful sentence: "Including, but not limited to depictions of sadomasochism, homoeroticism": here homoeroticism is not distinct from homosexuality, but considered a more inclusive category; indeed, it provides for representations that depict homosexuality both explicitly and implicitly; hence, even the nuance of homosexuality is a site of danger (one might well wonder whether Plato's *Symposium* would receive funding under the guidelines now adopted by the National Endowment for the Arts and the National Endowment for the Humanities). But let us return to the progression of this sentence, for the "including but not limited to" established a determinate juridical object and an indeterminate one as well, and this rhythm repeats itself throughout the sentence. Sadomasochism is presumed to be clearly and collectively identifiable in its distinction from other sorts of sexual activities, but "homoeroticism" is, I take it, a term that concedes the indeterminate status of this sexuality, for it is not simply the acts that qualify as homosexual under the law, but the ethos, the spreading power of this sexuality, which must also be rooted out.

"The exploitation of children" comes next, at which point I begin to wonder: what reasons are there for grouping these three categories together? Do they lead to each other, as if the breaking of one taboo necessitates a virtual riot of perversion? Or is there, implicit in the sequencing and syntax of this legal text, a figure of the homosexual, apparently male, who practices sadomasochism and preys on young boys, or who practices sadomasochism with young boys, a homosexuality which is perhaps defined as sadomasochism and the exploitation of children? Perhaps this is an effort to define restrictively the sexual exploiter of children *as* the sadomasochistic male homosexual in order, quite conveniently, to locate the source of child sexual abuse outside the home, safeguarding the family as the unregulated sexual property of the father?[4] On one level, the figure of such a homosexual is Mapplethorpe whom the *Washington Post* describes as producing "photographs, some of which are homoerotic or sado-masochistic, and some that show children exposing themselves" ("Obscenity"). And yet, the figure of Mapplethorpe is already a stand-in for the figure of the homosexual male, so that the target is a representation of homosexuality which, according to the representational theory Helms presumes, *is* in some sense the homosexual *himself*.

If the legal statute relies on this figure of the male homosexual, then perhaps the legal statute can be understood as its own kind of fantasy. The "subject" of fantasy, according to Laplanche and Pontalis, is dissimulated in the syntax of the scene. This law contains as the tacit structure of its elliptical syntax a figure of homosexuality whose figurings, whose "representations," are to be forbidden.

In other words, this is a figure who can only be figured by Helms, who belongs to him, as it were, and who will be forbidden to figure anything or anyone in return. Is this a figure that the law contrives in order to prohibit, or perhaps, prohibits in order to produce – time and again – for its own . . . satisfaction? Is this a production of a figure that it itself outlaws from production, a vehement and public way of drawing into public attention the very figure that is supposed to be banned from public attention and public funds? What kind of sadomasochistic performance is this that brings into phantasmatic relief the very object that it seeks to subordinate, revile, debase, and denigrate? Is this not, paradoxically, a public flogging and debasement of the homosexual that is finally necrophilic as well, considering the fact that Mapplethorpe, who is made to stand for homosexuality in general, is but recently dead from AIDS?

In a sense, the Helms amendment in its final form can be read as precisely the kind of pornographic exercise that it seeks to renounce. According to the logic which would identify representations with injurious acts, Helms's amendment ought to be understood as an injury against those whom it demeans through its depiction. According to its own logic, Helms's amendment should then prohibit itself from becoming law. Although a wonderful turn of the screw to contemplate, it is not finally the argumentative tactic that I would promote. The phantasmatic construction of the homosexual in Helms's terms is not unlike the phantasmatic construction of women in pornography, but in each case, the question needs to be asked, at what juncture does that phantasmatic construction call its own ontological claim into question, reveal its own tenuousness, confess its own impossibility? There is no doubt that Helms's fantasy of homosexuality takes place within the scene of child molestation and sadomasochism; let us remember that this is his fantasy, though surely not his alone. Consider that the stability of the homosexual real as a social signification is always negotiated through fantasy; to point at Mapplethorpe's representations as the graphic articulation of homosexuality *soi-même*, is a state-sanctioned pointing (both a referring and a restraining) which effectively produces and stabilizes the homosexual real; in other words, it is a syntactically regulated phantasmatic production which assumes and preempts the claim of the real.

Helms not only extends those legal precedents that categorize homosexuality as obscenity, but, rather, authorizes and orchestrates through those legal statutes a restriction of the very terms by which homosexuality is culturally defined. One interpretation could claim that this tactic is simply an occasion for Helms to assault the gay male artistic community, or gay men generally, as well as the sexual practices phantasmatically imposed upon them. The political response is then to develop a political resistance to this move by simply reversing the argument, claiming that gay men are not as he says, that Mapplethorpe is more significant and more properly artistic. It is not merely that Helms characterizes homosexuality unfairly, but that he constructs homosexuality itself through a set of exclusions that call to be politically interrogated.

One effect of this law, then, is to circumscribe the imaginability of homosexuality; in exchange for the variety of "representations" produced by Mapplethorpe and "others like him," there is only one representation that is now sanctioned, the one that is articulately prohibited by Helms's law. Homosexuality becomes thinkable only as the forbidden and sadomasochistic exchange between intergenerational male partners. This prohibition is thus a production, one that takes place through reductive and exclusionary principles that regulate the thinkability or imaginability of homosexuality itself. In a sense, lesbian sexuality is not even thought of as the forbidden, for to be forbidden is still to be produced as a prohibited or censored object; whereas male homosexuality is thought as the forbidden, lesbian sexuality cannot even enter into the parameters of thought itself; lesbianism is here the phantasm of the phantasm. It would be naive, however, to assume that the Helms amendment, though phantasmatically obsessed with men, would not be deployed against depictions of female homoeroticism.[5] and that anyone in academics and in the arts who wishes to study representations of homosexuality or homoeroticism in the history of literature, in history, in popular culture, in sexology, in psychoanalysis, or even in the law, as I am doing now, will likewise now be ruled out of NEA and NEH funding.

By focusing on the homoeroticism of the photographs, the anxiety over interracial homo- and heterosexual exchange is contained and permanently deferred. The naked Black men characterized by Mapplethorpe engage a certain racist romanticism of Black men's excessive physicality and sexual readiness, their photographic currency as a sexual sign. Perhaps the most offensive dimension of Mapplethorpe's work, it is never that which is explicitly named as the offense by Helms; the fear of miscegenation operates tacitly here as well, disavowed, contained, and deferred by the stated spectre of "homoeroticism" or the generalized possibility of "individuals engaged in sex acts."

In a paradoxical alliance with Dworkin, I am writing here in opposition to what I take to be violent and violating representations; what Helms performs with the help of MacKinnon/Dworkin is a kind of representational violence. But whereas Dworkin would counter this violent reduction with a call for censorship, that is a restriction which can only displace and reroute the violence it seeks to forestall. If prohibitions invariably *produce and proliferate* the representations that they seek to control, then the political task is to promote a proliferation of representations, sites of discursive production, which might then contest the authoritative production produced by the prohibitive law. This kind of preemptive exclusion is enacted in the name of a prohibition that seeks to end the ostensibly injurious power of representation;

and yet, this prohibition can work only through producing and proliferating precisely the kind of reductive and phantasmatic representations that it seeks to forestall.

In the *History of Sexuality: Volume I*, Foucault argues for the provisional political efficacy of a "reverse-discourse" that is inadvertently mobilized by the very regulatory structures that would render that reversal impossible. The example he uses is, not coincidentally, that of "homosexuality." The juridical discourse of the medico-legal alliance at the end of the nineteenth century, he argues, seeks to establish homosexuality as a medical category and to institute homo-sexuality as a kind of identity.[6] Fortuitously, the institution of the category of homosexuality provides a discursive site for the homosexual resistance to its pathologization; hence, homosexuals now have the discursive occasion to resignify and valorize the terms of that identity and to organize against the medico-juridical alliance. Foucault's analysis presupposes that the discursive life of such identity categories always exceeds the purposes to which they are originally put; in this sense, Foucault reappropriates Nietzsche's notion of a "sign-chain" in which the original purposes to which a discursive sign is devised are reversed and proliferated throughout the history of its usages [hence, also the necessity of a "genealogy" to trace the meanderings of such terms, rather than a unilinear "history"]. The very uncontrollability of dis-course, its penchant for superseding and reversing the purposes for which it is instrumentally deployed, provides for the possibility, if not the necessity, of regulatory regimes producing the very terms by which their purposes are undermined.

Although Foucault points to "homosexuality" as subject to a "reverse-discourse," that is, a reappropriation and resignification, it is clear that for "reversal" to become politically undermining, it must be followed by "proliferation," where what is proliferated is not the self-identical figure of homosexuality, but, rather, a set of figures which refuse to replicate each other faithfully. In other words, it is not enough to effect a dialectical exchange whereby the group consolidated by the term "homosexuality," or for that matter, "feminism," tries to control the meaning of that term; such a tactic could only replace a negatively signified identity term with an equally reduc-tive, but positively signified identity term. In opposition to the prohibition of Mapplethorpe and his figures and to the homophobic figuration of Mapplethorpe, *ACT UP* in San Francisco produced and distributed a wide array of Mapplethorpe photographs as posters which counseled gay men on safe sex practices. The resistance to Helms cannot be the regulatory production of a singular or unified figure of homosexuality, for that figuration can always and only suppress the proliferation of non-self-identical semantic sites of homosexuality that punctuate the contemporary discursive field. Although "proliferation" is often understood exclusively as the depoliticizing effect of late capitalism, it is also precisely the possibility of deploying politically that domain of discursive excess produced by the identity categories at the center of a reverse-discourse. The singular and authoritative homophobic figuration of homosexuality, which works through the violence of a synthesis (all gay men are "x") and an erasure of multiple cultural formations of lesbianisms and which defers and contains racist erotic fears, cannot be opposed by remaining within the terms of that binary fight, but by displacing the binary itself through producing again and again precisely the discursive *uncontrollability* of the terms that are suppressed by regulatory violence.

In a sense, I have been arguing some very different points, using fantasy and the phantasmatic as a point of critical departure. The fixed subject-position of "women" functions within the feminist discourse in favor of censorship as a phantasm that suppresses multiple and open possibilities for identification, a phantasm, in other words, that refuses its own possibilities as fantasy through its self-stabilization as the real. Feminist theory and politics cannot regulate the representation of "women" without producing that very "representation"; and if that is in some sense a discursive inevitability of representational politics, then the task must be to safeguard the open productivity of those categories, whatever the risk.

As I have tried to argue elsewhere (*Gender Trouble*), every description of the "we" will always do more than describe; it will constitute and construct an imaginary unity and contrived totality, a phantasmatic ideal, which makes the "representability" of the we into a permanent impossibility. This might be understood linguistically as the inevitable performativity of the representational claim; the categories of identity instate or bring into "the real" the very phenomenon that they claim to name only after the fact. This is not a simple performative, but one which operates through exclusionary operations that come back to haunt the very claim of representability that it seeks to make.

The Helms amendment reenforces the category of identity as a site of political crisis; who and what wields the power to define the homosexual real? This kind of crisis has been produced as well by the anti-pornography discourse: what is the figure of "women" to which it objects, and the figure of "women" in the name of whom the objection is articulated? How does the analysis of pornography delimit in advance the terms of identity to be contested? My recommendation is not to solve this crisis of identity politics, but to proliferate and intensify this crisis. This failure to master the foundational identity categories of feminism or gay politics is a political necessity, a failure to be safeguarded for political reasons.[7] The task is not to resolve or restrain the tension, the crisis, the phantasmatic excess induced by the term, but to affirm

identity categories as sites of inevitable rifting, in which the phantasmatic fails
to preempt the linguistic prerogative of the real. It is the incommensurability of
the phantasmatic and the real that requires at this political juncture to be
safeguarded; the task, then, is to make that rift, that insistent rifting, into the
persistently ungrounded ground from which feminist discourse emerges.

In other words, it is important to risk losing control of the ways in which the
categories of women and homosexuality are represented, even in legal terms,
to safeguard the uncontrollability of the signified. In my view, it is in the very
proliferation and deregulation of such representations – in the production of a
chaotic multiplicity of representations – that the authority and prevalence of
the reductive and violent imagery produced by Jesse Helms and other pornographic industries will lose their monopoly on the ontological indicator, the
power to define and restrict the terms of political identity.

Notes

I thank Karin Cope, Ruth Leys, and Jeff Nunokawa for helping me to think through
this essay.

1   In the original version of the Helms amendment, an anti-discrimination clause was
    added to an obscenity clause. In a sense, the Helms bill imitates the MacKinnon/
    Dworkin strategy to restrict or censor pornographical materials through (a)
    broadening obscenity statutes and (b) establishing pornography as an instance of
    discrimination on the basis of sex. In the original version of the Helms amendment,
    the following clause qualifies the kinds of materials to be excluded from federal
    funding: "that denigrates, debases or reviles a person, group, or class of citizens on
    the basis of race, creed, sex, handicap, age or national origin." Here Helms clearly
    appeals to the legal precedent of construing pornography as sex discrimination. In a
    subsequently deleted section, it appears that he wanted to extend the MacKinnon
    formulation in such a way that materials offensive to members of certain religions
    could also be construed as discriminatory actions.
        In an amendment to Title 7, Chapter 139 the Minneapolis code of ordinances
    (#385.130), discrimination on the basis of sex is said to include "sexual harassment
    and pornography"; in an included special finding, the amendment reads in part:
    "Pornography is a systematic practice of exploitation and subordination based on
    sex which differentially harms women. This harm includes dehumanization, sexual
    exploitation, physical injury, intimidation, and inferiority presented as entertain-
    ment ... [it] promote[s] rape, battery and prostitution ... "; "pornography" is de-
    fined as the "graphic sexually explicit subordination of women": this phrase will be
    reworked slightly by the Helms amendment.
        Obscenity in the Helms amendment is extended to include depictions of
    "Homoeroticism, sadomasochism and child molestation" as well as "individuals

engaged in sex acts": in the Minneapolis code, "obscene" is given the following legal definition: (i) That the average person, applying contemporary community standards, would find that the work, taken as a whole, appeals to the prurient interest in sex of the average person; (ii) That the work depicts or describes, in a patently offensive manner, sexual conduct specifically defined by the clause (b); [clause "b" includes such acts as sexual intercourse, "actual or simulated," "sado-masochistic abuse," "masturbation," "physical contact or simulated physical contact with the clothed or unclothed pubic areas or buttocks of a human male or female ... "]; (iii) That the work, taken as a whole, lacks serious literary, artistic, political or scientific value." The Indianapolis code (#20.120), reads similarly, but under "b" reads, "the material depicts or describes patently offensive representations or descriptions of ultimate sex acts, normal or perverted, actual or simulated, or patently offensive representations or descriptions of masturbation, excretory functions, and lewd exhibitions of the genitals."

The amendment "a" to the Minneapolis Title 7 declares that pornography is discrimination against women. The Indianapolis ordinance, which was passed in 1984, was found unconstitutional in federal court and rescinded.

2   *"Mais le fantasme n'est pas l'objet du désir, il est la scène. Dans le fantasme, en effet, le sujet ne vise pas l'objet désiré ou son signe, le figure lui-même pris dans la séquence d'images. Il ne se représente pas l'objet désiré mais il est représenté participant à la scène, sans que, dans les formes les plus proches du fantasme originaire, une place puisse lui être assignée (d'où le danger, dans la cure, des interprétations qui y prétendent). Conséquences: tout en étant toujours présent dans le fantasme, le sujet peut y être sous une forme désubjectivée, c'est-à-dire dans la syntaxe même de la séquence en question."* Fantasme 74.

3   Significantly, the determination of obscenity in US law since the advent of obscenity statutes in 1957 has almost always appealed to "contemporary community standards," a phrase that is used in the Minneapolis and Indianapolis ordinances and which emerged in the recent controversies over the Mapplethorpe show in Cincinnati courts. The MacKinnon tactic has been, it seems, to extend the obscenity statutes by including pornography as part of sex discrimination. The effect of extending anti-discrimination statutes is not only (a) to diversify the legal tactics through which the putative injuries of pornography can be redressed by establishing sex discrimination as a separate basis for complaint, but (b) to insure that the anti-pornography statutes are not applied differentially against protected groups like homosexuals. Hence, the anti-discrimination clause in the Minneapolis bill states clearly that "affectional preference" is protected against discrimination, and even goes so far as to protect "transsexuals" against discrimination via pornography.

The anti-discrimination statute also can be understood to provide a legal safe-guard against the invocation of the obscenity statute for discriminatory purposes. Insofar as the obscenity statute seeks recourse to "community standards" which would almost always (and presently in Cincinnati) culminate in the judgment that any and all representations of homosexuality or homoeroticism are obscene, the extended anti-discrimination clause seeks to protect the rights, which obviously include free speech, of homosexual minorities and others, even when "community standards" would find the self-representational "free speech" of those groups to fall unconditionally under the rubric of obscenity.

In a sense, the recourse to these two different legal bases, obscenity and discrimination, always risks a collision between them. And in the case in which "community standards" *conflict* with the protection of homosexual free speech, community standards, precisely because the sanction of the community outweighs the constitutional claims of the minorities, will invariably win. Moreover, if depictions are construed as discriminatory and injurious, then the legal precedent has been set (and exploited now by Helms) to claim that any and all depictions of homoeroticism are injurious to those whose moral sensibilities are offended in the process of viewing these depictions. Hence, Helms sought (unsuccessfully) to establish that the depiction of homoeroticism et al. *discriminates* against members of certain unspecified religions. Realizing, it seems, that this very statute might discriminate on the basis of religion, he supplies an absurd supplement that protects the rights of members of non-religions as well.

4   In the Mapplethorpe exhibition, "The Perfect Moment," which was to show at various art spaces partially financed by the National Endowment for the Arts, and which serves as the basis for the Helms criticism, there are two photographs of children. One, "Honey" (1976), is a picture of a young girl, around five years old, sitting on a bench with one leg up and one leg crossed in front of her. She is looking somewhat indifferently into the camera; she has no underpants on, and the thin line that marks the closed labia revealed by her sitting position is marked primarily by its unremarkability. An aesthetic formalist and photographic realist, Mapplethorpe's photos work to enforce principles of symmetry and linear order. The vertical line that is the labia is paralleled on either side by the vertical lines of the sides of the bench, by the line between her arm and her dress and, predictably, the side-lines of the canvas itself. The focal point of the photograph is effectively distributed across these lines, and the labia line effectively shields the vagina from view.

The other photograph is of a boy, seven or eight years old, "Jesse McBride" (1976). It is equally languorous, suggesting as in the above the final unremarkability (and perhaps innocence) of nudity. As in the above, this photo of Jesse sitting nude on the top of a velvet chair, is an exemplar of the symmetrical distribution of formal elements. His two arms rest comfortably against the velvet chair, his two legs fall against the chair, and his small and decidedly *un*erect penis lounges peacefully against the velvet as well. I would call this composition, "appendages against velvet." Both figures look straight into the camera, without shame or sexuality, as if to ask (for us now), "what is the big deal?" In a sense, the photos engage a pornographic convention only to debunk it: the search for eroticism is rerouted and diffused through the insistence on formal symmetry. In this way, the photos of children parallel and extend the photographic technique of Mapplethorpe's still life photos of flowers.

5   Recently it seems that letters emanating from certain Congressional quarters inquiring into the federal funding of lesbian poets and writers have been circulating "confidentially." Mab Segrest and others have begun to wage a lesbian-based campaign against Helms.

6   Prior to this move, he argues, there are various homosexual acts and pleasures, but they are not yet taken as symptoms or evidence of a certain typological identity. The forces that would pathologize homosexuality institute that category as an identity, a move which invokes the distinction between "normal" identity *qua* heterosexuality and deviant or deformed identity, now occupied by the (male) homosexual.

7   In other words, I want to resist both the claim that feminism is being "ruined" by its fragmentations, a position which implicitly or explicitly establishes the dispensability of some crucial constituency, and the claim that fragmentation ought to be overcome through the postulation of a phantasmatically unified ideal.

Works Cited

Bartkowski, Frances. 1989. *Feminist Utopias*. Lincoln: University of Nebraska Press.

Butler, Judith. 1990. *Gender Trouble: Feminism and the Subversion of Identity*. New York: Routledge.

Dworkin, Andrea. 1981. *Pornography: Men Possessing Women*. New York: Seal.

English, Dierdre. 1980. "The Politics of Porn: Can Feminists Walk the Line?" *Mother Jones* (April): 20–50.

Haraway, Donna. 1989. *Primate Visions: Gender, Race, and Nature in the World of Modern Science*. New York: Routledge.

HR 2788 and HR 4825. Department of Interior and Related Agencies Appropriations bill for FY 1990. 1989.

Indianapolis code of ordinances #20. 117–20.150. 1984.

Laplanche, Jean, and J.-B. Pontalis. 1985. *Fantasme originaire*. Paris: Hachette.

——— 1986. *Formations of Fantasy*, ed. Victor Burgin, James Donald, and Cora Kaplan. London: Methuen.

——— 1967. *Vocabulaire de la psychoanalyse*. Paris: Presses Universitaires de France.

"Obscenity Measure Approved." 1989. *Washington Post* 21 Sept.: 1.

Public Law 101–121 (103 Stat 701). 1989.

Rose, Jacqueline. 1987. *Sexuality in the Field of Vision*. London: Verso.

"Senate Votes to Bar U.S. Support of 'Obscene or Indecent' Artwork." 1989. *New York Times* 27 July: 1.

Title 7. Ch. 139. Minneapolis code of ordinances #385.130. amendment "a." 1987.

7

Endangered/Endangering: Schematic Racism and White Paranoia (1993)

Introduction

Butler's article appeared in a collection of essays published shortly after the brutal beating of Rodney King by Los Angeles police in 1991 and the announcement of the trial verdict in 1992. In her contribution, Butler focuses on the amateur video in which a defenseless King is shown being brutalized by police. According to Butler, the jurors who watched this video during the trial were not engaged in a simple act of seeing, but, their "readings" (the verb Butler prefers to "seeing" because it makes no implicit claim to objectivity or neutrality) were constrained in advance by the racist, homophobic episteme in which they took place. As in *Bodies That Matter*, the existence of a prediscursive body is rejected, and it is assumed that there is no unmarked field of vision through which "black" and "white" bodies are neutrally viewed. Instead, the body as "read" in the video is the *effect* of what Butler calls the phantasmatic production of the white violence and homophobic paranoia which are projected onto the black male body – homophobic because as Butler points out, the white man's racist fear of the black male body is generated by the possibility of sexual exchange. This is race in the field of vision, the seeing or rather, the reading, of blackness which occurs within what Frantz Fanon calls the historico-racial schema. Indeed, the saturated discursive field determines in advance how the black body will be perceived and constructed by the white viewer.

In Butler's article on the photographer Robert Mapplethorpe (pp. 183–203), fantasy is characterized as a means of agency which may convert the putative "degradation" of pornography into a scene of feminist or queer subversion. There is no such force at work during the Rodney King trial and its aftermath, since the "black bodies" Butler describes seem powerless to resist the fears and fantasies which the paranoid homophobic white viewer projects onto them. Here, the onus seems to lie with readers and jurors, who must learn how to recognize and read what Butler calls "a specific social modality of repetition compulsion" in which racist and homophobic impulses are projected onto the black body in a racially and sexually saturated episteme.

From Robert Gooding-Williams (ed.), *Reading Rodney King/Reading Urban Uprising*, pp. 15–22. New York: Routledge, 1993. Reproduced by permission of Routledge, an imprint of Taylor & Francis Books, Inc.

The defense attorneys for the police in the Rodney King case made the argument that the policemen were endangered, and that Rodney King was the source of that danger. The argument they made drew from many sources: comments he made, acts he refused to perform on command, and the highly publicized video recording taken on the spot and televised widely before and during the trial. During the trial, the video was shown at the same time that the defense offered a commentary, and so we are left to presume that some convergence of word and picture produced the "evidence" for the jurors in the case. The video shows a man being brutally beaten, repeatedly, and without visible resistance; and so the question is, How could this video be used as evidence that the body being beaten was *itself* the source of danger, the threat of violence, and, further, that the beaten body of Rodney King bore an intention to injure, and to injure precisely those police who either wielded the baton against him or stood encircling him? In the Simi Valley courtroom, what many took to be incontrovertible evidence *against* the police was presented instead to establish police vulnerability, that is, to support the contention that Rodney King was endangering the police. Later, a juror reported that she believed that Rodney King was in "total control" of the situation. How was this feat of interpretation achieved?

That it *was* achieved is not the consequence of ignoring the video, but, rather, of reproducing the video within a racially saturated field of visibility. If racism pervades white perception, structuring what can and cannot appear within the horizon of white perception, then to what extent does it interpret in advance "visual evidence"? And how, then, does such "evidence" have to be read, and read publicly, *against* the racist disposition of the visible which will prepare and achieve its own inverted perceptions under the rubric of "what is seen"?

In the above, without hesitation, I wrote, "the video shows a man being brutally beaten." And yet, it appears that the jury in Simi Valley claimed that what they "saw" was a body threatening the police, and saw in those blows the reasonable actions of police officers in self-defense. From these two interpretations emerges, then, a contest within the visual field, a crisis in the certainty of what is visible, one that is produced through the saturation and schematization of that field with the inverted projections of white paranoia. The visual representation of the black male body being beaten on the street by the policemen and their batons was taken up by that racist interpretive framework to construe King as the *agent* of violence, one whose agency is phantasmatically implied as the narrative precedent and antecedent to the frames that are shown. Watching King, the white paranoiac forms a sequence of narrative intelligibility that consolidates the racist figure of the black man: "He *had* threatened them, and now he is being justifiably restrained." "If they cease hitting him, he *will* release his violence, and now is being justifiably restrained." King's palm turned away from his body, held above his own head, is read *not* as self-protection but as the incipient moments of a physical threat.

How do we account for this *reversal* of gesture and intention in terms of a racial schematization of the visible field? Is this a specific transvaluation of agency proper to a racialized episteme? And does the possibility of such a reversal call into question whether what is "seen" is not always already in part a question of what a certain racist episteme produces as the visible? For if the jurors came to see in Rodney King's body a danger *to* the law, then this "seeing" requires to be read as that which was culled, cultivated, regulated – indeed, policed – in the course of the trial. This is not a simple seeing, an act of direct perception, but the racial production of the visible, the workings of racial constraints on what it means to "see." Indeed, the trial calls to be read not only as instruction in racist modes of seeing but as a repeated and ritualistic production of blackness (a further instance of what Ruth Gilmore, in describing the video beating, calls an act of "nation building"). This is a seeing which is a reading, that is, a *contestable* construal, but one which nevertheless passes itself off as "seeing," a reading which became for that white community, and for countless others, the same as seeing.

If what is offered here over and against what the jury saw is a different seeing, a different ordering of the visible, it is one that is also contestable – as we saw in the temporary interpretive triumph of the defense attorneys' construal of King as endangering. To claim that King's victimization is *manifestly* true is to assume that one is presenting the case to a set of subjects who *know how to see*; to think that the video "speaks for itself" is, of course, for many of us, obviously true. But if the field of the visible is racially contested terrain, then it will be politically imperative to read such videos aggressively, to repeat and publicize such readings, if only to further an antiracist hegemony over the visual field. It may appear at first that over and against this heinous failure to see police brutality, it is necessary to restore the visible as the sure ground of evidence. But what the trial and its horrific conclusions teach us is that there is no simple recourse to the visible, to visual evidence, that it still and always calls to be read, that it is already a reading, and that in order to establish the injury on the basis of the visual evidence, an aggressive reading of the evidence is necessary.

It is not, then, a question of negotiating between what is "seen," on the one hand, and a "reading" which is imposed upon the visual evidence, on the other. In a sense, the problem is even worse: to the extent that there is a racist organization and disposition of the visible, it will work to circumscribe what qualifies as visual evidence, such that it is in some cases impossible to establish the "truth" of racist brutality through recourse to visual evidence. For when the visual is fully schematized by racism, the "visual evidence" to which one refers will always and only refute the conclusions based upon it; for it is possible within this racist episteme that no black person can seek recourse to the visible as the sure ground of evidence. Consider that it *was* possible to draw a line of inference from the black male body motionless and beaten on the street to the conclusion that this very body was in "total control," rife with "dangerous intention." The visual field is not neutral to the question of race; it is itself a racial formation, an episteme, hegemonic and forceful.

> In the white world the man of color encounters difficulties in the development of his bodily schema. Consciousness of the body is solely a negating activity. It is a third-person consciousness. The body is surrounded by an atmosphere of certain uncertainty. I know that if I want to smoke, I shall have to reach out my right arm and take the pack of cigarettes lying at the other end of the table. The matches, however, are in the drawer on the left, and I shall have to lean back slightly. And all of these movements are made not out of habit but out of implicit knowledge. A slow composition of my *self* as a body in the middle of a spatial and temporal world – which seems to be the schema. . . . Below the corporeal schema I had sketched [there is] a historico-racial schema. The elements I had used had been provided for me . . . by the other, the white man, who had woven me out of a thousand details, anecdotes, stories. I thought that what I had in hand was to construct a physiological self, to balance space, to localize sensations, and here I was called on for more.
>   "Look, a Negro!" It was an external stimulus that flicked over me as I passed by. I made a tight smile.
>   "Look, a Negro!" It was true. It amused me.
>   "Look, a Negro!" The circle was drawing a bit tighter.
>   I made no secret of my amusement.
>   "Mama, see the Negro! I'm frightened!" Frightened!"
>   Frightened! Now they were beginning to be afraid of me. I made up my mind to laugh myself to tears but laughter had become impossible.[1]

Frantz Fanon offers here a description of how the black male body is constituted through fear, and through a naming and a seeing: "Look, a Negro!" where the "look" is both a pointing and a seeing, a pointing out what there is to see, a pointing which circumscribes a dangerous body, a racist indicative which relays its own danger to the body to which it points. Here the "pointing" is not only an indicative, but the schematic foreshadowing of an accusation, one which carries the performative force to constitute that danger which it fears and defends against. In his clearly masculinist theory, Fanon demarcates the subject as the black male, and the Other as the white male, and perhaps we ought for the moment to let the masculinism of the scene stay in place; for there is within the white male's racist fear of the black male body a clear anxiety over the possibility of sexual exchange; hence, the repeated references to Rodney King's "ass" by the surrounding policemen, and the homophobic circumscription of that locus of sodomy as a kind of threat.

In Fanon's recitation of the racist interpellation, the black body is circumscribed as dangerous, prior to any gesture, any raising of the hand, and the infantilized white reader is positioned in the scene as one who is helpless in relation to that black body, as one definitionally in need of protection by his/her mother or, perhaps, the police. The fear is that some physical distance will be crossed, and the virgin sanctity of whiteness will be endangered by that proximity. The police are thus structurally placed to protect whiteness against violence, where violence is the imminent action of that black male body. And because within this imaginary schema, the police protect whiteness, their own violence cannot be read as violence; because the black male body, prior to any video, is the site and source of danger, a threat, the police effort to subdue this body, even if in advance, is justified regardless of the circumstances. Or rather, the conviction of that justification rearranges and orders the circumstances to fit that conclusion.

What struck me on the morning after the verdict was delivered were reports which reiterated the phantasmatic production of "intention," the intention inscribed in and read off Rodney King's frozen body on the street, his intention to do harm, to endanger. The video was used as "evidence" to support the claim that the frozen black male body on the ground receiving blows was himself producing those blows, about to produce them, was himself the imminent threat of a blow and, therefore, was himself responsible for the blows he received. That body thus received those blows in return for the ones it was about to deliver, the blows which were that body in its essential gestures, even as the one gesture that body can be seen to make is to raise its palm outward to stave off the blows against it. According to this racist episteme, he is hit in exchange for the blows he never delivered, but which he is, by virtue of his blackness, always about to deliver.

Here we can see the splitting of that violent intentionality off from the police actions, and the investment of those very intentions in the one who receives the blows. How is this splitting and attribution of violent intentionality possible? And how was it *reproduced* in the defense attorneys' racist pedagogy, thus implicating the defense attorneys in a *sympathetic* racist affiliation with the police, inviting the jurors to join in that community of victimized victimizers? The attorneys proceeded through cultivating an identification with white paranoia in which a white community is always and only protected by the police, against a threat which Rodney King's body emblematizes, quite apart from any action it can be said to perform or appear ready to perform. This is an action that the black male body is always already performing within that white racist imaginary, has always already performed prior to the emergence of any video. The identification with police paranoia culled, produced, and consolidated in that jury is one way of reconstituting a white racist imaginary that postures *as if* it were the unmarked frame of the visible field, laying claim to the authority of "direct perception."

The interpretation of the video in the trial had to work the possible sites of identification it offered: Rodney King, the surrounding police, those actively beating him, those witnessing him, the gaze of the camcorder and, by implication, the white bystander who perhaps feels moral outrage, but who is also watching from a distance, suddenly installed at the scene as the undercover newsman. In a sense, the jury could be convinced of police innocence only through a tactical orchestration of those identifications, for in some sense, they *are* the white witness, separated from the ostensible site of black danger by a circle of police; they *are* the police, enforcers of the law, encircling that body, beating him, once again. They are perhaps King as well, but whitewashed: the blows he suffers are taken to be the blows they *would* suffer if the police were not protecting them from him. Thus, the physical danger in which King is recorded is transferred to them; they identify with that vulnerability, but construe it as their own, the vulnerabilty of whiteness, thus refiguring him as the threat. The danger that they believe themselves always to be in, by virtue of their whiteness (whiteness as an episteme operates despite the existence of two nonwhite jurors). This completes the circuit of paranoia: the projection of their own aggression, and the subsequent regarding of that projection as an external threat.

The kind of "seeing" that the police enacted, and the kind of "seeing" that the jury reenacted, is one in which a further violence is performed by the disavowal and projection of that violent beating. The actual blows against Rodney King are understood to be fair recompense, indeed, defenses against, the dangers that are "seen" to emanate from his body. Here "seeing" and attributing are indissoluble. Attributing violence to the object of violence is part of the very mechanism that recapitulates violence, and that makes the jury's "seeing" into a complicity with that police violence.

The defense attorneys broke the video down into "stills," freezing the frame, so that the gesture, the raised hand, is torn from its temporal place in the visual narrative. The video is not only violently decontextualized, but violently recontextualized; it is played without a simultaneous sound track which, had it existed, would have been littered with racial and sexual slurs against Rodney King. In the place of reading that testimony alongside the video, the defense attorneys offered the frozen frame, the magnification of the raised hand as the hyperbolic figure of racial threat, interpreted again and again as a gesture foreshadowing violence, a gesture about to be violent, the first sign of violence, violence itself. Here the anticipatory "seeing" is clearly a "reading," one which reenacts the disavowal and paranoia that enable and defend the brutality itself.

Over against this reading is required an aggressive counterreading, one which the prosecutors failed to perform, one which might expose through a different kind of reiteration of what Fanon called "the historico-racial schema" through which the "seeing" of blackness takes place.[2] In other words, it is necessary to read not only for the "event" of violence, but for the racist schema that orchestrates and interprets the event, which splits the violent intention off from the body who wields it and attributes it to the body who receives it.

If the raised gesture can be read as evidence that supports the contention that Rodney King is "in control," "totally" of the entire scene, indeed, as evidence of his own threatening intentions, then a circuit is phantasmatically produced whereby King is the origin, the intention, and the object of the selfsame brutality. In other words, if it is *his* violence which impels the causal sequence, and it is his body which receives the blows, then, in effect, he beats himself: he is the beginning and the end of the violence, he brings it on himself. But if the brutality which he is said to embody or which the racial schema ritualistically fabricates as the incipient and inevitable "intention" of his body, if this brutality is that of the white police, then this is a brutality that the police enact and displace *at once*, and Rodney King, who appears for them as the origin and potential instrument of all danger in the scene, has become reduced to a phantasm of white racist aggression, a phantasm that *belongs* to that white racist aggression as the externalized figure of its own distortion. He becomes, within that schema, nothing other than the site at which that racist violence fears and beats the specter of its own rage. In this sense, the circuit of violence attributed to Rodney King is itself the circuit of white racist violence which violently disavows itself only to brutalize the specter that embodies its own intention. This is the phantasm that it ritualistically produces at the site of the racialized other.

Is it precisely because this black male body is on the ground that the beating becomes intensified? For if white paranoia is also to some degree homophobia, then is this not a brutalization performed as a desexualization or, rather, as a punishment for a conjectured or desired sexual aggression? The image of the police standing over Rodney King with their batons might be read as a sexual degradation which ends up miming and inverting the imagined scene of sexual violation that it appears to want and to loathe; the police thus deploy the "props" and "positions" of that scene in the service of its aggressive denial.

The reversal and displacement of dangerous intention mentioned above continued to be reiterated after the verdict: first, in the violence that took place in Los Angeles in which the majority of individuals killed were black and in the streets, killed by the police, thus replaying, intensifying, and extending the scope of the violence against Rodney King. The intensification of police violence against people of color can be read as evidence that the verdict was taken as further state sanction for racist police violence; second, in remarks made by Mr. Bush on the day after the verdict was announced in which he condemned public violence, noting first the lamentability of public violence against property(!), and holding responsible, once again, those black bodies on the street, as if the figure of the brutalized black body had, as anticipated, risen and raised its forces against the police. The groups involved in street violence thus were construed paradoxically as the originators of a set of killings that may well have left those very bodies dead, thus exonerating the police and the state *again*, and performing an identification with the phantasmatic endangerment of the white community in Simi Valley; a third, in the media scanning of street violence, the refusal to read how and where and why fires were lit, stores burned, indeed, what was being articulated in and through that violence. The bestialization of the crowds, consolidated by scanning techniques which appeared to "hunt down" people of color and figure their violence as "senseless" or "barbaric," thus recapitulated the racist production of the visual field.

If the jury's reading of the video reenacted the phantasmatic scene of the crime, reiterating and re-occupying the always already endangered status of the white person on the street, and the response to the reading, now inscribed as verdict, was to re-cite the charge and to reenact and enlarge the crime, it achieved this in part through a transposition and fabrication of dangerous intention. This is hardly a full explanation of the causes of racist violence, but it does, perhaps, constitute a moment in its production. It can perhaps be described as a form of white paranoia which projects the intention to injure that it itself enacts, and then repeats that projection on increasingly larger scales, a specific social modality of repetition compulsion, which we still need to learn how to read, and which as a "reading," performed in the name of law, has obvious and consequential effects.

Notes

1 Frantz Fanon, "The Fact of Blackness," in *Black Skin; White Masks*, trans. Charles Lam Markmann (New York: Grove Press, 1967), 111–12.
2 I do not mean to suggest by "white racist episteme" a static and closed system of seeing, but rather an historically self-renewing practice of reading which, when left uninterrupted, tends to extend its hegemonic force. Clearly, terms like "white paranoia" do not describe in any totalizing way "how white people see," but are offered here as theoretical hyperboles which are meant to advance a strategically aggressive counter-reading.

8

Burning Acts, Injurious Speech
(1997)

Introduction

What are the consequences of what Butler calls "the decentering of the subject" in legal cases, particularly those involving hate speech and "obscenity"? In *Gender Trouble* Butler deploys Friedrich Nietzsche's insight that "there is no 'being' behind doing, acting, becoming; the 'doer' is merely a fiction imposed on the doing – the doing itself is everything."[1] If this is the case, then who or what should the law prosecute when cases of (for example) race hate are brought to court? Moreover, if we agree with Butler and Derrida that authorial intentions are not binding and that contexts are "non-saturable," then the notion that certain words are necessarily and inevitably wounding is thrown into doubt. Seizing on J. L. Austin's unstable distinction between constative and performative utterances, in *Excitable Speech* Butler characterizes *How To Do Things With Words* as "an amusing catalogue of failed performatives." *Excitable Speech*, on the other hand, is an attempt to maximize the subversive potential of failed performatives which may *never* be "successful" in enacting what they name.

"Excitable speech" is a legal term referring to utterances deemed to be beyond their speaker's control, but since utterances take place within discursive contexts which precede and exceed the utterer, Butler asserts that all speech is excitable. As in her previous work, the speaking subject in *Excitable Speech* is a "belated metalepsis," i.e. a substitution which doesn't precede discourse but which is the effect of discourses which precede it. As before, Butler's Foucauldianism leads her to conclude that in the contexts of hate speech and obscenity, the law produces the subject it subsequently prosecutes – indeed, it produces that subject in order to prosecute it. *Bodies That Matter* began to explore the subversive potential of failed interpellations, and in chapter 1 of *Excitable Speech* Butler extends this discussion by returning to the Althusserian scene. Since we know from *Bodies That Matter* that interpellation is not "a simple performative," it follows that the subject does not have to respond to the policeman's call by obediently turning around and recognizing itself. Indeed, the "excitability" of speech means that there are any number of subversive and radical ways of turning around and responding to the call

Chapter 1, pp. 43–69, 169–73 (notes) from *Excitable Speech: A Politics of the Performative*. New York: Routledge, 1997. Reproduced by permission of Routledge, an imprint of Taylor & Francis Books, Inc.

of the law. Unlike Althusser, Butler does not take for granted the sovereign power of the interpellative utterance to bring into being what it names. Instead, she complements her acknowledgment that naming is constitutive of the subject with Foucault's insight that "[t]he time of discourse is not the time of the subject." This disjunction between discourse and the linguistically constituted subject leads Butler to posit a revised version of Althusserian interpellation in which the subject is still "hailed" but does not have to turn around in order to be constituted as a subject.

Whereas Althusser assumes the "divine" performative power of the policeman's voice, Butler characterizes the interpellative call as an infelicitous performative "which regularly misses its mark." Furthermore, *Excitable Speech* begins to probe the subject's necessary attachment to subjection, in other words, her/his desire to turn around when hailed by the law or its agent, an issue she considers at more length in chapter 4 of *The Psychic Life of Power* (reprinted below, pp. 000–0). If interpellation is a failed performative, Butler also doubts that words "do" what they say in other respects, particularly in the contexts of hate speech, so-called obscenity, and gay self-expression in the military, the three types of speech with which she is centrally concerned in *Excitable Speech*. "What gives hate speech the power to constitute the subject with such efficacy?" she asks. To question the assumption that hate speech (or any kind of speech for that matter) is always "effective" is not an attempt to minimize the pain that is suffered as a consequence of insult, nor does it remove responsibility from the speaker; rather, it is to suggest that the possibility of failure will provide what Butler calls "the condition of a critical response." Although she accepts that words *do* wound and that there may be occasions when recourse to the law will be necessary, Butler advocates minimizing legal and state intervention in such cases, since this will tighten the controls exercised by law and state over what are deemed to be "acceptable" representations. Moreover, when the law *does* intervene, hate speech is re-cited and rehearsed in the court room by the legislators who are supposed to proscribe it. Power proliferates rather than merely prohibiting, an argument Butler also deploys in her article on Robert Mapplethorpe and the Helms Amendment (see pp. 183–203).

There is nothing "objective" or "neutral" about legal discourse in such cases, and the first chapter of *Excitable Speech*, "Burning Acts, Injurious Speech" (included below) focuses on the anti-gay prejudice and racism underlying the legal prosecution of cases of race hate and "obscenity." Whereas acts of race hate such as burning a cross on the lawn of a black family are deemed to be speech acts and therefore come under the protection of the First Amendment to the US Constitution, US courts of law have judged pornographic representations to be content-less, *not* speech but conduct – in other words "utterances" which "do" what they depict.[2] As Butler points out, what appears to be a tacit governmental sanction for racist violence contrasts tellingly and troublingly with the extension of legal controls over "obscenity" in cases of homosexual representation.

In the Mapplethorpe piece and in *Excitable Speech*, Butler pits herself against Catharine MacKinnon, Senator Jesse Helms, and other pro-censorship campaigners with the following three-pronged argument: (i) if speech is *not* conduct, then pornography does not constitute an act of violence against women – rather, it is an allegory of impossible heterosexuality; (ii) prohibition preserves rather than prevents the desire it aims to censor; (iii) no word or representation is inevitably wounding and all language is "excitable," vulnerable to subversive appropriation and re-citation. The third point is important, since it means that "excitable" speech is "ex-*citable*," i.e. it may be wrested from its prior contexts and cited so that it signifies against its utterer's intentions and expectations. In *Excitable Speech* as in *Bodies That Matter*, Butler engages Derrida's notion of the citationality and essential iterability of the sign. Rejecting Austin's view that context and convention fix and determine meaning, Butler asserts that there is potential for agency in what she calls the sign's unanticipated futures, while the force of the performative lies in its capacity to rupture. If performative utterances are not as successful as Austin and pro-censorship advocates claim they are (so that they are not really performatives as such), then these terms will be vulnerable to catachresis and appropriation, subversive future deployments which signal unanticipated futures for deconstructive thinking.

As before, subversive praxis rises out of oppression in what Butler calls "a social and cultural struggle of language...in which agency is derived from injury and injury countered through that very derivation." Speech may be resignified, and it is possible to effect linguistic and semantic breaks with prior histories and contexts. So if one accepts Foucault's postulation that "discourse is not life; its time is not yours," it will be possible to appropriate and re-cite a word such as "queer" in ways which will rob that word of its historic power to wound (this does not mean that subversive redeployment is a straight-forward matter, or that *all* words may be resignified in this way). Moreover, within a Foucauldian model of power as multiple, diffuse, and dispersed, it would be relatively futile to prosecute a single speaker who is neither in control of nor uniquely responsible for his/her ex-citable utterance. As always for Butler, agency begins where sovereignty wanes, and injurious language must be countered by insurrectionary speech in spite of the risk that such a repetition involves. Such resignifications will be the means of instituting (or "forcing" as Butler puts it) change.

Excitable Speech is divided into an introduction and four relatively short chapters. Chapter 1, "Burning Acts, Injurious Speech," in which Butler discusses the anomalous legal treatment of hate speech and "obscene" sexual representations, is reprinted here.

The title of J. L. Austin's *How to Do Things with Words* poses the question of performativity as what it means to say that "things might be done with words." The problem of performativity is thus immediately bound up with a question of transitivity. What does it mean for a word not only to name, but also in some sense to perform and, in particular, to perform what it names? On the one hand, it may seem that the word – for the moment we do not know which word or which kind of word – enacts what it names; where the "what" of "what it names" remains distinct from the name itself and the performance of that "what." After all, Austin's title questions how to do things *with* words, suggesting that words are instrumentalized in getting things done. Austin, of course, distinguishes between illocutionary and perlocutionary acts of speech, between actions that are performed by virtue of words, and those that are performed as a consequence of words. The distinction is tricky, and not always stable. According to the perlocutionary view, words are instrumental to the accomplishment of actions, but they are not themselves the actions which they help to accomplish. This form of the performative suggests that the words and the things done are in no sense the same. But according to his view of the illocutionary speech act, the name performs *itself*, and in the course of that performing becomes a thing done; the pronouncement is the act of speech at the same time that it is the speaking of an act. Of such an act, one cannot reasonably ask for a "referent," since the effect of the act of speech is not to refer beyond itself, but to perform itself, producing a strange enactment of linguistic immanence.

The title of Austin's manual, *How to Do Things With Words*, suggests that there is a perlocutionary kind of doing, a domain of things done, and then an instrumental field of "words," indeed, that there is also a deliberation that precedes that doing, and that the words will be distinct from the things that they do.

But what happens if we read that title with an emphasis on the illocutionary form of speech, asking instead what it might mean for a word "to do" a thing, where the doing is less instrumental than it is transitive. Indeed, what would it mean for a thing to be "done by" a word or, for that matter, for a thing to be "done in" by a word? When and where, in such a case, would such a thing become disentangled from the word by which it is done or done in, and where and when would that conjunction between word and thing appear indissoluble? If a word in this sense might be said to "do" a thing, then it appears that the word not only signifies a thing, but that this signification will also be an enactment of the thing. It seems here that the meaning of a performative act is to be found in this apparent coincidence of signifying and enacting.

And yet it seems that this "act-like" quality of the performative is itself an achievement of a different order, and that de Man was clearly on to something when he asked whether a trope is not animated at the moment when we claim that language "acts," that language posits itself in a series of distinct acts, and that its primary function might be understood as this kind of periodic acting. Significantly, I think, the common translation of Nietzsche's account of the metaleptic relation between doer and deed rests on a certain confusion about the status of the "deed." For even there, Nietzsche will claim that certain forms of morality require a subject and institute a subject as the consequence of that requirement. This subject will be installed as prior to the deed in order to assign blame and accountability for the painful effects of a certain action. A being is hurt, and the vocabulary that emerges to moralize that pain is one which isolates a subject as the intentional originator of an injurious deed; Nietzsche understands this, first, as the moralization by which pain and injury are rendered equivalent and, second, as the production of a domain of painful effects suffused with conjectured intention. At such a moment the subject is not only fabricated as the prior and causal origin of a painful effect that is recast as an injury, but the action whose effects are injurious is no longer an action, the continuous present of "a doing," but is reduced to a "singular act."

The following citation from *On the Genealogy of Morals* is usually read with an emphasis on the retroactive positing of the doer prior to the deed; but note that simultaneous with this retroactive positing is a moral resolution of a continuous "doing" into a periodic "deed": "there is no 'being' behind the doing, effecting, becoming: 'the doer' is merely a fiction added to the deed — the deed is everything." "... es gibt kein 'Sein' hinter dem Tun, Wirken, Werden; 'der Täter' ist zum Tun blos hinzugedichtet – das Tun ist alles." In the German, there is no reference to an "act" – *die Tat* – but only to a "doing" – *das Tun*, and to the word for a culprit or wrong-doer, *der Täter*, which translates merely as a "doer."[1] Here the very terms by which "doing" is retroactively fictionalized (*hinzugedichtet*) as the intentional effect of a "subject," establishes the notion of a "doer" primarily as a wrong-doer. Furthermore, in order to attribute accountability to a subject, an origin of action in that subject is fictively secured. In the place of a "doing" there appears the grammatical and juridical constraint on thought by which a subject is produced first and foremost as the accountable originator of an injurious deed. A moral causality is thus set up between the subject and its act such that both terms are separated off from a more temporally expansive "doing" that appears to be prior and oblivious to these moral requirements.

For Nietzsche, the subject appears only as a consequence of a demand for accountability; a set of painful effects is taken up by a moral framework that seeks to isolate the "cause" of those effects in a singular and intentional agent, a moral framework that operates through a certain economy of paranoid fabrication and efficiency. *The question, then, of who is accountable for a given injury precedes and initiates the subject, and the subject itself is formed through being nominated to inhabit that grammatical and juridical site.*

In a sense, for Nietzsche, the subject comes to be only within the requirements of a moral discourse of accountability. The requirements of blame figure the subject as the "cause" of an act. In this sense, there can be no subject without a blameworthy act, and there can be no "act" apart from a discourse of accountability and, according to Nietzsche, without an institution of punishment.

But here it seems that Nietzsche's account of subject-formation in *On the Genealogy of Morals* exposes something of its own impossibility. For if the "subject" is first animated through accusation, conjured as the origin of an injurious action, then it would appear that the accusation has to come *from* an interpellating performative that precedes the subject, one that presupposes the prior operation of an efficacious speaking. Who delivers that formative judgment? If there is an institution of punishment within which the subject is formed, is there not also a figure of the law who performatively sentences the subject into being? Is this not, in some sense, the conjecturing by Nietzsche of a prior and more powerful subject? Nietzsche's own language elides this problem by claiming that "der Täter ist zum Tun blos hinzugedichtet." This passive verb formation, "hinzugedichtet," poetically or fictively added on to, appended, or applied, leaves unclear who or what executes this fairly consequential formation.

If, on the occasion of pain, a subject is belatedly attributed to the act as its origin, and the act then attributed to the subject as its effect, this double attribution is confounded by a third, namely, the attribution of an injurious consequence to the subject and its act. In order to establish injurious consequence within the domain of accountability, is it necessary to install a subject, and to establish the singularity and discreteness of the act itself as well as the efficacy of the act to produce injury? If the injury can be traced to a specifiable act, it qualifies as an object of prosecution: it can be brought to court and held accountable. Does tracing the injury to the act of a subject and privileging of the juridical domain as the site to negotiate social injury not unwittingly stall the analysis of how precisely discourse produces injury by taking the subject and its spoken deed as the proper place of departure? And when it is words that wound, to borrow Richard Delgado's phrase, how are we to understand the relation between the word and the wound? If it is not a causal relation, and not the materialization of an intention, is it perhaps a kind of discursive transitivity that needs to be specified in its historicity and its violence? What is the relation between this transitivity and the power to injure?

In Robert Cover's impressive essay, "Violence and the Word," he elaborates the violence of legal interpretation as "the violence that *judges* deploy as instruments of a modern nation-state."[2] "Judges," he contends, "deal pain and death," "for as the judge interprets, using the concept of punishment, she also acts – through others – to restrain, hurt, render helpless, even kill the prisoner" [note the unfortunate implication of liberal feminism when it decides to legislate the feminine as the universal]. Cover's analysis is relevant to the question of prosecuting hate speech precisely because it underscores the power of the *judiciary* to enact violence through speech. Defenders of hate speech prosecution have had to shift the analysis to acknowledge that agents other than governments and branches of government wield the power to injure through words. Indeed, an analogy is set up between state action and citizen action such that both kinds of actions are understood to have the power to deny rights and

liberties protected by the Equal Protection Clause of the Constitution. Consequently, one obstacle to contemporary efforts to legislate against hate speech is
that the "state action doctrine" qualifies recourse to the Equal Protection
Clause in such instances, presuming as it does that only governments can be
the agents of harmful treatment that results in a deprivation of rights and
liberties.[3] To argue that citizens can effectively deprive *each other* of such rights
and liberties through words that wound requires overcoming the restrictions
imposed by the state action doctrine.[4]

Whereas Cover emphasizes the *juridical* power to inflict pain through language, recent jurisprudence has shifted the terms away from the interpretive
violence enacted by nation-states and toward the violence enacted by citizen-
subjects toward members of minority groups. In this shift, it is not simply that
citizens are said to act like states, but the power of the state is refigured as a
power wielded by a citizen-subject. By "suspending" the state action doctrine,
proponents of hate speech prosecution may also suspend a critical understanding of state power, relocating that power as the agency and effect of the citizen-
subject. Indeed, if hate speech prosecution will be adjudicated by the state, in
the form of the judiciary, the state is tacitly figured as a neutral instrument of
legal enforcement. Hence, the "suspension" of the state action doctrine may
involve both a suspension of critical insight into state power and state violence
in Cover's sense, but also a displacement of that power onto the citizen and the
citizenry, figured as sovereigns whose speech now carries a power that operates
like state power to deprive other "sovereigns" of fundamental rights and
liberties.[5]

In shifting the emphasis from the harm done by the state to the harm done
by citizens and non-state institutions against citizens, a reassessment of how
power operates in and through discourse is also at work. When the words that
wound are not the actions of the nation-state – indeed, when the nation-state
and its judiciary are appealed to as the arbiter of such claims made by citizens
against one another – how does the analysis of the violence of the word
change? Is the violence perpetrated by the courts unwittingly backgrounded
in favor of a politics that presumes the fairness and efficacy of the courts in
adjudicating matters of hate speech? And to what extent does the potential for
state violence become greater to the degree that the state action doctrine is
suspended?

The subject as sovereign is presumed in the Austinian account of performativity: the figure for the one who speaks and, in speaking performs what she/he
speaks, as the judge or some other representative of the law. A judge pronounces a sentence and the pronouncement is the act by which the sentence
first becomes binding, as long as the judge is a legitimate judge and the
conditions of felicity are properly met. The one who speaks the performative

effectively is understood to operate according to uncontested power. The doctor who receives the child and pronounces – "It's a girl" – begins that long string of interpellations by which the girl is transitively girled: gender is ritualistically repeated, whereby the repetition occasions both the risk of failure and the congealed effect of sedimentation. Kendall Thomas makes a similar argument that the subject is always "raced," transitively racialized by regulatory agencies from its inception.[6] The power to "race" and, indeed, the power to gender, precedes the "one" who speaks such power, and yet the one who speaks nevertheless appears to have that power.

If performativity requires a power to effect or enact what one names, then who will be the "one" with such a power, and how will such a power be thought? How might we account for *the injurious word* within such a framework, the word that not only names a social subject, but constructs that subject in the naming, and constructs that subject through a violating interpellation? Is it the power of a "one" to effect such an injury through the wielding of the injurious name, or is that a power accrued through time which is concealed at the moment that a single subject utters its injurious terms? Does the "one" who speaks the term *cite* the term, thereby establishing him or herself as the author while at the same time establishing the derivative status of that authorship? Is a community and history of such speakers not magically invoked at the moment in which that utterance is spoken? And if and when that utterance brings injury, is it the utterance or the utterer who is the cause of the injury, or does that utterance perform its injury through a transitivity that cannot be reduced to a causal or intentional process originating in a singular subject?

Indeed, is iterability or citationality not precisely this: *the operation of that metalepsis by which the subject who "cites" the performative is temporarily produced as the belated and fictive origin of the performative itself?* The subject who utters the socially injurious words is mobilized by that long string of injurious interpellations: the subject achieves a temporary status in the citing of that utterance, in performing itself as the origin of that utterance. That subject-effect, however, is the consequence of that very citation; it is derivative, the effect of a belated metalepsis by which that invoked legacy of interpellations is dissimulated as the subject and the "origin" of its utterance. If the utterance is to be prosecuted, where and when would that prosecution begin, and where and when would it end? Would this not be something like the effort to prosecute a history that, by its very temporality, cannot be called to trial? If the function of the subject as fictive origin is to occlude the genealogy by which that subject is formed, the subject is also installed in order to assume the burden of responsibility for the very history that subject dissimulates; the juridicalization of history, then, is achieved precisely through the search for subjects to prosecute who might be

held accountable and, hence, temporarily resolve the problem of a fundamentally unprosecutable history.

This is not to say that subjects ought not to be prosecuted for their injurious
speech; I think that there are probably occasions when they should. But what is
precisely being prosecuted when the injurious word comes to trial and is it
finally or fully prosecutable?

That words wound seems incontestably true, and that hateful, racist, misogynist, homophobic speech should be vehemently countered seems incon-
trovertibly right. But does understanding from where speech derives its power
to wound alter our conception of what it might mean to counter that
wounding power? Do we accept the notion that injurious speech is attributable
to a singular subject and act? If we accept such a juridical constraint on thought
– the grammatical requirements of accountability – as a point of departure,
what is lost from the political analysis of injury? Indeed, when political
discourse is fully collapsed into juridical discourse, the meaning of political
opposition runs the risk of being reduced to the act of prosecution.

How is the analysis of the discursive historicity of power unwittingly
restricted when the subject is presumed as the point of departure for such an
analysis? A clearly theological construction, the postulation of the subject as the
causal origin of the performative act is understood to generate that which it
names; indeed, this divinely empowered subject is one for whom the name
itself is generative. According to the biblical rendition of the performative,
"Let there be light!," it appears that by virtue of *the power of a subject or its will* a
phenomenon is named into being. Although the sentence is delivered in the
subjunctive, it qualifies as a "masquerading" performative in the Austinian
sense. In a critical reformulation of the performative, Derrida makes clear in
relation to Austin that this power is not the function of an originating will but
is always derivative:

> Could a performative utterance succeed if its formulation did not repeat a
> "coded" or iterable utterance, or in other words, if the formula I pronounce in
> order to open a meeting, launch a ship or a marriage were not identifiable as
> conforming with an iterable model, if it were not then identifiable in some way
> as a "citation"? . . . [I]n such a typology, the category of intention will not
> disappear; it will have its place, but from that place it will no longer be able to
> govern the entire scene and system of utterance [*l'énonciation*].[7]

To what extent does discourse gain the authority to bring about what it
names through citing the linguistic conventions of authority, conventions that
are themselves legacies of citation? Does a subject appear as the author of its
discursive effects to the extent that the citational practice by which he/she is

conditioned and mobilized remains unmarked? Indeed, could it be that the production of the subject as originator of his/her effects is precisely a consequence of this dissimulated citationality?

If a performative provisionally succeeds (and I will suggest that "success" is always and only provisional), then it is not because an intention successfully governs the action of speech, but only because that action echoes prior actions, and *accumulates the force of authority through the repetition or citation of a prior and authoritative set of practices*. It is not simply that the speech act takes place *within* a practice, but that the act is itself a ritualized practice. What this means, then, is that a performative "works" to the extent that *it draws on and covers over* the constitutive conventions by which it is mobilized. In this sense, no term or statement can function performatively without the accumulating and dissimulating historicity of force.

When the injurious term injures (and let me make clear that I think it does), it works its injury precisely through the accumulation and dissimulation of its force. The speaker who utters the racial slur is thus citing that slur, making linguistic community with a history of speakers. What this might mean, then, is that precisely the iterability by which a performative enacts its injury establishes a permanent difficulty in locating final accountability for that injury in a singular subject and its act.

In two recent cases, the Supreme Court has reconsidered the distinction between protected and unprotected speech in relation to the phenomenon of "hate speech." Are certain forms of invidious speech to be construed as "fighting words," and if so, are they appropriately considered to be a kind of speech unprotected by the First Amendment? In the first case, *R.A.V. v. St. Paul*, 112 S. Ct. 2538, 120 L. Ed. 2d 305 (1992), the ordinance in question was one passed by the St. Paul City Council in 1990, and read in part as follows:

> Whoever places on public or private property a symbol, object, appellation, characterization or graffiti, including, but not limited to, a burning cross or Nazi swastika, which one knows or has reasonable grounds to know arouses anger, alarm, or resentment in others, on the basis of race, color, creed, religion or gender commits disorderly conduct and shall be guilty of a misdemeanor.[8]

A white teenager was charged under this ordinance after burning a cross in front of a black family's house. The charge was dismissed by the trial court but reinstated by the Minnesota State Supreme Court; at stake was the question whether the ordinance itself was "substantially overbroad and impermissably content based." The defense contended that the burning of the cross in front of the black family's house was to be construed as an example of protected speech. The State Supreme Court overturned the decision of the trial court, arguing first that the burning of the cross could not be construed as protected speech because it constituted "fighting words" as defined in *Chaplinsky v. New Hampshire*, 315 U.S. 568, 572 (1942), and second, that the reach of the ordinance was permissible considering the "compelling government interest in protecting the community against bias-motivated threats to public safety and order." *In Re Welfare of R.A.V.*, 464 N.W.2 507, 510 (Minn. 1991).

The United States Supreme Court reversed the State Supreme Court decision, reasoning first that the burning cross was not an instance of "fighting words," but a "viewpoint" within the "free marketplace of ideas" and that such "viewpoints" are categorically protected by the First Amendment."[9] The majority on the High Court (Scalia, Rehnquist, Kennedy, Souter, Thomas) then offered a *second* reason for declaring the ordinance unconstitutional, a judicially activist contribution which took many jurists by surprise: the justices severely restricted the possible doctrinal scope of "fighting words" by claiming it unconstitutional to impose prohibitions on speech solely on the basis of the "content" or "subjects addressed" in that speech. In order to determine whether words are fighting words, there can be no decisive recourse to the content and the subject matter of what is said.

One conclusion on which the justices appear to concur is that the ordinance imposed overbroad restrictions on speech, given that forms of speech *not* considered to fall within the parameters of fighting words would nonetheless be banned by the ordinance. But while the Minnesota ordinance proved too broad for all the justices, Scalia, Thomas, Rehnquist, Kennedy, and Souter took the opportunity of this review to severely restrict any future application of the fighting words doctrine. At stake in the majority opinion is not only when and where "speech" constitutes some component of an injurious act such that it loses its protected status under the First Amendment, but what constitutes the domain of "speech" itself.

According to a rhetorical reading of this decision – distinguished from a reading that follows established conventions of legal interpretation – the court might be understood as asserting its state-sanctioned linguistic power to determine what will and will not count as "speech" and, in the process, enacting a potentially injurious form of juridical speech. What follows, then, is a reading which considers not only the account that the Court gives of how and when speech becomes injurious, but considers as well the injurious potential of the account itself as "speech" considered in a broad sense. Recalling Cover's claim that legal decisions can engage the nexus of language and violence, consider that the adjudication of what will and will not count as protected speech will itself be a kind of speech, one which implicates the state in the very problem of discursive power with which it is invested to regulate, sanction, and restrict such speech.

In the following, then, I will read the "speech" in which the decision is articulated against the version of "speech" officially circumscribed as protected content in the decision. The point of this kind of reading is not only to expose a contradictory set of rhetorical strategies at work in the decision, but to consider the power of that discursive domain which not only produces what will and will not count as "speech," but which regulates the political field of contestation through the tactical manipulation of that very distinction. Furthermore, I want to argue that the very reasons that account for the injuriousness of such acts, construed as speech in a broad sense, are precisely what render difficult the prosecution of such acts. Lastly, I want to suggest that the court's speech carries with it its *own* violence, and that the very institution that is invested with the authority to adjudicate the problem of hate speech recirculates and redirects that hatred in and as its own highly consequential speech, often by coopting the very language that it seeks to adjudicate.

The majority opinion, written by Scalia, begins with the construction of the act, the burning of the cross; and one question at issue is whether or not this act constitutes an injury, whether it can be construed as "fighting words" or whether it communicates a content which is, for better or worse, protected by First Amendment precedent. The figure of burning will be repeated throughout the opinion, first in the context in which the burning cross is construed as the free expression of a viewpoint within the marketplace of ideas, and, second, in the example of the burning of the flag, which could be held illegal were it to violate an ordinance prohibiting outside fires, but which could not be held to be illegal if it were the expression of an idea. Later Scalia will close the argument through recourse to yet another fire: "Let there be no mistake about our belief that burning a cross in someone's front yard is reprehensible." "But," Scalia continued, "St. Paul has sufficient means at its disposal to prevent such behavior without adding the First Amendment to the fire." *R.A.V.v. St. Paul*, 112 S. Ct. at 2550, 120 L. Ed. 2d at 326.

Significantly, Scalia here aligns the act of cross-burning with those who defend the ordinance, since both are producing fires, but whereas the cross-burner's fire is constitutionally protected speech, the ordinance-maker's language is figured as the incineration of free speech. The analogy suggests that the ordinance is itself a kind of cross-burning, and Scalia then draws on the very destructive implications of cross-burning to underscore his point that the ordinance itself is destructive. The figure thus affirms the destructiveness of the cross-burning that the decision itself effectively denies, the destructiveness of the act that it has just elevated to the status of protected verbal currency within the marketplace of ideas.

The Court thus transposes the place of the ordinance and the place of the cross-burning, but also figures the First Amendment in an analogous relation to the black family and its home which in the course of the writing has become reduced to "someone's front yard." The stripping of blackness and family from the figure of the complainant is significant, for it refuses the dimension of social power that constructs the so-called speaker and the addressee of the speech act in question, the burning cross. And it refuses as well the racist history of the convention of cross-burning by the Ku Klux Klan which marked, targeted, and, hence, portended a further violence against a given addressee. Scalia thus figures himself as quenching the fire which the ordinance has lit, and which is being stoked with the First Amendment, apparently in its totality. Indeed, compared with the admittedly "reprehensible" act of burning a cross in "someone's" front yard, the ordinance itself appears to conflagrate in much greater dimensions, threatening to burn the book which it is Scalia's duty to uphold; Scalia thus champions himself as an opponent of those who would set the constitution on fire, cross-burners of a more dangerous order.[10]

The lawyers arguing for the legality of the ordinance based their appeal on the fighting words doctrine. This doctrine, formulated in *Chaplinsky v. New Hampshire*, 315 U.S. 568, 572 (1942), argued that speech acts unprotected by the Constitution are those which are not essential to the communication of ideas: "such utterances are no essential part of any exposition of ideas, and are of such slight social value as a step to truth that any benefit that may be derived from them is clearly outweighed by the social interest in order and morality." Scalia takes this phrasing to legitimate the following claim: "the unprotected features of the words are, despite their verbal character, essentially a 'non-speech' element of communication." *R.A.V. v. St. Paul*, 112 S. Ct. at 2545, 120 L. Ed. 2d at 319. In his efforts to protect all contents of communication from proscription, Scalia establishes a distinction between the content and the vehicle of that expression; it is the latter which is proscribable, and the former which is not. He continues, "fighting words are thus analogous to a noisy sound truck." *Id*. What is injurious, then, is the sound, but not the message, indeed, "the government may not regulate use based on hostility – or favoritism – towards the underlying message expressed." *Id*.

The connection between the signifying power of the burning cross and Scalia's regressive new critical distinction between what is and is not a speech element in communication is nowhere marked in the text.[11] Scalia assumes that the burning cross is a message, an expression of a viewpoint, a discussion of a "subject" or "content": in short, that the act of burning the cross is fully and exhaustively translatable into a *constative* act of speech; the burning of the cross which is, after all, on the black family's lawn, is thus made strictly analogous – and morally equivalent – to an individual speaking in public on whether or not there ought to be a fifty-cent tax on gasoline. Significantly, Scalia does not tell us what the cross would say if the cross could speak, but he does insist that what the burning cross is doing is expressing a viewpoint, discoursing on a content which is, admittedly, controversial, but for that very reason, ought not to be proscribed. Thus the defense of cross-burning as free speech rests on an unarticulated analogy between that act and a public constation. This speech is not a doing, an action or an injury, even as it is the enunciation of a set of "contents" that might offend.[12] The injury is thus construed as one that is registered at the level of sensibility, which is to say that it is an offense that is one of the risks of free speech.

That the cross burns and thus constitutes an incendiary destruction is not considered as a sign of the intention to reproduce that incendiary destruction at the site of the house or the family; the historical correlation between cross-burning and marking a community, a family, or an individual for further violence is also ignored. How much of that burning is translatable into a declarative or constative proposition? And how would one know exactly what constative claim is being made by the burning cross? If the cross is the expression of a viewpoint, is it a declaration as in, "I am of the opinion that black people ought not to live in this neighborhood" or even, "I am of the opinion that violence ought to be perpetrated against black people," or is it a perlocutionary performative, as in imperatives and commands which take the form of "Burn!" or "Die!"? Is it an injunction that works its power metonymically not only in the sense that the fire recalls prior burnings which have served to mark black people as targets for violence, but also in the sense that the fire is understood to be transferable from the cross to the target that is marked by the cross? The relation between cross-burning and torchings of both persons and properties is historically established. Hence, from this perspective, the burning cross assumes the status of a direct address and a *threat* and, as such, is construed either as the incipient moment of injurious action *or* as the statement of an intention to injure.[13]

Although Justice Stevens agreed with the decision to strike down the Minnesota ordinance, he takes the occasion to rebuke Scalia for restricting the fighting words doctrine. Stevens reviews special cases in which conduct may be prohibited by special rules. Note in the following quotation how the cross-burning is nowhere mentioned, but the displacements of the figure of fire appear in a series of examples which effectively transfer the need for protection *from racist speech* to the need for protection *from public protest against racism.* Even within Stevens's defense of proscribing conduct, a phantasmatic figure of a menacing riot emerges:

> Lighting a fire near an ammunition dump or a gasoline storage tank is especially dangerous; such behavior may be punished more severely than burning trash in a

vacant lot. Threatening someone because of her race or religious beliefs may cause particularly severe trauma or touch off a riot, and threatening a high public official may cause substantial social disruptions; such threats may be punished more severely than threats against someone based on, say, his support of a particular athletic team. *R.A.V.v. St. Paul*, 112 S. Ct. at 2561, 120 L Ed. 2d at 340.

Absent from the list of fires above is the burning of the cross in question. In the place of that prior scene, we are asked first to imagine someone who would light a fire near a gas tank, and then to imagine a more innocuous fire in a vacant lot. But with the vacant lot, we enter the metaphor of poverty and property, which appears to effect the unstated transition to the matter of blackness[14] introduced by the next line, "threatening someone because of her race or religious beliefs...": *because* of her race is not the same as "on the basis of" her race and leaves open the possibility that the race causally induces the threat. The threat appears to shift mid-sentence as Stevens continues to elaborate a second causality: this threat "may cause particularly severe trauma or touch off a riot" at which point it is no longer clear whether the threat which warrants the prohibition on conduct refers to the "threatening someone because of her race or religious beliefs" or to the riot that might result therefrom. What immediately follows suggests that the limitations on rioters has suddenly become more urgent to authorize than the limitation on those who would threaten this "her" "because of her race...." After "or touch off a riot," the sentence continues, "and threatening a high official may cause substantial social disruption...," as if the racially marked trauma had already led to a riot and an attack on high officials.

This sudden implication of the justices themselves might be construed as a paranoid inversion of the original cross-burning narrative. That original narrative is nowhere mentioned, but its elements have been redistributed throughout the examples; the fire which was the original "threat" against the black family is relocated first as an incendiary move against industry, then as a location in a vacant lot, and then reappears tacitly in the riot which now appears to follow from the trauma and threaten public officials. The fire which initially constituted the threat against the black family becomes metaphorically transfigured as the threat that blacks in trauma now wield against high officials. And though Stevens is on record as endorsing a construction of "fighting words" that would include cross-burning as *un*protected speech, the language in which he articulates this view deflects the question to that of the state's right to circumscribe conduct to protect itself against a racially motivated riot.[15]

The circumscription of content explicitly discussed in the decision appears to emerge through a production of semantic excess in and through the metonymic chain of anxious figuration. The separability of content from sound, for instance, or of content from context, is exemplified and illustrated through figures which signify in excess of the thesis which they are meant to support. Indeed, to the extent that, in the Scalia analysis, "content" is circumscribed and purified to establish its protected status, that content is secured through the production and proliferation of "dangers" from which it calls to be protected. Hence, the question of whether or not the black family in Minnesota is entitled to protection from public displays such as cross-burnings is displaced onto the question of whether or not the "content" of free speech is to be protected from those who would burn it. The fire is thus displaced from the cross to the legal instrument wielded by those who would protect the family from the fire, but then to the black family itself, to blackness, to the vacant lot, to rioters in Los Angeles who explicitly oppose the decision of a court and who now represent the incendiary power of the traumatized rage of black people who would burn the judiciary itself. But, of course, that construal is already a reversal of the narrative in which a court delivers a decision of acquittal for the four policemen indicted for the brutal beating of Rodney King, a decision that might be said to "spark" a riot which calls into question whether the claim of having been injured can be heard and countenanced by a jury and a judge who are extremely susceptible to the suggestion that a black person is always and only endangering, but never endangered. And so the High Court might be understood in its decision of June 22, 1992, to be taking its revenge on Rodney King, protecting itself against the riots in Los Angeles and elsewhere which appeared to be attacking the system of justice itself. Hence, the justices identify with the black family who sees the cross burning and takes it as a threat, but they substitute themselves for that family, and reposition blackness as the agency behind the threat itself.[16]

The decision enacts a set of metonymic displacements which might well be read as anxious deflections and reversals of the injurious action at hand; indeed, the original scene is successively reversed in the metonymic relation between figures such that the fire is lit by the ordinance, carried out by traumatized rioters on the streets of Los Angeles, and threatens to engulf the justices themselves.

Mari Matsuda and Charles Lawrence also write of this text as enacting a rhetorical reversal of crime and punishment: "The cross burners are portrayed as an unpopular minority that the Supreme Court must defend against the power of the state. The injury to the Jones family is appropriated and the cross burner is cast as the injured victim. The reality of ongoing racism and exclusion is erased and bigotry is redefined as majoritarian condemnation of racist views."[17]

Significantly, the justices revisited *R.A.V.v. St. Paul* in a more recent decision, *Wisconsin v. Mitchell*, 113 S. Ct. 2194, 14 L. Ed. 2d 436 (1993), in which the court unanimously decided that racist speech could be included as evidence that a victim of a crime was intentionally selected because of his/her race and could constitute one of the factors that come into play in determining whether an enhanced penalty for the crime is in order. *Wisconsin v. Mitchell* did not address whether racist speech is injurious, but only whether speech that indicates that the victim was selected on the basis of race could be brought to bear in determining penalty enhancement for a crime which is itself not a crime of speech, as it were. Oddly, the case at hand involved a group of young black men, including Todd Mitchell who had just left the film, *Mississippi Burning*. They decided to "move on" some white people, and proceeded to beat a young white man who had approached them on the street. Rehnquist is quick to note that these young men were discussing a scene from the film, one in which "a white man beat a young black boy who was praying." Rehnquist then goes on to quote Mitchell whose speech will become consequential in the decision: "Do you all feel hyped up to move on some white people" and later, "You all want to fuck somebody up? There goes a white boy; go get him." *Wisconsin v. Mitchell*, 113 S. Ct. at 2196-7, 120 L. Ed. 2d at 442 (citing Brief for Petitioner). Now, the irony of this event, it seems, is that the film narrates the story of three civil rights workers (two white and one black) who are murdered by Klansmen who regularly threaten with burning crosses and firebombs any townspeople who appear to help the Justice Department in their search for the bodies of the slain civil rights activists and then their murderers. The court system is first figured within the film as sympathetic to the Klan, refusing to imprison the murdering Klansmen, and then as setting improper restraints on the interrogation. Indeed, the Justice Department official is able to entrap the Klansman only by acting against the law, freely brutalizing those he interrogates. This official is largely regarded as rehabilitating masculinity on the side of what is right over and against a liberal "effeminization" represented by judicial due process. But perhaps most important, while the effective official acts in the name of the law, he also acts against the law, and purports to show that his unlawfulness is the only efficacious way to fight racism. The film thus appeals to a widespread lack of faith in the law and its proceduralism, reconstructing a lawless white masculinity even as it purports to curb its excesses.

In some ways, the film shows that violence is the consequence of the law's failure to protect its citizens, and in this way allegorizes the reception of the judicial decisions. For if the film shows that the court will fail to guarantee the rights and liberties of its citizens, and only violence can counter racism, then the street violence that literally follows the film reverses the order of that allegory. The black men who leave the film and embark upon violence in the street find themselves in a court that not only goes out of its way to indict the film – which is, after all, an indictment of the courts – but implicitly goes on to link the street violence to the offending representation, and effectively to link the one through the other.

The court seeks to decide whether or not the selection of the target of violence is a racially motivated one by quoting Todd Mitchell's speech. This speech is then taken to be the consequence of having watched the film, indeed, to be the very extension of the speech that constitutes the text of the film. But the Court itself is implicated in the extended text of the film, "indicted" by the film as complicit with racial violence. Hence, the punishment of Mitchell and his friends – and the attribution of racially selective motives to them – reverses the "charges" that the film makes against the Court. In *R.A.V.v. St. Paul*, the Court makes a cameo appearance in the decision as well, reversing the agency of the action, substituting the injured for the injurer, and figuring itself as a site of vulnerability.

In each of these cases, the Court's speech exercises the power to injure precisely by virtue of being invested with the authority to adjudicate the injurious power of speech. The reversal and displacement of injury in the name of "adjudication" underscores the particular violence of the "decision," one which becomes both dissimulated and enshrined once it becomes word of law. It may be said that all legal language engages this potential power to injure, but that insight supports only the argument that it will be all the more important to gain a reflective understanding of the specificities of that violence. It will be necessary to distinguish between those kinds of violence that are the necessary conditions of the binding character of legal language, and those kinds which exploit that very necessity in order to redouble that injury in the service of injustice.

The arbitrary use of this power is evidenced in the contrary use of precedents on hate speech to promote conservative political goals and thwart progressive efforts. Here it is clear that what is needed is not a better understanding of speech acts or the injurious power of speech, but the strategic and contradictory uses to which the Court puts these various formulations. For instance, this same Court has been willing to countenance the expansion of definitions of obscenity, and to use the very rationale proposed by some arguments in favor of hate-crime legislation to augment its case to exclude obscenity from protected speech.[18] Scalia refers to *Miller v. California* (1973) as the case which installs obscenity as an exception to the categorical protection of content through recourse to what is "patently offensive," and then remarks that in a later case, *New York v. Ferber*, 458 U.S. 747 (1982), in exempting child pornography from protection, there was no "question here of censoring a particular literary theme." *R.A.V.v. St. Paul*, 112 S. Ct at 2543, 120 L. Ed. 2d at 318. What constitutes the "literary" is thus circumscribed in such a way that child pornography is excluded from both the literary and the thematic. Although it seems that one must be able to recognize the genre of child

pornography, to identify and delimit it in order to exempt it from the categorical protection of content, the identifying marks of such a product can be
neither literary nor thematic. Indeed, the Court appears in one part of its
discussion to accept the controversial position of Catharine MacKinnon, which
claims that certain verbal expressions constitute sex discrimination, when it says
"sexually derogatory 'fighting words' . . . may produce a violation of Title VII's
general prohibition against sexual discrimination in employment practices" *Id.*
at 2546, 120 L. Ed. 2d at 321. But here the court is clear that it does not
prohibit such expressions on the basis of their content, but only on the basis of
the effects that such expressions entail.

I would suggest that the contemporary conservative sensibility exemplified
by the court and right-wing members of Congress is also exemplified in the
willingness to expand the domain of obscenity and, to that end, to enlarge the
category of the pornographic and to claim the unprotected status of both, and
so, potentially, to position obscenity to become a species of "fighting words,"
that is, to accept that graphic sexual representation is injurious. This is underscored by the rationale used in *Miller v. California* in which the notion of
"appealing to prurience" is counterposed to the notion of "literary, artistic,
political, or scientific value." Here the representation that is deemed immediately and unobjectionably injurious is excluded from the thematic and the
valuable and, hence, from protected status.

This same rationale has been taken up by Jesse Helms and others to argue
that the National Endowment for the Arts is under no obligation to fund
obscene materials, and then to argue that various lesbian performers and gay
male photographers produce work that is obscene and lacking in literary value.
Significantly, it seems, the willingness to accept the nonthematic and unobjectionably injurious quality of graphic sexual representations, when these representations cannot be said to leave the page or to "act" in some obvious way,
must be read against the unwillingness to countenance the injuriousness of the
burning cross in front of the black family's house. That the graphic depiction of
homosexuality, say, can be construed as nonthematic or simply prurient,
figured as a sensuousness void of meaning, whereas the burning of the cross,
to the extent that it communicates a message of racial hatred, might be
construed as a sanctioned point in a public debate over admittedly controversial
issues, suggests that the rationale for expanding the fighting words doctrine to
include unconventional depictions of sexuality within its purview has been
strengthened, but that the rationale for invoking fighting words to outlaw racist
threats is accordingly weakened. This is perhaps a way in which a heightened
sexual conservatism works in tandem with an increasing governmental sanction

for racist violence, but in such a way that whereas the "injury" claimed by the viewer of graphic sexual representation is honored as fighting words, the injury sustained by the black family with the burning cross out front, like the injury of Rodney King, proves too ambiguous, too hypothetical to abrogate the ostensible sanctity of the First Amendment.[19] And it is not simply that prohibitions against graphic sexual representation will be supported by this kind of legal reasoning, whereas racist injury will be dignified as protected speech, but that racially marked depictions of sexuality will be most susceptible to prosecution, and those representations that threaten the pieties and purities of race and sexuality will become most vulnerable.

Two remarks of qualification: first, some critical race theorists such as Charles Lawrence will argue that cross-burning is speech, but that not all speech is to be protected, indeed, not all speech *is* protected, and that racist speech conflicts with the Equal Protection Clause because it hinders the addressed subject from exercising his/her rights and liberties. Other legal scholars, in critical race studies, such as Richard Delgado, will argue for expanding the domain of the fighting words restriction on First Amendment rights. Matsuda and Mackinnon, following the example of sex discrimination jurisprudence, will argue that it is impossible to distinguish between conduct and speech, that hateful remarks are injurious actions. Oddly enough, this last kind of reasoning has reappeared in the recent policy issued on gays in the military, where the statement "I am a homosexual" is considered to be a "homosexual act." [. . .] According to this policy, the act of coming out is implicitly construed as fighting words. Here it seems that one must be reminded that the prosecution of hate speech in a court runs the risk of giving that court the opportunity to impose a further violence of its own. And if the court begins to decide what is and is not violating speech, that decision runs the risk of constituting the most binding of violations.

For, as in the case with the burning cross, it was not merely a question of whether the court knows how to read the threat contained in the burning cross, but whether the court itself signifies along a parallel logic. For this has been a court that can only imagine the fire engulfing the First Amendment, sparking the riot which will fray its own authority. And so it protects itself against the imagined threat of that fire by protecting the burning cross, allying itself with those who would seek legal protection from a spectre wrought from their own fantasy. Thus the court protects the burning cross as free speech, figuring those it injures as the site of the true threat, elevating the burning cross as a deputy for the court, the local protector and and token of free speech: with so much protection, what do we have to fear?

From Hate Speech to Pornography

MacKinnon herself understands this risk of invoking state power, but in her recent book, *Only Words* (1993), she argues that state power is on the side of the pornographic industry; and that the construction of women within pornography in subordinate positions is, effectively, a state-sanctioned construction. [...] I offer an analysis of the putative performativity of pornography here to show how the construal of the visual image as illocutionary speech effectively sidesteps the First Amendment by claiming that pornography is sovereign conduct.

MacKinnon has argued that pornography is a kind of hate speech, and that the argument in favor of restricting hate speech ought to be based on the argument in favor of restricting pornography. This analogy rests upon the assumption that the visual image in pornography operates as an imperative, and that this imperative has the power to realize that which it dictates. The problem, for MacKinnon, is *not* that pornography reflects or expresses a social structure of misogyny, but that it is an institution with the performative power to bring about that which it depicts. She writes that pornography not only substitutes for social reality, but that that substitution is one which creates a social reality of its own, the social reality of pornography. This self-fulfilling capacity of pornography is, for her, what gives sense to the claim that pornography *is* its own social context. She writes,

> Pornography does not simply express or interpret experience; it substitutes for it. Beyond bringing a message from reality, it stands in for reality. . . . To make visual pornography, and to live up to its imperatives, the world, namely women, must do what the pornographers want to "say." Pornography brings its conditions of production to the consumer. . . . Pornography makes the world a pornographic place through its making and use, establishing what women are said to exist as, are seen as, are treated as, constructing the social reality of what a woman is and can be in terms of what can be done to her, and what a man is in terms of doing it. (25)

In the first instance, pornography substitutes for experience, implying that there is an experience which is supplanted, and supplanted thoroughly, through pornography. Hence, pornography takes the place of an experience and thoroughly constitutes a new experience understood as a totality; by the second line this second-order experience is rendered synonymous with a second order "reality," which suggests that in this universe of pornography there is no distinction between an experience of reality and reality. MacKinnon herself makes clear that this systemic conflation of the two takes place within a reality which is itself a mere substitution for another reality, one which is figured as more original, perhaps one which furnishes the normative or utopian measure by which she judges the pornographic reality that has taken its place. This visual field is then figured as speaking, indeed, as delivering imperatives, at which point the visual field operates as a subject with the power to bring into being what it names, to wield an efficacious power analogous to the divine performative. The reduction of that visual field to a speaking figure, an authoritarian speaker, rhetorically effects a different substitution than the one that MacKinnon describes. She substitutes a set of linguistic imperatives for the visual field, implying not only a full transposition of the visual into the linguistic, but a full transposition of visual depiction into an efficacious performative.

When pornography is then described as "constructing the social reality of what a woman is," the sense of "construction" needs to be read in light of the above two transpositions. That construction can be said to work, that is, "to produce the social reality of what a woman is," only if the visual can be transposed into the linguistically efficacious in the way that she suggests. Similarly, the analogy between pornography and hate speech works to the extent that the pornographic image can be transposed into a set of efficacious spoken imperatives. In MacKinnon's paraphrase of how the pornographic image speaks, she insists that the image says, "do this," where the commanded act is an act of sexual subordination, and where, in the doing of that act, the social reality of woman is constructed precisely as the position of the sexually subordinate. Here "construction" is not simply the doing of the act – which remains, of course, highly ambiguous in order perhaps to ward off the question of an equivocal set of readings – but *the depiction* of that doing, where the depiction is understood as the dissimulation and fulfillment of the verbal imperative, "do this." For MacKinnon, no one needs to speak such words because the speaking of such words already functions as the frame and the compulsory scripting of the act; in a sense, to the extent that the frame orchestrates the act, it wields a performative power; it is conceived by Mac-Kinnon as encoding the will of a masculine authority, and compelling a compliance with its command.

But does the frame impart the will of a preexisting subject, or is the frame something like the derealization of will, the production and orchestration of a phantasmatic scene of willfulness and submission? I don't mean to suggest a strict distinction between the phantasmatic and the domain of reality, but I do mean to ask, to what extent does the operation of the phantasmatic within the construction of social reality render that construction more frail and less determinative than MacKinnon would suggest? In fact, although one might well agree that a good deal of pornography is offensive, it does not follow that its offensiveness consists in its putative power to construct (unilaterally, exhaustively) the social reality of what a woman is. To return for a moment to MacKinnon's own language, consider the way in which the hypothetical insists itself into the formulation of the imperative, as if the force of her own assertions about the force of pornographic representation tends toward its own undoing: "pornography establish[es] ... what women are said to exist, *are seen as*, are treated *as* ... " Then, the sentence continues: "constructing the social reality of what a woman is": here to be treated as a sexual subordinate is to be constructed as one, and to have a social reality constituted in which that is precisely and only what one is. But if the "as" is read as the assertion of a likeness, it is not for that reason that assertion of a metaphorical collapse into identity. Through what means does the "as" turn into an "is," and is this the doing of pornography, or is it the doing of the very *depiction* of pornography that MacKinnon provides? For the "as" could also be read as "as if" – "as if one were" – which suggests that pornography neither represents nor constitutes what women are, but offers an allegory of masculine willfulness and feminine submission (although these are clearly not its only themes), one which repeatedly and anxiously rehearses its own *un*realizability. Indeed, one might argue that pornography depicts impossible and uninhabitable positions, compensatory fantasies that continually reproduce a rift between those positions and the ones that belong to the domain of social reality. Indeed, one might suggest that pornography is the text of gender's unreality, the impossible norms by which it is compelled, and in the face of which it perpetually fails. The imperative "do this" is less delivered than "depicted," and if what is depicted is a set of compensatory ideals, hyperbolic gender norms, then pornography charts a domain of unrealizable positions that hold sway over the social reality of gender positions, but do not, strictly speaking, constitute that reality; indeed, it is their failure to constitute it that gives the pornographic image the phantasmatic power that it has. In this sense, to the extent that an imperative is "depicted" and not "delivered," it fails to wield the power to construct the social reality of what a woman is. This failure, however, is the occasion for an allegory of such an imperative, one that concedes the unrealizability of that imperative from the start, and which, finally, cannot overcome the unreality that is its condition and its lure. My call, as it were, is for a feminist reading of pornography that resists the literalization of this imaginary scene, one which reads it instead for the incommensurabilities between gender norms and practices that it seems compelled to repeat without resolution.

In this sense, it makes little sense to figure the visual field of pornography as a subject who speaks and, in speaking, brings about what it names; its authority is decidedly less divine; its power, less efficacious. It only makes sense to figure the pornographic text as the injurious act of a speaker if we seek to locate accountability at the prosecutable site of the subject. Otherwise our work is more difficult, for what pornography delivers is what it recites and exaggerates from the resources of compensatory gender norms, a text of insistent and faulty imaginary relations that will not disappear with the abolition of the offending text, the text that remains for feminist criticism relentlessly to read. To read such texts against themselves is to concede that the performativity of the text is not under sovereign control. On the contrary, if the text acts once, it can act again, and possibly against its prior act. This raises the possibility of resignification as an alternative reading of performativity and of politics.

Notes

Introduction

1 *On the Genealogy of Morals*, 29.
2 This is J. L. Austin's distinction between illocutionary and perlocutionary utterances, i.e. utterances which do what they say (illocutionary) or those which lead to a consequence as a result of utterance (perlocutionary).

Burning Acts

1 I greatly appreciate the thoughtful readings given to this chapter in an earlier form by Wendy Brown, Robert Gooding-Williams, Morris Kaplan, Robert Post, and Hayden White. Any inaccuracies and all misreadings are, of course, my responsibility alone. I thank Jane Malmo for help with preparing the manuscript.
2 This criminal sense of an actor is to be distinguished both from the commercial and theatrical terms (*Händlerin* and *Schauspielerin*, respectively).
3 Robert M. Cover, "Violence and the Word," 96 *Yale Law Journal* 1595, 1601 n I (1986).
4 "The [state action] doctrine holds that although someone may have suffered harmful treatment of a kind that one might ordinarily describe as a deprivation of liberty or a denial of equal protection of the laws, that occurrence excites no constitutional concern unless the proximate active perpetrators of the harm include persons exercising the special authority or power of the government of a state." Frank Michelman, "Conceptions of Democracy in American Constitutional Argument: The Case of Pornography Regulation," 56 *Tennessee Law Review* 291, 306 (1989).
5 Charles Lawrence III, "If He Hollers Let Him Go: Regulating Racist Speech on Campus," in *Words that Wound: Critical Race Theory, Assaultive Speech and the First Amendment*, ed. Mari J. Matsuda, Charles R. Lawrence III, Richard Delgado, and Kimberlé Williams Crenshaw (Boulder, col.: Westview Press, 1993), p. 65.
6 I thank Robert Post for this last analogy, suggested to me in conversation.
7 Kendall Thomas, "The Eclipse of Reason: A Rhetorical Reading of 'Bowers v. Hardwick'," 79 *Virginia Law Review*, 1805–1832 (Oct. 1993).

8   Jacques Derrida, "Signature, Event, Context," in *Limited Inc.*, ed. Gerald Graff, tr. Samuel Weber and Jeffrey Mehlman (Evanston, Ill. 1988), p. 18.

9   St. Paul Bias Motivated Crime Ordinance, Section 292.02 Minn. Legis. Code (1990).

10   Charles R. Lawrence III argues that "it is not just the prevalence and strength of the idea of racism that make the unregulated marketplace of ideas an untenable paradigm for those individuals who seek full and equal personhood for all. The real problem is that the idea of the racial inferiority of nonwhites infects, skews, and disables the operation of a market." In "If He Hollers Let Him Go: Regulating Racist Speech on Campus," in *Words That Wound*, p. 77.

11   The lawyers defending the application of the ordinance to the cross-burning episode made the following argument:

> . . . we ask the Court to reflect on the "content" of the "expressive conduct" represented by a "burning cross." It is no less than the first step in an act of racial violence. It was and unfortunately still is the equivalent of [the] waving of a knife before the thrust, the pointing of a gun before it is fired, the lighting of the match before the reason, the hanging of the noose before the lynching. It is not a political statement, or even a cowardly statement of hatred. It is the first step in an act of assault. It can be no more protected than holding a gun to a victim['s] head. It is perhaps the ultimate expression of "fighting words."

> *R.A.V.v. St. Paul*, 112 S. Ct. at 2569–70, fn. 8, 120 L. Ed. 2d at 320 (App. to Brief for Petitioner).

12   The new critical assumption to which I refer is that of the separable and fully formal unity that is said to characterize a given text.

13   All of the Justices concur that the St. Paul ordinance is overbroad because it isolates "subject-matter" as offensive, and (a) potentially prohibits discussion of such subject-matters even by those whose political sympathies are with the ordinance, and (b) fails to distinguish between the subject-matter's injuriousness and the context in which it is enunciated.

14   Justice Stevens, in a decision offered separately from the argument offered by the majority, suggests that the burning cross is precisely a threat, and that whether a given "expression" is a threat can only be determined *contextually*. Stevens bases his conclusion on *Chaplinsky*, which argued that one of the characteristics that justifies the constitutional status of fighting words is that such words "by their very utterance inflict injury or tend to incite an immediate breach of the peace." *Chaplinsky v. New Hampshire*, 315 U.S. 568,572 (1942).

Here Stevens argues, first, that certain kinds of contents have always been proscribable, and, second, that the fighting words doctrine has depended for its very implementation on the capacity to discriminate among kinds of contents (i.e., political speech is more fully protected than obscene speech, etc.), but also, third, that fighting words that are construed as a threat are in themselves injurious, and that it is this injurious character of speech, and not a separable "context" that is at issue. As he continues, however, Stevens is quick to point out that whether or not an expression is injurious is a matter of determining the force of an expression within a given context. This determination will never be fully predictable, precisely because, one assumes, contexts are also not firmly delimitable. Indeed, if one considers not only historical circumstance, but the historicity of the utterance itself, it follows that the demarcation of relevant context will be as fraught as the demarcation of injurious content.

Stevens links content, injurious performativity, and context together when he claims, objecting to both Scalia and White, that there can be no categorical approach to the question of proscribability: "few dividing lines in First Amendment laws are straight and unwavering, and efforts at categorization inevitably give rise only to fuzzy boundaries . . . the quest for doctrinal certainty through the definition of categories and subcategories is, in my opinion, destined to fail." *R.A.V.v. St. Paul*, 112 S. Ct. at 2561, 120 L. Ed. 2d, at 346. Furthermore, he argues, "the meaning of any expression and the legitimacy of its regulation can only be determined in context." *Id.*

At this point in his analysis, Stevens cites a metaphoric description of "the word" by Justice Holmes, a term which stands synecdochally for "expression" as it is broadly construed within First Amendment jurisprudence: the citation from Holmes runs as follows: "a word is not a crystal, transparent and unchanged, it is the skin of a living through and may vary greatly in color and content according to the circumstances and the time in which it is used" (11–12). We might consider this figure not only as a racial metaphor which describes the "word" as a "skin" that varies in "color," but also in terms of the theory of semantics it invokes. Although Stevens believes that he is citing a figure which will affirm the historically changing nature of an "expression's" semantic "content," denoted by a "skin" that changes in color and content according to the historical circumstance of its use, it is equally clear that the epidermal metaphor suggests a living and disembodied thought which remains dephenomenalized, the noumenal quality of life, the living spirit in its skinless form. Skin and its changing color and content thus denote what is historically changing, but they also are, as it were, the signifiers of historical change. The racial signifier comes to stand not only for changing historical circumstances in the abstract, but for the specific historical changes marked by explosive racial relations.

15   Toni Morrison remarks that poverty is often the language in which black people are spoken about.

16   The above reading raises a series of questions about the rhetorical status of the decision itself. Kendall Thomas and others have argued that the figures and examples used in judicial decisions are as central to its semantic content as the explicit propositional claims that are delivered as the conclusions of the argumentation. In a sense, I am raising two kinds of rhetorical questions here, one has to do with the "content" of the decision, and the other with the way in which the majority ruling, written by Scalia, itself delimits what will and will not qualify as

the content of a given public expression in light of the new restrictions imposed on fighting words. In asking, then, after the rhetorical status of the decision itself, we are led to ask how the rhetorical status of the decision presupposes a theory of semantics that undermines or works against the explicit theory of semantics argued for and in the decision itself.

Specifically, it seems, the decision itself draws on a distinction between the verbal and non-verbal parts of speech, those which Scalia appears to specify as "message" and "sound." *R.A.V.v. St. Paul*, 120 L. Ed. 2d 305, 319–21. For Scalia, only the sound of speech is proscribable or, analogously, that sensuous aspect of speech deemed inessential to the alleged ideality of semantic content. Although Justice Stevens rejects what he calls this kind of "absolutism," arguing instead that the proscribability of content can only be determined in context, he nevertheless preserves a strict distinction between the semantic properties of an expression and the context, including historical circumstance, but also conditions of address. For both Scalia and Stevens, then, the "content" is understood in its separability from both the non-verbal and the historical, although in the latter case, determined in relation to it.

17   The decision made in the trial of the policemen in Simi Valley relied on a similar kind of reversal of position, whereby the jury came to believe that the policemen, in spite of their graphic beating of King, were themselves the endangered party in the case.

18   Matsuda and Lawrence, "Epilogue," *Words that Wound*, p. 135.

19   *Chaplinsky* makes room for this ambiguity by stipulating that some speech loses its protected status when it constitutes "no essential part of any exposition of ideas." This notion of an inessential part of such an exposition forms the basis of a 1973 ruling, *Miller v. California*, 413 U.S. 15, extending the unprotected status of obscenity. In that ruling the picture of a model sporting a political tattoo, constructed by the court as "anti-government speech," is taken as *un*protected precisely because it is said, "taken as a whole to lack serious literary, artistic, political, or scientific value." Such a representation, then, is taken to be "no essential part of any exposition of ideas." But here, you will note that "no essential part" of such an exposition has become "no valuable part." Consider then Scalia's earlier example of what remains unprotected in speech, that is, the noisy sound truck, the semantically void part of speech which, he claims, is the "nonspeech element of communication." Here he claims that only the semantically empty part of speech, its pure sound, is unprotected, but that the "ideas" which are sounded in speech most definitely are protected. This loud street noise, then, forms no essential part of any exposition but, perhaps more poignantly, forms no valuable part. Indeed, we might speculate that whatever form of speech is unprotected will be reduced by the justices to the semantically empty sounding title of "pure noise." Hence, the film clip of the ostensibly nude model sporting an anti-government tattoo would be nothing but pure noise, not a message, not an idea, but the valueless soundings of street noise.

20   Kimberlé Crenshaw marks this ambivalence in the law in a different way, suggesting that the courts will discount African-American forms of artistic expression as

artistic expression and subject such expression to censorship precisely because of racist presumptions about what counts as artistic. On the other hand, she finds the representation of women in these expressions to be repellant, and so feels herself to be "torn" between the two positions. See "Beyond Racism and Misogyny: Black Feminism and 2 Live Crew," in *Words That Wound*.

21   Note the subsumption of the declaration that one is a homosexual under the rubric of offensive conduct: "Sexual orientation will not be a bar to service unless manifested by homosexual conduct. The military will discharge members who engage in homosexual conduct, which is defined as a homosexual act, a statement that the member is homosexual or bisexual, or a marriage or attempted marriage to someone of the same gender." "The Pentagon's New Policy Guidelines on Homosexuals in the Military," *The New York Times* (July 20, 1993), p. A14.

Part III
Subjection, Kinship, and Critique

9

Melancholy Gender/Refused Identification (1997)

Introduction

In previous work, Butler has deployed psychoanalytic and Foucauldian paradigms to analyse the formation of gendered and sexed identities within a law that operates through the performative interpellation of the subject. *The Psychic Life of Power* continues and extends the analysis of subjection, here defined as the processes of subordination whereby one becomes a subject. Steering a careful middle course between reductive voluntarism and foreclosed determinism, Butler contends that the subject depends on power for its formation, so that it is the effect of prior power as well as the potential site for a radically conditioned (and conditional?) form of agency. In other words, the subject is not merely the effect of power, but it is both formative and forming, while agency is facilitated by the power that it exceeds. As Butler writes in her introduction to *The Psychic Life of Power*, agency is "the assumption of a purpose *unintended* by power, one that could not have been derived logically or historically." Agency depends on power; it is complicit with it, so that exceeding power is not synonymous with escaping from it: indeed, the subject remains bound to power, so that both the subject and the scene of agency depend on what constrains them for their very constitution.

The Psychic Life of Power thus presents a Foucauldian analysis of the regulatory formation of the psyche, as well as undertaking a psychoanalytic investigation into the psychic forms assumed by power as it effects the subject. Implicit throughout these discussions is the question as to what possibilities for agency are available to the subject in postliberatory times, possibilities that Butler discerns in the subject's paradoxical dependence on a discourse it does not choose.

The analysis of what Butler calls the subject's structuring attachment to subjection begins with the encounter between Hegel's lord and bondsman, progressing through accounts of the subject in Nietzsche, Freud, Foucault, and Althusser. What is common to these thinkers in Butler's readings of them is the structure of self-incarceration she discerns in modern formulations of reflexivity. In particular, Butler is attentive to the ways in which the subject turns against itself by passionately attaching itself to the law that

Chapter 5, pp. 132–50, 211–12 (notes) from *The Psychic Life of Power: Theories in Subjection*. Stanford: Stanford University Press, 1997. Originally published in *Psychoanalytic Dialogues* 5:5.2 (1995), pp. 165–94. Reprinted by permission of The Analytic Press as copyright holder and publisher.

subjects it, and she asserts that the prohibitions instituted by the law – specifically, as in *Gender Trouble*, the prohibition against homosexual desire – are constitutive of a subject that *requires* subjection in certain crucial senses. In *Subjects of Desire*, Butler insisted that negation, loss, and melancholia are preconditions for the emergence of the subject; *Gender Trouble* and *Bodies That Matter* developed these insights by placing them in a psychoanalytic framework, and chapter 5 of *The Psychic Life of Power* ("Melancholy Gender/Refused Identification," reprinted here) returns to Freud's "Mourning and Melancholia" and *The Ego and the Id* to analyze further the ways in which melancholic identification is crucial to the gendering of the ego.

Butler argues that the formation of gendered and sexed identities involves the foreclosure and loss of same-sex attachments and the preservation and incorporation of that loss. Gender is composed of what is inarticulate or impermissible in sexuality, and homosexuality is preserved in the structure of renunciation. Returning to arguments put forward in *Bodies That Matter*, Butler now makes the transition from considering melancholy as a psychic economy to theorizing the production of melancholy as one of power's regulatory operations. Similarly, Butler extends her theorizations of performative gender by linking psychoanalysis to gender performativity, and performativity to melancholia, connections that lead her to formulate performativity as the "acting out" of unresolved grief, whereby performative genders (both straight and gay) are allegories of heterosexual/homosexual melancholia. Homosexual and heterosexual identities are founded on repudiated identifications that nonetheless preserve and sustain what has been repudiated on the surface of the body through incorporation. And yet, towards the end of chapter 5 Butler characterizes the logic of repudiation she has charted as logic in drag, a necessary overstatement. Crucially, she believes that identification does not necessarily have to oppose desire, while desire is not inevitably dependent on repudiation. "Perhaps the economy of desire always works through refusal and loss of some kind, but it is not as a consequence an economy structured by a logic of non-contradiction," she writes in response to Adam Phillips' commentary on the chapter, and she acknowledges that there may be other "compelling accounts" of homosexuality (and heterosexuality) which do not have repudiation as their basis.

Indeed, as in *Gender Trouble* and *Bodies That Matter*, Butler emphasizes the productive, proliferative nature of power, and in chapter 3 of *The Psychic Life of power* the insistence on the generative nature of prohibition informs her psychoanalytic critique of Foucault and her Foucauldian critique of Althusser. While Foucault's characterization of the psyche as an imprisoning effect fails to take account of the psychic resistance to power, Althusser's doctrine of interpellation mistakenly assumes interpellation's sovereign power, thereby overlooking the subject's willingness to turn around in response to the "call" of the law. In *Bodies That Matter* and *Excitable Speech*, Butler diverges from Althusser's descriptions of the sovereign interpellator, the obedient interpellee and the efficacy of the interpellative: *The Psychic Life of Power* also questions the power of the interpellative call, arguing that in its pursuit of social recognition and social identity, the subject is engaged in a willing embrace of the law. According to Butler, Althusser's own passionate pursuit of the law after murdering his wife is an example of reverse interpellation in which a man (Althusser in this case) rushes into the street and shouts out "Hey, you there!" to a police officer. Althusser's proclamation of his own guilt exemplifies the two-way nature of interpellation and the way in which the law becomes the object of a passionate attachment – what Butler calls "a strange scene of love."

Although the failure of interpellation is productive, Butler also recognizes that the subject's passionate attachment to the law necessarily limits her/his critique of it. However, like Homi K. Bhabha, she regards melancholia as a means of potential revolt rather than a site of passive self-abnegation: the melancholic acceptance and embracing of one's own incoherence and alterity facilitates an epistemological encounter with the other, while psychic survival involves acknowledging that one's emergence as a subject is inaugurated through loss. As in previous works, Butler insists on the constitutive, productive nature of melancholia, asserting that it is only by recognizing the other as oneself that one becomes anything at all. Power does not act unilaterally upon a passive subject, and the failure of interpellation furnishes the conditions of possibility for the constitution of the subject. The subject's relationship to power is ambivalent, paradoxical and *necessary*, and the subject both resists and embraces a multiplicitous law without which it is unable to survive.

Chapter 5, "Melancholy Gender/Refused Identification" is included below, without Adam Phillips' commentary or Butler's response.

In grief the world becomes poor and empty; in melancholia it is the ego itself.
                                                    – Freud, "Mourning and Melancholia"

How is it then that in melancholia the super-ego can become a gathering-place for the death instincts?
                                                    – Freud, *The Ego and the Id*

It may at first seem strange to think of gender as a kind of melancholy, or as one of melancholy's effects. But let us remember that in *The Ego and the Id* Freud himself acknowledged that melancholy, the unfinished process of grieving, is central to the formation of the identifications that form the ego. Indeed, identifications formed from unfinished grief are the modes in which the lost object is incorporated and phantasmatically preserved in and as the ego. Consider in conjunction with this insight Freud's further remark that "the ego is first and foremost a bodily ego,"[1] not merely a surface, but "the projection of a surface." Further, this bodily ego assumes a gendered morphology, so that the bodily ego is also a gendered ego. I hope first to explain the sense in which a melancholic identification is central to the process whereby the ego assumes a gendered character. Second, I want to explore how this analysis of the melancholic formation of gender sheds light on the predicament of living within a culture which can mourn the loss of homosexual attachment only with great difficulty.

Reflecting on his speculations in "Mourning and Melancholia," Freud writes in *The Ego and the Id* that in the earlier essay he had supposed that "an object which was lost has been set up again inside the ego – that is, that an object-cathexis had been replaced by an identification. At that time, however," he continued, "we did not appreciate the full significance of this process and did not know how common and how typical it is. Since then we have come to understand that this kind of substitution has a great share in determining the form taken by the ego and that it makes an essential contribution toward building up what is called its 'character'" (p. 28). Slightly later in the same text, Freud expands this view: "when it happens that a person has to give up a sexual object, there quite often ensues an alteration of his ego which can only be described as a setting up of the object inside the ego, as it occurs in melancholia" (29). He concludes this discussion by speculating that "it may be that this identification is the sole condition under which the id can give up its objects . . . it makes it possible to suppose that the character of the ego is a precipitate of abandoned object-cathexes and that it contains the history of those object-choices" (29). What Freud here calls the "character of the ego" appears to be the sedimentation of objects loved and lost, the archaeological remainder, as it were, of unresolved grief.

What is perhaps most striking about his formulation here is how it reverses his position in "Mourning and Melancholia" on what it means to resolve grief. In the earlier essay, Freud assumes that grief can be resolved through a de-cathexis, a breaking of attachment, as well as the subsequent making of new attachments. In *The Ego and the Id*, he makes room for the notion that melancholic identification may be a *prerequisite* for letting the object go. By claiming this, he changes what it means to "let an object go," for there is no final breaking of the attachment. There is, rather, the incorporation of the attachment *as* identification, where identification becomes a magical, a psychic form of preserving the object. Insofar as identification is the psychic preserve of the object and such identifications come to form the ego, the lost object continues to haunt and inhabit the ego as one of its constitutive identifications. The lost object is, in that sense, made coextensive with the ego itself. Indeed, one might conclude that melancholic identification permits the loss of the object in the external world precisely because it provides a way to *preserve* the object as part of the ego and, hence, to avert the loss as a complete loss. Here we see that letting the object go means, paradoxically, not full abandonment of the object but transferring the status of the object from external to internal. Giving up the object becomes possible only on the condition of a melancholic internalization or, what might for our purposes turn out to be even more important, a melancholic *incorporation*.

If in melancholia a loss is refused, it is not for that reason abolished. Internalization preserves loss in the psyche; more precisely, the internalization of loss is part of the mechanism of its refusal. If the object can no longer exist in the external world, it will then exist internally, and that internalization will be a way to disavow the loss, to keep it at bay, to stay or postpone the recognition and suffering of loss.

Is there a way in which *gender* identifications or, rather, the identifications that become central to the formation of gender, are produced through melancholic identification? It seems clear that the positions of "masculine" and "feminine," which Freud, in *Three Essays on the Theory of Sexuality* (1905), understood as the effects of laborious and uncertain accomplishment, are established in part through prohibitions which *demand the loss* of certain sexual attachments, and demand as well that those losses *not* be avowed, and *not* be grieved. If the assumption of femininity and the assumption of masculinity proceed through the accomplishment of an always tenuous heterosexuality, we might understand the force of this accomplishment as mandating the abandonment of homosexual attachments or, perhaps more trenchantly, *preempting* the possibility of homosexual attachment, a foreclosure of possibility which produces a domain of homosexuality understood as unlivable passion and ungrievable loss. This heterosexuality is produced not only through implementing the prohibition on incest but, prior to that, by enforcing the prohibition on homosexuality. The oedipal conflict presumes that heterosexual desire has already been *accomplished*, that the distinction between heterosexual and homosexual has been enforced (a distinction which, after all, has no necessity); in this sense, the prohibition on incest presupposes the prohibition on homosexuality, for it presumes the heterosexualization of desire.

To accept this view we must begin by presupposing that masculine and feminine are not dispositions, as Freud sometimes argues, but indeed accomplishments, ones which emerge in tandem with the achievement of heterosexuality. Here Freud articulates a cultural logic whereby gender is achieved and stabilized through heterosexual positioning, and where threats to heterosexuality thus become threats to gender itself. The prevalence of this heterosexual matrix in the construction of gender emerges not only in Freud's text, but in the cultural forms of life that have absorbed this matrix and are inhabited by everyday forms of gender anxiety. Hence, the fear of homosexual desire in a woman may induce a panic that she is losing her femininity, that she is not a woman, that she is no longer a proper woman, that if she is not quite a man, she is like one, and hence monstrous in some way. Or in a man, the terror of homosexual desire may lead to a terror of being construed as feminine, feminized, of no longer being properly a man, of being a "failed" man, or being in some sense a figure of monstrosity or abjection.

I would argue that phenomenologically there are many ways of experiencing gender and sexuality that do not reduce to this equation, that do not presume that gender is stabilized through the installation of a firm heterosexuality, but for the moment I want to invoke this stark and hyperbolic construction of the relation between gender and sexuality in order to think through the question of ungrieved and ungreivable loss in the formation of what we might call the gendered character of the ego.

Consider that gender is acquired at least in part through the repudiation of homosexual attachments; the girl becomes a girl through being subject to a prohibition which bars the mother as an object of desire and installs that barred object as a part of the ego, indeed, as a melancholic identification. Thus the identification contains within it both the prohibition and the desire, and so embodies the ungrieved loss of the homosexual cathexis. If one is a girl to the extent that one does not want a girl, then wanting a girl will bring being a girl into question; within this matrix, homosexual desire thus panics gender.

Heterosexuality is cultivated through prohibitions, and these prohibitions take as one of their objects homosexual attachments, thereby forcing the loss of those attachments.[2] If the girl is to transfer love from her father to a substitute object, she must, according to Freudian logic, first renounce love for her mother, and renounce it in such a way that both the aim and the object are foreclosed. She must not transfer that homosexual love onto a substitute feminine figure, but renounce the possibility of homosexual attachment itself. Only on this condition does a heterosexual aim become established as what some call a sexual orientation. Only on the condition of this foreclosure of homosexuality can the father and substitutes for him become objects of desire, and the mother become the uneasy site of identification.

Becoming a "man" within this logic requires repudiating femininity as a precondition for the heterosexualization of sexual desire and its fundamental ambivalence. If a man becomes heterosexual by repudiating the feminine, where could that repudiation live except in an identification which his heterosexual career seeks to deny? Indeed, the desire for the feminine is marked by that repudiation: he wants the woman he would never be. He wouldn't be caught dead being her: therefore he wants her. She is his repudiated identification (a repudiation he sustains as at once identification and the object of his desire). One of the most anxious aims of his desire will be to elaborate the difference between him and her, and he will seek to discover and install proof of that difference. His wanting will be haunted by a dread of being what he wants, so that his wanting will also always be a kind of dread. Precisely because what is repudiated and hence lost is preserved as a repudiated identification, this desire will attempt to overcome an identification which can never be complete.

Indeed, he will not identify with her, and he will not desire another man. That refusal to desire, that sacrifice of desire under the force of prohibition, will incorporate homosexuality as an identification with masculinity. But this masculinity will be haunted by the love it cannot grieve, and before I suggest how this might be true, I'd like to situate the kind of writing that I have been offering as a certain cultural engagement with psychoanalytic theory that belongs neither to the fields of psychology nor to psychoanalysis, but which nevertheless seeks to establish an intellectual relationship to those enterprises.

Thus far, I have been offering something like an exegesis of a certain psychoanalytic logic, one that appears in some psychoanalytic texts but which these texts and others also sometimes contest. I make no empirical claims, nor attempt a survey of current psychoanalytic scholarship on gender, sexuality, or melancholy. I want merely to suggest what I take to be some productive convergences between Freud's thinking on ungrieved and ungrievable loss and the predicament of living in a culture which can mourn the loss of homosexual attachment only with great difficulty.

This problematic is made all the more acute when we consider the ravages of AIDS, and the task of finding a public occasion and language in which to grieve this seemingly endless number of deaths. More generally, this problem makes itself felt in the uncertainty with which homosexual love and loss is regarded: is it regarded as a "true" love, a "true" loss, a love and loss worthy and capable of being grieved, and thus worthy and capable of having been lived? Or is it a love and a loss haunted by the specter of a certain unreality, a certain unthinkability, the double disavowal of the "I never loved her, and I never lost her," uttered by a woman, the "I never loved him, I never lost him," uttered by a man? Is this the "never-never" that supports the naturalized surface of heterosexual life as well as its pervasive melancholia? Is it the disavowal of loss by which sexual formation, including gay sexual formation, proceeds?

If we accept the notion that the prohibition on homosexuality operates throughout a largely heterosexual culture as one of its defining operations, then the loss of homosexual objects and aims (not simply this person of the same gender, but *any* person of the same gender) would appear to be foreclosed from the start. I say "foreclosed" to suggest that this is a preemptive loss, a mourning for unlived possibilities. If this love is from the start out of the question, then it cannot happen, and if it does, it certainly did not. If it does, it happens only under the official sign of its prohibition and disavowal.[3] When certain kinds of losses are compelled by a set of culturally prevalent prohibitions, we might expect a culturally prevalent form of melancholia, one which signals the internalization of the ungrieved and ungrievable homosexual cathexis. And where there is no public recognition or discourse through which such a loss might be named and mourned, then melancholia takes on cultural dimensions of contemporary consequence. Of course, it comes as no surprise that the more hyperbolic and defensive a masculine identification, the more fierce the ungrieved homosexual cathexis. In this sense, we might understand both "masculinity" and "femininity" as formed and consolidated through identifications which are in part composed of disavowed grief.

If we accept the notion that heterosexuality naturalizes itself by insisting on the radical otherness of homosexuality, then heterosexual identity is purchased through a melancholic incorporation of the love that it disavows: the man who insists upon the coherence of his heterosexuality will claim that he never loved another man, and hence never lost another man. That love, that attachment becomes subject to a double disavowal, a never having loved, and a never having lost. This "never-never" thus founds the heterosexual subject, as it were; it is an identity based upon the refusal to avow an attachment and, hence, the refusal to grieve.

There is perhaps a more culturally instructive way of describing this scenario, for it is not simply a matter of an individual's unwillingness to avow and hence to grieve homosexual attachments. When the prohibition against homosexuality is culturally pervasive, then the "loss" of homosexual love is precipitated through a prohibition which is repeated and ritualized throughout the culture. What ensues is a culture of gender melancholy in which masculinity and femininity emerge as the traces of an ungrieved and ungrievable love; indeed, where masculinity and femininity within the heterosexual matrix are strengthened through the repudiations that they perform. In opposition to a conception of sexuality which is said to "express" a gender, gender itself is here understood to be composed of precisely what remains inarticulate in sexuality.

If we understand gender melancholy in this way, then perhaps we can make sense of the peculiar phenomenon whereby homosexual desire becomes a source of guilt. In "Mourning and Melancholia" Freud argues that melancholy is marked by the experience of self-beratement. He writes, "If one listens carefully to the many and various self-accusations of the melancholic, one cannot in the end avoid the impression that often the most violent of them are hardly at all applicable to the patient himself, but that with insignificant modifications they do fit someone else, some person whom the patient loves, has loved or ought to love . . . the self-reproaches are reproaches against a loved object which have been shifted on to the patient's own ego."[4]

Freud goes on to conjecture that the conflict with the other which remains unresolved at the time the other is lost reemerges in the psyche as a way of continuing the quarrel. Indeed, anger at the other is doubtless exacerbated by the death or departure which occasions the loss. But this anger is turned inward and becomes the substance of self-beratement.

In "On Narcissism," Freud links the experience of guilt with the turning back into the ego of homosexual libido.[5] Putting aside the question of whether libido can be homosexual or heterosexual, we might rephrase Freud and consider guilt as the turning back into the ego of homosexual attachment. If the loss becomes a renewed scene of conflict, and if the aggression that follows from that loss cannot be articulated or externalized, then it rebounds upon the ego itself, in the form of a super-ego. This will eventually lead Freud to link melancholic identification with the agency of the super-ego in *The Ego and the Id*, but already in "On Narcissism" we have some sense of how guilt is wrought from ungrievable homosexuality.

The ego is said to become impoverished in melancholia, but it appears as poor precisely through the workings of self-beratement. The ego-ideal, what Freud calls the "measure" against which the ego is judged by the super-ego, is precisely the ideal of social rectitude defined over and against homosexuality. "This ideal," Freud writes, "has a social side: it is also the common ideal of a family, a class or a nation. It not only binds the narcissistic libido, but also a considerable amount of the person's homosexual libido, which in this way becomes turned back into the ego. The dissatisfaction due to the non-fulfillment of this ideal liberates homosexual libido, which is transformed into a sense of guilt (dread of the community)" (81).

But the movement of this "transformation" is not altogether clear. After all, Freud will argue in *Civilization and Its Discontents* that these social ideals are transformed into a sense of guilt through a kind of internalization which is not, ultimately, mimetic. In "On Narcissism," it is not that one treats oneself as harshly as one was treated but rather that the aggression toward the ideal and its unfulfillability is turned inward, and this self-aggression becomes the primary structure of conscience: "by means of identification [the child] takes the unattackable authority into himself" (86).

In this sense, in melancholia the super-ego can become a gathering place for the death instincts. As such, it is not necessarily the same as those instincts or their effect. In this way, melancholia attracts the death instincts to the super-ego, the death instincts being understood as a regressive striving toward organic equilibrium, and the self-beratement of the super-ego being understood to make use of that regressive striving for its own purposes. Melancholy is both the refusal of grief and the incorporation of loss, a miming of the death it cannot mourn. Yet the incorporation of death draws upon the death instincts to such a degree that we might well wonder whether the two can be separated from one another, whether analytically or phenomenologically.

The prohibition on homosexuality preempts the process of grief and prompts a melancholic identification which effectively turns homosexual desire back upon itself. This turning back upon itself is precisely the action of self-beratement and guilt. Significantly, homosexuality is *not* abolished but preserved, though preserved precisely in the prohibition on homosexuality. In *Civilization and Its Discontents*, Freud makes clear that conscience requires the continuous sacrifice or renunciation of instinct to produce the peculiar satisfaction that conscience requires; conscience is never assuaged by renunciation, but is paradoxically strengthened ("renunciation breeds intolerance").[6] Renunciation does not abolish the instinct; it deploys the instinct for its own purposes, so that prohibition, and the lived experience of prohibition as repeated renunciation, is nourished precisely by the instinct that it renounces. In this scenario, renunciation requires the very homosexuality that it condemns, not as its external object, but as its own most treasured source of sustenance. The act of renouncing homosexuality thus paradoxically strengthens homosexuality, but it strengthens homosexuality precisely *as* the power of renunciation. Renunciation becomes the aim and vehicle of satisfaction. And it is, we might conjecture, precisely the fear of setting homosexuality loose from this circuit of renunciation that so terrifies the guardians of masculinity in the US military. What would masculinity "be" without this aggressive circuit of renunciation from which it is wrought? Gays in the military threaten to undo masculinity only because this masculinity is made of repudiated homosexuality.[7]

Some suggestions I made in *Bodies That Matter*[8] can facilitate the transition from the consideration of melancholia as a specifically psychic economy to the production of the circuitry of melancholia as part of the operation of regulatory power. If melancholia designates a sphere of attachment that is not explicitly produced as an object of discourse, then it erodes the operation of language that not only posits objects, but regulates and normalizes objects through that positing. If melancholia appears at first to be a form of containment, a way of internalizing an attachment that is barred from the world, it also establishes the psychic conditions for regarding "the world" itself as contingently organized through certain kinds of foreclosures.[9]

Having described a melancholy produced through the compulsory production of heterosexuality, thus, a heterosexual melancholy that one might read in the workings of gender itself, I want now to suggest that rigid forms of gender and sexual identification, whether homosexual or heterosexual, appear to spawn forms of melancholy. I would like first to reconsider the theory of gender as performative that I elaborated in *Gender Trouble*, and then to turn to the question of gay melancholia and the political consequences of ungrievable loss.

There I argued that gender is performative, by which I meant that no gender is "expressed" by actions, gestures, or speech, but that the performance of gender produces retroactively the illusion that there is an inner gender core. That is, the performance of gender retroactively produces the effect of some true or abiding feminine essence or disposition, so that one cannot use an expressive model for thinking about gender. Moreover, I argued that gender is produced as a ritualized repetition of conventions, and that this ritual is socially compelled in part by the force of a compulsory heterosexuality. In this context, I would like to return to the question of drag to explain in clearer terms how I understand psychoanalysis to be linked with gender performativity, and how I take performativity to be linked with melancholia.

It is not enough to say that gender is performed, or that the meaning of gender can be derived from its performance, whether or not one wants to rethink performance as a compulsory social ritual. Clearly there are workings of gender that do not "show" in what is performed as gender, and to reduce the psychic workings of gender to the literal performance of gender would be a mistake. Psychoanalysis insists that the opacity of the unconscious sets limits to the exteriorization of the psyche. It also argues – rightly, I think – that what is exteriorized or performed can only be understood by reference to what is barred from performance, what cannot or will not be performed.

The relation between drag performances and gender performativity in *Gender Trouble* goes something like this: when a man is performing drag as a woman, the "imitation" that drag is said to be is taken as an "imitation" of femininity, but the "femininity" that he imitates is not understood as being itself an imitation. Yet if one considers that gender is acquired, that it is assumed in relation to ideals which are never quite inhabited by anyone, then femininity is an ideal which everyone always and only "imitates." Thus, drag imitates the imitative structure of gender, revealing gender itself to be an imitation. However attractive this formulation may have seemed, it didn't address the question of how certain forms of disavowal and repudiation come to organize the performance of gender. How is the phenomenon of gender melancholia to be related to the practice of gender performativity?

Moreover, given the iconographic figure of the melancholic drag queen, one might ask whether there is not a dissatisfied longing in the mimetic incorporation of gender that is drag. Here one might ask also after the disavowal which occasions the performance and which performance might be said to enact, where performance engages "acting out" in the psychoanalytic sense. If melancholia in Freud's sense is the effect of an ungrieved loss,[10] performance, understood as "acting out," may be related to the problem of unacknowledged loss. If there is an ungrieved loss in drag performance, perhaps it is a loss that is refused and incorporated in the performed identification, one which reiterates a gendered idealization and its radical uninhabitability. This is, then, neither a territorialization of the feminine by the masculine nor a sign of the essential plasticity of gender. It suggests that the performance allegorizes a loss it cannot grieve, allegorizes the incorporative fantasy of melancholia whereby an object is phantasmatically taken in or on as a way of refusing to let it go. Gender itself might be understood in part as the "acting out" of unresolved grief.

The above analysis is a risky one because it suggests that for a "man" performing femininity, or for a "woman" performing masculinity (the latter is always, in effect, to perform a little less, given that femininity is cast as the spectacular gender), there is an attachment to – and a loss and refusal of – the figure of femininity by the man, or the figure of masculinity by the woman. It is important to underscore that, although drag is an effort to negotiate cross-gendered identification, cross-gendered identification is not the only paradigm for thinking about homosexuality, merely one among others. Drag allegorizes some set of melancholic incorporative fantasies that stabilize *gender*. Not only are a vast number of drag performers straight, but it would be a mistake to think that homosexuality is best explained through the performativity that is drag. What does seem useful in this analysis, however, is that drag exposes or allegorizes the mundane psychic and performative practices by which hetero-sexualized genders form themselves through renouncing the *possibility* of homosexuality, a foreclosure which produces both a field of heterosexual objects and a domain of those whom it would be impossible to love. Drag thus allegorizes *heterosexual melancholy*, the melancholy by which a masculine gender is formed from the refusal to grieve the masculine as a possibility of love; a feminine gender is formed (taken on, assumed) through the incorpora-tive fantasy by which the feminine is excluded as a possible object of love, an exclusion never grieved, but "preserved" through heightened feminine iden-tification. In this sense, the "truest" lesbian melancholic is the strictly straight woman, and the "truest" gay male melancholic is the strictly straight man.

What drag does expose, however, is that in the "normal" constitution of gender presentation, the gender that is performed is constituted by a set of disavowed attachments, identifications which constitute a different domain of the "unperformable." Indeed, what constitutes the *sexually* unperformable may – but need not – be performed as *gender identification*.[11] To the extent that homosexual attachments remain unacknowledged within normative hetero-sexuality, they are not merely constituted as desires which emerge and subse-quently become prohibited; rather, these desires are proscribed from the start. And when they do emerge on the far side of the censor, they may well carry the mark of impossibility with them, performing, as it were, as the impossible within the possible. As such, they will not be attachments that can be openly grieved. This is, then, less a *refusal* to grieve (the Mitscherlich formulation that accents the choice involved) than a preemption of grief performed by the absence of cultural conventions for avowing the loss of homosexual love. And this absence produces a culture of heterosexual melancholy, one which can be read in the hyperbolic identifications by which mundane heterosexual masculinity and femininity confirm themselves. The straight man *becomes* (mimes, cites, appropriates, assumes the status of) the man he "never" loved and "never" grieved; the straight woman *becomes* the woman she "never" loved and "never" grieved. It is in this sense, then, that what is most apparently performed as gender is the sign and symptom of a pervasive disavowal.

Gay melancholia, however, also contains anger that can be translated into political expression. It is precisely to counter this pervasive cultural risk of gay melancholia (what the newspapers generalize as "depression") that there has been an insistent publicization and politicization of grief over those who have died from AIDS. The Names Project Quilt is exemplary, ritualizing and repeating the name itself as a way of publically avowing limitless loss.[12]

Insofar as the grief remains unspeakable, the rage over the loss can redouble by virtue of remaining unavowed. And if that rage is publically proscribed, the melancholic effects of such a proscription can achieve suicidal proportions. The emergence of collective institutions for grieving are thus crucial to survival, to reassembling community, to rearticulating kinship, to reweaving sustaining relations. Insofar as they involve the publicization and dramatization of death – as in the case of "die-ins" by Queer Nation – they call for being read as life-affirming rejoinders to the dire psychic consequences of a grieving process culturally thwarted and proscribed.

Melancholy can work, however, within homosexuality in specific ways that call for rethinking. Within the formation of gay and lesbian identity, there may be an effort to disavow a constitutive relationship to heterosexuality. When this disavowal is understood as a political necessity in order to *specify* gay and lesbian identity over and against its ostensible opposite, heterosexuality, that cultural practice paradoxically culminates in a weakening of the very constituency it is meant to unite. Not only does such a strategy attribute a false and monolithic status to heterosexuality, but it misses the political opportunity to work on the weakness in heterosexual subjectivation and to refute the logic of mutual exclusion by which heterosexism proceeds. Moreover, a full-scale denial of the interrelationship can constitute a rejection of heterosexuality that is to some degree an identification *with* a rejected heterosexuality. Important to this economy, however, is the refusal to recognize this identification that is, as it were, already made, a refusal which absently designates the domain of a specifically gay melancholia, a loss which cannot be recognized and, hence, cannot be mourned. For a gay or lesbian identity position to sustain its appearance as coherent, heterosexuality must remain in that rejected and repudiated place. Paradoxically, its heterosexual *remains* must be *sustained* precisely through insisting on the seamless coherence of a specifically gay identity. Here it should become clear that a radical refusal to identify suggests that on some level an identification has already taken place, an identification has been made and disavowed, whose symptomatic appearance is the insistence, the overdetermination of the identification that is, as it were, worn on the body that shows.

This raises the political question of the cost of articulating a coherent identity position by producing, excluding, and repudiating a domain of abjected specters that threaten the arbitrarily closed domain of subject positions. Perhaps only by risking the *incoherence* of identity is connection possible, a political point that correlates with Leo Bersani's insight that only the decentered subject is available to desire.[13] What cannot be avowed as a constitutive identification for any given subject position runs the risk not only of becoming externalized in a degraded form, but repeatedly repudiated and subject to a policy of disavowal.

The logic of repudiation that I've charted here is in some ways a hyperbolic theory, a logic in drag, as it were, which overstates the case, but overstates it for a reason. There is no necessary reason for identification to oppose desire, or for desire to be fueled by repudiation. This remains true for heterosexuality and homosexuality alike, and for forms of bisexuality that take themselves to be composite forms of each. Indeed, we are made all the more fragile under the pressure of such rules, and all the more mobile when ambivalence and loss are given a dramatic language in which to do their acting out.

Notes

This paper was first presented at the Division 39 Meetings of the American Psychological Association in New York City in April 1993. It was subsequently published with the replies from and to Adam Phillips in *Psychoanalytic Dialogues: A Journal of Relational Perspectives* 5 no. 2 (1995): 165–94.

1   Sigmund Freud, *The Ego and the Id*, in *The Standard Edition of the Complete Psychological Works of Sigmund Freud*, ed. and trans. James Strachey, 24 vols. (London: Hogarth, 1953–74), 19: 16.

2   Presumably, sexuality must be trained away from things, animals, parts of all of the above, and narcissistic attachments of various kinds.

3   The notion of foreclosure has become Lacanian terminology for Freud's notion of *Verwerfung*. Distinguished from repression understood as an action by an already-formed subject, foreclosure is an act of negation that founds and forms the subject. See the entry "Forclusion" in J. Laplanche and J.-B. Pontalis, *Vocabulaire de la psychanalyse* (Paris: Presses Universitaires de France, 1967), pp. 163–7.

4   Sigmund Freud, "Mourning and Melancholia," *Standard Edition*, 14: 169.

5   Sigmund Freud, "On Narcissism: An Introduction," *Standard Edition*, 14: 81–2.

6   See Freud, *Civilization and Its Discontents*, trans. James Strachey, (New York: Norton, 1977), pp. 81–92.

7   See "Contagious Word: 'Homosexuality' and the Military," in my *Excitable Speech* (New York: Routledge, 1996).

8   See my *Bodies That Matter* (New York: Routledge, 1993), pp. 169–77.

9   The following argument is taken from my *Bodies That Matter*, pp. 233–6.

10 See "Freud and the Melancholia of Gender" in my *Gender Trouble: Feminism and the Subversion of Identity* (New York: Routledge, 1990).

11 This is not to suggest that an exclusionary matrix rigorously distinguishes between how one identifies and how one desires; it is quite possible to have overlapping identification and desire in heterosexual or homosexual exchange, or in a bisexual history of sexual practice. Furthermore, "masculinity" and "femininity" do not exhaust the terms for either eroticized identification or desire.

12 See Douglas Crimp, "Mourning and Militancy," *October* 51 (Winter 1989): 97–107.

13 Leo Bersani, *The Freudian Body: Psychoanalysis and Art* (New York: Columbia University Press, 1986), pp. 64–6, 112–13.

10

Competing Universalities (2000)

Introduction

This sequence of essay exchanges emerged from conversations between Butler and the two political theorists Ernesto Laclau and Slavoj Žižek about poststructuralism, psychoanalysis, and hegemony. In their joint introduction the thinkers state their shared commitment to a Left political project and their affinity to Marxism, but although all three value the "failure" of the subject as a form of democratic contestation, Butler, Laclau, and Žižek diverge as much as they converge in their theorizations of the subject. The book is dialogical (indeed, dialectical), and the theorists interrogate one another's arguments in each of their three contributions. Broadly speaking their essays address the following questions: how is power deployed? (hegemony); is it possible or politically useful to assume universal norms and values? (universality); are there useful political outcomes in *not* assuming such universals? (contingency). At the beginning of the book, each thinker is allotted ten specific questions which identify the issues they wish to consider in the exchanges that follow. Among other concerns, Butler's questions address the compatibility of psychoanalysis and politics in general and Lacanianism and hegemony in particular; the future of feminism; the possibility of agency; the role of Kantianism, universalism, and historicism in the theoretical field; the necessity of autocritique for the critical theorist.

Butler's three contributions, "Restaging the Universal: Hegemony and the Limits of Formalism," "Competing Universalities," and "Dynamic Conclusions," continue to reject what she calls "empty universals" as formalistic, oppressive and exclusionary. Instead, Butler emphasizes the political value of strategic contingency which may lead to "perverse reiterations" of (specifically heterosexual) norms. What might be called "the politics of the perverse" will be familiar from earlier work where Butler insists on power's instability and its vulnerability to re-contextualization and re-citation. "Reiteration" has always been a point of theoretical and political leverage for Butler, and her contributions to *Contingency* continue to exploit the vulnerability of hegemonic terms and structures to appropriation and redeployment. Accordingly, in her second contribution Butler affirms

Extracts from pp. 143–8, 151–8, 159–62, 175–81 in Judith Butler, Ernesto Laclau, Slavoj Žižek, *Contingency, Hegemony, Universality: Contemporary Dialogues on the Left.* London: Verso, 2000. Reprinted by permission of Verso.

the necessity of seeking out the incoherencies of universality in a political practice which in her third essay she calls "affirmative deconstruction."

Asserting the need to keep political conflict alive, Butler's view is firmly anti-assimilationist: even though what she calls "the shiny new gay citizen" may desire access to institutions such as marriage and the military which currently exclude them, Butler claims that joining such institutions is not a useful political tactic because it effectively strengthens them. A more radical but risky strategy would be to "starve" these hegemonic structures of their ideological power by rejecting them. In a clear departure from *Gender Trouble, Bodies That Matter*, and *Excitable Speech*, Butler seems suspicious of attempts to occupy the dominant terms of discourse, and rather than appropriation, she now talks in terms of what she calls "a performativity proper to refusal." Similarly, like Gayatri Chakravorty Spivak, in her more recent work does not endorse strategic essentialism because of the potential violence of its ontological (albeit strategic) foreclosures. See the *jac* interview, reprinted below, pp. 325–56, where Butler claims that she is now less sanguine about the possibility of a "radical unmooring" than she was when she wrote *Bodies That Matter*.

The kind of performativity Butler now advocates will *not* involve occupying dominant terms in order to subvert them from within, and rather than appropriating specific heterosexual norms (marriage, for example) broader ontological "forms of alliance and exchange" such as sexuality and gender must be radically reiterated. Deconstruction and psychoanalysis still underpin a political project in which Butler seeks out the unintended meanings and non-intentional effects of discourse, and as always, the interpellative failures and subversive reterritorializations occur *within* the hegemonic regulatory schema, so that resistance and domination are implicated and perhaps even impossible to distinguish from each other.

Affirmative deconstruction as Butler describes it is similarly difficult to define – neither strategy nor practice exactly, but a coalition of action and thought whereby the terms by which we are constituted and oppressed may be genealogized, appropriated, and re-deployed. The democratic political project is necessarily incomplete, what Butler in a non-teleological spirit calls "the open-ended futurity of hegemony," and like Marx, Butler believes that democracy is necessarily unrealizable since if it were realized it would no longer be democracy or democratic. Stating her alliance with those contemporary critical thinkers who represent "the valorization of unrealizability" (Homi K. Bhabha, Jacques Derrida, Drucilla Cornell, Gayatri Chakravorty Spivak, as well as Žižek and Laclau), Butler also argues for the importance of "let[ting] the signifier congeal at the moment of use" even as it is acknowledged that signifiers are "under erasure," unstable, vulnerable to re-citation. Translation rather than metalanguage, contingency and the local rather than universality and the global, will provide the conditions of possibility for an ongoing democratic project of contestation whereby the terms that constitute us are simultaneously deployed, deconstructed, and reiterated. According to Butler, it is at the level of language that political struggle takes place, and "truth" (there may indeed be such a thing) can only be affirmed in language which reveals its vulnerability to affirmative reinscription and re-contextualization – perhaps not "truth" at all as many would understand it.

The extracts included here are taken from "Competing Universalities," Butler's second contribution to the book, where she discusses the issues of sexual difference, Lacanians and gay parenting, and gay marriage.

The Doubling of Sexual Difference

There are surely some feminists who would agree with the primacy given to sexual difference, but I am not one of them. The formulation casts sexual difference in the first instance as more fundamental than other kinds of differences, and it gives it a structural status, whether transcendental in the garden-variety or "quasi-" mode, which purports to be significantly different from the concrete formulations it receives within the horizon of historical meaning. When the claim is made that sexual difference at this most funda-mental level is merely formal (Shepherdson[1]) or empty (Žižek), we are in the same quandary as we were in with ostensibly formal concepts such as univer-sality: is it fundamentally formal, or does it *become* formal, become available to a formalization on the condition that certain kinds of exclusions are performed which enable that very formalization in its putatively transcendental mode?

This becomes an important consideration when we recognize that the spheres of "ideality" which Žižek attributes to the symbolic order – the structures that govern symbolizability – are also structural features of the analysis, not contingent norms that have become rarefied as psychic ideals. Sexual difference is, thus, in his view, (1) non-symbolizable; (2) the occasion for contesting interpretations of what it is; (3) symbolizable in ideal terms, where the ideality of the ideal carries with it the original non-symbolizability of sexual difference itself. Here again the disagreement seems inevitable. Do we want to affirm that there is an ideal big Other, or an ideal small other, which is more fundamental than any of its social formulations? Or do we want to question whether any ideality that pertains to sexual difference is ever not constituted by actively reproduced gender norms that pass their ideality off as essential to a pre-social and ineffable sexual difference?

Of course, the reply from even my most progressive Lacanian friends is that I have no need to worry about this unnamable sexual difference that we nevertheless name, since it has no content but is purely formal, forever empty. But here I would refer back to the point made so trenchantly by Hegel against Kantian formalisms: the empty and formal structure is established precisely through the not fully successful sublimation of content as form. It is not adequate to claim that the formal structure of sexual difference is first and foremost without content, but that it comes to be "filled in" with content by a subsequent and anterior act. That formulation not only sustains a fully external relation between form and content, but works to impede the reading that might show us how certain kinds of formalisms are generated by a process of abstraction that is never fully free from the remainder of the content it refuses. The formal character of this originary, pre-social sexual difference in its ostensible emptiness is *accomplished* precisely through the reification by which a certain idealized and necessary dimorphism takes hold. The trace or remainder which formalism needs to erase, but which is the sign of its foundation in that which is anterior to itself, often operates as the clue to its unravelling. The fact that claims such as "cultural intelligibility requires sexual difference" or "there is no culture without sexual difference" circulate within the Lacanian discourse intimates something of the constraining normativity that fuels this transcendental turn, a normativity secured from criticism precisely because it officially announces itself as prior to and untainted by any given social operation of sexual difference. If Žižek can write, as he does: "the ultimate question is: which specific content has to be excluded so that the very *empty form* of universality emerges as the 'battlefield' for hegemony?" then he can certainly entertain the question: "which specific content has to be excluded so that the very *empty form* of sexual difference emerges as a battlefield for hegemony?"

Of course, as with any purely speculative position, one might well ask: who posits the original and final ineffability of sexual difference, and what aims does such a positing achieve? This most unverifiable of concepts is offered as the condition of verifiability itself, and we are faced with a choice between an uncritical theological affirmation or a critical social inquiry: do we accept this description of the fundamental ground of intelligibility, or do we begin to ask what kinds of foreclosures such a positing achieves, and at what expense?

If we were to accept this position, we could argue that sexual difference has a transcendental status even when sexed bodies emerge that do not fit squarely within ideal gender dimorphism. We could nevertheless explain intersexuality by claiming that the ideal is still there, but the bodies in question – contingent, historically formed – do not conform to the ideal, and it is their nonconformity that is the essential relation to the ideal at hand. It would not matter whether sexual difference is instantiated in living, biological bodies, for the ineffability and non-symbolizability of this most hallowed of differences would depend on no instantiation to be true. Or, indeed, we could, in trying to think about transsexuality, follow the pathologizing discourse of Catherine Millot,[2] who insists upon the primacy and persistence of sexual difference in the face of those lives which suffer under that ideality and seek to transform the fixity of that belief. Or take the extraordinarily regressive political claims made by Sylviane Agacinski, Irène Thèry, and Françoise Héritier in relation to contemporary

French efforts to extend legally sanctioned alliances to non-married individuals.[3] Agacinski notes that precisely because no culture can emerge without the presumption of sexual difference (as its ground and condition and occasion), such legislation must be opposed, because it is at war with the fundamental presuppositions of culture itself. Héritier makes the same argument from the perspective of Lévi-Straussian anthropology, arguing that efforts to counter nature in this regard will produce psychotic consequences.[4] Indeed, this claim was made so successfully that the version of the law that finally won approval in the French National Assembly explicitly denies the rights of gays and lesbians to adopt, fearing that the children produced and raised under such circumstances, counter to nature and culture alike, would be led into psychosis.

Héritier cited the notion of the "symbolic" that underlies all cultural intelligibility in the work of Lévi-Strauss. And Jacques-Alain Miller also joined in, writing that whereas it is certain that homosexuals should be granted acknowledgement of their relationships, it would not be possible to extend marriage-like legal arrangements to them, for the principle of fidelity for any conjugal pair is secured by the "the feminine presence," and gay men apparently lack this crucial anchor in their relationships.[5]

One might well argue that these various political positions which make use of the doctrine of sexual difference – some of which are derived from Lévi-Strauss, and some from Lacan – are inappropriate applications of the theory; and that if sexual difference were safeguarded as a truly empty and formal difference, it could not be identified with any of its given social formulations.

But we have seen above how difficult it is, even on the conceptual level, to keep the transcendental and the social apart. For even if the claim is that sexual difference cannot be identified with any of its concrete formulations or, indeed, its "contents," it is equally impossible to claim that it is radically extricable from any of them as well. Here we see something of the consequences of the vacillating status of the term. It is supposed to be (quasi-) transcendental, belonging to a "level" other than the social and symbolizable, yet if it grounds and sustains the historical and social formulations of sexual difference, it is their very condition and part of their very definition. Indeed, it is the non-symbolizable condition of symbolizability, according to those who accept this view.

My point, however, is that to be the transcendental condition of possibility for any given formulation of sexual difference is also to be, precisely, the *sine qua non* of all those formulations, the condition without which they cannot come into intelligibility. The "quasi-" that precedes the transcendental is meant to ameliorate the harshness of this effect, but it also sidesteps the question: what sense of transcendental is in use here? In the Kantian vein, "transcendental" can mean: the condition without which nothing can appear. But it can also mean: the regulatory and constitutive conditions of the appearance of any given object. The latter sense is the one in which the condition is not external to the object it occasions, but is its constitutive condition and the principle of its development and appearance. *The transcendental thus offers the criterial conditions that constrain the emergence of the thematizable.* And if this transcendental field is not considered to have a historicity – that is, is not considered to be a shifting episteme which might be altered and revised over time – it is unclear to me what place it can fruitfully have for an account of hegemony that seeks to sustain and promote a more radically democratic formulation of sex and sexual difference.

If sexual difference enjoys this quasi-transcendental status, then all the concrete formulations of sexual difference (second-order forms of sexual difference) not only implicitly refer back to the more originary formulation but are, in their very expression, constrained by this non-thematizable normative condition. Thus, sexual difference in the more originary sense operates as a radically incontestable principle or criterion that establishes intelligibility through foreclosure or, indeed, through pathologization or, indeed, through active political disenfranchisement. As non-thematizable, it is immune from critical examination, yet it is necessary and essential: a truly felicitous instrument of power. If it is a "condition" of intelligibility, then there will be certain forms that threaten intelligibility, threaten the possibility of a viable life within the sociohistorical world. Sexual difference thus functions not merely as a ground but as a defining condition that must be instituted and safeguarded against attempts to undermine it (intersexuality, transsexuality, lesbian and gay partnership, to name but a few).

Hence it is not merely a poor use of Lacan or of the symbolic order when intellectuals argue against non-normative sexual practices on the grounds that they are inimical to the conditions of culture itself. Precisely because the transcendental does not and cannot keep its separate place as a more fundamental "level," precisely because sexual difference as transcendental ground must not only take shape within the horizon of intelligibility but structure and limit that horizon as well, it functions actively and normatively to constrain what will and will not count as an intelligible alternative within culture. Thus, as a transcendental claim, sexual difference should be rigorously opposed by anyone who wants to guard against a theory that would prescribe in advance what kinds of sexual arrangements will and will not be permitted in intelligible culture. The inevitable vacillation between the transcendental and social functioning of the term makes its prescriptive function inevitable. [. . .]

The Fantasy in the Norm

In a Foucauldian perspective, one question is whether the very regime of power that seeks to regulate the subject does so by providing a principle of self-definition for the subject. If it does, and subjectivation is bound up with subjection in this way, then it will not do to invoke a notion of the subject as the ground of agency, since the subject is itself produced through operations of power that delimit in advance what the aims and expanse of agency will be. It does not follow from this insight, however, that we are all always-already trapped, and that there is no point of resistance to regulation or to the form of subjection that regulation takes. What it does mean, however, is that we ought not to think that by embracing the subject as a ground of agency, we will have countered the effects of regulatory power. The analysis of psychic life becomes crucial here, because the social norms that work on the subject to produce its desires and restrict its operation do not operate unilaterally. They are not simply imposed and internalized in a given form. Indeed, no norm can operate on a subject without the activation of fantasy and, more specifically, the phantasmatic attachment to ideals that are at once social and psychic. Psychoanalysis enters Foucauldian analysis precisely at the point where one wishes to understand the phantasmatic dimension of social norms. But I would caution against understanding fantasy as something that occurs "on one level" and social interpellation as something that takes place "on another level." These architectonic moves do not answer the question of the interrelation between the two processes or, indeed, how social normativity is not finally thinkable outside the psychic reality which is the instrument and source of its continuing effectivity. Norms are not only embodied, as Bourdieu has argued, but embodiment is itself a mode of interpretation, not always conscious, which subjects normativity itself to an iterable temporality. Norms are not static entities, but incorporated and interpreted features of existence that are sustained by the idealizations furnished by fantasy.

Whereas Žižek insists that at the heart of psychic life one finds a "traumatic kernel/remainder" which he describes alternately as material and ideal, the materiality to which he refers, however, has nothing to do with material relations. This traumatic kernel is not composed of social relations but functions as a limit-point of sociality, figured according to metaphors of materiality – that is to say, kernels and stains – but neither apparent nor legible outside of these figurations and not, strictly speaking, ideal, since it is not conceptualizable, and functions, indeed, as the limit of conceptualization as well. I wonder whether a Wittgensteinian approach to this question might simplify matters. We can agree that there is a limit to conceptualization and to any given formulation of sociality, and that we encounter this limit at various liminal and spectral moments in experience. But why are we then compelled to give a technical name to this limit, "the Real," and to make the further claim that the subject is constituted by this foreclosure? The use of the technical nomenclature opens up more problems than it solves. On the one hand, we are to accept that "the Real" means nothing other than the constitutive limit of the subject; yet on the other hand, why is it that any effort to refer to the constitutive limit of the subject in ways that do not use that nomenclature are considered a failure to understand its proper operation? Are we using the categories to understand the phenomena, or marshalling the phenomena to shore up the categories "in the name of the Father," if you will? Similarly, we can try to accept the watered-down notion of the symbolic as separable from normative kinship, but why is there all that talk about the place of the Father and the Phallus? One can, through definitional *fiat*, proclaim that the symbolic commits one to no particular notion of kinship or perhaps, more generally, to a fully empty and generalized conception of kinship, but then it is hard to know why the "positions" in this symbolic always revolve around an idealized notion of heterosexual parenting. Just as Jungians never did supply a satisfactory answer for why the term "feminine" was used when anyone of any gender could be the bearer of that principle, so Lacanians are hard-pressed to justify the recirculation of patriarchal kin positions as the capitalized "Law" at the same time as they attempt to define such socially saturated terms in ways that immunize them from all sociality or, worse, render them as the pre-social (quasi-)transcendental condition of sociality as such. The fact that my friends Slavoj and Ernesto claim that the term "Phallus" can be definitionally separated from phallogocentrism constitutes a neologistic accomplishment before which I am in awe. I fear that their statement rhetorically refutes its own propositional content, but I shall say no more.

Whereas I accept the psychoanalytic postulate, eschewed by some prevalent forms of ego psychology, that the subject comes into being on the basis of foreclosure (Laplanche), I do not understand this foreclosure as the vanishing point of sociality. Although it might be inevitable that individuation requires a foreclosure that produces the unconscious, a remainder, it seems equally inevitable that the unconscious is not presocial, but *a certain mode in which the unspeakably social endures.* The unconscious is not a psychic reality purified of social content that subsequently constitutes a necessary gap in the domain of conscious, social life. *The unconscious is also an ongoing psychic condition in which norms are registered in both normalizing and non-normalizing ways, the postulated site of their fortification, their undoing and their perversion, the unpredictable trajectory of their appropriation in identifications and disavowals that are not always consciously or deliberately performed.* The foreclosures that found – and destabilize – the subject are articulated through trajectories of power, regulatory ideals which constrain what will and will not be a person, which tend to separate the person from the animal, to distinguish between two sexes, to craft identification in the direction of an "inevitable" heterosexuality and ideal morphologies of gender, and can also produce the material for tenacious identifications and disavowals in relation to racial, national and class identities that are very often difficult to "argue" with or against.

Psychoanalysis cannot conduct an analysis of psychic reality that presumes the autonomy of that sphere unless it is willing to naturalize the forms of social power that produce the effect of that autonomy. Power emerges in and as the formation of the subject: to separate the subject-generating function of foreclosure from the realm of productive power is to disavow the way in which social meanings become interpreted as part of the very action of unconscious psychic processes. Moreover, if the ideals of personhood that govern self-definition on preconscious and unconscious levels are themselves produced through foreclosures of various kinds, then the panic, terror, trauma, anger, passion, and desire that emerge in relation to such ideals cannot be understood without reference to their social formulations. This is not to say that social forms of power produce subjects as their simple effects, nor is it to claim that norms are internalized as psychic reality along behaviourist lines. It is to emphasize, however, the way that social norms are variously lived as psychic reality, suggesting that key psychic states such as melancholia or mania, paranoia and fetishism, not only assume specific forms under certain social conditions, but have no underlying essence other than the specific forms they assume. The specificity of the psyche does not imply its autonomy.

The prospect of engaging in sexual relations that might invite social condemnation can be read in any number of ways, but there is no way to dispute the operation of the social norm in the fantasy. Of course, the norm does not always operate in the same way: it may be that the sexual practice is desired precisely because of the opprobrium it promises, and that the opprobrium is sought because it promises, psychically, to restore a lost object, a parental figure, or indeed a figure of the law, and to restore a connection through the scene of punishment (much of melancholia is based upon this self-vanquishing wish). Or it may be that the sexual practice is desired precisely because it acts as a defence against another sort of sexual practice that is feared or disavowed, and that the entire drama of desire and anticipated condemnation operates to deflect from another, more painful psychic consequence. In any of these cases, the norm operates to structure the fantasy, but it is also, as it were, put to use in variable ways by the psyche. Thus, the norm structures the fantasy, but does not determine it; the fantasy makes use of the norm, but does not create it.

If that sexual practice turned out to be, say, anal penetration, and the person who lives a vexed relation to it turns out to be a man in some generic sense, then many questions can emerge: is the fantasy to perform or to receive it, to perform and receive it both at once; is the fantasy also operating as a substitute for another fantasy, one which has an unacceptable aggression at its core, or which involves incestuous desire? What figure does the social norm assume within the fantasy, and is the identification with the desire and with the law both at once, so that it is not easy to say where the "I" might be simply located within the scenography of the fantasy? And if one finds oneself in a debilitated state in relation to this fantasy, suffering paranoia and shame, unable to emerge in public, interact with others, do we not need an explanation for this kind of suffering that takes into account not only the social power of the norm, but the exacerbation of that social power as it enters into and shapes the psychic life of fantasy? Here it would not be possible to postulate the social norm on one side of the analysis, and the fantasy on the other, for the *modus operandi* of the norm is the fantasy, and the very syntax of the fantasy could not be read without an understanding of the lexicon of the social norm. The norm does not simply enter into the life of sexuality, as if norm and sexuality were separable: the norm is sexualized and sexualizing, and sexuality is itself constituted, though not determined, on its basis. In this sense, the body must enter into the theorization of norm and fantasy, since it is precisely the site where the desire for the norm takes shape, and the norm cultivates desire and fantasy in the service of its own naturalization.

One Lacanian temptation is to claim that the law figured in the fantasy is the Law in some capitalized sense, and that the small appearance indexes the operation of the larger one. This is the moment in which the theory of psychoanalysis becomes a theological project. And although theology has its place, and ought not to be dismissed, it is perhaps important to acknowledge that this is a credo of faith. To the extent that we mime the gestures of genuflection that structure this practice of knowledge, we do perhaps come to believe in them, and our faith becomes an effect of this mimetic practice. We could, with Žižek, claim that a primordial faith preconditions the gestures of genuflection we make, but I would suggest that all that is necessary to start on this theological venture is the desire for theology itself, one that not all of us share. Indeed, what seems more poignant here for psychoanalysis as both theory and clinical practice is to see what transformations social norms undergo as they assume various forms within the psyche, what specific forms of suffering they induce, what clues for relief they also, inadvertently, give.

Or let us consider various forms of self-mutilation that have the apparent aim of marring or even destroying the body of the subject. If the subject is a woman, and she takes responsibility for a seduction that lured her father away from her mother (and her mother away from her), or took her brother away from her sister (and both away from her), then it may be that the mutilation serves as an attempt to annihilate the body which she understands as the source of her guilt and her loss. But it may also be that she does not seek to annihilate the body, but only to scar it, to leave the marks for all to see, and so to communicate a sign, perform the corporeal equivalent to a confessional and a supplication. Yet these marks may not be readable to those for whom they are (ambivalently) intended, and so the body communicates the signs that it also fails to communicate, and the "symptom" at hand is one of a body dedicated to an illegible confession. If we abstract too quickly from this scene, and decide that there is something about the big Other operating here, something quasi-transcendental or a priori that is generalizable to all subjects, we have found a way to avoid the rather messy psychic and social entanglement that presents itself in this example. The effort to generalize into the a priori conditions of the scene takes a short cut to a kind of universalizing claim that tends to dismiss or devalue the power of social norms as they operate in the scene: the incest taboo, the nuclear family, the operation of guilt in women to thwart the putatively aggressive consequences of their desire, women's bodies as mutilated signs (an unwitting playing out of the Lévi-Straussian identification of women with circulating signs in *The Elementary Structures of Kinship*).

Žižek has in part made his mark in contemporary critical studies by raising Lacan out of the realm of pure theory, showing how Lacan can be understood through popular culture, and how popular culture conversely indexes the theory of Lacan. Žižek's work is full of rich examples from popular culture and various kinds of ideologies and their complicated "jokes," but these examples serve to illustrate various principles of psychic reality without ever clarifying the relation between the social example and the psychic principle. Although the social examples serve as the occasions for insights into the structures of psychic reality, we are not given to understand whether the social is any more than a lens for understanding a psychic reality that is anterior to itself. The examples function in a mode of allegory that presumes the separability of the illustrative example from the content it seeks to illuminate. Thus, this relation of separation recapitulates the architectonic tropes of two levels that we have seen before. If this kind of separation between the psychic and the social is not appropriately called Cartesian, I would be glad to find another term to describe the dualism at work here.

This extended discussion does not yet make clear the place of psychoanalysis for a broader conception of politics. Žižek has contributed immeasurably to this project by showing us how disidentification operates in ideological interpellation, how the failure of interpellation to capture its object with its defining mark is the very condition for a contest about its meanings, inaugurating a dynamic essential to hegemony itself. It seems clear that any effort to order the subject through a performative capture whereby the subject becomes synonymous with the name it is called is bound to fail. Why it is bound to fail remains an open question. We could say that every subject has a complexity that no single name can capture, and so refute a certain form of nominalism. Or we could say that there is in every subject something that cannot be named, no matter how complicated and variegated the naming process becomes (I believe that this is Žižek's point). Or we could think a bit more closely about the name, in the service of what kind of regulatory apparatus it works, whether it works alone, whether in order to "work" at all it requires an iteration that introduces the possibility of failure at every interval. It is important to remember, however, that interpellation does not always operate through the name: this silence might be meant for you. And the discursive means by which subjects are ordered fails not only because of an extra-discursive something that resists assimilation into discourse, but because discourse has many more aims and effects than those that are actually intended by its users. As an instrument of non-intentional effects, discourse can produce the possibility of identities that it means to foreclose. Indeed, the articulation of foreclosure is the first moment of its potential undoing, for the articulation can become rearticulated and countered once it is launched into a discursive trajectory, unmoored from the intentions by which it is animated.

In the case of foreclosure, where certain possibilities are ruled out so that cultural intelligibility can be instituted, giving discursive form to the foreclosure can be an inaugurating moment of its destabilization. The unspeakable speaks, or the speakable speaks the unspeakable into silence, but these speech acts are recorded in speech, and speech becomes something else by virtue of having been broken open by the unspeakable. Psychoanalysis enters here to the extent that it insists upon the efficacy of unintended meaning in discourse. And although Foucault failed to see his affinity with psychoanalysis, he clearly understood that the "inadvertent consequences" produced by discursive practices not fully controlled by intention have disruptive and transformative effects. In this sense, psychoanalysis helps us to understand the contingency and risk intrinsic to political practice – that certain kinds of aims which are deliberately intended can become subverted by other operations of power to effect consequences that we do not endorse (e.g. the feminist anti-pornography movement in the US saw its cause taken up by right-wing Republicans, to the dismay of – we hope – some of them). Conversely, attacks by one's enemies can paradoxically boost one's position (one hopes), especially when the broader public has no desire to identify with the manifest aggression represented by their tactics. This does not mean that we ought not to delineate goals and devise strategies, and just wait for our foes to shoot themselves in their various feet. Of course, we should devise and justify political plans on a collective basis. But this will not mean that we would be naive in relation to power to think that the institution of goals (the triumphs of the civil rights movement) will not be appropriated by its opponents (California's civil rights initiative) to dismantle those accomplishments (the decimation of affirmative action).

Conditions of Possibility for Politics – and then some

The possibilities of these reversals and the feared prospect of a full co-optation by existing institutions of power keep many a critical intellectual from engaging in activist politics. The fear is that one will have to accept certain notions which one wants to subject to critical scrutiny. Can one embrace a notion of "rights" even as the discourse tends to localize and obscure the broader workings of power, even as it often involves accepting certain premises of humanism that a critical perspective would question? Can one accept the very postulate of "universality," so central to the rhetoric of democratic claims to enfranchisement? The demand for "inclusion" when the very constitution of the polity ought to be brought into question? Can one call into question the way in which the political field is organized, and have such a questioning accepted as part of the process of self-reflection that is central to a radical democratic enterprise? Conversely, can a critical intellectual use the very terms that she subjects to criticism, accepting the pre-theoretical force of their deployment in contexts where they are urgently needed?

It seems important to be able to move as intellectuals between the kinds of questions that predominate these pages, in which the conditions of possibility for the political are debated, and the struggles that constitute the present life of hegemonic struggle: the development and universalization of various new social movements, the concrete workings of coalitional efforts and, especially, those alliances that tend to cross-cut identitarian politics. It would be a mistake to think that these efforts might be grouped together under a single rubric, understood as "the particular" or "the historically contingent," while intellectuals then turn to more fundamental issues that are understood to be clearly marked off from the play of present politics. I am not suggesting that my interlocutors are guilty of such moves. Laclau's work, especially his edited volume *The Making of Political Identities*,[6] takes on this question explicitly. And Žižek has also emerged as one of the central critics of the political situation in the Balkans, more generally, and is engaged, more locally, in the political life of Slovenia in various ways. Moreover, it seems that the very notion of hegemony to which we are all more or less committed demands a way of thinking about social movements precisely as they come to make a universalizing claim, precisely when they emerge within the historical horizon as the promise of democratization itself. But I would caution that establishing the conditions of possibility for such movements is not the same as engaging with their internal and overlapping logics, the specific ways in which they appropriate the key terms of democracy, and directing the fate of those terms as a consequence of that appropriation.

The lesbian and gay movement, which in some quarters has extended to include a broad range of sexual minorities, has faced a number of questions regarding its own assimilation to existing norms in recent years. Whereas some clamoured for inclusion in the US military, others sought to reformulate a critique of the military and question the value of being included there. Similarly, whereas throughout some areas of Europe (especially France and Holland) and the US some activists have sought to extend the institution of marriage to non-heterosexual partners, others have sustained an active critique of the institution of marriage, questioning whether state recognition of mon-ogamous partners will in the end delegitimate sexual freedom for a number of sexual minorities. One might say that the advances that are sought by main-stream liberal activists (inclusion in the military and in marriage) are an extension of democracy and a hegemonic advance to the extent that lesbian and gay people are making the claim to be treated as equal to other citizens with respect to these obligations and entitlements, and that the prospect of their inclusion in these institutions is a sign that they are at present carrying the universalizing promise of hegemony itself. But this would not be a salutary conclusion, for the enstatement of these questionable rights and obligations for some lesbians and gays establishes norms of legitimation that work to remargi-nalize others and foreclose possibilities for sexual freedom which have also been long-standing goals of the movement. The naturalization of the military–marriage goal for gay politics also marginalizes those for whom one or the other of these institutions is anathema, if not inimical. Indeed, those who oppose both institutions would find that the way in which they are represented by the "advance of democracy" is a violation of their most central political commitments. So how would we understand the operation of hegemony in this highly conflicted situation?

First of all, it seems clear that the political aim is to mobilize against an identification of marriage or military rights with the universalizing promise of the gay movement, the sign that lesbians and gays are becoming human according to universally accepted postulates. If marriage and the military are to remain contested zones, as they surely should, it will be crucial to maintain a political culture of contestation on these and other parallel issues, such as the legitimacy and legality of public zones of sexual exchange, intergenerational sex, adoption outside marriage, increased research and testing for AIDS, and transgender politics. All of these are debated issues, but where can the debate, the contest, take place? *The New York Times* is quick to announce that lesbians and gays have advanced miraculously since Stonewall, and many of the major entertainment figures who "come out" with great enthusiasm also communicate that the new day has arrived. The Human Rights Campaign, the most well-endowed gay rights organization, steadfastly stands in a patriotic salute before the flag. Given the overwhelming tendency of liberal political culture to regard the assimilation of lesbians and gays into the existing institutions of marriage and the military as a grand success, how does it become possible to keep an open and politically efficacious conflict of interpretations alive?

This is a different question from asking after the conditions of possibility for hegemony and locating them in the pre-social field of the Real. And it will not do simply to say that all these concrete struggles exemplify something more profound, and that our task is to dwell in that profundity. I raise this question not to counterpose the "concrete" to "theory," but to ask: what are the specifically theoretical questions raised by these concrete urgencies? In addition to providing an inquiry into the ideal conditions of possibility for hegemony, we also need to think about its conditions of efficacy, how hegemony becomes realizable under present conditions, and to rethink realizability in ways that resist totalitarian conclusions. The open-endedness that is essential to democratization implies that the universal cannot be finally identified with any particular content, and that this incommensurability (for which we do not need the Real) is crucial to the futural possibilities of democratic contestation. To ask after the new grounds of realizability is not to ask after the "end" of politics as a static or teleological conclusion: I presume that the point of hegemony on which we might concur is precisely the ideal of a possibility that exceeds every attempt at a final realization, one which gains its vitality precisely from its non-coincidence with any present reality. What makes this non-coincidence vital is its capacity to open up new fields of possibility and; thus, to instill hope where a sense of fatality is always threatening to close down political thinking altogether. [. . .]

The Practice of Logic, the Politics of Discourse, and Legitimating the Liminal

One of the pressing instances of this problem is to be found in the current Euro-American debate on same-sex legal alliances or marriages. It is important to counter the homophobic arguments marshalled against these proposals, and I have indicated above how these arguments work in the French context to deny important legal entitlements to lesbian and gay people. But the most pressing question is whether this ought to be the primary goal of the lesbian and gay movement at the present time, and whether it constitutes a radical step towards greater democratization or an assimilationist politics that mitigates against the movement's claim to be working in the direction of substantive social justice. In the bid to gain rights to marry, the mainstream gay political movement has asked that an existing institution open its doors to same-sex partners, that marriage no longer be restricted to heterosexuals. It has further argued that this move will make the institution of marriage more egalitarian, extending basic rights to more citizens, overcoming arbitrary limits to the process by which such rights are universalized. We might be tempted to applaud, and think that this represents something of the radically universalizing effects of a particular movement. But consider the fact that a critique of this strategy claims that the petition to gain entry into the institution of marriage (or the military) extends the power of the very institution and, in extending that power, exacerbates the distinction between those forms of intimate alliance that are legitimated by the state, and those that are not. This critique further claims that certain kinds of rights and benefits are secured only through establishing marital status, such as the right to adopt (in France, in certain parts of the US) or the entitlement to a partner's health benefits, or the right to receive inheritance from another individual, or indeed the right to executive medical decision-making or the right to receive the body of one's dead lover from the hospital. These are only some of the legal consequences of marital status; there are, of course, several other kinds of legitimation that are cultural and economic; and the tax code also stipulates some ways in which profitability can be secured more easily through establishing marital status, including the ability to claim dependants in the US. Thus the successful bid to gain access to marriage effectively strengthens marital status as a state-sanctioned condition for the exercise of certain kinds of rights and entitlements; it strengthens the hand of the state in the regulation of human sexual behaviour; and it emboldens the distinction between legitimate and illegitimate forms of partnership and kinship. Moreover, it seeks to reprivatize sexuality, removing it from the public sphere and from the market, domains where its politicization has been very intense.[7]

Thus the bid to gain access to certain kinds of rights and entitlements that are secured by marriage by petitioning for entrance into the institution does not consider the alternative: to ask for a delinking of precisely those rights and entitlements from the institution of marriage itself. We might ask: what form of identification mobilizes the bid for marriage, and what form mobilizes its opposition, and are they radically distinct? In the first case, lesbian and gay people see the opportunity for an identification with the institution of marriage and so, by extension, common community with straight people who inhabit that institution. And with whom do they break alliance? They break alliance with people who are on their own without sexual relationships, single mothers or single fathers, people who have undergone divorce, people who are in relationships that are not marital in kind or in status, other lesbian, gay, and transgender people whose sexual relations are multiple (which does not mean unsafe), whose lives are not monogamous, whose sexuality and desire do not have the conjugal home as their (primary) venue, whose lives are considered less real or less legitimate, who inhabit the more shadowy regions of social reality. The lesbian/gay alliance with these people – and with this condition – is broken by the petition for marriage. Those who seek marriage identify not only with those who have gained the blessing of the state, but with the state itself. Thus the petition not only augments state power, but accepts the state as the necessary venue for democratization itself.

So, the claim to extend the "right" of marriage to non-heterosexual people may appear at first to be a claim that works to extend existing rights in a more universalizing direction, but to the extent that those universalizing effects are those that emanate from the state legitimation of sexual practice, the claim has the effect of widening the gap between legitimate and illegitimate forms of sexual exchange. Indeed, the only possible route for a radical democratization of legitimating effects would be to relieve marriage of its place as the precondition of legal entitlements of various kinds. This kind of move would actively seek to dismantle the dominant term, and to return to non-state-centered forms of alliance that augment the possibility for multiple forms on the level of culture and civil society. Here it should become clear that I am not, in this instance, arguing for a view of political performativity which holds that it is necessary to occupy the dominant norm in order to produce an internal subversion of its terms. Sometimes it is important to refuse its terms, to let the term itself wither, to starve it of its strength. And there is, I believe, a performativity proper to refusal which, in this instance, insists upon the reiteration of sexuality beyond the dominant terms. What is subject to reiteration is not "marriage" but sexuality, forms of intimate alliance and exchange, the social basis for the state itself. As increasing numbers of children are born outside marriage, as increasing numbers of households fail to replicate the family norm, as extended kinship systems develop to care for the young, the ill and the aging, the social basis for the state turns out to be more complicated and less unitary than the discourse on the family permits. And the hope would be, from the point of view of performativity, that the discourse would eventually reveal its limited descriptive reach, avowed only as one practice among many that organize human sexual life.

I have been referring to this political dilemma in terms which suggest that what is most important is to make *certain kinds of claims*, but I have not yet explained what it is to make a claim, what form a claim takes, whether it is always verbal, how it is performed. It would be a mistake to imagine that a political claim must always be articulated in language; certainly, media images make claims that are not readily translatable into verbal speech. And lives make claims in all sorts of ways that are not necessarily verbal. There is a phrase in US politics, which has its equivalents elsewhere, which suggests something about the somatic dimension of the political claim. It is the exhortation: "Put your body on the line." The line is usually understood to be the police line, the line over which you may not step without the threat of police violence. But it is also the line of human bodies in the plural which make a chain of sorts and which, collectively, exert the physical force of collective strength. It is not easy, as a writer, to put one's body on the line, for the line is usually the line that is written, the one that bears only an indirect trace of the body that is its condition. The struggle to think hegemony anew is not quite possible, however, without inhabiting precisely that line where the norms of legitimacy, increasingly adjudicated by state apparatuses of various kinds, break down, where liminal social existence emerges in the condition of suspended ontology. Those who should ideally be included within any operation of the universal find themselves not only outside its terms but as the very outside without which the universal could not be formulated, living as the trace, the spectral remainder, which does not have a home in the forward march of the universal. This is not even to live as the particular, for the particular is, at least, constituted within the field of the political. It is to live as the unspeakable and the unspoken for, those who form the blurred human background of something called "the population." To make a claim on one's own behalf assumes that one speaks the language in which the claim can be made, and speaks it in such a way that the claim can be heard. This differential among languages, as Gayatri Chakravorty Spivak[8] has argued, is the condition of power that governs the global field of language. Who occupies that line between the speakable and the unspeakable, facilitating a translation there that is not the simple augmentation of the power of the dominant? There is nowhere else to stand, but there is no "ground" there, only a reminder to keep as one's point of reference the dispossessed and the unspeakable, and to move with caution as one tries to make use of power and discourse in ways that do not renaturalize the political vernacular of the state and its status as the primary instrument of legitimating effects. Another universality emerges from the trace that only borders on political legibility: the subject who has not been given the prerogative to be a subject, whose *modus vivendi* is an imposed catachresis. If the spectrally human is to enter into the hegemonic reformulation of universality, a language between languages will have to be found. This will be no metalanguage, nor will it be the condition from which all languages hail. It will be the labor of transaction and translation which belongs to no single site, but is the movement between languages, and has its final destination in this movement itself. Indeed, the task will be not to assimilate the unspeakable into the domain of speakability in order to house it there, within the existing norms of dominance, but to shatter the confidence of dominance, to show how equivocal its claims to universality are, and, from that equivocation, track the break-up of its regime, an opening towards alternative versions of universality that are wrought from the work of translation itself. Such an opening will not only relieve the state of its privileged status as the primary medium through which the universal is articulated, but re-establish as the conditions of articulation itself the human trace that formalism has left behind, the left that is Left.

Notes

1   Charles Shepherdson, *Vital Signs: Nature, Culture, Psychoanalysis*, New York: Routledge 2000.
2   See Catherine Millot, *Horsexe: Essay on Transsexuality*, trans. Kenneth Hylton (Brooklyn, NY: Autonomedia, 1990).
3   See Sylviane Agacinski, "Questions autour de la filiation," le Forum, *Ex Aequo* (July 1998), an interview on her recent book, *Politique des sexes* (Paris: Éditions du Seuil, 1998). There she claims not only explicitly that no "civil pact of solidarity" ought to be accorded to gay people because their relationships are "private," not "social," but that heterosexuality constitutes "une origine mixte... qui est naturelle, est aussi un fondement culturel et symbolique" (p. 24). Irène Thèry has made a similar argument in her numerous public presentations against the PACS in France, a legal effort to accord limited legal rights to non-married couples. See Thèry, *Couple, filiation et parenté aujourd' hui* (Paris: Odile Jacob, 1998). Héritier has made perhaps the boldest arguments in favor of the symbolic, arguing that heterosexuality is coextensive with the symbolic order, that no culture can emerge without this particular formation of sexual difference as its foundation, and that the PACS and other such efforts seek to undo the foundations of culture itself.
4   For a more general understanding of her view that sexual difference and heterosexual parenting are essential to all culturally viable forms of kinship, see Françoise Héritier, *Masculin/Féminin: La pensée de la différence* (Paris: Odile Jacob, 1996). See also her remarks in "Aucune société n'admet de parenté homosexuelle," *La Croix* (November 1998). I thank Eric Fassin for guiding me through some of this material.
5   See the response supplied by Miller to Éric Laurent's essay "Normes nouvelles de 'l'homosexuality'," in "L'inconscient homosexuel," *La Cause freudienne: revue de psychanalyse*, p. 37:

À mon avis, il existe, chez les homosexuels, des liens affectifs de longue durée qui justifient parfaitement, selon des modalités à étudier, leur reconnaissance juridique, si les sujets le souhaitent. Savoir si cela doit s'appeler mariage ou pas est une autre question. Ces liens ne sont pas exactement du même modèle que les liens affectifs hétérosexuels. En particulier, quand ils unissent deux hommes, on ne trouve pas l'exigence de fidélité érotique, sexuelle, introduite pour le couple hétérosexuel par un certain nombre de facteurs – du côté féminin dans un certain registre, dans un autre registre par les exigences du partenaire masculin. (pp. 12–13)

In my opinion, there are in homosexual relations long-term emotional ties which perfectly justify, in accordance with juridical clauses to be studied, their legal recognition, if the subjects so desire. Whether this ought to be called marriage or not is another question. These ties are not exactly of the same model as heterosexual emotional ties. In particular, when they unite two men, we do not find the demand for erotic, sexual fidelity that is introduced into the heterosexual couple by a certain number of factors – from the feminine side in a certain register; in another register by the demands of the male partner.

6   Ernesto Laclau, ed., *The Making of Political Identities* (London and New York: Verso, 1994).
7   See Michael Warner, "Normal and Normaller," *GLQ* 5.2 (1999); and Janet Halley, "Recognition, Rights, Regulation, Normalization," unpublished MS. The politicization of sexuality in the public sphere was evidenced in the Stonewall riots in New York, for instance, where the rights of gay people to congregate had been violated by the New York City Police Department. Violent police action against sexual minorities continues in several countries, including the US. In Brazil, in August 1998, military policemen tortured, humiliated, and drowned two transvestite sex workers. Mexico reports the death of 125 gay people between April 1995 and May 1998. The International Gay and Lesbian Human Rights Commission keeps an active file on the myriad forms of public violence that continues on an international level against lesbians, gays, and transgendered people. The unionization of prostitutes by Coyote and similar organizations has also been crucial for advocating for safe working conditions for sex workers. Communities of sexual minorities whose relations of sexual exchange take place outside of conjugal or semi-conjugal forms run the more general risk of being pathologized and marginalized as marriage assumes the status of a normative ideal within the gay movement.
8   Gayatri Chakravorty Spivak, "Can the Subaltern Speak?" in *Marxism and the Interpretation of Culture*, ed. Cary Nelson and Lawrence Grossberg (Urbana: University of Illinois Press, 1988).

11

Promiscuous Obedience (2000)

Introduction

What would have been the outcome if Antigone and not her father-brother Oedipus had provided the starting point for psychoanalysis? This question, originally posed by George Steiner, is taken up by Butler in her three Wellek Library Lectures delivered at the University of California, Irvine, in 1998 and published two years later as *Antigone's Claim: Kinship Between Life and Death*. Unravelling the tangled nexus of kinship relations in Sophocles' representation of this highly dysfunctional and complicated family, Butler perceives what she calls a promising fatality at the heart of the kinship norm. In Sophocles' play, Antigone has been sentenced to death by her uncle King Creon for defying his edict against giving her brother Polyneices a proper burial. Polyneices was killed in battle by his cousin, and Antigone's fiancé is Creon's son Haemon, another cousin of hers. Antigone herself is the daughter of Oedipus and Jocasta, but since her father had the famous misfortune of marrying his mother by mistake, Oedipus (now dead) was also her brother, a double relationship which Butler notes introduces an ambiguity into Antigone's use of the word "brother," by which she could be referring to Polyneices, Oedipus, or a third brother, Eteocles. Privileging her relationship to Polyneices above all others, Antigone goes ahead and performs the burial rites in defiance of Creon's prohibition. For this "crime" she is condemned to be buried alive, but Antigone preempts her execution by committing suicide, prompting the suicides of her fiancé-cousin and aunt, and thereby further rupturing this troubled family unit.

According to Butler, previous analyses of the play by commentators such as G. W. F. Hegel, Claude Lévi-Strauss, Jacques Lacan, and Luce Irigaray have overlooked the interrelationship of family and state exemplified by Antigone's appropriation of her uncle Creon's authoritative discourse. By "crossing over" the gender of sovereignty in her discursive self-assertions (and indeed the sovereignty of gender is also crossed over as Antigone opts for death by burial rather than marriage) Antigone exposes the contingency of both kinship and gender norms, simultaneously causing gender trouble and what Butler calls "kinship trouble." Taking Antigone rather than Oedipus as the origin of psychoanalytic theory does not mean that love for the mother and murderous impulses

Chapter 3, pp. 57–82, 92–7 from *Antigone's Claim: Kinship Between Life and Death*. New York: Columbia University Press, 2000. Reprinted by permission of Columbia University Press.

towards the father would be replaced by a love relationship with one's cousin and an erotic attachment to one's brother: rather, an "Antigone complex" would denote the *complex*, multiple nature of kinship relations (or complexes) which cannot be configured according to universal structural or symbolic norms. This is the "promiscuity" Butler notes in the title of her third chapter ("Promiscuous Obedience," reprinted below), where the word denotes the way in which Antigone's plural affiliations exceed universalist psychoanalytic and structuralist assumptions about kinship.

Such limiting accounts of the play have effectively "entombed" its promiscuous significations, but if Antigone has been twice buried – by King Creon and by theorists such as Lacan who metaphorically "entrap" her within their universalizing theories – Butler effectively disinters Antigone by returning to the "buried question" of the symbolic, "the question of whether or not that symbolic is a 'totality' as Lévi-Strauss claimed and as Hyppolite feared." Releasing Antigone from the "curse" of the structuralist symbolic with the "kiss" of psychoanalysis and Foucauldianism, Butler's reading of the play emphasizes how the polymorphous and promiscuous perverse is structurally necessary to kinship norms. "The perverse" here is exemplified by Antigone's nonconformity, the incestuous nature of her relations with cousin and brother, her double affiliation to father and cousin, her choice of death rather than marriage and maternity. And yet these multiple departures from heterosexual norms arise out of and are structured by taboos which we know from Butler's previous work are themselves proliferative and productive. This idea was formulated in *Gender Trouble* and *Bodies That Matter*, and like these two books, *Antigone's Claim* continues to insist on the generative nature of the law. In the first lecture, Butler wants to know whether the prohibition against incest can operate effectively without producing the spectre of its transgression: "Do such rules produce conformity, or do they also produce a set of social configurations that exceed and defy the rules by which they are occasioned?" As usual, Butler answers these questions via Foucault's formulations of power and the law. While psychoanalysis has neglected the question of how new forms of kinship arise out of the incest taboo, Butler arguest that taboo and the law are structured on the basis of the aberrations and perversions such laws supposedly proscribe.

What passes for ontological and familial intelligibility is founded on prohibition, but Butler argues that *Antigone* constitutes a challenge to both. What we might call "Antigone's trace" (Butler's specter of transgression as cited above) is discernible in those family complexes which are not bound by blood affiliations and which do not conform to heterosexual kinship norms. The term "radical kinship" may describe single- or multi-parent families, caring and buddying relationships, and African-American family structures which Butler (following Orlando Patterson) claims have been consigned to a "social death" since slavery. Furthermore Butler discerns a parity between Creon's proscription of Antigone's mourning for her brother and a culture in which it is forbidden to mourn men and women who have died of AIDS.

However, hope is to be found in Antigone, that not-quite-queer heroine whose promiscuous affiliations and fatal aberrations reveal the instability and contingency of heterosexual kinship norms and structures. Just as Antigone refuses to be entombed by uncle or theorists, the incest taboo and the taboos against same-sex relationships resist universalization and "structuralization," leading instead to radical proliferations and the de-instating of heterosexuality. This is the focus of Butler's third chapter, reprinted here, where Antigone's challenge to kinship norms is taken to provide the grounds for a radical reenactment of those norms in defiance of the prohibitions and proscriptions of the law.

In George Steiner's study of the historical appropriations of *Antigone*, he poses a controversial question he does not pursue: What would happen if psycho-analysis were to have taken Antigone rather than Oedipus as its point of departure?[1] Oedipus clearly has his own tragic fate, but Antigone's fate is decidedly postoedipal. Although her brothers are explicitly cursed by her father, does the curse also work on her and, if so, through what furtive and implicit means? The chorus remarks that something of Oedipus' fate is surely working through her own, but what burden of history does she bear? Oedipus comes to know who his mother and father are but finds that his mother is also his wife. Antigone's father is her brother, since they both share a mother in Jocasta, and her brothers are her nephews, sons of her brother-father, Oedipus. The terms of kinship become irreversibly equivocal. Is this part of her tragedy? Does this equivocity of kinship lead to fatality?

Antigone is caught in a web of relations that produce no coherent position within kinship. She is not, strictly speaking, outside kinship or, indeed, unin-telligible. Her situation can be understood, but only with a certain amount of horror. Kinship is not simply a situation she is in but a set of practices that she also performs, relations that are reinstituted in time precisely through the practice of their repetition. When she buries her brother, it is not simply that she acts from kinship, as if kinship furnishes a principle for action, but that her action is the action of kinship, the performative repetition that reinstates kinship as a public scandal. Kinship is what she repeats through her action; to redeploy a formulation from David Schneider, it is not a form of being but a form of doing.[2] And her action implicates her in an aberrant repetition of a norm, a custom, a convention, not a formal law but a lawlike regulation of culture that operates with its own contingency.

If we recall that for Lacan the symbolic, that set of rules that govern the accession of speech and speakability within culture, is motivated by the father's words, then the father's words are surely upon Antigone; they are, as it were, the medium within which she acts and in whose voice she defends her act. She transmits those words in aberrant form, transmitting them loyally and betraying them by sending them in directions they were never intended to travel. The words are repeated, and their repeatability relies on the deviation that the repetition performs. The aberration that is her speech and her act facilitates such transmissions. Indeed, she is transmitting more than one discourse at once, for the demands that are upon her come from more than one source: her brother also petitions her to give him a decent burial, a demand that in some ways conflicts with the curse that Oedipus has laid upon his son, to die at battle and be received by the underworld. These two demands converge and produce a certain interference in the transmitting of the paternal word. After all, if the father is the brother, then what finally is the difference between them? And what is to elevate the demand of Oedipus over the demand of Polyneices?

The words are upon her, but what does that mean? How does a curse come to inform the action that fulfills the prophecy inherent in the curse? What is the temporality of the curse such that the actions that she takes create an equivocation between the words that are upon her, that she suffers, and the act that she herself performs? How are we to understand the strange *nomos* of the act itself? How does the word of the Other become one's own deed, and what is the temporality of this repetition in which the deed that is produced as a result of the curse is also in some ways an aberrant repetition, one that affirms that the curse produces unanticipated consequences?

Oedipus, of course, unknowingly sleeps with his mother and slays his father, and is driven into the wilderness accompanied by Antigone. In *Oedipus at Colonus* the two of them, along with a small party of followers, are given shelter by Theseus in a land governed by Athens. Oedipus learns that his sons have explicitly forbidden his return to Thebes and also learns that they have turned against one another in a bitter battle for the throne. Toward the end of that play, the second of the trilogy, Polyneices visits Oedipus and calls upon him to return. Oedipus not only refuses but levels a curse against Polyneices, that "you shall never conquer in war your native land; . . . but shall perish by your brother's hand, and kill him who drove you out!" (1385–1393).

Antigone stands by, importuning her father to show benevolence toward Polyneices, and fails. And it remains unclear whether the brother whose act will kill him is Eteocles who delivers the fatal blow, or Oedipus, whose curse both predicts and mandates the blow itself. Polyneices, despite Antigone's protest, decides nevertheless to go into battle with Eteocles, and Antigone is left, crying out "My heart is broken!" She then speaks a line that prefigures her own knowing approach to her own fate: "Brother, how can anyone *not* mourn, seeing you set out to death so clear before you go with open eyes to death!" (Grene 1645–1649). Indeed, Antigone will and – given the chronology of the plays – "already has" undergone precisely the fate she predicts for her brother, to enter death knowingly.

Antigone not only loses her brother to her father's curse, words that quite literally yield the force of annihilation, but she then loses her father to death by the curse that is upon him. Words and deeds become fatally entangled in the familial scene. The acts of Polyneices and Eteocles seem to fulfill and enact the father's words, but his words – and his deeds – are also compelled by a curse upon him, the curse of Laius. Antigone worries over their fate even as she embarks upon her own course of action for which death is a necessary conclusion. Her desire to save her brothers from their fate is overwhelmed, it seems, by her desire to join them in their fate.

Before he dies, Oedipus makes several utterances that assume the status of a curse. He condemns her, but the force of the condemnation is to bind her to him. His words culminate in her own permanent lovelessness, one that is mandated by Oedipus' demand for loyalty, a demand that verges on incestuous possessiveness: "From none did you have love more than from this man, without whom you will now spend the remainder of your life" (1617–1619). His words exert a force in time that exceeds the temporality of their enunci-ation: they demand that for all time she have no man except for the man who is dead, and though this is a demand, a curse, made *by* Oedipus, who positions himself as her only one, it is clear that she both honors and disobeys this curse as she displaces her love for her father onto her brother. Indeed, she takes her brother to be her only one – she would risk defying the official edict for no kin but Polyneices. Thus she betrays Oedipus even as she fulfills the terms of his curse. She will only love a man who is dead, and hence she will love no man. She obeys his demand, but promiscuously, for he is clearly not the only dead man she loves and, indeed, not the ultimate one. Is the love for the one dissociable from the love for the other? And when it is her "most precious brother" for whom she commits her criminal and honorable act, is it clear that this brother is Polyneices, or could it be Oedipus?

Knowing that he is dying, Oedipus asks, "And will they even shroud my body in Theban soil?" (406) and learns that his crime makes that impossible. He is thus buried by Theseus out of everyone else's sight, including Antigone's. Then, Antigone, in the play by that name, mimes the act of the strong and true Theseus and buries her brother out of sight, making sure that Polyneices' shade is composed of Theban dust. Antigone's assertive burial, which she performs twice, might be understood to be for both, a burial that at once reflects and institutes the equivocation of brother and father. They are, after all, already interchangeable for her, and yet her act reinstitutes and reelaborates that interchangeability.

Although Sophocles wrote *Antigone* several years before *Oedipus at Colonus*, the action that takes place in the former *follows* the action of the latter. What is the significance of this belatedness? Are the words that goad the action understandable only in retrospect? Can the implications of the curse, under-stood as extended action, be understood only retrospectively? The action predicted by the curse for the future turns out to be an action that has been happening all along, such that the forward movement of time is precisely what is inverted through the temporality of the curse. The curse establishes a temporality for the action it ordains that predates the curse itself. The words bring into the future what has always already been happening.

Antigone is to love no man except the man who is dead, but in some sense she is also a man. And this is also the title that Oedipus bestows upon her, a gift or reward for her loyalty. When Oedipus is banished, Antigone cares for him, and in her loyalty, is referred to as a "man" (*aner*). Indeed, she follows him loyally into the wilderness, but at some point that following imperceptibly turns into a scene in which *she* leads *him*: "Follow, follow me this way with your unseeing steps, father, where I lead you!" (183–184).

Indeed, she is at once cursed with a loyalty to a dead man, a loyalty that makes her manly, compels her to acquire the attribute that carries his approbation such that desire and identification are acutely confounded in a melancholic bind. Oedipus clearly understands gender as something of a curse itself, since one of the ways in which he condemns his sons is by leveling his accusation through the trope of an orientalizing gender inversion:

> Those two conform together to the customs that prevail in Egypt in their nature and the nurture of their lives! For there the males sit in their houses working at the loom, and their consorts provide the necessities of life out of doors. And in your case, my children, those who ought to perform this labour sit at home and keep the house like maidens, and you two *in their place* bear the burdens of your unhappy father's sorrows.   *(337–344, my emphasis)*

Later, Oedipus maintains that Ismene and Antigone have quite literally taken the place of their brothers, acquiring masculine gender along the way. Addressing his sons, he says:

> If I had not begotten these daughters to attend me, I would not be living, for all you did for me. But as it is they preserve me, they are my nurses, they are men, not women, when it comes to working for me; but you are sons of some other, and no sons of mine.   *(1559–1563)*

His daughters thus become his sons, but these same children (Antigone and Ismene), he maintains earlier, are also his "sisters" (328). And so we've arrived at something like kinship trouble at the heart of Sophocles. Antigone has, then, already taken the place of her brother; when she breaks with Ismene, it mirrors the break that Polyneices has made with Eteocles, thus acting, we might say, as brothers do. By the time this drama is done, she has thus taken the place of nearly every man in her family. Is this an effect of the words that are upon her?

Indeed, words exercise a certain power here that is not immediately clear. They act, they exercise performative force of a certain kind, sometimes they are clearly violent in their consequences, as words that either constitute or beget violence. Indeed, sometimes it seems that the words act in illocutionary ways, enacting the very deed that they name in the very moment of the naming. For Hölderlin, this constitutes something of the murderous force of the word in Sophocles. Consider this moment in which the chorus in *Oedipus at Colonus* reminds Oedipus of his crime, a verbal narration *of* the deed that becomes the violent punishment *for* the deed. They not only narrate the events but deliver the accusation, compel his acknowledgment, and inflict a punishment through their interrogatory address:

> CHORUS: Unhappy one, what then? You murdered... your father?
> OEDIPUS: Woe! You have struck me a second blow, anguish upon anguish!
> CHORUS: You killed him!   *(542–545)*

Thus Oedipus is verbally struck by the chorus for having struck and slain his father; the accusation verbally repeats the crime, strikes again where Oedipus is already hurt and where he is thus hurt again. He says, "You strike again," and they strike again, strike with words, repeating, "You killed him"; and the chorus who speaks is ambiguously addressed as "God in heaven," speaking with the force that divine words do. Such scenes no doubt prompted Hölderlin to remark upon the fatality of words in his "Anmerkungen zur Antigone": "The word becomes mediately factic in that it grasps the sensuous body. The tragic Greek word is fatally factic [tödlichfaktisch], because it actually seizes the body that murders."[3]

It is not just that the words kill Oedipus in some linguistic and psychic sense but those words, the ones composing the prior curse of Laius upon him, move him toward incest and murder. In murdering, he fulfills or completes the words that were upon him; his action becomes indissociable from the spoken act, a condition we might say of both the curse that dramatic action reflects and the structure of dramatic action itself. These are words that one transmits, but they are not autonomously generated or maintained by the one who speaks them. They emerge from, in Hölderlin's terms, an inspired or possessed mouth (*aus begeistertem Munde*) and seize the body that murders. They are spoken to Oedipus, but he also restages his trauma, as it were, as his words seize and kill his sons, seize them and make them murderous, and as his words also seize and gender as manly the body of his daughter, Antigone. And they do this precisely by becoming words that act in time, words whose temporality exceeds the scene of their utterance, becoming the desire of those they name, repetitious and conjuring, conferring only retrospectively the sense of a necessary and persistent past that is confirmed by the utterance that predicts it, where prediction becomes the speech act by which an already operative necessity is confirmed.

The relation between word and deed becomes hopelessly entangled in the familial scene; every word transmutes into event or, indeed, "fatal fact," in Hölderlin's phrase. Every deed is the apparent temporal effect of some prior word, instituting the temporality of tragic belatedness, that all that happens has already happened, will come to appear as the always already happening, a word and a deed entangled and extended through time through the force of repetition. Its fatality is, in a sense, to be found in the dynamic of its temporality and its perpetual exile into non-being that marks its distance from any sense of home.[4] According to Hölderlin, this prodigious performativity of the word is tragic both in the sense of fatal and theatrical. Within the theater, the word is acted, the word as deed takes on a specific meaning; the acute performativity of words in this play has everything to do with the words taking place within a play, as acted, as acted out.

There are, of course, other contexts in which words become indissociable from deeds, such as department meetings or family gatherings. The particular force of the word as deed within the family or, more generally, as it circuits within kinship, is enforced as law (nomos). But this enforcement does not happen without a reiteration – a wayward, temporal echo – that also puts the law at risk of going off its course.

And if we were to return to psychoanalysis through the figure of Antigone, how might our consideration of this play and this character lay out the possibility of an aberrant future for psychoanalysis, as that mode of analysis becomes appropriated in contexts that could not be anticipated? Psychoanalysis traces the wayward history of such utterances and makes its own lawlike pronouncements along the way. Psychoanalysis might be one mode of interpreting the curse, the apparently predictive force of the word as it bears a psychic history that cannot fully enter narrative form. The encrypted word that carries an irrecoverable history, a history that, by virtue of its very irrecoverability and its enigmatic afterlife in words, bears a force whose origin and end cannot be fully determined.

That the play Antigone predates its prehistory, is written decades before Oedipus at Colonus, indicates how the curse operates within an uncertain temporality. Uttered before the events, its force is only known retroactively; its force precedes its utterance, as if the utterance paradoxically inaugurates the necessity of its prehistory and of what will come to appear as always already true.

But how surefire is a curse? Is there a way to break it? Or is there, rather, a way in which its own vulnerability might be exposed and exploited? The one who within the present recites the curse or finds oneself in the midst of the word's historical effectivity does not precisely ventriloquize words that are received from a prior source. The words are reiterated, and their force is reenforced. The agency that performs this reiteration knows the curse but misunderstands the moment in which she participates in its transmission.

To what extent is this notion of the curse operating in the conception of a symbolic discourse that is transmitted in certain but unpredictable forms by the speaking subject? And to the extent that the symbolic reiterates a "structural" necessity of kinship, does it relay or perform the curse of kinship itself? In other words, does the structuralist law report on the curse that is upon kinship or does it deliver that curse? Is structuralist kinship the curse that is upon contemporary critical theory as it tries to approach the question of sexual normativity, sociality, and the status of law? And, moreover, if we are seized by this inheritance, is there a way to transmit that curse in aberrant form, exposing its fragility and fracture in the repetition and reinstitution of its terms? Is this breaking from the law that takes place in the reinstituting of the law the condition for articulating a future kinship that exceeds structuralist totality, a poststructuralism of kinship?[5]

The Antigonean revision of psychoanalytic theory might put into question the assumption that the incest taboo legitimates and normalizes kinship based in biological reproduction and the heterosexualization of the family. Although psychoanalysis has often insisted that normalization is invariably disrupted and foiled by what cannot be ordered by regulatory norms, it has rarely addressed the question of how new forms of kinship can and do arise on the basis of the incest taboo. From the presumption that one cannot – or ought not to – choose one's closest family members as one's lovers and marital partners, it does not follow that the bonds of kinship that *are* possible assume any particular form.

To the extent that the incest taboo contains its infraction within itself, it does not simply prohibit incest but rather sustains and cultivates incest as a necessary specter of social dissolution, a specter without which social bonds cannot emerge. Thus the prohibition against incest in the play *Antigone* requires a rethinking of prohibition itself, not merely as a negative or privative operation of power but as one that works precisely through proliferating through displacement the very crime that it bars. The taboo, and its threatening figuration of incest, delineates lines of kinship that harbor incest as their ownmost possibility, establishing "aberration" at the heart of the norm. Indeed, my question is whether it can also become the basis for a socially survivable aberration of kinship in which the norms that govern legitimate and illegitimate modes of kin association might be more radically redrawn.

Antigone says "brother," but does she mean "father"? She asserts her public right to grieve her kin, but how many of her kin does she leave ungrieved?

Considering how many are dead in her family, is it possible that mother and father and repudiated sister and other brother are condensed there at the site of the irreproducible brother? What kind of psychoanalytic approach to Antigone's act would foreclose in advance any consideration of overdetermination at the level of the object? This equivocation at the site of the kinship term signals a decidedly postoedipal dilemma, one in which kin positions tend to slide into one another, in which Antigone is the brother, the brother is the father, and in which psychically, linguistically, this is true regardless of whether they are dead or alive; for anyone living in this slide of identifications, their fate will be an uncertain one, living within death, dying within life.

One might simply say in a psychoanalytic spirit that Antigone represents a *perversion* of the law and conclude that the law requires perversion and that, in some dialectical sense, the law is, therefore, perverse. But to establish the structural necessity of perversion to the law is to posit a static relation between the two in which each entails the other and, in that sense, is nothing without the other. This form of negative dialectics produces the satisfaction that the law is *invested* in perversion and that the law is not what it seems to be. It does not help to make possible, however, other forms of social life, inadvertent possibilities produced by the prohibition that come to undermine the conclusion that an invariant social organization of sexuality follows of necessity from the prohibitive law. What happens when the perverse or the impossible emerges in the language of the law and makes its claim precisely there in the sphere of legitimate kinship that depends on its exclusion or pathologization?[6]

In Slavoj Žižek's brief account of Antigone offered in *Enjoy Your Symptom!*,[7] he suggests that Antigone's "no!" to Creon is a feminine and destructive act, one whose negativity leads to her own death. The masculine act is apparently more affirmative for him, the act by which a new order is founded (46). By saying "no" to the sovereign, she excludes herself from the community and is not survivable in that exile. Yet it seems that masculine reparation and building are an effort to cover over that "traumatic rupture" caused by feminine negation. Here it seems that Antigone is once again elevated to a feminine position (unproblematically) and then understood to have constituted the founding negation for the polis, the site of its own traumatic dissolution that the subsequent polity seeks to cover over. But does Antigone simply say "no"? Surely there are negations that riddle her speech, but she also approximates the stubborn will of Creon and circumscribes a rival autonomy by her negation. Later, Žižek will make clear that Antigone counters Creon not with reasons but with a tautology that is nothing other than her brother's name: "The 'law' in the name of which Antigone insists upon Polyneices' right to burial is this law of the 'pure' signifier.... It is the Law of the name that fixes our identity" (91–92). But does Antigone call her brother by his name, or does she, at the moment in which she seeks to give him precedence, call him by a kinship term that is, in fact and in principle, interchangeable? Will her brother ever have one name?

What is the contemporary voice that enters into the language of the law to disrupt its univocal workings? Consider that in the situation of blended families, a child says "mother" and might expect more than one individual to respond to the call. Or that, in the case of adoption, a child might say "father" and might mean both the absent phantasm she never knew as well as the one who assumes that place in living memory. The child might mean that at once, or sequentially, or in ways that are not always clearly disarticulated from one another. Or when a young girl comes to be fond of her stepbrother, what dilemma of kinship is she in? For a woman who is a single mother and has her child without a man, is the father still there, a spectral "position" or "place" that remains unfilled, or is there no such "place" or "position"? Is the father absent, or does this child have no father, no position, and no inhabitant? Is this a loss, which assumes the unfulfilled norm, or is it another configuration of primary attachment whose primary loss is not to have a language in which to articulate its terms? And when there are two men or two women who parent, are we to assume that some primary division of gendered roles organizes their psychic places within the scene, so that the empirical contingency of two same-gendered parents is nevertheless straightened out by the presocial psychic place of the Mother and Father into which they enter? Does it make sense on these occasions to insist that there are symbolic positions of Mother and Father that every psyche must accept regardless of the social form that kinship takes? Or is that a way of reinstating a heterosexual organization of parenting at the psychic level that can accommodate all manner of gender variation at the social level? Here it seems that the very division between the psychic or symbolic, on the one hand, and the social, on the other, occasions this preemptory normalization of the social field.

I write this, of course, against the background of a substantial legacy of feminist theory that has taken the Lévi-Straussian analytic of kinship as the basis for its own version of structuralist and poststructuralist psychoanalysis and the theorization of a primary sexual difference. It is, of course, one function of the incest taboo to prohibit sexual exchange among kin relations or, rather, to establish kin relations precisely on the basis of those taboos. The question, however, is whether the incest taboo has also been mobilized to *establish* certain forms of kinship as the only intelligible and livable ones. Thus one hears, for instance, the legacy of this tradition in psychoanalysis invoked by psychoanalysts in Paris in recent months against the prospect of "contracts of alliance," construed by conservatives as a bid for gay marriage. Although the rights of gay people to adopt children were not included in the proposed contracts, those who opposed the proposal fear that such contracts might lead to that eventuality and argue that any children raised in a gay family would run the immanent threat of psychosis, as if some structure, necessarily named "Mother" and necessarily named "Father" and established at the level of the symbolic, was a necessary psychic support against an engorgement by the Real. Similarly, Jacques-Alain Miller argued that whereas he was clear that homosexual relations deserve recognition, they should not qualify for marriage because two men together, deprived of the feminine presence, would not be able to bring fidelity to the relationship (a wonderful claim made against the backdrop of our presidential evidence of the binding power of marriage on heterosexual fidelity). Yet other Lacanian practitioners who trace the sources of autism in the "paternal gap" or "absence" similarly predict psychotic consequences for children with lesbian parents.

These views commonly maintain that alternative kinship arrangements attempt to revise psychic structures in ways that lead to tragedy again, figured incessantly as the tragedy of and for the child. No matter what one ultimately thinks of the political value of gay marriage, and I myself am a skeptic here for political reasons I outline elsewhere,[8] the public debate on its legitimacy becomes the occasion for a set of homophobic discourses that must be resisted on independent grounds. Consider that the horror of incest, the moral revulsion it compels in some, is not that far afield from the same horror and revulsion felt toward lesbian and gay sex, and is not unrelated to the intense moral condemnation of voluntary single parenting, or gay parenting, or parenting arrangements with more than two adults involved (practices that can be used as evidence to support a claim to remove a child from the custody of the parent in several states in the United States). These various modes in which the oedipal mandate fails to produce normative family all risk entering into the metonymy of that moralized sexual horror that is perhaps most fundamentally associated with incest.

The abiding assumption of the symbolic, that stable kinship norms support our abiding sense of culture's intelligibility, can be found, of course, outside of the Lacanian discourse. It is invoked in popular culture, by psychiatric "experts" and policy makers to thwart the legal demands of a social movement that threatens to expose the aberration at the heart of the heterosexual norm. It is quite possible to argue in a Lacanian vein that the symbolic place of the mother can be multiply occupied, that it is never identified or identifiable with an individual, and that this is what distinguishes it as symbolic. But why is the symbolic place singular and its inhabitants multiple? Or consider the liberal gesture in which one maintains that the place of the father and the place of the mother are necessary, but hey, anyone of any gender can fill them. The structure is purely formal, its defenders say, but note how its very formalism secures the structure against critical challenge. What are we to make of an inhabitant of the form that brings the form to crisis? If the relation between the inhabitant and the form is arbitrary, it is still structured, and its structure works to domesticate in advance any radical reformulation of kinship.[9]

The figure of Antigone, however, may well compel a reading that challenges that structure, for she does not conform to the symbolic law and she does not prefigure a final restitution of the law. Though entangled in the terms of kinship, she is at the same time outside those norms. Her crime is confounded by the fact that the kinship line from which she descends, and which she transmits, is derived from a paternal position that is already confounded by the manifestly incestuous act that is the condition of her own existence, which makes her brother her father, which begins a narrative in which she occupies, linguistically, every kin position *except* "mother" and occupies them at the expense of the coherence of kinship and gender.

Although not quite a queer heroine, Antigone does emblematize a certain heterosexual fatality that remains to be read. Whereas some might conclude that the tragic fate she suffers is the tragic fate of any and all who would transgress the lines of kinship that confer intelligibility on culture, her example, as it were, gives rise to a contrary sort of critical intervention: What in her act is fatal for heterosexuality in its normative sense? And to what other ways of organizing sexuality might a consideration of that fatality give rise?

Following schools of cultural anthropology inflected by Marxian analysis and Engels's famous study of the origin of the family, a school of feminist anthropologists have taken distance from the Lévi-Straussian model – a critique exemplified perhaps most powerfully by Gayle Rubin,[10] Sylvia Yanagisako, Jane Collier, Michelle Rosaldo,[11] and David Schneider.[12] The critique of the structuralist account, however, is not the end of kinship itself. Understood as a socially alterable set of arrangements that has no cross-cultural structural features that might be fully extracted from its social operations, kinship signifies any number of social arrangements that organize the reproduction of material life, that can include the ritualization of birth and death, that provide bonds of intimate alliance both enduring and breakable, and that regulate sexuality through sanction and taboo. In the 1970s socialist feminists sought to make use of the unwaveringly social analysis of kinship to show that there is no ultimate basis for normative heterosexual monogamous family structure in nature, and we might now add that it has no similar basis in language. Various utopian projects to revamp or eliminate family structure have become important components of the feminist movement and, to some extent, have survived in contemporary queer movements as well, the support for gay marriage notwithstanding.

Consider, for instance, Carol Stack's *All Our Kin* that shows that despite governmental efforts to label fatherless families as dysfunctional, those black urban kinship arrangements constituted by mothers, grandmothers, aunts, sisters, and friends who work together to raise children and reproduce the material conditions of life are extremely functional and would be seriously misdescribed if measured against an Anglo-American standard of familial normalcy.[13] The struggle to legitimate African-American kinship dates back to slavery, of course. And Orlando Patterson's book *Slavery and Social Death* makes the significant point that one of the institutions that slavery annihilated for African-Americans was kinship.[14] The slave-master invariably owned slave families, operating as a patriarch who could rape and coerce the women of the family and effeminize the men; women within slave families were unprotected by their own men, and men were unable to exercise their role in protecting and governing women and children. Although Patterson sometimes makes it seem that the primary offense against kinship was the eradication of paternal rights to women and children within slave families, he nevertheless offers us the important concept of "social death" to describe this aspect of slavery in which slaves are treated as dying within life.

"Social death" is the term Patterson gives to the status of being a living being radically deprived of all rights that are supposed to be accorded to any and all living human beings. What remains uninterrogated in his view, and that I believe resurfaces in his contemporary views on family politics, is precisely his objection to slave men being deprived by slavery of an ostensibly "natural" patriarchal position within the family. Indeed, his use of Hegel supports this point. Angela Davis made a radically different point in *The Black Scholar* several years ago when she underscored the vulnerability of black women to rape both within the institution of slavery and its aftermath, and argued that the family has not served as an adequate protection against sexualized racial violence.[15] Moreover, one can see in the work of Lévi-Strauss the implicit slide between his discussion of kinship groups, referred to as clans, and his subsequent writing on race and history in which the laws that govern the reproduction of a "race" become indissociable from the reproduction of the nation. In these latter writings, he implies that cultures maintain an internal coherence precisely through rules that guarantee their reproduction, and though he does not consider the prohibition of miscegenation, it seems to be presupposed in his description of self-replicating cultures.[16]

The critique of kinship within anthropology has centered on the fiction of bloodlines that work as a presupposition for kinship studies throughout the past century. And yet, the dissolution of kinship studies as an interesting or legitimate field of anthropology does not have to lead to a dismissal of kinship altogether. Kath Weston makes this clear in her book *Families We Choose*, where she replaces the blood tie as the basis for kinship with consensual affiliation.[17] We might see new kinship in other forms as well, ones where consent is less salient than the social organization of need: something like the buddy system that the Gay Men's Health Clinic in New York has established for caring for those who live with HIV and AIDS would similarly qualify as kinship, despite the enormous struggle to gain recognition by legal and medical institutions for the kin status of those relations, manifested for instance by the inability to assume medical responsibility for one another or, indeed, to be permitted to receive and bury the dead.

This perspective of radical kinship, which sought to extend legitimacy to a variety of kinship forms, and which, in fact, refused the reduction of kinship to family, came under criticism by some feminists in the aftermath of the 1960s "sexual revolution," producing, I would suggest, a theoretical conservatism that is currently in tension with contemporary radical sexual politics. It is why, for instance, it would be difficult to find a fruitful engagement at the present time between the new Lacanian formalisms and the radical queer politics of, for example, Michael Warner and friends. The former insists on fundamental notions of sexual difference, which are based on rules that prohibit and regulate sexual exchange, rules we can break only to find ourselves ordered by them anew. The latter calls into question forms of sexual foundationalism that cast viable forms of queer sexual alliance as illegitimate or, indeed, impossible and unlivable. At its extreme, the radical sexual politics turns against psychoanalysis or, rather, its implicit normativity, and the neoformalists turn against queer studies as a "tragically" utopian enterprise.

I remember hearing stories about how radical socialists who refused monogamy and family structure at the beginning of the 1970s ended that decade by filing into psychoanalytic offices and throwing themselves in pain on the analytic couch. And it seemed to me that the turn to psychoanalysis and, in particular, to Lacanian theory was prompted in part by the realization by some of those socialists that there were some constraints on sexual practice that were necessary for psychic survival and that the utopian effort to nullify prohibitions often culminated in excruciating scenes of psychic pain. The subsequent turn to Lacan seemed to be a turn away from a highly constructivist and malleable account of social law informing matters of sexual regulation to one that posits a presocial law, what Juliet Mitchell once called a "primordial law" (something she no longer does), the law of the Father, which sets limits upon the variability of social forms and which, in it most conservative form, mandates an exogamic, heterosexual conclusion to the oedipal drama. That this constraint is understood to be beyond social alteration, indeed, to constitute the condition and limit of all social alterations, indicates something of the theological status it has assumed. And though this position often is quick to claim that although there is a normative conclusion for the oedipal drama, the norm cannot exist without perversion, and only through perversion can the norm be established. We are all supposed to be satisfied with this apparently generous gesture by which the perverse is announced to be essential to the norm. The problem as I see it is that the perverse remains entombed precisely there, as the essential and negative feature of the norm, and the relation between the two remains static, giving way to no rearticulation of the norm itself.

In this light, then, it is perhaps interesting to note that Antigone, who concludes the oedipal drama, fails to produce heterosexual closure for that drama, and that this may intimate the direction for a psychoanalytic theory that takes Antigone as its point of departure. Certainly, she does not achieve another sexuality, one that is *not* heterosexuality, but she does seem to deinstitute heterosexuality by refusing to do what is necessary to stay alive for Haemon, by refusing to become a mother and a wife, by scandalizing the public with her wavering gender, by embracing death as her bridal chamber and identifying her tomb as a "deep dug home" (*kataskaphes oikesis*). If the love toward which she moves as she moves toward death is a love for her brother and thus, ambiguously, her father, it is also a love that can only be consummated by its obliteration, which is no consummation at all. As the bridal chamber is refused in life and pursued in death, it takes on a metaphorical status and, as metaphor, its conventional meaning is transmuted into a decidedly nonconventional one. If the tomb is the bridal chamber, and the tomb is chosen over marriage, then the tomb stands for the very destruction of marriage, and the term "bridal chamber" (*numpheion*) represents precisely the negation of its own possibility. The word destroys its object. In referring to the institution it names, the word performs the destruction of the institution. Is this not the operation of ambivalence in language that calls into question Antigone's sovereign control of her actions?

Although Hegel claims that Antigone acts with no unconscious, perhaps hers is an unconscious that leaves its trace in a different form, indeed that becomes readable precisely in her travails of referentiality. Her naming practice, for instance, ends up undoing its own ostensible aims. When she claims that she acts according to a law that gives her most precious brother precedence, and she appears to mean "Polyneices" by that description, she means more than she intends, for that brother could be Oedipus and it could be Eteocles, and there is nothing in the nomenclature of kinship that can successfully restrict its scope of referentiality to the single person, Polyneices. The chorus at one point seeks to remind her that she has more than one brother, but she continues to insist on the singularity and non-reproducibility of this term of kinship. In effect, she seeks to restrict the reproducibility of the word "brother" and to link it exclusively to the person of Polyneices, but she can do this only by displaying incoherence and inconsistency.[18] The term continues to refer to those others she would exclude from its sphere of application, and she cannot reduce the nomenclature of kinship to nominalism. Her own language exceeds and defeats her stated desire, thereby manifesting something of what is beyond her intention, of what belongs to the particular fate that desire suffers in language. Thus she is unable to capture the radical singularity of her brother through a term that, by definition, must be transposable and reproducible in order to signify at all. Language thus disperses the desire she seeks to bind to him, cursing her, as it were, with a promiscuity she cannot contain.

In this way Antigone does not achieve the effect of sovereignty she apparently seeks, and her action is not fully conscious. She is propelled by the words that are upon her, words of her father's that condemn the children of Oedipus to a life that ought not to have been lived. Between life and death, she is already living in the tomb prior to any banishment there. Her punishment precedes her crime, and her crime becomes the occasion for its literalization.

How do we understand this strange place of being between life and death, of speaking precisely from that vacillating boundary? If she is dead in some sense and yet speaks, she is precisely the one with no place who nevertheless seeks to claim one within speech, the unintelligible as it emerges within the intelligible, a position within kinship that is no position.

Although Antigone tries to capture. kinship through a language that defies the transposability of the terms of kinship, her language loses its consistency – but the force of her claim is not therefore lost. The incest taboo did not work to foreclose the love that it should have between Oedipus and Jocasta, and it is arguably faltering again for Antigone. The condemnation follows Oedipus' act and his recognition, but for Antigone, the condemnation works as foreclosure, ruling out from the start any life and love she might have had.

When the incest taboo works *in this sense* to foreclose a love that is not incestuous, what is produced is a shadowy realm of love, a love that persists in spite of its foreclosure in an ontologically suspended mode. What emerges is a melancholia that attends living and loving outside the livable and outside the field of love, where the lack of institutional sanction forces language into perpetual catachresis, showing not only how a term can continue to signify outside its conventional constraints but also how that shadowy form of signification takes its toll on a life by depriving it of its sense of ontological certainty and durability within a publicly constituted political sphere.

To accept those norms as coextensive with cultural intelligibility is to accept a doctrine that becomes the very instrument by which this melancholia is produced and reproduced at a cultural level. And it is overcome, in part, precisely through the repeated scandal by which the unspeakable nevertheless makes itself heard through borrowing and exploiting the very terms that are meant to enforce its silence.

Do we say that families that do not approximate the norm but mirror the norm in some apparently derivative way are poor copies, or do we accept that the ideality of the norm is undone precisely through the complexity of its instantiation? For those relations that are denied legitimacy, or that demand new terms of legitimation, are neither dead nor alive, figuring the nonhuman at the border of the human. And it is not simply that these are relations that cannot be honored, cannot be openly acknowledged, and cannot therefore by publicly grieved, but that these relations involve persons who are also restricted in the very act of grieving, who are denied the power to confer legitimacy on loss. In this play, at least, Antigone's kin are condemned prior to her crime, and the condemnation she receives repeats and amplifies the condemnation that animates her actions. How does one grieve from within the presumption of criminality, from within the presumption that one's acts are invariably and fatally criminal?

Consider that Antigone is trying to grieve, to grieve openly, publicly, under conditions in which grief is explicitly prohibited by an edict, an edict that assumes the criminality of grieving Polyneices and names as criminal anyone who would call the authority of that edict into question. She is one for whom open grieving is itself a crime. But is she guilty only because of the words that are upon her, words that come from elsewhere, or has she also sought to destroy and repudiate the very bonds of kinship that she now claims entitlement to grieve? She is grieving her brother, but part of what remains unspoken in that grief is the grief she has for her father and, indeed, her other brother. Her mother remains almost fully unspeakable, and there is hardly a trace of grief for her sister, Ismene, whom she has explicitly repudiated. The "brother" is no singular place for her, though it may well be that all her brothers (Oedipus, Polyneices, Eteocles) are condensed at the exposed body of Polyneices, an exposure she seeks to cover, a nakedness she would rather not see or have seen. The edict demands that the dead body remain exposed and ungrieved, and though Antigone seeks to overcome the edict, it is not entirely clear all of what she grieves or whether the public act she performs can be the site of its resolution. She calls her loss her brother, Polyneices, insists on his singularity, but that very insistence is suspect. Thus her insistence on the singularity of her brother, his radical irreproducibility, is belied by the mourning she fails to perform for her two other brothers, the ones she fails to reproduce publicly for us. Here it appears that the prohibition against mourning is not simply imposed upon her but is enjoined independently without direct pressure by public law.

Her melancholia, if we can call it that, seems to consist in this refusal to grieve that is accomplished through the very public terms by which she insists on her right to grieve. Her claim to entitlement may well be the sign of a melancholia at work in her speech. Her loud proclamations of grief presuppose a domain of the ungrievable. The insistence on public grieving is what moves her away from feminine gender into hubris, into that distinctively manly excess that makes the guards, the chorus, and Creon wonder: Who is the man here? There seem to be some spectral men here, ones that Antigone herself inhabits, the brothers whose place she has taken and whose place she transforms in the taking. The melancholic, Freud tell us, registers his or her "plaint," levels a juridical claim, where the language becomes the event of the grievance, where, emerging from the unspeakable, language carries a violence that brings it to the limits of speakability.

We might ask what remains unspeakable here, not in order to produce speech that will fill the gap but to ask about the convergence of social prohibition and melancholia, how the condemnations under which one lives turn into repudiations that one performs, and how the grievances that emerge against the public law also constitute conflicted efforts to overcome the muted rage of one's own repudiations. In confronting the unspeakable in *Antigone*, are we confronting a socially instituted foreclosure of the intelligible, a socially instituted melancholia in which the unintelligible life emerges in language as a living body might be interred into a tomb?

Indeed, Giorgio Agamben has remarked that we live increasingly in a time in which populations with full citizenship exist within states; their ontological status as legal subjects is suspended. These are not lives that are being genocidally destroyed, but neither are they being entered into the life of the legitimate community in which standards of recognition permit for an attainment of humanness.[19] How are we to understand this realm, what Hannah Arendt described as the "shadowy realm," which haunts the public sphere, which is precluded from the public constitution of the human, but which is human in an apparently catachrestic sense of that term?[20] Indeed, how are we to grasp this dilemma of language that emerges when "human" takes on that doubled sense, the normative one based on radical exclusion and the one that emerges in the sphere of the excluded, not negated, not dead, perhaps slowly dying, yes, surely dying from a lack of recognition, dying, indeed, from the premature circumscription of the norms by which recognition as human can be conferred, a recognition without which the human cannot come into being but must remain on the far side of being, as what does not quite qualify as that which is and can be? Is this not a melancholy of the public sphere?

Arendt, of course, problematically distinguished the public and the private, arguing that in classical Greece the former alone was the sphere of the political, that the latter was mute, violent, and based on the despotic power of the patriarch. Of course, she did not explain how there might be a prepolitical despotism, or how the "political" must be expanded to describe the status of a population of the less than human, those who were not permitted into the interlocutory scene of the public sphere where the human is constituted through words and deeds and most forcefully constituted when its word becomes its deed. What she failed to read in *The Human Condition* was precisely the way in which the boundaries of the public and political sphere were secured through the production of a constitutive outside. And what she did not explain was the mediating link that kinship provided between the public and private spheres. The slaves, women, and children, all those who were not property-holding males were not permitted into the public sphere in which the human was constituted through its linguistic deeds. Kinship and slavery thus condition the public sphere of the human and remain outside its terms. But is that the end of the story?

Who then is Antigone within such a scene, and what are we to make of her words, words that become dramatic events, performative acts? She is not of the human but speaks in its language. Prohibited from action, she nevertheless acts, and her act is hardly a simple assimilation to an existing norm. And in acting, as one who has no right to act, she upsets the vocabulary of kinship that is a precondition of the human, implicitly raising the question for us of what those preconditions really must be. She speaks within the language of entitlement from which she is excluded, participating in the language of the claim with which no final identification is possible. If she is human, then the human has entered into catachresis: we no longer know its proper usage. And to the extent that she occupies the language that can never belong to her, she functions as a chiasm within the vocabulary of political norms. If kinship is the precondition of the human, then Antigone is the occasion for a new field of the human, achieved through political catachresis, the one that happens when the less than human speaks as human, when gender is displaced, and kinship founders on its own founding laws. She acts, she speaks, she becomes one for whom the speech act is a fatal crime, but this fatality exceeds her life and enters the discourse of intelligibility as its own promising fatality, the social form of its aberrant, unprecedented future.

Notes

1   George Steiner, *Antigones* (reprint, New Haven: Yale University Press, 1996), p. 18.
2   David Schneider, *A Critique of the Study of Kinship* (Ann Arbor: University of Michigan Press, 1984), p. 131.

3   "Das Wort mittelbarer faktisch wird, indem es den sinnlicheren Körper ergreift. Das griechischtragische Wort ist tödlichfaktisch, weil der Leib, den es ergreift, wirklich tötet," in "Anmerkungen zur Antigone" in *Friedrich Hölderlin, Werke in einem Band* (Munich: Hanser Verlag, 1990), p. 64. All English citations are from "Remarks on Antigone," *Friedrich Hölderlin: Essays and Letters*, ed. and trans. Thomas Pfau (Albany: State University of New York Press, 1977). See also Philippe Lacoue-Labarthe, *Métaphrasis suivi de la théâtre de Hölderlin* (Paris: Presses Universitaires de France, 1988), pp. 63–73.

4   Heidegger offers a sustained meditation on Hölderlin's translation of *Antigone* (1803), as well as his "Remarks on Antigone" with respect to the various ways that Hölderlin brings forward Antigone's "uncanniness." The proximity to death underscored in the "Remarks on Antigone" corresponds in large measure to Heidegger's reading of Antigone as one whose exile from the hearth establishes her essential relation to a sense of being that is beyond human life. This participation in what is non-living turns out to be something like the condition of living itself. As in the reading supplied by Jacques Lacan, Heidegger also claims that "[Antigone] names being itself" (118), and that this proximity to being involves a necessary estrangement from living beings even as it is the ground of their very emergence.

      Similarly, Heidegger understands the "unwritten law" to which Antigone refers as a relationship to being and to death:

> Antigone assumes as what is fitting that which is destined to her from the realm of whatever prevails beyond the higher gods (Zeus) and beyond the lower gods. . . . Yet this refers neither to the dead, nor to her blood-relationship with her brother. What determines Antigone is that which first bestows ground and necessity upon the distinction of the dead and the priority of blood. What that is, Antigone, and that also means the poet, leaves without a name. Death and human being, human being and embodied life (blood) in each case belong together. "Death" and "blood" in each case name different and extreme realms of human being.

From Martin Heidegger, *Hölderlin's Hymn "The Ister"*, trans. William McNeill and Julia Davis (Bloomington: Indiana University Press, 1996), p. 117.

5   There have been several important works within anthropology in the last few decades showing the limitations of structuralist paradigms for thinking the problem of kinship, including Marilyn Strathern, *Reproducing the Future: Essays on Anthropology, Kinship, and the New Reproductive Technologies* (New York: Routledge, 1992). In *Gender and Kinship: Essays Toward a Unified Analysis*, ed. Jane Fishburne Collier and Sylvia Junko Yanagisako (Stanford: Stanford University Press, 1987), the editors argue against a view of kinship that focuses exclusively on symbolic relations at the expense of social action. Perspectives in that volume that seek to elaborate the complex social conditions of kinship relations against both functionalist and purely structuralist accounts are to be found in the important contributions by John

Comaroff, Rayna Rapp, Marilyn Strathern, and Maurice Bloch. See also Sylvia Junko Yanagisako, "The Analysis of Kinship Change," in *Transforming the Past: Tradition and Kinship Among Japanese Americans* (Stanford: Stanford University Press, 1985), where she faults both structuralist and functionalist accounts for failing to give a dynamic understanding of kin relations. David Schneider, in *A Critique of the Study of Kinship*, elaborates how the theoretical models of kinship elaborated by Fortes, Leach, and Lévi-Strauss impose theoretical constraints on ethnographic perception, failing to account for societies that failed to approximate the theoretical norm and that, regardless of their claim not to take biological relations of reproduction as the point of departure of kinship study, still make that assumption operate as a fundamental premise of their work (see pp. 3–9, 133–77). In particular, the work of Pierre Clastres in France made dramatically and vociferously, clearly drawing in part on the prior work of Marshall Sahlins, argues that the sphere of the social could not be reduced to the workings of kinship, and cautions against any effort to treat kinship rules as supplying the principles of intelligibility for any social order. He writes, for instance, that it is not possible to reduce relations of power to those of exchange: "Power relates . . . to the . . . essential structural levels of society: that is, it is at the very heart of the communicative universe" (37). In *Society Against the State*, trans. Robert Hurley (New York: Zone, 1987), pp. 27–49, Clastres argues for relocating the "exchange of women" within relations of power. And in "Marxists And Their Anthropology," he offers a searing criticism of Maurice Godelier on the matter of kinship and the state. There he argues that the principle function of kinship is not to institute the incest taboo nor to exemplify relations of production, but to transmit and reproduce the "name" of the relative, and that "the function of nomination, inscribed in kinship, determines the entire sociopolitical being of primitive society. It is there that the tie between kinship and society is located." See Pierre Clastres, *Archaeology of Violence*, trans. Jeanine Herman (New York: Semiotext(e), 1994), p. 134.

For a notion of kinship as embodied practice, see also Pierre Bourdieu, *The Logic of Practice*, trans. Richard Nice (Stanford: Stanford University Press, 1990), pp. 34–5.

6   Here I am not suggesting that the perverse simply inhabits the norm as something that remains autonomous, but neither am I suggesting that it is dialectically assimilated into the norm itself. It might be understood to signal the impossibility of maintaining a sovereign lock on any claim to legitimacy, since the reiteration of the claim outside of its legitimated site of enunciation shows that the legitimate site is not the source of its effectivity. Here I am indebted to what I take to be Homi Bhabha's significant reformulation dispersed throughout his work of both speech act theory and the Foucaultian notion of discourse developed in the latter's *Archaeology of Knowledge*.

7   Slavoj Žižek, *Enjoy Your Symptom!* (New York: Routledge, 1992).

8   See my contribution, "Competing Universalities," to Judith Butler, Ernesto Laclau, and Slavoj Žižek, *Universality, Hegemony, Contingency* (London: Verso, 2000). Reprinted on pp. 00–00 of this volume.

9   It has been one strategy here to argue that the incest taboo does not always
    produce normative family, but it is perhaps more important to realize that the
    normative family that it does produce is not always what it seems. There is, for
    instance, clearly merit in the analysis offered by Linda Alcoff and others that
    heterosexual incest within heterosexually normative families is an extension rather
    than abrogation of patriarchal prerogative within heterosexual normativity. Pro-
    hibition is not fully or exclusively privative, that is, just as prohibition requires *and*
    produces the specter of crime it bars. And for Alcoff, in an interesting Foucaultian
    move, the prohibition offers the cover that protects and abets the practice of
    incest. But is there any reason to check the productivity of the incest taboo here,
    at this dialectical inversion of its aim? See Linda Alcoff, "Survivor Discourse:
    Transgression or Recuperation?" *signs* 18, no. 2 (Winter 1993): 260–91. See also
    for a very interesting and brave Foucaultian discussion of the criminalization of
    incest, Vikki Bell, *Interrogating Incest: Feminism, Foucault, and the Law* (London:
    Routledge, 1993).

10 Gayle Rubin, "The Traffic in Women: Notes on the 'Political Economy' of Sex,"
    in *Toward an Anthropology of Women*, ed. Rayna R. Reiter (New York: Monthly
    Review Press, 1975).

11 See *Gender and Kinship*, ed. Collier and Yanagisako. For an excellent critique of
    gender-based approaches to kinship, which shows how the uncritical presumption
    of marriage underwrites the anthropological approach to kinship, see John Borne-
    man, "Until Death Do Us Part: Marriage/Death in Anthropological Discourse,"
    American Ethnologist 23, no. 2 (1996): 215–38.

12 David Schneider, *A Critique of the Study of Kinship; American Kinship* (Chicago:
    University of Chicago Press, 1980).

13 Carol Stack, *All Our Kin: Strategies for Survival in a Black Community* (New York:
    Harper and Row, 1974).

14 See, in particular, the very interesting use of Hegel in his discussion of the
    dehumanization in slavery in Orlando Patterson, *Slavery and Social Death: A
    Comparative Study*, pp. 97–101. For Patterson's illuminating discussion of Antig-
    one, see *Freedom, Volume 1: Freedom in the Making of Western Culture* (New York:
    Basic Books, 1991), pp. 106–32.

15 Angela Davis, "Rape, Racism, and the Myth of the Black Rapist," reprinted in
    Women, Race, and Class (New York: Random House, 1981), pp. 172–201.

16 Claude Lévi-Strauss, *Race et histoire* (Paris: Denoël, 1987); *Structural Anthropology,
    Volume 2*, trans. Monique Layton (New York: Basic Books, 1974), pp. 323–62.

17 Kath Weston, *Families We Choose: Lesbians, Gays, Kinship* (New York: Columbia
    University Press, 1991).

18 Like Lacan, Derrida appears to accept the singularity of Antigone's relationship to
    her brother, one that Hegel describes, as we have already seen, as a relationship
    without desire. Although Derrida does not read the play, *Antigone*, in *Glas*, he does
    read the figure of Antigone in Hegel, working within the terms of that reading to
    show how Antigone comes to mark the radical outside to Hegel's own systematic
    thinking and Hegel's own "fascination by a figure inadmissable within the system"

(151). Although I agree that neither the figure nor the play of Antigone can be readily assimilated into either the framework of *The Phenomenology of Spirit* or the *The Philosophy of Right*, and although the play is curiously applauded in the *Aesthetics* as "the most magnificent and appeasing work of art," it would be a mistake to take her persistent unreadability within the Hegelian perspective as a sign of her final or necessary unreadability.

19 Giorgio Agamben, *Homo Sacer: Sovereign Power and Bare Life*, trans. Daniel Heller-Roazen (Stanford: Stanford University Press, 1998).

20 Hannah Arendt, *The Human Condition* (Chicago: University of Chicago Press, 1969), part 1.

12

What is Critique? An Essay on Foucault's Virtue (2000)

Introduction

Originally delivered as the Raymond Williams Lecture at Cambridge University, Butler's self-styled "essay" on self-stylization as a form of critique begins and ends with two different but related questions: first, what is it to offer a critique, and last, who will count as a subject and what will count as a life? The fact that questions frame this piece is significant, since critique as it emerges in Butler's reading of Foucault's "What Is Critique?" and his *The History of Sexuality: Volume II: The Use of Pleasure*, is an ethical mode of self-making in which the limits of epistemology and ontology are interrogated without recourse to answers or definitions. Asking questions that one has no intention of answering throws into relief frameworks of knowledge and power as they are currently configured, while existing at the limits of ontology and epistemology also involves risking one's certainty, indeed, risking oneself.

In both the works from which Butler draws here, Foucault characterizes critique as a mode of ethical self-questioning that is akin to virtue, where virtue does not denote obedience to the law but its opposite – a critical and *questioning* relation to the norms by which subjects are constituted. For both Butler and Foucault, virtue is a practice of self-making and self-transformation which opposes itself to the established order by interrogating the terms by which subjects are currently constituted. As always, these interrogations take place within existing discursive structures, so that rather than a refusal of morality, virtue is "a specific stylization of morality" where "stylization" is opposed to codification and "fixture."

It is through such practices of self-stylization and self-transformation that the limits of knowledge and being are exposed, which means that critique involves investigating the relationship between power and knowledge. The critical practice of self-stylization does not involve the formation of new selves in contradistinction to discourse and the law, since on the contrary, it is a suspension of ontological certainty. Moreover, the self-stylization in which the subject is engaged will be contingent upon the law whose limits are thereby exposed. Addressing some of her critics' objections, Butler asserts that such ontological risk-taking is neither nihilism nor a "sexy" brush with evil merely for the sake

From David Ingram (ed.), *The Political*, pp. 212–26. Oxford: Blackwell, 2001. Reprinted by permission of Blackwell Publishing Ltd.

of it, but a necessary resistance to discursive norms which have congealed into givens. The practice of ethical self-making that is described in "What Is Critique?" sounds very like the modes of resistance formulated in earlier work – the strategies of parody and drag outlined in *Gender Trouble* and *Bodies That Matter* for example, where Butler asserts that the performative rehearsal of subject-positions will reveal the contingency and instability of heterosexual norms. Retrospectively then, earlier descriptions of subversion – the paradoxical practice of self-making in desubjugation, the occupying of subject-positions only in order to reveal their instability and untenability – assume the contours of critique as it is described in this article.

As always, there is no discernible self who "does" these critical practices, so that critique as a practice of freedom should not be characterized as straightforward voluntarism. Just as in *Bodies That Matter*, there is no subject who gets up in the morning and peruses her/his "wardrobe" for a gender costume of choice for the day, so "What Is Critique?" addresses the question of agency by suggesting that voluntary insubordination and desubjugation always take place within the constraints of the constitutive fields whose limits are under investigation. On the first page of her lecture Butler asserts that critique is always a critique *of* some practice, discourse, episteme, institution, so that its form is determined by those practices, discourses, etc. As in Butler's previous work, there can be no recourse to a discursive "outside," since there is no such space or field; rather, the terms of discourse must be re-rehearsed and turned against themselves through radical appropriation.

Knowingly suspending any claim to ontological certainty by questioning the terms of subject-constitution is a risky business, but Foucault himself provides a working example of the practice in his "What Is Critique?" where he invokes "originary freedom" only to retract it immediately and to claim that he did not say it. What Butler calls Foucault's "oddly brave gesture" is a demonstration of originary freedom *sous rature* (an erasure that is replicated in Butler's own re-staging of Foucault's retracted term) which far from underscoring the notion of "original" freedom or an originating subject, marks the ontological suspension of both in the uttering/not-uttering of the phrase. Critique is thus a mode of questioning and conjecturing, a "saying something [e.g. 'originary freedom'] in the wondering," where no ontological commitment is made to the terms of the utterance or the question. We have come across the staging (as opposed to the assertion) of terms under erasure in previous work, and it is now clear that the questioning mode Butler frequently adopts is a critical practice with a deliberate political aim, rather than a stylistic tic or an epistemological evasion.

Again, interrogation is a risky practice since it is likely to expose the utterer-questioner to the denunciations of those who may have a vested interest in protecting ontological and epistemological certainties in order to conceal and congeal the operations of power/ knowledge. Both Butler and Foucault pose questions that are only approximately and contingently answered (what is critique? who will count as a subject? what will count as a life?), a practice that constitutes an ethical and a virtuous challenge to power. Indeed, we know that neither critique nor subject-formation can be described with any certainty or permanence, since both of these context-dependent practices are engaged in unraveling the definitions and the selves which currently pass for ontological norms.

The whole of Butler's essay, which is a slightly longer version of the lecture delivered in Cambridge in May 2000, is included below.

What is it to offer a critique? This is something that, I would wager, most of us understand in some ordinary sense. But matters become more vexing if we attempt to distinguish between a critique of this or that position and critique as a more generalized practice, one that might be described without reference to its specific objects. Can we even ask such a question about the generalized character of critique without gesturing toward an essence of critique? And if we achieved the generalized picture, offering something which approaches a philosophy of critique, would we then lose the very distinction between philosophy and critique that operates as part of the definition of critique itself? Critique is always a critique *of* some instituted practice, discourse, episteme, institution, and it loses its character the moment in which it is abstracted from its operation and made to stand alone as a purely generalizable practice. But if this is true, this does not mean that no generalizations are possible or that, indeed, we are mired in particularisms. On the contrary, we tread here in an area of constrained generality, one which broaches the philosophical, but must, if it is to remain critical, remain at a distance from that very achievement.

The essay I offer here is about Foucault, but let me begin by suggesting what I take to be an interesting parallel between what Raymond Williams and Theodor Adorno, in different ways, sought to accomplish under the name of "criticism" and what Foucault sought to understand by "critique." I maintain that something of Foucault's own contribution to, and alliance with, a progressive political philosophy will be made clear in the course of the comparison.

Raymond Williams worried that the notion of criticism has been unduly restricted to the notion of "fault-finding"[1] and proposed that we find a vocabulary for the kinds of responses we have, specifically to cultural works, "which [do] not assume the habit (or right or duty) of judgment." And what he called for was a more specific kind of response, one that did not generalize too quickly: "what always needs to be understood," he wrote, "is the specificity of the response, which is not a judgment, but a practice." I believe this last line also marks the trajectory of Foucault's thinking on this topic, since "critique" is precisely a practice that not only suspends judgment for him, but offers a new practice of values based on that very suspension.

So, for Williams, the practice of critique is not reducible to arriving at judgments (and expressing them). Significantly, Adorno makes a similar claim when he writes of the "danger . . . of judging intellectual phenomena in a subsumptive, uninformed and administrative manner and assimilating them into the prevailing constellations of power which the intellect ought to expose."[2] So, the task of exposing those "constellations of power" is impeded by the rush to "judgment" as the exemplary act of critique. For Adorno, the very operation of judgment serves to separate the critic from the social world at hand, a move which deratifies the results of its own operation, constituting a "withdrawal from praxis." Adorno writes that the critic's "very sovereignty, the claim to a more profound knowledge of the object, the separation of the idea from its object through the independence of the critical judgment threatens to succumb to the thing-like form of the object when cultural criticism appeals to a collection of ideas on display, as it were, and fetishizes isolated categories." For critique to operate as part of a praxis, for Adorno, is for it to apprehend the ways in which categories are themselves instituted, how the field of knowledge is ordered, and how what it suppresses returns, as it were, as its own constitutive occlusion. Judgments operate for both thinkers as ways to subsume a particular under an already constituted category, whereas critique asks after the occlusive constitution of the field of categories themselves. What becomes especially important for Foucault in this domain, is to try to think the problem of freedom and, indeed, ethics in general, beyond judgment: critical thinking constitutes this kind of effort.

In 1978 Foucault delivered a lecture entitled, "What is Critique?",[3] a piece that prepared the way for his more well-known essay, "What is Enlightenment?" (1984). He not only asks what critique is, but seeks to understand the kind of question that critique institutes, offering some tentative ways of circumscribing its activity. What remains perhaps most important about that lecture, and the more developed essay that followed, is the question form in which the matter is put. For the very question "what is critique?" is an instance of the critical enterprise in question, and so the question not only poses the problem – what is this critique that we supposedly do or, indeed, aspire to do? – but enacts a certain mode of questioning which will prove central to the activity of critique itself.

Indeed, I would suggest that what Foucault seeks to do with this question is something quite different from what we have perhaps come to expect from critique. Habermas made the operation of critique quite problematic when he suggested that a move beyond critical theory was required if we are to seek recourse to norms in making evaluative judgments about social conditions and social goals. The perspective of critique, in his view, is able to call foundations into question, denaturalize social and political hierarchy, and even establish perspectives by which a certain distance on the naturalized world can be had. But none of these activities can tell us in what direction we ought to move, nor can they tell us whether the activities in which we engage are realizing certain kinds of normatively justified goals. Hence, in his view, critical theory had to give way to a stronger normative theory, such as communicative action, in order to supply a foundation for critical theory, enabling strong normative judgments to be made,[4] and for politics not only to have a clear aim and normative aspiration, but for us to be able to evaluate current practices in terms of their abilities to reach those goals. In making this kind of criticism of critique, Habermas became curiously uncritical about the very sense of normativity he deployed. For the question "what are we to do?" presupposes that the "we" has been formed and that it is known, that its action is possible, and the field in which it might act is delimited. But if those very formations and delimitations have normative consequences, then it will be necessary to ask after the values that set the stage for action, and this will be an important dimension of any critical inquiry into normative matters.

And though the Habermasians may have an answer to this problem, my aim today is not to rehearse these debates nor to answer them, but to mark the distance between a notion of critique that is characterized as normatively impoverished in some sense, and another, which I hope to offer here, which is not only more complex than the usual criticism assumes but which has, I would argue, strong normative commitments that appear in forms that would be difficult, if not impossible, to read within the current grammars of normativity. Indeed, in this essay, I hope to show that Foucault not only makes an important contribution to normative theory, but that both his aesthetics and his account of the subject are integrally related to both his ethics and politics. Whereas some have dismissed him as an aesthete or, indeed, as a nihilist, I hope to suggest that the foray he makes into the topic of self-making and, by presupposition, into poeisis itself is central to the politics of desubjugation that he proposes. Paradoxically, self-making and desubjugation happen simultaneously when a mode of existence is risked which is unsupported by what he calls the regime of truth.

Foucault begins his discussion by affirming that there are various grammars for the term, "critique," distinguishing between a "high Kantian enterprise" called critique as well as "the little polemical activities that are called critique." Thus, he warns us at the outset that critique will not be one thing, and that we will not be able to define it apart from the various objects by which it itself is defined. "By its function," he writes "[critique] seems to be condemned to dispersion, dependency and pure heteronomy." "It only exists in relation to something other than itself."

Thus, Foucault seeks to define critique, but finds that only a series of approximations are possible. Critique will be dependent on its objects, but its objects will in turn define the very meaning of critique. Further, the primary task of critique will not be to evaluate whether its objects – social conditions, practices, forms of knowledge, power, and discourse – are good or bad, valued highly or demeaned, but to bring into relief the very framework of evaluation itself. What is the relation of knowledge to power such that our epistemological certainties turn out to support a way of structuring the world that forecloses alternative possibilities of ordering? Of course, we may think that we need epistemological certainty in order to state for sure that the world is and ought to be ordered a given way. To what extent, however, is that certainty orchestrated by forms of knowledge precisely in order to foreclose the possibility of thinking otherwise? Now, one might wisely ask, what good is thinking otherwise, if we don't know in advance that thinking otherwise will produce a better world? If we do not have a moral framework in which to decide with knowingness that certain new possibilities or ways of thinking otherwise will bring forth that world whose betterness we can judge by sure and already established standards? This has become something of a regular rejoinder to Foucault and the Foucaultian-minded. And shall we assume that the relative silence that has greeted this habit of fault-finding in Foucault is a sign that his theory has no reassuring answers to give? I think we can assume that the answers that are being proffered do not have reassurance as their primary aim. This is, of course, not to say what withdraws reassurance is, by definition, not an answer. Indeed, the only rejoinder, it seems to me, is to return to a more fundamental meaning of "critique" in order to see what may well be wrong with the question as it is posed and, indeed, to pose the question anew, so that a more productive approach to the place of ethics within politics might be mapped. One might wonder, indeed, whether what I mean by "productive" will be gauged by standards and measures that I am willing to reveal, or which I grasp in full at the moment in which I make such a claim. But here I would ask for your patience since it turns out that critique is a practice that requires a certain amount of patience in the same way that reading, according to Nietzsche, required that we act a bit more like cows than humans and learn the art of slow rumination.

Foucault's contribution to what appears as an impasse within critical and post-critical theory of our time is precisely to ask us to rethink critique as a practice in which we pose the question of the limits of our most sure ways of knowing, what Williams referred to as our "uncritical habits of mind" and what Adorno described as ideology (where the "unideological thought is that which does not permit itself to be reduced to 'operational terms' and instead strives solely to help the things themselves to that articulation from which they are otherwise cut off by the prevailing language"). One does not drive to the limits for a thrill experience, or because limits are dangerous and sexy, or because it brings us into a titillating proximity with evil. One asks about the limits of ways of knowing because one has already run up against a crisis within the epistemological field in which one lives. The categories by which social life are ordered produce a certain incoherence or entire realms of unspeakability. And it is from this condition, the tear in the fabric of our epistemological web, that the practice of critique emerges, with the awareness that no discourse is adequate here or that our reigning discourses have produced an impasse. Indeed, the very debate in which the strong normative view wars with critical theory may produce precisely that form of discursive impasse from which the necessity and urgency of critique emerges.

For Foucault, critique is "a means for a future or a truth that it will not know nor happen to be, it oversees a domain it would not want to police and is unable to regulate." So critique will be that perspective on established and ordering ways of knowing which is not immediately assimilated into that ordering function. Significantly, for Foucault, this exposure of the limit of the epistemological field is linked with the practice of virtue, as if virtue is counter to regulation and order, as if virtue itself is to be found in the risking of established order. He is not shy about the relation here. He writes, "there is something in critique that is akin to virtue." And then he says something which might be considered even more surprising: "this critical attitude [is] virtue in general."

There are some preliminary ways we can understand Foucault's effort to cast critique as virtue. Virtue is most often understood either as an attribute or a practice of a subject, or indeed a quality that conditions and characterizes a certain kind of action or practice. It belongs to an ethics which is not fulfilled merely by following objectively formulated rules or laws. And virtue is not only a *way* of complying with or conforming with preestablished norms. It is, more radically, a critical relation to those norms, one which, for Foucault, takes shape as a specific stylization of morality.

Foucault gives us an indication of what he means by virtue in the introduction to *The Use of Pleasure: The History of Sexuality, Volume Two*.[5] At this juncture he makes clear that he seeks to move beyond a notion of ethical philosophy that issues a set of prescriptions. Just as critique intersects with philosophy without quite coinciding with it, so Foucault in that introduction seeks to make of his own thought an example of a non-prescriptive form of moral inquiry. In the same way, he will later ask about forms of moral experience that are not rigidly defined by a juridical law, a rule or command to which the self is said mechanically or uniformly to submit. The essay that he writes, he tells us, is itself the example of such a practice, "to explore what might be changed, in its own thought, through the practice of a knowledge that is foreign to it." Moral experience has to do with a self-transformation prompted by a form of knowledge that is foreign to one's own. And this form of moral experience will be different from the submission to a command. Indeed, to the extent that Foucault interrogates moral experience here or elsewhere, he understands himself to be making an inquiry into moral experiences that are not primarily or fundamentally structured by prohibition or interdiction.

In the first volume of *The History of Sexuality*[6] he sought to show that the primary interdictions assumed by psychoanalysis and the structuralist account of cultural prohibitions cannot be assumed as historical constants. Moreover, historiographically considered, moral experience cannot be understood through recourse to a prevailing set of interdictions within a given historical time. Although there are codes to be studied, these codes must always be studied in relation to the modes of subjectivation to which they correspond. He makes the claim that the juridification of law achieves a certain hegemony within the thirteenth century, but that if one goes back to Greek and Roman classical cultures, one finds practices, or "arts of existence" which have to do with a cultivated relation of the self to itself.

Introducing the notion of "arts of existence," Foucault also reintroduces and reemphasizes "intentional and voluntary actions," specifically, "those actions by which men not only set themselves rules of conduct, but also seek to transform themselves in their singular being, and to make their life into an oeuvre." Such lives do not simply conform to moral precepts or norms in such a way that selves, considered preformed or readymade, fit themselves into a mold that is set forth by the precept. On the contrary, the self fashions itself in terms of the norm, comes to inhabit and incorporate the norm, but *the norm is not in this sense external to the principle by which the self is formed.* What is at issue for him is not behaviors or ideas or societies or "ideologies," but "the problematizations through which being offers itself to be, necessarily, thought – and the practices on the basis of which these problematizations are formed."

This last claim is hardly transparent, but what it suggests is that certain kinds of practices which are designed to handle certain kinds of problems produce, over time, a settled domain of ontology as their consequence, and this ontological domain, in turn, constrains our understanding of what is possible. Only with reference to this prevailing ontological horizon, itself instituted through a set of practices, will we be able to understand the kinds of relations to moral precepts that have been formed as well as those that are yet to be formed. For instance, he considers at length various practices of austerity, and he ties these to the production of a certain kind of masculine subject. The practices of austerity do not attest to a single and abiding prohibition, but work in the service of crafting a certain kind of self. Or put in a more precise way, the self, incorporating the rules of conduct that represent the virtue of austerity, creates itself as a specific kind of subject. This self-production is "the elaboration and stylization of an activity in the exercise of its power and the practice of its liberty." This was not a practice that opposed pleasure pure and simple, but a certain practice of pleasure itself, a practice of pleasure in the context of moral experience.

Thus, in section 3 of that same introduction, Foucault makes clear that it will not suffice to offer a chronicled history of moral codes, for such a history cannot tell us how these codes were lived and, more specifically, what forms of subject-formation such codes required and facilitated. Here he begins to sound like a phenomenologist. But there is, in addition to the recourse to the experiential means by which moral categories are grasped, a critical move as well, for the subjective relation to those norms will be neither predictable nor mechanical. The relation will be "critical" in the sense that it will not comply with a given category, but rather constitute an interrogatory relation to the field of categorization itself, referring at least implicitly to the limits of the epistemological horizon within which practices are formed. The point will not be to refer practice to a pregiven epistemological context, but to establish critique as the very practice that exposes the limits of that epistemological horizon itself, making the contours of the horizon appear, as it were, for the first time, we might say, in relation to its own limit. Moreover, the critical practice in question turns out to entail self-transformation in relation to a rule of conduct. How, then, does self-transformation lead to the exposure of this limit? How is self-transformation understood as a "practice of liberty," and how is this practice understood as part of Foucault's lexicon of virtue?

Let us begin first by understanding the notion of self-transformation at stake here, and then consider how it is related to the problem called "critique" which forms the focus of our deliberations here. It is, of course, one thing to conduct oneself in relation to a code of conduct, and it is another thing to form oneself as an ethical subject in relation to a code of conduct (and it will be yet another thing to form oneself as that which risks the orderliness of the code itself). The rules of chastity provide an important example for Foucault. There is a difference, for instance, in not acting on desires that would violate a precept to which one is morally bound and developing a practice of desire, so to speak, which is informed by a certain ethical project or task. The model according to which submitting to a rule of law is required would involve one in not acting in certain ways, installing an effective prohibition against the acting out of certain desires. But the model which Foucault seeks to understand and, indeed, to incorporate and exemplify, takes moral prescription to participate in the forming of a kind of action. Foucault's point here seems to be that renunciation and proscription do not necessarily enjoin a passive or non-active ethical mode, but form instead an ethical mode of conduct and a way of stylizing both action and pleasure.

I believe this contrast that Foucault lays out between a command-based ethics and the ethical practice which centrally engages the formation of the self sheds important light on the distinction between obedience and virtue that he offers in his essay, "What is Critique?" Foucault contrasts this yet to be defined understanding of "virtue" with obedience, showing how the possibility of this form of virtue is established through its difference from an uncritical obedience to authority.

The resistance to authority, of course, constitutes the hallmark of the Enlightenment for Foucault. And he offers us a reading of the Enlightenment which not only establishes his own continuity with its aims, but reads his own dilemmas back into the history of the Enlightenment itself. The account he provides is one that no "Enlightenment" thinker would accept, but this resistance would not invalidate the characterization at hand, for what Foucault seeks in the characterization of the Enlightenment is precisely what remains "unthought" within its own terms: hence, his is a critical history. In his view, critique begins with questioning the demand for absolute obedience and subjecting every governmental obligation imposed on subjects to a rational and reflective evaluation. Although Foucault will not follow this turn to reason, he will nevertheless ask what criteria delimit the sorts of reasons that can come to bear on the question of obedience. He will be particularly interested in the problem of how that delimited field forms the subject and how, in turn, a subject comes to form and reform those reasons. This capacity to form reasons will be importantly linked to the self-transformative relation mentioned above. To be critical of an authority that poses as absolute requires a critical practice that has self-transformation at its core.

But how do we move from understanding the reasons we might have for consenting to a demand to forming those reasons for ourselves, to transforming ourselves in the course of producing those reasons (and, finally, putting at risk the field of reason itself)? Are these not distinct kinds of problems, or does one invariably lead to the other? Is the autonomy achieved in forming reasons which serve as the basis for accepting or rejecting a pregiven law the same as the transformation of the self that takes place when a rule becomes incorporated into the very action of the subject? As we shall see, both the transformation of the self in relation to ethical precepts and the practice of critique are considered forms of "art," stylizations and repetitions, suggesting that there is no possibility of accepting or refusing a rule without a self who is stylized in response to the ethical demand upon it.

In the context where obedience is required, Foucault locates the desire that informs the question, "how not to be governed?" This desire, and the wonderment that follows from it, forms the central impetus of critique. It is of course unclear how the desire not to be governed is linked with virtue. He does make clear, however, that he is not posing the possibility of radical anarchy, and that the question is not how to become radically ungovernable.

It is a specific question that emerges in relation to a specific form of government: "how not to be governed *like that*, by that, in the name of those principles, with such and such an objective in mind and by means of such procedures, not like that, not for that, not by them."

This becomes the signature mark of "the critical attitude" and its particular virtue. For Foucault, the question itself inaugurates both a moral and political attitude, "the art of not being governed or, better, the art of not being governed like that and at that cost." Whatever virtue Foucault here circumscribes for us will have to do with objecting to that imposition of power, to its costs, to the way in which it is administered, to those who do that administering. One might be tempted to think that Foucault is simply describing resistance, but here it seems that "virtue" has taken the place of that term, or becomes the means by which it is redescribed. We will have to ask why. Moreover, this virtue is described as well as an "art," the art of not being governed "quite so much," so what is the relation between aesthetics and ethics at work here?

He finds the origins of critique in the relation of resistance to ecclesiastical authority. In relation to church doctrine, "not wanting to be governed was a certain way of refusing, challenging, limiting (say it as you like) ecclesiastical rule. It meant returning to the Scriptures... it meant questioning what kind of truth the Scriptures told." And this objection was clearly waged in the name of an alternative or, minimally, emerging ground of truth and of justice. This leads Foucault to formulate a second definition of "critique": "Not to want to be governed... not wanting to accept these laws because they are unjust because... they hide a fundamental illegitimacy."

Critique is that which exposes this illegitimacy, but it is not because critique has recourse to a more fundamental political or moral order. Foucault writes that the critical project is "confronted with government and the obedience it stipulates" and that what "critique means" in this context is "putting forth universal and indefeasible rights to which every government, whatever it may be, whether a monarch, a magistrate, an educator or a pater familias, will have to submit." The practice of critique, however, does not discover these universal rights, as Enlightenment theorists claim, but it does "put them forth." However, it does not put them forth as positive rights. The "putting forth" is an act which limits the power of the law, an act which counters and rivals the workings of power, power at the moment of its renewal. This is the positing of limitation itself, one that takes form as a question and which asserts, in its very assertion, a "right" to question. From the sixteenth century on, the question "how not to be governed" becomes specified as "What are the limits of the right to govern?" "'To not want to be governed' is of course not accepting as true... what an authority tells you is true, or at least not accepting it because an authority tells you that it is true, but rather accepting it only if one considers valid the reasons for doing so." There is of course a fair amount of ambiguity in this situation, for what will constitute a ground of validity for accepting authority? Does the validity derive from the consent to accept authority? If so, does consent validate the reasons offered, whatever they are? Or is it rather the case that it is only on the basis of a prior and discoverable validity that one offers one's consent? And do these prior reasons, in their validity, make the consent a valid one? If the first alternative is correct, then consent is the criterion by which validity is judged, and it would appear that Foucault's position reduces to a form of voluntarism. But perhaps what he is offering us by way of "critique" is an act, even a practice of freedom, which cannot reduce to voluntarism in any easy way. For the practice by which the limits to absolute authority are set is one that is fundamentally dependent on the horizon of knowledge effects within which it operates. The critical practice does not well up from the innate freedom of the soul, but is formed instead in the crucible of a particular exchange between a set of rules or precepts (which are already there) and a stylization of acts (which extends and reformulates that prior set of rules and precepts). This stylization of the self in relation to the rules comes to count as a "practice."

In Foucault's view, following Kant in an attenuated sense, the act of consent is a reflexive movement by which validity is attributed to or withdrawn from authority. But this reflexivity does not take place internal to a subject. For Foucault, this is an act which poses some risk, for the point will not only be to object to this or that governmental demand, but to ask about the order in which such a demand becomes legible and possible. And if what one objects to are the epistemological orderings that have established the rules of governmental validity, then saying "no" to the demand will require departing from the established grounds of its validity, marking the limit of the validity, which is something different and far more risky than finding a given demand invalid. In this difference, we might say, one begins to enter a critical relation to such orderings and the ethical precepts to which they give rise. The problem with those grounds that Foucault calls "illegitimate" is not that they are partial or self-contradictory or that they lead to hypocritical moral stands. The problem is precisely that they seek to foreclose the critical relation, that is, to extend their own power to order the entire field of moral and political judgment. They orchestrate and exhaust the field of certainty itself. How does one call into question the exhaustive hold that such rules of ordering have upon certainty without risking uncertainty, without inhabiting that place of wavering which exposes one to the charge of immorality, evil, aestheticism? The critical attitude is not moral according to the rules whose limits that very critical relation seeks to interrogate. But how else can critique do its job without risking the denunciations of those who naturalize and render hegemonic the very moral terms put into question by critique itself?

Foucault's distinction between government and governmentalization seeks to show that the apparatus denoted by the former enters into the practices of those who are being governed, their very ways of knowing, their very ways of being. To be governed is not only to have a form imposed upon one's existence, but to be given the terms within which existence will and will not be possible. A subject will emerge in relation to an established order of truth, but it can also take a point of view on that established order that retrospectively suspends its own ontological ground.

> If governmentalization is . . . this movement through which individuals are sub-jugated in the reality of a social practice through mechanisms of power that adhere to a truth, well, then! I will say that *critique is the movement by which the subject gives himself the right [le sujet se donne le droit] to question truth on its effects of power and question power on its discourses of truth.* (my emphasis)

Note here that the subject is said to "give himself that right," a mode of self-allocation and self-authorization that seems to foreground the reflexivity of the claim. Is this, then, a self-generated movement, one which shores up the subject over and against a countervailing authority? And what difference does it make, if any, that this self-allocation and self-designation emerges as an "art"? "Critique," he writes, "will be the art of voluntary insubordination, that of reflected intractability [*l'indocilité réfléchie*]." If it is an "art" in his sense, then critique will not be a single act, nor will it belong exclusively to a subjective domain, for it will be the stylized relation to the demand upon it. And the style will be critical to the extent that, as style, it is not fully determined in advance, it incorporates a contingency over time that marks the limits to the ordering capacity of the field in question. So the stylization of this "will" will produce a subject who is not readily knowable under the established rubric of truth. More radically, Foucault pronounces: "Critique would essentially insure the desubjugation [*désassujetissement*] of the subject in the context [*le jeu*] of what we could call, in a word, the politics of truth."

The politics of truth pertains to those relations of power that circumscribe in advance what will and will not count as truth, which order the world in certain regular and regulatable ways, and which we come to accept as the given field of knowledge. We can understand the salience of this point when we begin to ask: What counts as a person? What counts as a coherent gender? What qualifies as a citizen? Whose world is legitimated as real? Subjectively, we ask: Who can I become in such a world where the meanings and limits of the subject are set out in advance for me? By what norms am I constrained as I begin to ask what I may become? And what happens when I begin to become that for which there is no place within the given regime of truth? Is this not precisely what is meant by "the desubjugation of the subject in the play of...the politics of truth" (my translation)?

At stake here is the relation between the limits of ontology and epistemology, the link between the limits of what I might become and the limits of what I might risk knowing. Deriving a sense of critique from Kant, Foucault poses the question that is the question of critique itself: "Do you know up to what point you can know?" "Our liberty is at stake." Thus, liberty emerges at the limits of what one can know, at the very moment in which the desubjugation of the subject within the politics of truth takes place, the moment where a certain questioning practice begins that takes the following form: " 'What, therefore, am I', I who belong to this humanity, perhaps to this piece of it, at this point in time, at this instant of humanity which is subjected to the power of truth in general and truths in particular?" Another way of putting this is the following: "What, given the contemporary order of being, can I be?" If, in posing this question, liberty is at stake, it may be that staking liberty has something to do with what Foucault calls virtue, with a certain risk that is put into play through thought and, indeed, through language where the contemporary ordering of being is brought to its limit.

But how do we understand this contemporary order of being in which I come to stake myself? Foucault chooses here to characterize this historically conditioned order of being in a way that links him with the critical theory of the Frankfurt School, identifying "rationalization" as the governmentalizing effect on ontology. Allying himself with a Left critical tradition post-Kant, Foucault writes,

> From the Hegelian Left to the Frankfurt School, there has been a complete critique of positivism, rationalization, of techne and technicalization, a whole critique of the relationships between the fundamental project of science and techniques whose objective was to show the connections between science's naive presumptions, on one hand, and the forms of domination characteristic of contemporary society, on the other.

In his view, rationalization takes a new form when it comes into the service of bio-power. And what continues to be difficult for most social actors and critics within this situation is to discern the relationship between "rationalization and power." What appears to be a merely epistemic order, a way of ordering the world, does not readily admit of the constraints by which that ordering takes place. Nor does it eagerly show the way in which the intensification and totalization of rationalizing effects leads to an intensification of power.

Foucault asks, "How is it that rationalization leads to the furor of power?" Clearly, the capacity for rationalization to reach into the tributaries of life not only characterizes modes of scientific practice, "but also social relationships, state organizations, economic practices and perhaps even individual behaviors?" It reaches its "furor" and its limits as it seizes and pervades the subject it subjectivates. Power sets the limits to what a subject can "be," beyond which it no longer "is," or it dwells in a domain of suspended ontology. But power seeks to constrain the subject through the force of coercion, and the resistance to coercion consists in the stylization of the self at the limits of established being.

One of the first tasks of critique is to discern the relation "between mechanisms of coercion and elements of knowledge." Here again we seem confronted with the limits of what is knowable, limits which exercise a certain force without being grounded in any necessity, limits which can only be tread or interrogated by risking a certain security within an available ontology:

> Nothing can exist as an element of knowledge if, on the one hand, it . . . does not conform to a set of rules and constraints characteristic, for example, of a given type of scientific discourse in a given period, and if, on the other hand, it does not possess the effects of coercion or simply the incentives peculiar to what is scientifically validated or simply rational or simply generally accepted, etc.

He then continues to show that knowledge and power are not finally separable, but work together to establish a set of subtle and explicit criteria for thinking the world: "It is therefore not a matter of describing what knowledge is and what power is and how one would repress the other or how the other would abuse the one, but rather, a nexus of knowledge-power has to be described so that we can grasp what constitutes the acceptability of a system."

The critic thus has a double task, to show how knowledge and power work to constitute a more or less systematic way of ordering the world with its own "conditions of acceptability of a system," but also "to follow the breaking points which indicate its emergence." So not only is it necessary to isolate and identify the peculiar nexus of power and knowledge that gives rise to the field of intelligible things, but also to track the way in which that field meets its breaking point, the moments of its discontinuities, the sites where it fails to constitute the intelligibility for which it stands. What this means is that one looks both for the conditions by which the object field is constituted, but also for the limits of those conditions, the moments where they point up their contingency and their transformability. In Foucault's terms, "schematically speaking, we have perpetual mobility, essential fragility or rather the complex interplay between what replicates the same process and what transforms it."

Indeed, another way to talk about this dynamic within critique is to say that rationalization meets its limits in desubjugation. If the desubjugation of the subject emerges at the moment in which the episteme constituted through rationalization exposes its limit, then desubjugation marks precisely the fragility and transformability of the epistemics of power.

Critique begins with the presumption of governmentalization and then with its failure to totalize the subject it seeks to know and to subjugate. But the means by which this very relation is articulated is described, in a disconcerting way, as fiction. Why would it be fiction? And in what sense is it fiction? Foucault refers to "an historical – philosophical practice [in which] one had to make one's own history, fabricate history, as if through fiction [de faire comme par fiction], in terms of how it would be traversed by the question of the relationships between structures of rationality which articulate true discourse and the mechanisms of subjugation which are linked to it." There is thus a dimension of the methodology itself which partakes of fiction, which draws fictional lines between rationalization and desubjugation, between the know-ledge–power nexus and its fragility and limit. We are not told what sort of fiction this will be, but it seems clear that Foucault is drawing on Nietzsche and, in particular, the kind of fiction that genealogy is said to be.

You may remember that although it seems that for Nietzsche the genealogy of morals is the attempt to locate the origins of values, he is actually seeking to find out how the very notion of the origin became instituted. And the means by which he seeks to explain the origin is fictional. He tells a fable of the nobles, another about a social contract, another about a slave revolt in morality, and yet another about creditor and debtor relations. None of these fables can be located in space or time, and any effort to try to find the historical comple-ment to Nietzsche's genealogies will necessarily fail. Indeed, in the place of an account that finds the origin of values or, indeed, the origin of the origin, we read fictional stories about the way that values are originated. A noble says something is the case and it becomes the case: the speech act inaugurates the value, and becomes something like an atopical and atemporal occasion for the origination of values. Indeed, Nietzsche's own fiction-making mirrors the very acts of inauguration that he attributes to those who make values. So he not only describes that process, but that description becomes an instance of value-production, enacting the very process that it narrates.

How would this particular use of fiction relate to Foucault's notion of critique? Consider that Foucault is trying to understand the possibility of desubjugation within rationalization without assuming that there is a source for resistance that is housed in the subject or maintained in some foundational mode. Where does resistance come from? Can it be said to be the upsurge of some human freedom shackled by the powers of rationalization? If he speaks, as he does, of a will *not* to be governed, how are we to understand the status of that will?

In response to a query along these lines, he remarks,

> I do not think that the will not to be governed at all is something that one could consider an originary aspiration [*je ne pense pas en effet que la volonté de n'être pas gouverné du tout soit quelque chose que l'on puisse considérer comme une aspiration originaire*]. I think that, in fact, the will not to be governed is always the will not to be governed thusly, like that, by these people, at this price.

He goes on to warn against the absolutizing of this will that philosophy is always tempted to perform. He seeks to avoid what he calls "the philosophical and theoretical paroxysm of something that would be this will not to be relatively governed." He makes clear that accounting for this will involves him in a problem of the origin, and he comes quite close to ceding the terrain, but a certain Nietzschean reluctance prevails. He writes,

> I was not referring to something that would be a fundamental anarchism, that would be like an originary freedom [*qui serait comme la liberté originaire*], absolutely and wholeheartedly [*absolument et en son fond*] resistant to any governmentaliza-tion. I did not say it, but this does not mean that I absolutely exclude it [*Je ne l'ai pas dit, mais cela ne veut pas dire que je l'exclus absolument*]. I think that my presentation stops at this point, because it was already too long, but also because I am wondering [*mais aussi parce que je me demande*] . . . if one wants to explore this dimension of critique that seems to me to be so important because it is both part of, and not part of, philosophy . . . it is supported by something akin [*qui seraitou*] to the historical practice of revolt, the non-acceptance of a real government, on one hand, or, on the other, the individual refusal of governmentality.

Whatever this is that one draws upon as one resists governmentalization will be "*like* an originary freedom" and "something *akin to* the historical practice of revolt" (my emphasis). Like them, indeed, but apparently not quite the same. As for Foucault's mention of "originary freedom," he offers and withdraws it at once. "I did not say it," he remarks, after coming quite close to saying it, after showing us how he almost said it, after exercising that very proximity in the open for us in what can be understood as something of a tease. What discourse nearly seduces him here, subjugating him to its terms? And how does he draw from the very terms that he refuses? What art form is this in which a nearly collapsible critical distance is performed for us? And is this the same distance that informs the practice of wondering, of questioning? What limits of know-ing does he dare to broach as he wonders out loud for us? The inaugural scene of critique involves "*the art* of voluntary insubordination," and the voluntary or, indeed, "originary freedom" is given here, but in the form of a conjecture, in a form of art that suspends ontology and brings us into the suspension of disbelief.

Foucault finds a way to say "originary freedom," and I suppose that it gives him great pleasure to utter these words, pleasure and fear. He speaks them, but only through staging the words, relieving himself of an ontological commitment, but releasing the words themselves for a certain use. Does he refer to originary freedom here? Does he seek recourse to it? Has he found the well of originary freedom and drunk from it? Or does he, significantly, post it, mention it, say it without quite saying it? Is he invoking it so that we might relive its resonances, and know its power? The staging of the term is not its assertion, but we might say that the assertion is staged, rendered artfully, subjected to an ontological suspension, precisely so it might be spoken. And that it is this speech act, the one which for a time relieves the phrase "originary freedom" from the epistemic politics within which it lives which also performs a certain desubjugation of the subject within the politics of truth. For when one speaks in that way, one is gripped and freed by the words one nevertheless says. Of course, politics is not simply a matter of speaking, and I do not mean to rehabilitate Aristotle in the form of Foucault (although, I confess, that such a move intrigues me, and I mention it here to offer it as a possibility without committing myself to it at once). In this verbal gesture toward the end of his lecture, a certain freedom is exemplified, not by the reference to the term without any foundational anchor, but by the artful performance of its release from its usual discursive constraints, from the conceit that one might only utter it knowing in advance what its anchor must be.

Foucault's gesture is oddly brave, I would suggest, for it knows that it cannot ground the claim of original freedom. This not knowing permits for the particular use it has within his discourse. He braves it anyway, and so his mention, his insistence, becomes an allegory for a certain risk-taking that happens at the limit of the epistemological field. And this becomes a practice of virtue, perhaps, and not, as his critics profess, a sign of moral despair, precisely to the extent that the practice of this kind of speaking posits a value which it does not know how to ground or to secure for itself, posits it anyway, and thereby shows that a certain intelligibility exceeds the limits on intelligibility that power–knowledge has already set. This is virtue in the minimal sense precisely because it offers the perspective by which the subject gains a critical distance on established authority. But it is also an act of courage, acting without guarantees, risking the subject at the limits of its ordering. Who would Foucault be if he were to utter such words? What desubjugation does he perform for us with this utterance?

To gain a critical distance from established authority means for Foucault not only to recognize the ways in which the coercive effects of knowledge are at work in subject-formation itself, but to risk one's very formation as a subject. Thus, in "The Subject and Power,"[7] Foucault will claim "this form of power [that] applies itself to immediate, everyday life which categorizes the individual, marks him by his own individuality, attaches him to his own identity, imposes a law of truth on him which he must recognize and which others have to recognize in him." And when that law falters or is broken, the very possibility of recognition is imperiled. So when we ask how we might say "originary freedom," and say it in the wondering, we also put into question the subject who is said to be rooted in that term, releasing it, paradoxically, for a venture which might actually give the term new substance and possibility.

In concluding, I would simply return to the introduction to *The Use of Pleasure* where Foucault defines the practices that concern him, the "arts of existence," as having to do with a cultivated relation of the self to itself. This kind of formulation brings us closer to the strange sort of virtue that Foucault's anti-foundationalism comes to represent. Indeed, as I wrote earlier, when he introduces the notion of "arts of existence" Foucault also refers to such arts of existence as producing subjects who "seek to transform themselves in their singular being, and to make their life into an oeuvre." We might think that this gives support to the charge that Foucault has fully aestheticized existence at the expense of ethics, but I would suggest only that he has shown us that there can be no ethics, and no politics, without recourse to this singular sense of poeisis. The subject who is formed by the principles furnished by the discourse of truth is not yet the subject who endeavors to form itself. Engaged in "arts of existence," this subject is both crafted and crafting, and the line between how it is formed, and how it becomes a kind of forming, is not easily, if ever drawn. For it is not the case that a subject is formed and then turns around and begins suddenly to form itself. On the contrary, the formation of the subject is the institution of the very reflexivity that indistinguishably assumes the burden of formation. The "indistinguishability" of this line is precisely the juncture where social norms intersect with ethical demands, and where both are produced in the context of a self-making which is never fully self-inaugurated.

Although Foucault refers quite straightforwardly to intention and deliberation in this text, he also lets us know how difficult it will be to understand this self-stylization in terms of any received understanding of intention and deliberation. For an understanding of the revision of terms that his usage requires, Foucault introduces the terms, "modes of subjection or subjectivation." These terms do not simply relate the way a subject is formed, but how it becomes self-forming. This becoming of an ethical subject is not a simple matter of self-knowledge or self-awareness; it denotes a "process in which the individual delimits that part of himself that will form the object of his moral practice." The self delimits itself and decides on the material for its self-making, but the delimitation that the self performs takes place through norms which are, indisputably, already in place. Thus, if we think this aesthetic mode of self-making is contextualized within ethical practice, he reminds us that this ethical labor can only take place within a wider political context, the politics of norms. He makes clear that there is no self-forming outside of a mode of subjectivation, which is to say, there is no self-forming outside of the norms that orchestrate the possible formation of the subject.

We have moved quietly from the discursive notion of the subject to a more psychologically resonant notion of "self," and it may be that for Foucault the later term carries more agency than the former. The self forms itself, but it forms itself within a set of formative practices that are characterized as modes of subjectivations. That the range of its possible forms is delimited in advance by such modes of subjectivation does not mean that the self fails to form itself, that the self is fully formed. On the contrary, it is compelled to form itself, but to form itself within forms that are already more or less in operation and underway. Or, one might say, it is compelled to form itself within practices that are more or less in place. But if that self-forming is done in disobedience to the principles by which one is formed, then virtue becomes the practice by which the self forms itself in desubjugation, which is to say that it risks its deformation as a subject, occupying that ontologically insecure position which poses the question anew: who will be a subject here, and what will count as a life, a moment of ethical questioning which requires that we break the habits of judgment in favor of a riskier practice that seeks to yield artistry from constraint.

Notes

This essay was originally delivered, in shorter form, as the Raymond Williams Lecture at Cambridge University in May of 2000. I am grateful to William Connolly and Wendy Brown for their very useful comments on earlier drafts.

1   Raymond Williams, *Keywords* (New York: Oxford University Press, 1976), 75–6.
2   Theodor W. Adorno, "Cultural Criticism and Society," in *Prisms* (Cambridge, MA: MIT Press, 1984), 30.
3   Michel Foucault, "What is Critique?" in *The Politics of Truth*, ed. Sylvère Lotringer and Lysa Hochroth (New York: Semiotext(e), 1997), transcript by Monique

Emery, revised by Suzanne Delorme et al., translated into English by Lysa Hochroth. This essay was originally a lecture given at the French Society of Philosophy on 27 May 1978, subsequently published in *Bulletin de la Société française de la philosophie* 84:2 (1990), 35–63.

4 For an interesting account of this transition from critical theory to a theory of communicative action, see Seyla Benhabib, *Critique, Norm, and Utopia: A Study of the Foundations of Critical Theory* (New York: Columbia University Press, 1986), 1–13.

5 Michel Foucault, *The Use of Pleasure: The History of Sexuality, Volume Two* (New York: Pantheon Press, 1985).

6 Michel Foucault, *The History of Sexuality, Volume One* (New York: Random House, 1978).

7 Michel Foucault, "The Subject and Power," in Hubert L. Dreyfus and Paul Rabinow (eds), *Michel Foucault: Beyond Structuralism and Hermeneutics* (Chicago: University of Chicago Press, 1982), 208–28.

Part IV
Making Difficulty Clear

13

Changing the Subject: Judith Butler's Politics of Radical Resignification

Introduction

The interview format, which permits a diverse array of subjects to be raised without the constraints of structure or expected resolution, is particularly suited to Butler's non-teleological, interrogative mode of theorizing. In this recent interview, Butler addresses a number of key issues, touching briefly but usefully on language, agency, and performativity, among other areas. Towards the end of the interview, when Butler is invited to address specific misunderstandings and misinterpretations of her work, she takes the opportunity to identify her position as a critical intellectual who is engaged in questioning "basic" assumptions within an academy that seems to be politically stymied by its anti-intellectualism. For Butler on the other hand, the critical intellectual's work is *always* political, since it involves laboring on difficult texts that do not yield their meaning easily, and thereby engender in the reader a critical attitude towards the social world as it is currently constituted.

   This insight leads Butler to reflect on the question of her style, a subject on which she has been taken to task by critics who object to what they deem to be the obscurity and élitism of her prose. Acknowledging that the apparent "difficulty" of her writing may produce anxiety in her readers, Butler identifies the prose style she deploys as a strategy resembling what Foucault has called "a politics of discomfort" which is *designed* to estrange and upset. This does not mean that Butler sets out to annoy her readers by adopting a style that is incomprehensible or "untranslatable"; rather, her prose implicitly invites us to question our schemes of intelligibility by extending the linguistic and epistemological horizons we may take for granted, prompting us to ask "what it is to be a human...a really fundamental question." Early in her academic career, Butler learned from Hegel and Heidegger that readers' assumptions could be effectively challenged via the media of grammar and style, since calling "ordinary" language into question also invites a consideration of how we structure the world on that basis, and by doing so brings "newness" into that world. On the other hand, a text's "radical

Interview with Gary A. Olson and Lynn Worsham, from *jac* 20:4 (2000), pp. 731–65. Reprinted by permission of Lynn Worsham and Gary A. Olson.

accessibility" may foster parochialism and complacency, so that for Butler, making the ordinary world seem strange (rather than unintelligible) constitutes a move towards a more capacious understanding of otherness.

In fact, Butler regards the issue of style as "one of the most profound pedagogical problems of our time," and yet in this interview she also addresses other important subjects, including issues surrounding critique, agency, and "race." Although at times she responds directly to criticisms and objections, Butler does not set out to "define" herself; indeed, her theoretical identifications remain as multiple as ever as she notes a number of critical shifts which have taken place in her thought – her retreat from Monique Wittig's position on the violence of naming, for example, as well as her new doubts about the political efficacy of "the radical unmooring" of the subject. Such autocritique and theoretical plurality exemplify the mode of political insurrection Butler dubs "critical subversion," as, rather than seeking to liberate herself from existing norms and their corresponding linguistic terms (an impossible endeavor), she replays and recites them in order to reveal the instability of those norms. Thus, notwithstanding her acknowledgment of the inevitable violence of naming, Butler adopts the terms that are given to (or thrown at) her, playfully appropriating categories such as "lesbian," "woman," and "queer" while refusing to be defined by them, precipitating a crisis for established power through subversive reiteration. Like Sophocles' Antigone as she is characterized in *Antigone's Claim*, Butler is engaged in the risky but politically necessary practices of citation and critique, which, by suspending ontological and epistemological certainties, may lead to the more capacious understanding of difference for which she calls towards the end of the interview.

The complete text of the interview is reprinted here, but space does not permit the inclusion of the editorial preface with which it was originally published.

Q. Recently, *Philosophy and Literature* awarded you a prize for "bad writing." Many of your readers, however, find your prose to be richly textured and carefully crafted. Do you think consciously about the problems of writing as you are composing? Do you think of yourself as a writer?

A. I think that in general one thinks consciously about what one is composing but that what one is composing also happens in a way that exceeds one's own consciousness of what one does. So, for example, after I finish writing something I can look back and see that I have made implicit citations to other styles of writing without knowing that that's what I have done, or that I've tried to achieve something by pushing grammar in certain ways because what I was trying to think about couldn't quite be contained within the grammar that was available to me at the time. There's a *certain* level of consciousness to my writing process. I write and edit as I go along, and I'm not even sure one can, strictly speaking, distinguish between writing and editing. I know that people say that writing comes first and then editing comes later, but I think that's actually not true. It may actually be the reverse that's true: one edits in order to write.

I was trained in continental philosophy, and that meant that I spent a considerable amount of time reading Hegel and took numerous seminars on Heidegger; the difficulty of the language was in some ways essential to the philosophical views that were being expressed. For instance, when Hegel talks about the "speculative sentence," he is trying to work against the propositional form as it's been received. When he says, "The subject is spirit," the first inclination, the one that received grammar in some sense prepares us for, is to establish "the subject" as the subject of the sentence, and then "spirit" becomes one way of determining or qualifying that subject. But, of course, what he wants us to be able to do is to reverse that sentence, to recognize something about how the "is" functions: it doesn't just point linearly in one direction; rather, it points in both directions at once. He wants us to be able to experience the simultaneity of that sentence as it functions in its double directionality. Now that's a very hard thing to do given how profoundly inclined we are by what Nietzsche called the "seductions of grammar" to read in a linear way. Reading Heidegger as a young person and trying to figure out what it is he was trying to do with his neologisms and his coinages also influenced me. Some people, such as Bourdieu, have dismissed it completely, but I think there was and remains a rather profound effort there to call into question ordinary language and the ways in which we structure the world on its basis, an analysis of the kinds of occlusions or concealments that take place when we take ordinary language to be a true indicator of reality as it is and as it must be.

So, submitting myself to what were profound grammatical challenges – challenges to grammar, challenges to ordinary language – was part of my own formation, and it was very exhilarating. I would even say that such texts were in a way the high modernism of the continental philosophical tradition, in that you have a similar experience as if you were to pick up the works of Mallarmé, or Celan, or even Proust: there are times when you think, "My God, what's happened to the sentence? Where's the sentence?" There's something in the life of the sentence that's become new or odd or estranging in some fundamental way – and I went for that. I was very much seduced by what I think was a high modernist notion that some newness of the world was going to be opened up through messing with grammar as it has been received. What concerns me is that this impulse – which I consider to be important to critical thinking and to an openness to what is new – has been disparaged by those who believe that we have a certain responsibility to write not only in an accessible way, but within the terms of already accepted grammar. What concerns me is that the critical relation to ordinary grammar has been lost in this call for radical accessibility. It's not that I'm in favor of difficulty for difficulty's sake; it's that I think there is a lot in ordinary language and in received grammar that constrains our thinking – indeed, about what a person is, what a subject is, what gender is, what sexuality is, what politics can be – and that I'm not sure we're going to be able to struggle effectively against those constraints or work within them in a productive way unless we see the ways in which grammar is both producing and constraining our sense of what the world is.

Q. That reminds us of your recent piece in the *New York Times*, in which you explain the role of the contemporary tradition of critical theory, pointing out that "difficult language can change a tough world." You argue that language that challenges common sense can "help point the way to a more socially just world." Yet, many commentators, both within the academy and in the public sector, have taken aim at academic discourse in general, particularly that discourse (as you point out) that focuses on topics such as sexuality, race, nationalism, and the workings of capitalism. What do you believe is really at stake in these criticisms? Is this debate really about "good writing"?

A. No, I don't believe it's a debate about good writing. Sure, there is a problem when writing in the academy becomes so rarefied or so specialized that it speaks only to an in-crowd or to a group of people who are initiated into the protocols of the discourse. I've certainly seen that. There were times when deconstructive literary criticism became so internal to itself that unless you were trained in the exact same way and had read all the same texts and knew all the same allusions and understood all the same rhetorical gestures it was going to be a very odd and strange and alienating enterprise. I understand that. I believe it is important that intellectuals with a sense of social responsibility be able to shift registers and to work at various levels, to communicate what they're communicating in various ways. I think I probably do that, both in my writing and in my teaching, but it's always possible to seize upon the more specialized moments of my writing and to say that it is somehow exemplary – and that is unfair.

I'm interested in why there is an upsurge of anti-intellectualism in the academy right now. Is there guilt about being an intellectual? Is there guilt about being an intellectual because we don't know what effects, if any, the intellectual (especially the intellectual in the humanities) can have on the larger social world? There are some people on the left in the academy who believe that all you have to do is make certain verbal gestures and be publicly identified with certain kinds of verbal gestures in order to qualify as a politically minded intellectual. That is, you don't actually work in labor politics or give time to gay and lesbian activism or any of the rest; you simply identify publicly with certain stands. But even this is a haunted and guilty moment because the intellectual who believes that political satisfaction is to be gained through the public performance of certain kinds of verbal gestures is still not sure what effect that has. One gets to know in effect that one is being identified with certain positions, and so one gets *positioned*, you might say, within the academic landscape as a "leftist," as a "progressive," or as something else. Part of it is a structural problem in that people in the humanities no longer know whether they're central to the academy; they know that they're derided by the outside, and they don't know how to articulate how their work can have concrete effects on the lives of the students and the world in which they live. And there's a certain scapegoating occurring. Those intellectuals who speak in a rarefied way are being scapegoated, are being purged, are being denounced precisely because they represent a certain anxiety about everyone's effect – that is, what effect are *any* of us having, and what effect *can* we have? So, there might be an identification and a projection occurring: the persons who are being scapegoated probably remind the scapegoaters too much of their own dilemma.

It's unfortunate because I believe it has to be the case (certainly since Marx it *has* been the case) that becoming a critical intellectual involves working hard on difficult texts. Capitalism is itself a difficult text. From Marx through Adorno, we learned that capitalism is an extremely difficult text: it does not show itself as transparent; it gives itself in enigmatic ways; it calls for interpretive hermeneutic effort. There is no question about it. We think things are the way they must be because they've become naturalized. The life of the commodity structures our world in ways that we take for granted. And what was Marx's point? Precisely to make the taken-for-granted world seem spectral, strange. And how does that work? It only works by taking received opinion and received *doxa* and really working through it. It means undergoing something painful and difficult: an estrangement from what is most familiar. Adorno understood this. In *Minima Moralia* he talks about the painfulness of passing through difficult language but how it is absolutely essential to developing a critical attitude toward the constituted social world if we're not to take the constituted social world – that is to say the social world – as it is given, as it is rendered not only *familiar* but *natural* for us. That's a painful process, and not everybody wants to undergo it.

It may well be that we want to construct a fiction called "the public sphere," or a fiction called "common sense," or a fiction called "accessible meaning" that would allow us to think and feel for a moment as if we all inhabit the same linguistic world. What does it mean to dream of a common sense? What does it mean to want that today, at the beginning of the twenty-first century, when there's enormous conflict at the level of language? When Serbian and Croatian are now claiming they are separate languages? When speaking even in a Berkeley classroom means speaking across inflection, across dialect, across genres of academic writing to students for whom English is very often a second language? Every classroom I've ever been in is a hermeneutic problem. It's not as if there's a "common" language. I suppose if I were to speak in the language of the television commercial, I might get a kind of uniform recognition – at least for a brief moment – but I'm not going to be able to presuppose a common language in my classroom. I was teaching Rousseau's *Essay on the Origin of Languages* to a lecture course in modern rhetorical theory – it's a beautiful essay, very paradoxical, very complicated – and at one point Rousseau takes issue with the common conception of what onomatopoesis means. He says that you think that it is an instance in which the word we use in language approximates the sound that we hear in the world. So, for instance, the word *meow* actually sounds very much like the noise that the cat makes. We assume that language in some sense represents a pre-linguistic sound and that it is fully mimetic at that moment, that it's fully representative, that it's as close to a certain kind of mimetic proximity as one can get between language and thing. But, he says, it's not true. Cats say various things (or speak various ways or make various sounds) in various languages, and it's more the case that the word we have for the sound prepares us to hear the sound in a certain way. This is a very Wittgensteinian point, really – a pre- or proto-Wittgensteinian point.

So, I looked up at my classroom of eighty students and asked, "How many of you speak another language besides English?" Probably fifty-five of them raised their hands. And I asked, "Okay, what languages do you speak?" We went around the room, and there were probably sixteen languages represented in the class: Korean, Chinese, Japanese, Urdu, French, German, Spanish, Portuguese, and more. Then I asked, "What do cats say in your languages?" And we got sixteen *different* sounds, all of which claimed to be onomatopoetic. And the assumption in every single language was that *this* is what cats truly sound like. So the point was made, and it was fabulous. Cats say, "mah." Cats say, "mew." They say, "eee." Cats say lots of things. You have no idea what they say. Now, this was not just a lesson about how Rousseau was right; it was a lesson about multilingualism in the classroom. What does it mean to say that there is *a* language that is common, that everyone understands, and that it is somehow our social responsibility to speak? It seems to me that our social responsibility is to become attuned to the fact that there is *no* common language anymore. Or if there is a common language, it is the language of a commercialism that seeks to extend the hegemony of commercial American English, and to do it in a way that violently effaces the problem of multilingualism. This is one of the most profound pedagogical problems of our time, if not one of the most profound political problems of our time.

Q. In *Bodies That Matter* you write, "To call a presupposition into question is not the same as doing away with it; rather, it is to free it from its metaphysical lodgings in order to understand what political interests were secured in and by that metaphysical placing, and thereby to permit the term to occupy and to serve very different political aims." This statement seems to characterize your critical practice in general. Do you agree?

A. Yes, I do agree. That was an important thing to say. People are very much afraid of criticism; they think criticism is destructive. I wonder, though, whether it's not time to rethink what we mean by critique and the tradition of critique that was established really with Kant and that goes through critical theory and that emerges quite interestingly in Foucault (I think his short piece, "What Is Critique?" is generally under-read) and in Walter Benjamin when he writes about the critique of violence, for instance. That sense of critique has to be dissociated from a sense of destruction or pure negation. What it's really about is opening up the possibility of questioning what our assumptions are and somehow encouraging us to live in the anxiety of that questioning without closing it down too quickly. Of course, it's not for the sake of anxiety that one should do it (I don't think one should do anything for the sake of anxiety), but it's because anxiety accompanies something like the witnessing of new possibilities. It is important to call things into question. That does not mean one does away with them; it just means that one asks important questions: "What purposes have they served? What purposes can they serve? How can this term be mobilized beyond its established context to assume new meanings in new contexts?" The qualification I would add now, seven years later, is that although one can very often take a term like "masculine" and dislodge it from its metaphysical moorings – one can say, for example, that "masculine" does not necessarily apply exclusively to ostensibly anatomically male bodies and that it can function in another way, like, let's say, in the way that Judith Halberstam talks about "female masculinities" – it is important to question what of the prior context is brought forward as a kind of residue or trace. It is also important to question what new ontological effects the term can achieve, because to liberate it from its prior moorings in an established ontology is not to say that it will not acquire a new one.

Spivak understood this when she reneged on her notion of "strategic essentialism." She at first thought she'd be able to use a term like "Third-World woman" and just have it be strategic rather than metaphysically grounded. It didn't have to describe her (or anyone else) fully or exhaustively; it could be relieved of its descriptive function. But, of course, it *does* begin to describe, because the author who strategically intends it as "X, Y, or Z" has also to recognize that the semantic life of the term will exceed the intention of the strategist and that as it travels through discourse, it can take on new ontological meanings and become established in ways that one never intended. So, I guess I would be a little less optimistic about the possibility of a radical unmooring than I was in 1993.

Q. In *The Psychic Life of Power*, you try to open a space for agency that avoids the liberal humanist concept of self and that finds in subordination and subjection the very conditions for agency. Would you explain this apparent paradox for readers not yet familiar with your work?

A. Much of the poststructuralist writing that came into this country in the 1970s and 1980s had a very strong antihumanist or posthumanist bent, and it was particularly interesting to see how the notions of the self that for the most part have been popular in the American philosophical tradition are ones that assume an agency to the self and that resonate strongly with forms of American individualism and notions of self-making. When Lacan came along, for instance, and said that the subject is produced on the condition of a foreclosure, he meant, quite clearly, that there would always be a lack of self-understanding for any subject; that there would be no way to recover one's origins or to understand oneself fully; that one would be, to the extent that one is a subject, always at a distance from oneself, from one's origin, from one's history; that some part of that origin, some part of that history, some part of that sexuality would always be at a radical distance. And it would have to be, because the foreclosure of the past, and the foreclosure of whatever we're talking about when we talk about what is prior to foreclosure, is the condition of the formation of the subject itself. So, I come into being on the condition that I am radically unknowing about my origins, and that unknowingness is the condition of my coming into being – and it afflicts me. And if I seek to undo that, I also lose myself as a subject; I become undone, and I become psychotic as a result.

A formulation like that surely limits our sense of self-knowing, and it also means that when we do things or when we act intentionally, we are always in some sense motivated by an unconscious that is not fully available to us. I can say, "I will this; I do this; I want this," but it may be that the effects of my doing are quite different from what I intend, and it's at that moment that I realize that I am also driven by something that is prior to and separate from this conscious and intentional "I." In some ways, that was great for a lot of people because they thought, "Oh, look, we no longer have the mastery of the ego; we no longer believe that the self is supreme or sovereign. The self is in its origin split. The self is always to some extent unknowing. Its action is always governed by aims that exceed its intentions." So there seemed to be an important limiting of the notion of the ego, the notion of individualism, the notion of a subject who was master of his – usually his – destiny. And instead we started to see that the subject might be subject to things other than itself: to drives, to an unconscious, to effects of a language. The latter was very important to Lacan: the subject is born into a network of language and uses language but is also used *by* it; it speaks language, but language speaks it. Lacanian thought involved a kind of humility and de-centering of the subject that many people prized because it seemed also to release the subject from the hold of its own mastery and to give it over to a world of desire and language that was bigger than itself. It gets connected to others in a very profound way through that de-centering.

Of course, the critique of this notion emerged on political grounds, and it questioned whether we haven't undone agency altogether. Can I ever say that I will do X and Y and truly do them and keep my word and be effective in the world and have my signature attached to my deed? I think that I have always been a little bit caught between an American political context and a French intellectual one, and I've sought to negotiate the relation between them. I would oppose the notion that my agency is nothing but a mockery of agency. I don't go that far. And I also don't think that the foreclosures that produce the subject are fixed in time in the way that most Lacanians do. They really understand foreclosure as a kind of founding moment. My sense is that it is always the case that the subject is produced through certain kinds of foreclosure – certain things become impossible for it; certain things become irrecoverable – and that this makes for the possibility of a temporarily coherent subject who can act. But I also want to say that its action can very often take up the foreclosure itself; it can renew the meaning and the effect of foreclosure. For instance, many people are inaugurated as subjects through the foreclosure of homosexuality; when homosexuality returns as a possibility, it returns precisely as the possibility of the unraveling of the subject itself: "I would not be I if I were a homosexual. I don't know who I would be. I would be undone by that possibility. Therefore, I cannot come in close proximity to that which threatens to undo me fundamentally." Miscegenation is another moment – it's when you suddenly realize that a white subject assumes that its whiteness is absolutely essential to its capacity to be a subject at all: "If I must be in this kind of proximity to a person of color, I will become undone in some radical way." We see forms of segregation and phobic forms of organizing social reality that keep the fiction of those subjects intact.

Now, I think it's possible sometimes to undergo an undoing, to submit to an undoing by virtue of what spectrally threatens the subject, in order to reinstate the subject on a new and different ground. What have I done? Well, I've taken the psychoanalytic notion of foreclosure, and I've made it specifically social. Also, instead of seeing that notion as a founding act, I see it as a temporally renewable structure – and as temporally renewable, subject to a logic of iteration, which produces the possibility of its alteration. So, I both render social and temporalize the Lacanian doctrine of foreclosure in a way that most Lacanians don't like – not all, but most. I am also trying to say that while we are constituted socially in limited ways and through certain kinds of limitations, exclusions and foreclosures, we are not constituted for all time in that way; it is possible to undergo an alteration of the subject that permits new possibilities that would have been thought psychotic or "too dangerous" in an earlier phase of life.

So, in answer to the question "How is it that subordination and subjection are the very conditions for agency?" the short answer is that I am clearly born into a world in which certain limitations become the possibility of my subjecthood, but those limitations are not there as structurally static features of my self. They are subject to a renewal, and I perform (mainly unconsciously or implicitly) that renewal in the repeated acts of my person. Even though my agency is conditioned by those limitations, my agency can also thematize and alter those limitations to some degree. This doesn't mean that I will get over limitation – there is always a limitation; there is always going to be a foreclosure of some kind or another – but I think that the whole scene has to be understood as more dynamic than it generally is.

Q. You note that discussions of subject formation resonate with "a larger cultural and political predicament, namely, how to take an oppositional relation to power that is, admittedly, implicated in the very power one opposes. Often this postliberatory insight has led to the conclusion that all agency here meets its impasse." Your notion of the postliberatory will be of special interest to scholars in rhetoric and composition, in that the literature is saturated with a discourse of "resistance," "liberatory learning," and "critical consciousness." Is your theory of the necessary relation between subjection and subject formation implied in what you mean by the postliberatory?

A. First, let's make a distinction between a certain conception of liberation and other conceptions of radical change or critical alteration. I suppose that I follow Foucault to a certain degree here in wondering whether *liberation* as a term promises us a radical freedom from constraint that in the end is impossible and that will just redeliver us to new constraints and plunge us into forms of political cynicism. So, if liberation isn't the way to think radical social change, what is? Radical social change has to be understood in light of the fact that we are radically constituted culturally, and as we approach the problem of what to change and how to change, we are already within the confines of a language, a discourse, and an institutional apparatus that will orchestrate for us what will or will not be deemed possible. Now, there are some hard-core structuralists, even structuralist Marxists, who would say that anything we seek to change within the contemporary order will simply augment the power of the order and that we're coopted and contained in advance. Jameson sometimes falls into that mode. It's as if one says, "You think *that's* subversion, and you think *that's* criticism? Actually, it's nothing other than an extension of an existing power regime – end of story." Now, what I want to be able to say is, "Sure, we *are* extending the contemporary power regime by our ostensible subversion, but there's extending the power regime and there's extending the power regime." Extending it does not mean extending it always in the same form; it could mean reiterating it in new forms. Extending is not a mechanical process. We need to understand power as something that produces unanticipated effects, that we can certainly extend power but that we can extend it into an unknown future.

I've been working on *Antigone* in the last couple of years, and I've been particularly interested in the fact that Antigone is so often understood as a completely oppositional figure. Most of the critical literature reads the play in one way: there's Creon who represents the State and Antigone who represents resistance, individualism, and kinship. But if you read the play carefully, you see that time and again her language is actually mirroring *his* and that she is more like *him* than she is like any other character in the play. She tries to mirror his speech acts, and she in some sense is involved in what I would understand to be a mimetic practice, a critical mimesis in relation to his discourse. Now, you could answer despairingly and just say, "Oh, I see, so Antigone is nothing more than Creon or an example of Creon's power." But I think that characterization would be false. She's exploiting the language of sovereignty in order to produce a new public sphere for a woman's voice – a sphere that doesn't actually exist at that time. The citation of power that she performs is a citation that, yes, is mired in established power – it's mired in the conventions of established power – but it also uses that citation in order to produce the possibility of a political speech act for a woman in the name of her desire that is radically delegitimated by the State itself. She produces, one might say, a new basis for legitimating speech precisely through deterritorializing or citing the norms of power in a radically new context. She's not free of power, and she's not even free of traditional forms of power, but in the mode of citation she does produce a radical crisis for established power. This seems to me to be an example of political insurrection that is based on a citation of existing norms and that also produces something new. I don't call it "liberation." It's a "critical subversion," a "radical resignification." It does not engage the fantasy of transcending power altogether, although it does work within the hope and the practice of replaying power, of restaging it again and again in new and productive ways.

Q. In *Gender Trouble*, you write that "it is no longer clear that feminist theory ought to try to settle the questions of primary identity in order to get on with the task of politics. Instead, we ought to ask what political possibilities are the consequence of a radical critique of the categories of identity?" This critique is one that you yourself initiated with the publication of *Gender Trouble*. Do you believe that feminist theorists have moved in that direction? Do we now have a more nuanced understanding of identity?

A. Yes, we do, and I'm not sure everybody's happy about that. (First, it's important to note that Denise Riley's *Am I That Name?* predated *Gender Trouble*, and it made the argument in a way that I definitely profited from.) Yes, at some point feminist theory probably agreed that it was no longer useful to come up with an essentialist description of what women are, if "essentialism" means a category that adequately describes the range of women's experience and that attempts to unify that experience in some way. There have been some innovative efforts to try to rethink what essentialism is if it is no longer making the claim to be descriptive. Strategic essentialism was one way to do that. And many scholars who drew on the work of Luce Irigaray sought to rethink what essentialism is (often within the pages of the journal *differences*) in order to hold out some possibility for talking about feminine specificity without basing it on a descriptive claim, or a denial of women's complexity, or anything of the sort. But I'm not sure these attempts got very far. They certainly produced some interesting work, and I learned from it. But my argument was made in a theoretical mode in relationship to feminism and the emerging field of queer theory. At the same time, there were other people who were making the argument against the unified subject of feminism on very different grounds. Certainly, bell hooks made the argument in *Ain't I a Woman*. Patricia Hill Collins made it in a different way. Kimberlé Crenshaw made it with her notion of "intersectionality" – the feminine subject must always be complicated. Spivak made it quite radically. So, the argument was made from different quarters at different times. I don't think *Gender Trouble* is solely responsible, but it is one moment in that movement.

As to the question of whether we now have a more nuanced understanding of identity, there's a lot of interesting psychoanalytic work that has complicated our understanding of identification and desire. For example, Jessica Benjamin has only become more interesting with the years. Her most recent work opens up very interesting questions about how multiple identifications coexist within a child, how the pre-Oedipal domain is an extremely important one, and how the task of the adult is to somehow recapture or become attuned anew to pre-Oedipality. That's very interesting, and she's done great clinical work on it – and scholarly work as well. Feminist film theory, too, has become more complicated in recent years. Film critics don't always assume that the woman's gaze is heterosexual, or that it's looking at the man, or that it's identifying with the feminine person (it could be identifying with Cary Grant). There's been a lot of theoretical complication that has produced a field of gender studies that is sometimes distinct from feminism precisely because of this complication. It's not necessarily woman-centered because it doesn't know what a "woman" is or must be. I know that this produces tensions within the academy, but I believe that in part it's a good sign – it's a sign of a certain kind of opening up.

Q. Well, let us follow up on this point. You comment that to understand the concept "women" as "a permanent site of contest, or as a feminist site of agonistic struggle, is to presume that there can be no closure on the category and that, for politically significant reasons, there ought never to be. That the category can never be descriptive is the very condition of its political efficacy." Yet, as you point out, many kinds of feminism have been thoroughly committed to the category "women." What critical practices can be used to circumvent the categorical violence of naming "women" or "men"?

A. There is no circumventing the categorical violence of naming "women" or "men." Wittig, in her early years, wanted us not to use these terms anymore. She even wanted to change hospital practices, questioning why it is necessary to name a child a "boy" or a "girl" when it comes into the world. (I actually heard her say this in public at one point.) She also thought that we should not accept the given terms for anatomy, so that if asked if you have a vagina, for instance, you just say, "No." She felt that this would be a form of radical resistance to how vernacular language structures the body in ways that prepare it for heterosexual reproduction. There is a necessary violence that must be committed in the act of naming. I was probably more Wittigian in that way at the time that I wrote *Gender Trouble*. I now think, "Sure, you say it; you must say it; you use that language; you become dirtied by the language; you know you're lying; you know it's false, but you do use it." And you live with the consequences of this catachresis, this use of a term to describe something in a radically improper way. When asked, "Are you a woman or a man?" as I was asked two weeks ago, I said that I *am* a woman – although I accompanied my affirmation with a certain bewildered laughter. My interlocutor had to live with that as part of the speech act itself. So, yes, that's the answer. I commit this violence against myself in the name of a certain kind of politics that would be ill-served if I were not to use that language.

There are, however, obligations. The assertion of identity can never become the end of politics itself. This is a terrible American conceit – the idea that if you accomplish your identity, you are there; that you've achieved recognition, status, legitimation; and that that's the end of your struggle, as if becoming visible, becoming sayable is the end of politics. That's not the case because what that perspective fails to do is to ask, "What are the conditions of sayability, of speakability, of visibility? Does one want a place within them? Does one want to be assimilated to them? Or does one want to ask some more profound questions about how political structures work to delimit what visibility will be and what sayability will be?" Those critical questions cannot be asked if the only thing you want is to achieve visibility and sayability within the existing order. So, I have a real problem with identity becoming the aim of politics itself. To have a conference in Beijing on "women's human rights" is great. You must have such events, and there must be lots of people who go, but we must constantly question what it means that we gather there under that rubric and what that rubric can mean – and not just in an abstract way. For example, when we're talking about sexual autonomy, and reproductive freedom, and anti-rape laws, and discrimination, and rights to divorce, etc., we need to ask, "How is gender being positioned? How is it being defined in relationship to those various practices? And how is it being defined internationally?" I don't think that when you say that there's going to be an international conference on women's rights that everybody comes to that conference agreeing on what a "woman" is. Nor do you ask in advance that they achieve consensus. And, of course, there was a crisis at the Beijing conference. In what's called the "pre-con-proposal," the pre-conference writings, the organizers wanted to use the language of gender to talk about what a woman is, but the Vatican denounced the word *gender*. Many Catholic countries also voiced their opposition to any platform that used the word *gender* because that would suggest that women are not defined by their biological roles as mothers, and it would also suggest that those biological roles are not mandated by theology. And if you made a distinction between theology, biology, and cultural meaning, that was considered to be a very dangerous form of Western relativism. So the very word *gender* became extremely controversial: "Are they saying that there are more than two genders?" Then the Vatican came out against Anne Fausto-Sterling, and there was a big argument about that. But my sense is that, yes, you use the words. If *gender* is the word that produces that argument, then use that word. If *woman* is the word that produces that argument, great. Those are the conflicts that have to be put on the table, and such words are very useful. And the more public the conflicts, the more divisive they are, the better it is.

Q. Theorists such as Gayatri Spivak and you yourself have warned that feminists should not posit a universal patriarchy that is the same across all cultures, nor should they posit a universal oppression of women. You write, "Feminist critique ought to explore the totalizing claims of a masculine signifying economy, but also remain self-critical with respect to the totalizing gestures of feminism. The effort to identify the enemy as singular in form is a reverse-discourse that uncritically mimics the strategy of the oppressor instead of offering a different set of terms." Is there any sense of universality that feminists can strategically employ, or is an appeal to universality always a totalizing gesture regardless of one's strategic intentions?

A. I'm going to suggest that there are ways of seeking recourse to universality that are quite important and necessary, but I'm also going to say that they are not "strategic." In fact, in the book that I just finished writing with Ernesto Laclau and Slavoj Žižek, *Contingency, Hegemony, Universality*, we discuss universality at length. In *Gender Trouble*, I could only see the violent and exclusionary character of universality, so I was extremely skeptical of any claims to universality. The claim to universality seemed to me to be by definition totalizing. But I have become more convinced in recent years that there is an open-ended sense to universality that can be affirmed. I did some work in gay and lesbian human rights (in fact, I was the chair of the International Gay and Lesbian Human Rights Commission) that was really rough for me because so much of the human rights discourse had intense international and universalist dimensions to it, which I had to deal with. And I learned many things about the discourse of universality. The first thing I learned was from Charlotte Bunch, oddly enough. She talks about women's human rights, and she says that we can say as a universal that women and men ought to be treated equally, but we do not know what that means in any given context. For her, it's an abstraction that remains to be specified: what equality will prove to be will differ radically from context to context. So, the pragmatic dimension of the politics ends up particularizing the problem of universality in a very interesting way. And we could take that even further. What does it mean to claim "universal" human rights in an American context, in an upper-class American context, in a working-class American context? What does it mean to claim it in another country? What does it mean to claim it in an international convention where the problem of translation is at work? What does it mean to claim it in a movement where there are various different cultural and linguistic practices at work that will take up the notion of universality very differently? It doesn't mean it cannot be said, but what becomes clear is that it's "empty" when it's said; it only comes to life when it is applied and redeployed in ways that cannot be fully anticipated by anyone who strategically mobilizes it.

My sense is that universality takes on its life precisely when it exceeds the strategic intentions of its speaker and that it is extremely mobile. What does and does not count as a universal, as the universal reach of human obligation and right? That is a question that is constantly on the table. For instance, when the Vatican says that it is very interested in human rights but that homosexuality is an assault on "the human," what it is in effect saying is that homosexual humans are destroying the human by virtue of their homosexuality, and the rights that pertain to humans do not pertain to them because they have in some sense disqualified themselves from the human by virtue of their homosexuality. If the homosexual then, nevertheless, gets up out of her or his abject state and says, "I am human, and I deserve some rights," then in that moment there's a certain paradox: universality is actually being asserted precisely by the one who represents what must be foreclosed for universality to take place. This is one who's outside of the legitimating structure of universality but who nevertheless speaks in its terms and makes the claim without prior legitimation in order to assume legitimation as a performative consequence of the claim itself.

It seems to me that this is the position that gay rights activists are in time and time again, often in relation to other human rights activist groups. It took a long time, for instance, for Human Rights Watch or the ACLU or Amnesty International or other organizations to bring gay questions into human rights issues because they were afraid that they would lose the ability to have connections with certain countries, so they made the case for human rights on other grounds. So what does this mean? It means that the notion of universality is in crisis. As Laclau points out, any notion of universality is based on a foreclosure: there must be something that is not included within the universal; there must be something that is outside of it for the universal to make sense; there must be something that is particular, that is not assimilable into the universal. What happens when that particular – that particular identity that cannot lay claim to the universal and who may not – nevertheless lays claim to the universal? It seems to me that the very notion of universality is brought into an extremely productive crisis and that we get what might be understood as spectral invocations of the universal among those who have no established, legitimate right to make the claim.

So, I like the idea that universality is a discourse that is driven into crisis again and again by the foreclosures that it makes and that it's forced to rearticulate itself. Where I agree with the project of hegemony that Laclau and Mouffe lay out is that for me the process of a universality that is brought into crisis again and again by what is outside of itself is an open-ended one. Universality, in that sense, would not be violent or totalizing; it would be an open-ended process, and the task of politics would be to keep it open, to keep it as a contested site of persistent crisis and not to let it be settled.

Q. Extending Althusser's notion of interpellation, you posit that *conscience* is central to subject formation, in that the hailed individual inevitably turns around to encounter the interpellating force. In *The Psychic Life of Power*, you write, "'Submission' to the rules of the dominant ideology might then be understood as a submission to the necessity to prove innocence in the face of accusation, a submission to the demand for proof, an execution of that proof, and acquisition of the status of subject in and through compliance with the terms of the interrogative law. To become a 'subject' is thus to have been presumed guilty, then tried and declared innocent. Because this declaration is not a single act, but a status incessantly *reproduced*, to become 'subject' is to be

continuously in the process of acquitting oneself of the accusation of guilt."
Although you draw primarily on Freud and Nietzsche to construct this theory,
it seems also to allude to Judeo-Christian notions of guilt, conscience, and "the
law of the father." Would you clarify why you think a theory of conscience is
necessary to explain subject formation?

A. The basic presupposition of the argument that you're citing – there are
other arguments that I have for this, too – is that part of what it means to be a
subject is to be born into a world in which norms are already acting on you
from the very beginning. What are those norms? There's a certain regulation of
the subject from the outset: you're born in a hospital (or somewhere else),
you're given a name, you're ordered in that particular way; you're assigned a
gender, and very often a race; you're inculcated quite quickly into a name and
therefore a lineage (if you stay with the biological mother or both biological
mother and father); you're immediately submitted to a calculative logic –
weight and height – which becomes the cause of trauma for the rest of your
life. And there are a set of fantasies that are immediately imposed: what this will
be if it is a boy, what it will be if it is a girl, what it will be, how it will relate to
the family, how it will or will not be the same as others. Very often – at least in
Judaism, which is my context – you are given a name that recalls someone who
is dead, so already you are the site of a mourning; and you cannot anticipate
what the effects of *that* will be. And as the subject is reared, certain civilizing
norms are imposed: how to eat; how to defecate; how to speak; how to do all
these things correctly and in the right time and place; how distinctions between
public and private are established; how sexuality is managed, controlled,
structured, sequestered. There is a set of legitimating norms, and they all
come with their punishments or their costs, so that as the child emerges into
subjecthood, it emerges in relationship to a set of norms that give it its place, its
legitimacy, its lovability, its promise of security; and it risks all of these things
when it abdicates those norms. What is punishment for the child but the
perceived withdrawal of love? And that's great, that's terrific, that's how it
works. The child learns how to do that which will somehow bring forth love
(or perhaps learns how to instigate the withdrawal of love for another reason);
there is some negotiation with love at the level of learning norms, and this is
inevitable to the extent that a child will, of necessity, despite its best judgment,
be passionately attached to whoever is bringing it up. That is, of course, the
humiliation of all humans: that we love these beings who happen to be our
parents or who happen to be our caregivers, and it's terrible to find that we
have absolutely no choice but to love them and that the love is absolute. It's a
deep humiliation, I think, for any thinking human. This is not just the
relationship of the child to an external norm or to a norm that is imposed by
someone or to a relationship to an Other who comes to stand for normativity

in some way. To the extent that the child develops the capacity to take itself as an object, to regulate itself, to think about itself, to make a decision for itself, it develops a reflexivity that has already taken that norm in in some way. So, it's not always in consultation with the external exemplification of the norm.

So, how does the norm become internalized, and internalized as a feature of the self? I would suggest that to become a subject is precisely to be one who has internalized the regulatory principles and who regulates one's self. There is no subject who does not have this capacity for reflexivity, and this reflexivity does not exist without the internalization of that norm. But what do I mean by the "internalization of the norm"? A lot of behavioral psychology assumes that norms are more or less mechanically internalized, but I think that they can in fact take all kinds of forms, that they enter into the fantasy life of an individual and, as part of fantasy, take on shapes and forms and meanings and intensities that are in no sense mimetically related to how they're existing in the outside world. It would be a mistake, for example, to say that if there is a severe parent there will be a severe superego. I'm not sure that this is at all true; in fact, sometimes the most severe superegos are those that are formed in relationship to radically *absent* parents as a way of producing a proximity in compensation for what was in fact not there. So, I think there is, as it were, a psychic life of power – which is not the same as a social life of power, but the two are radically implicated in one another.

When you ask why a theory of conscience is necessary to explain subject formation, let me say that conscience is the relation to oneself that is formed in a way as a substitute and as a transfiguration of primary relations to others, and it is the moment when reflexivity emerges as a structure of the subject that is relatively independent of its relation to concrete existing social others. Nietzsche says it more strongly. He says that I only begin to think about myself as an object when I am asked to be accountable for something I have done, that the question of accountability is actually what inaugurates reflexivity. It's a very, very strong claim, and there are many people who totally disagree with him and with me. Object relations theorists take me aside and say, "Judy, you've got to get out of this." And it *is* theological, and it probably comes from my own Judaism, but I do find it interesting that I become an object to myself at the moment in which I am accountable to an Other. The relation to myself that takes place is psychic and is complicated and does not necessarily replicate my relation to the Other; the I who takes myself to task is not the same as the Other who takes me to task. I may do it more severely; I may do it in ways the Other never would. And that incommensurability is crucial, but there is no subject yet without the specificity of that reflexivity. You might even say that the subject becomes inaugurated at the moment when the social power that acts on it, that interpellates it, that brings it into being through these norms is successfully implanted within the subject itself and when the subject becomes the site of the reiteration of those norms, even through its own psychic apparatus. I suppose that this would be why conscience is essential to the inception of the subject.

Q. Sounds like the voice of the Other within yourself.
A. Yes, which, of course, *is* and *is not* the Other.

Q. You've written quite a bit about melancholia, saying at one point that there are culturally instituted forms of it. In recent *JAC* interviews, Chantal Mouffe and Homi Bhabha have also discussed the social dimensions of emotions, and they've argued that passion is central to progressive political action. What do you feel is the role of passion, emotion, affective states in the formation of political agency?
A. One way to answer this to interrogate the relationship of politics to loss, since loss is what occasions melancholia and since loss is what melancholia seeks to deny in a certain way. It's clear, for instance, that many political movements are fueled by the sense of a loss that has already taken place or that is expected to take place. It could be a loss of autonomy, it could be a loss of land, it could be the violent loss of relatives in a war; but many political passions emerge from an experience of loss that comes to understand itself as collective. What becomes difficult to read sometimes is how these passions then get transmuted into certain kinds of political claims that don't always reflect them in a clear way. For instance, take something that is notoriously difficult, like Israeli military aggression. It seems to me that it is based in a profound sense of mournfulness, in a rage that comes from a limitless sense of mournfulness and a sense of precariousness that is not always possible to read and that in certain ways is not acknowledged as the anxiety over loss that it is. The transmutation of mourning into aggression is something that Freud talked about as part of melancholia, and it was something that he thought could only be undone by returning melancholia to mourning, to the extent that that's possible. There would have to be a more overt way of acknowledging loss; aggression is, to a certain extent, an effort to deny loss.

There are enormous anxieties, for instance, about the loss of place that are being undergone by white South Africans or white landowners in Zimbabwe that probably take the form of certain kinds of legal and political agendas; it would be interesting to figure out how the loss of privilege or the loss of dominance translates into political action. Or look at affirmative action in the state of California, the decimation of that agenda that took place not so long ago. There's no way to grasp what happened there without first understanding that white people knew damn well that they were very soon not to be the majority in this state. What does it mean for them to lose that place? Affirmative action seemed nothing other than ceding that place or hastening the loss of that majority status. I'm not sure what kind of political culture we would have to live in where the psychological dimensions and the passionate dimensions of our political investments actually got analyzed. It seems to me that we act out our passions rather quickly and unselfconsciously – in this culture, at least – and that the field of popular psychology tends to de-politicize rather than to function as a commentary on our political culture. I suppose I have some nostalgia for the Frankfurt School's efforts to try to bring politics and psychology together in a certain way.

Q. In *Bodies that Matter*, you take pains to clarify your notion of performativity: "There is a tendency to think that sexuality is either constructed or determined; to think that if it is constructed, it is in some sense free, and if it is determined, it is in some sense fixed. These oppositions do not describe the complexity of what is at stake in any effort to take account of the conditions under which sex and sexuality are assumed. The 'performative' dimension of construction is precisely the forced reiteration of norms. In this sense, then, it is not only that there are constraints to performativity; rather, constraint calls to be rethought as the very condition of performativity. Performativity is neither free play nor theatrical self-presentation; nor can it be equated with performance. Moreover, constraint is not necessarily that which sets a limit to performativity; constraint is, rather, that which impels and sustains performativity." For our readers, all of whom are interested in the workings of rhetoric, would you elaborate on the rhetoric of performativity?

A. Let's think about the difference between performativity and performance. I was somewhat surprised that people took performativity to be nothing other than performance when they read *Gender Trouble*. In that book, I used the example of the drag queen to try to make the case that the performance of gender that the drag queen offers is no less real and no less true than the performance of gender that any ordinary man or woman might perform, that it gives us a kind of allegory of the mundane performance of gender, and that we are all, all the time, as it were, performing gender. The drag show is a moment in which that performance is rendered explicit. It's not an aberration from the norm; it shows us how the norm actually functions, how the norm is instituted through our bodies, through our stylistics, through our bodily gestures. Then the tendency was to think, "Oh great, now we can perform gender differently," which led to the notion of radical free agency: "Oh, let's get up and put on a new gender today," or "Let's have a collective meeting and decide what gender we should perform and go perform it on the street and alter things radically." Now, I don't mind that. I think that's great. And I love my students who are performing their gender in various ways, and I have elaborate e-mail correspondences with various genders throughout the world, and I'm grateful for them. It makes my life better, and it makes everybody live a little more easily. So, I'm not opposed to performance, and in fact performance is a crucial part of performativity, but there's something else that's going on: the performance of a gender is also compelled by norms that I do not choose. I work within the norms that constitute me. I do something with them. Those norms are the condition of my agency, and they also limit my agency; they are that limit *and* that condition at the same time. What I can do is, to a certain extent, conditioned by what is available for me to do within the culture and by what other practices are and by what practices are legitimating.

Then there is the question of how performance is taken up or read or interpreted. That's always very interesting. When I'm in Hawaii, I'm sometimes treated as a grandmother, which I think is extremely funny. Why is it that I'm constituted as a grandmother? It's one of the things that happen. In other places, I am assumed to be a man. Gender performativity is not just drawing on the norms that constitute, limit, and condition me; it's also delivering a performance within a context of reception, and I cannot fully anticipate what will happen. Once I gave a talk in Germany and it was reported in the *Frankfurter Rundschau* that as I stood at the podium explaining the difference between masculine and feminine, I looked like a young Italian man. They said that I used my hands to gesture in certain ways and that I had a manly haircut. In Paris my haircut probably would not look manly but would look like any other woman's short haircut, and it would even function within a certain conception of femininity; but in Frankfurt, for whatever reason, it looked masculine. That I was *Italian* was interesting. Since there aren't very many Jews in Frankfurt, I suppose you could look at this nose and my skin tone and say that I'm Italian – some weird Mediterranean, non-Aryan something. This really interesting interpellation – which, of course, is not what I intended – might have to be understood as something like the effect of various cultural norms as they produce something like the readability of a person. And I think this happens again and again: performativity – gender performativity, in particular – produces hermeneutic rifts, questions of whether a common understanding is even possible. It can actually lead to massive cultural misunderstanding, to real dissonant meanings and interpretations.

So, yes, there is an aspect of performance, but that does not mean that the meaning of the performance is established by the intention of the actor – hardly. What are being performed are the cultural norms that condition and limit the actor in the situation; but also in play are the cultural norms of reception, which may or may not accord with the ones that are constituting a situation so that we actually have a retrospective of constitution of the performance through the norms of reception – and this can produce really interesting problems of cultural translation and cultural misunderstanding. And those problems are very productive. That gender is a site of cultural translation (and I think it probably is) accords with my argument that woman is a site of contest and so why wouldn't gender performativity be a site of contested meanings as well?

Q. You state in *Gender Trouble* that you do not believe that there is a "radical disjunction" between heterosexuality and homosexuality, that there are "structures of psychic homosexuality within heterosexual relations, and structures of psychic heterosexuality within gay and lesbian sexuality and relationships." In other words, heterosexuality is not "the only compulsory display of power that informs sexuality." Also, we noticed that you were cited recently in the *New York Times Magazine* in a story about Barry Winchell, a soldier who had dated a pre-operative transsexual and who was consequently bludgeoned to death by another soldier. In describing the transsexual, Calpernia Addams, the author of the story writes, "Just as Addams is not yet female and no longer purely male, as a couple they were not wholly straight or acceptably gay. Rather they occupied a rare middle ground encompassing both, and neither: socially heterosexual, sexually homosexual, uncomfortably on the margins of all worlds" (26). Does this case serve as an example of the way in which the structures of psychic homosexuality and heterosexuality occur together in heterosexual or homosexual relations?

A. Well, let me comment about the Barry Winchell story, and that will lead me to a more direct answer to your question. What's interesting about this case is that Barry Winchell was involved with a transgendered person who remains anatomically male (to the extent that we can say that) but whose rather seamless gender presentation is in fact as a woman – with a woman's name and everything. So, when gay legal activists sought to take the military to trial on this question, claiming that this was gay-bashing, the only coherent way they could make that argument was by claiming that this was a relationship between two men, since if it were a heterosexual relationship it could not be gay-bashing. So they decided that they would reconstitute the woman as a man, reduce her as it were to her anatomy and therefore violate her self-understanding and her self-naming practice for the sake of the political and legal issue. Of course, the question comes up: "Why is it that gay rights activism has to assume that its primary goal is to defend homosexual relations, where 'homosexual relations' are understood as relations between people of the same gender?" The law itself is very complicated, since the legal precedents within which such an activist group is functioning would define homosexuality as a sexual relationship between two people of the same gender. But what I would like to see is a system of jurisprudence that understands something of the complexity of gender that is at work in homosexual and heterosexual relations and in bisexuality, since a bisexual would also prove a problem for the law in a discrimination case.

I have always been drawn to the concept of "sexual minorities," a notion that Gayle Rubin introduced many years ago. This term is not identity-based: it isn't that we're struggling for people who are gay or lesbian or transgendered; we're struggling for all kinds of people who for whatever reason are not immediately captured or legitimated by the available norms and who live with the threat of violence or the threat of unemployment or the threat of dispossession of some kind by virtue of their aberrant relation to the norm. What worries me is that many mainstream gay organizations have become very identity-based; coming out has become a very big thing because that's the moment of rendering visible your identity. The problem is that among that kind of bourgeois politics – and it is an intensely bourgeois politics that has taken over the gay movement – the point is to get good-looking people on television who say, "I'm a lawyer, or I'm a doctor, and I just happen to be X or Y. And the fact that I'm X or Y should not get in the way of my being accepted in society." Of course, that's just to say, "I'm an identity that needs to be included within American pluralism." But there are a lot of folks who aren't going to be able to stand up and say they are X or Y, or who might even say they are X or Y and their assertion would be disputed. So, for instance, this woman who is anatomically male in part – or who may be mixed; she has breast implants, so perhaps she is in transition – could get up and say that she's a woman, but that is going to be a really rough speech act for a lot of people to accept. There will be some who say, "No, you are not." It would be profoundly infelicitous. She may try her best. She may try to go to the Women's Music Festival in Michigan and may be returned to her home. She may go to the doctor's office and hear that she's "wrong." She may try to make certain legal claims under the status of "woman" – or even under, say, Title IX – and she may be dismissed. She may try to compete in athletics, and she may be dismissed. So, we're talking about a speech act that again and again runs up against a refusal to accept its claim. What's most painful in the Barry Winchell story is that the very activists whom one might expect to be trying to produce a world in which this woman's speech act would be accepted are in fact denying her, undermining her, violating her by keeping her out of the media and by trying to suppress that aspect of the story in order to make the legal claim that they want to make.

So, one important question here is: "What happens when identity politics gets instituted in the law and becomes a very rigid structure so that the capacity for making a claim or seeking redress becomes effectively dictated by very narrow identity terms?" Who's left out at that point? It seems to me that in the zeal to achieve legal redress within existing legal terms, we as a movement have actually failed to take stock of who we are as a community and who we want to represent and how. There's something terribly, terribly sad there. In the relationship of heterosexual and homosexual, we have to make a distinction. Many transgendered people understand themselves to have issues with the gender that they've been assigned and often want to alter that to another gender, or even alter it to the point where they are "transsexual" or "transgendered" *rather than* "male" or "female." It's possible to have *transgender* as a term that is neither one nor the other but that denotes something like a transition that has no end. Kate Bornstein has been quite vocal in trying to open that up as a possibility. This is an interesting move because the conventional critique of transgender has been that it accepts the most orthodox notions of gender and wants to reconstitute them. In fact, there is a gender-subversive strain within transgender that needs to be understood a little bit more clearly. But many people who are transgendered do not therefore have a question about what their sexuality is, and that's very complicated. In the same way, people who are perhaps very mobile in their sexualities – who are bi or who are alternately straight and gay, who are a bottom in a straight scene and a top in a gay scene – may feel that the available language for their sexuality is inadequate. They may find themselves profoundly estranged or annoyed by identity language as it circulates within public culture, but they may have absolutely no question about their gender; the question of gender assignment is not an issue. It may well be that the sexual issue doesn't challenge their sense of gender at all. I think it's rare but I think it's true, in the same way that many transgendered people really think the issue is gender and not sexuality.

So the case that you're offering to me is a complicated one. The interesting question at this level is, "What does it mean for a man to be in love with a drag performer, someone who's not just performing on stage but who is transgendered throughout life, who still has male genitals and who may well engage those genitals in sexual activity?" Anatomy is a *condition* of sexual fantasy, but it also gets radically transfigured by sexual fantasy, so I think we would be making a big mistake if we thought that the sex between Barry Winchell and his lover was straight or was gay. I'm not sure we can say. I'm not sure we *should* say. It may well be that it is romantically and even sexually very straight for both of them, extremely straight, even though there are two penises in play. That just means that the *meaning* of the penis is going to be transfigured within the sexual scene. Or that penis may well be put *out* of play; we don't know what kind of play it was in. But if it's put *into* play, the question is, "In the service of what sexual fantasy is it put into play?" For example, think about *Boys Don't Cry*. Are we going to say that Teena Brandon/Brandon Teena was having straight sex with her girlfriend/his girlfriend? Or is it lesbian sex? My sense is that their sex puts the distinction into crisis and that it is probably all the more interesting and exciting by virtue of the fact that it eludes the categories that are available for it. Where's anatomy in that? In some ways, Brandon's anatomy is put out of play (some parts of it are), and yet there is also obviously a body that's put into play. We get the breasts that are strapped, the vagina that is not accessible, the dildo that enters and that is, we might say, a kind of phantasmatic extension of the body – all of which would seem to be making this sex pretty male, pretty straight; but we also get lips and arms and thighs and lots of other body parts at play. I think that we would not be able to answer in any easy way the question, "Is this straight or is this gay?" There might be what Brandon says. There might be what Brandon's lover says. There might also be a certain cultural reading that is possible that would take into account what they say but would not be completely wedded to what they say. But I think the reason why we are kind of stopped at these moments is that we realize that there is a certain crossing going on such that these human beings cannot be easily reduced to either category, straight or gay. Of course, there's much more to be said about this question.

Q. You take issue with Luce Irigaray's contention that sexual difference is *the* question of our time, saying that she positions sexual difference as more fundamental than any other form of difference. You posit instead that it might be more productive to "consider the assumption of sexual positions, the disjunctive ordering of the human as 'masculine' or 'feminine,' as taking place not only through a heterosexualizing symbolic with its taboo on homo-sexuality, but through a complex set of racial injunctions which operate in part through the taboo on miscegenation." Further, you remind us that "the reproduction of the species will be articulated as the reproduction *of* relations of reproduction, that is, as the cathected site of a racialized version of the species in pursuit of hegemony through perpetuity, that requires and produces a normative heterosexuality in its service." Would you say, then, that the ordering and regulating of sexuality is a racial or even racist project?
A. It's a very complicated issue. What is most interesting to me about this topic right now is the relationship between the incest taboo as it functions to make the case not only for the institution of gender as masculine and feminine but also for the institution of heterosexuality as a necessary social form, and the taboo against miscegenation, which works to make sure that families remain racially discrete and that gender mixing does not take place as a result of reproduction. For the most part, they have been theorized separately. We get the theorization of the incest taboo through Lévi-Strauss and what follows from that analysis. Then we have historical scholarship on miscegenation,

which talks a lot about American slavery (especially what happens between slaves and slave owners) and about how miscegenation is both taboo and also a kind of taboo that is regularly broken – in the same way that we might say that the incest taboo is regularly broken. What *hasn't* been done and what I would like to see done is another kind of work. When Lévi-Strauss makes his argument in *The Elementary Structures of Kinship* that the incest taboo is the basis of culture and that it mandates exogamy, that it mandates marriage outside the clan, I wonder whether his notion of the clan could also be understood in terms of the notion of race. I mean that in the following way: marriage must take place outside the clan, there must be exogamy, but there must be a limit to exogamy; that is, it must be outside the clan but not outside of a certain racial self-understanding or racial commonality. So, it seems to me that the incest taboo mandates exogamy, but the taboo against miscegenation limits the exogamy that the incest taboo mandates.

Of course, one can see that Lévi-Strauss is in some sense making marriage into one of the most elementary structures of culture itself, because it's not just that women are exchanged but that they're exchanged through marriage, and the marriage bond is what opens up symbolic modes of communication between two clans. This has been very worrisome, by the way, in contemporary French debates on the family and marriage and whether single or gay people can have medically assisted reproductive technology and whether they can adopt children. For the most part, the French have said no because they believe that heterosexual marriage is essential to culture itself and that such options would destroy – Destroy! – culture. Indeed, an anthropologist, Françoise Héritier, who is the bona fide representative of the Lévi-Straussian position, is the one who has gone in front of the *Assemblée nationale* to say that heterosexual marriage must remain the basis of culture. So we've seen a massively conservative move there.

Let's take the French case. The effort to shore up marriage as the essential moment of culture takes place in a context in which there are many married people who live separately, who are in what they call a state of *démariage* (which is a term I love; it's almost like the deconstruction of marriage). The French are also dealing with a new Europe in which there are many people in France who are no longer "French" in the old, white sense of French. So, Frenchness itself is coming under crisis. The very culture – for which they think marriage is the linchpin – is in crisis because it's becoming profoundly multiracial and multilingual. Lots of young kids are having sexual relations with their friends who are from Turkey or from Arab countries or from North Africa, and who knows what's going on with miscegenation? So, this shoring up of the family as the essence of culture is also the shoring up of family as the essential moment of *French* culture, of its racial purity: "We must keep marriage in order to transmit

Frenchness and its national and racial purity." We might even read this kind of new orthodoxy on marriage, which the structuralists are responsible for to some degree, as a panicked response to the possibility of miscegenation: it's not just that gay people are going to adopt and that you'll get something like the dislocation of heterosexuality from its primary place, but that the family itself may end up not transmitting culture as we know it. It may end up transmitting a *new* culture or cultural hybridity or cultural complexity, or we may find that what is North African has become essential to French culture and that colonialism has reversed itself through the intimacies of family life. So, it's important that we understand both how the mandating of heterosexuality and the mandating of heterosexual marriage are linked with notions of cultural transmission that are invariably linked with questions of what race that culture will be, questions of racial transmission and racial purity. One can see it most intensely in some of these European scenes, but I'm quite sure we could do such an analysis domestically as well.

Q. You point out that an injurious term "works its injury precisely through the accumulation and dissimulation of its force. The speaker who utters the racial slur is thus citing that slur, making linguistic community with a history of speakers. What this might mean, then, is that precisely the iterability by which a performative enacts its injury establishes a permanent difficulty in locating final accountability for that injury in a singular subject and its act." Would you expand on how iterability does its rhetorical work?

A. As an example, consider the word *queer*, which thirty years ago (even twenty, even fifteen years ago) was considered profoundly derogatory and frightening as a speech act. I remember living in great fear of the word, knowing I was eligible for it, thinking that once it actually landed on me I would be branded forever and that the stigma would do me in completely. Ten or twelve years ago when *queer* started to happen as a term, people would ask, "What do you think, should we produce a journal called *Queer Theory*?" I thought, "My God, do we have to use that word?" I was still in its grip. I was still thinking, "Must we take on this word? Isn't it too injurious? Why do we need to repeat it at all?" I still think there are words that are in fact so injurious that it's very hard to imagine that they could be repeated in a productive way; however, I did note that using the word *queer* again and again as part of an affirmative practice in certain contexts helped take it out of an established context of being exclusively injurious, and it became about reclaiming language, about a certain kind of courage, about a certain kind of opening up of the term, about the possibility of transforming stigmatization into something more celebratory. So, I became convinced that it's fine. Now I hear administrators in the University of California system wondering whether it would be appropriate to include "queer studies" in this or that instructional unit, and they don't blanch. Of course, there are certain places even in this very city [Berkeley/San Francisco] where we couldn't use the term or people would be quite upset, or where it would in fact incite violence of some kind. It is interesting to me that we're in a linguistic landscape in which it functions variably: you don't know, when you say it, what it's going to do.

And, of course, to whom does the word belong? I remember once walking on a street in Berkeley and some kid leaned out of a window and asked, "Are you a lesbian?" Just like that. I replied, "Yes, I *am* a lesbian." I returned it in the affirmative. It was a completely impulsive moment. It was an interpellation from nowhere. Of course, what such a questioner is really asking is, "Are you this thing that I fear and loathe? Do you dare to say yes to this thing that you apparently are, at least on the basis of what you look like? And I have power over you to the extent that I am now seeking to expose you through the question I pose to you." To the extent that I was able very quickly to turn around and say, "Yes, I am a lesbian," the power of my interrogator was lost. My questioner was then left in a kind of shock, having heard somebody gamely, proudly take on the term – somebody who spends most of her life deconstructing the term in other contexts. It was a very powerful thing to do. It wasn't that I authored that term: I received the term and gave it back; I replayed it, reiterated it. Whose speech act was that? Is it my speech act? Is it the other person's speech act? Did I recite the other person's speech act in my own? Did I extend it? Were we in an odd moment of community at that moment – kind of remaking language together? It's as if my interrogator were saying, "Hey, what do we do with the word *lesbian*? Shall we still use it?" And I said, "Yeah, let's use it *this* way!" Or it's as if the interrogator hanging out the window were saying, "Hey, do you think the word *lesbian* can only be used in a derogatory way on the street?" And I said, "No, it can be claimed on the street! Come join me!" We were having a negotiation. And what have I given back to that person? Well, I don't know. Will this person make the same interrogation again? Maybe my questioner really wanted to know: "Hey, are you a lesbian?" "Will this person claim or not claim?" That was the question being posed to me: "Are you gonna claim or are you not gonna claim?" "I'm gonna claim." "Oh, you're gonna claim. It can be claimed?" "Yeah, it can be claimed!" "Oh, look, it can be claimed!" It could be that this person then notes that this is not going to work anymore. Or that it is possible to claim. Who knows, maybe that person is claiming. Maybe that person needed a little help to claim. We don't know. But it's an interesting moment because it brings into relief something about how the question will function. Will this word serve injury, or will it serve another purpose? There is a certain challenge that is delivered with something like hate speech. "Are you a lesbian?" Is that hate speech? I don't know. I think in fact that my interrogator was actually asking *me* whether it was hate speech: "Is this hate speech that I am delivering to you right now?" "No, it doesn't have to be hate speech."

So, when we're thinking about how iterability does its rhetorical work, we probably make a mistake when we think that it's the word that causes the injury, when actually there is always a question of what purpose that word will serve. We can re-link it to injury, we can de-link it, we can try to interrogate how it is linked and de-linked, but the whole purpose of reiterating injurious language is to show that the relationship of the word itself to the injury that it performs is finally arbitrary. I worry that many people focus on injurious language, on racist or homophobic speech, thinking that the language is the source of the injury when the source of the injury is actually in racism or homophobia – which is much more profound and much more complicated. To single out language seems to me to single out one mode of its conveyance (and an arbitrary one at that) and probably to miss the larger struggle at stake.

Q. Well, that's a point you make in *Excitable Speech* when you say there is an inverting. You say that rather than an act of regulation that occurs after an offensive speech act, censorship is "a way of *producing* speech, constraining in advance what will and will not become acceptable speech." That is, in the conventional view censorship appears to follow the utterance of offensive speech, but in your view censorship *produces* offensive speech: the temporal relation is inverted. Nonetheless, you do acknowledge that speech *can* injure people. While we agree that the State should not be allowed any power to censor words and images, we wonder if you believe that there is *any* role that the State should play in protecting citizens from hateful speech and images?

A. I do. There's a difference between coming up with a typology of words and images that are of necessity injurious, and actually looking at the way in which they function as social practices in very specific contexts. For instance, in *Excitable Speech* I cite the example of the burning cross on the black family's lawn in *R.A.V. v. St. Paul*; that is *massively* injurious, a threat to their lives. We understand that this is operating as a threat of violence according to conventions. I would not argue that it is an arbitrary sign in that case. Although we could say that the wood and the fire do not in themselves "mean" anything, we can say that wood placed in that way, formed as a cross, burning on a black family's lawn, is a racist act – and it is a threat of violence. It seems to me appalling to understand that as "free expression." And that there are people who have made that argument is just appalling to me. No, that's not appropriate. That's where the State needs to intervene. There's no question about it. What worries me is that the State will call *that* "free expression" and will say that coming out in the military is not: that coming out is "an action," "conduct." So then the question becomes: "What are we to do with the fact that we live under a State apparatus that will abuse its power in that way, that will use the speech/conduct distinction in such a way as to allow racists their free expression while throttling the expression of gay desire?" We have a big problem: what to give to the courts and what not to give to the courts, or how to formulate it in such a way that the hands of the courts are tied so that they can't use their discretion in a way that produces such noxious results.

That's a set of critical questions about what to do when there are fundamentally conservative aims that are coursing through the State apparatus and that are manipulating this distinction in certain ways. For instance, there are various elements of sexual and racial harassment policies that I accept, that I helped to draft for my university, and that I believe ought to be instituted. I think, however, that it's not enough to know that a professor had a liaison with a student. So I wouldn't support the MacKinnon view that those relations are structurally imbalanced and therefore exploitative by their very definition. I would need to know a lot more. I would be very context-bound about trying to understand what meaning that liaison had, what consequences it had, whether there was a threat of punishment, whether it was undermining the student's ability to function and complete the course work, whether there are charges that are being vindictively and retroactively produced. Most sexual harassment officers – at least the ones I have talked to – understand that there's nothing you can derive a priori from that scene.

The same is true with utterance. An utterance in a classroom that one student understands as racist may well have another meaning, implication, or intention; and precisely because we live in disjunct linguistic locations, the capacity for radically different interpretations, for interpreting words that are not intended in certain ways as having certain intentions, is very possible. It's a sign of the fact that we do not speak a common language. Such attributions are possible all the time; sometimes you can establish why they are racist, or sexist, or impermissible, but I don't think you can derive either from a typology of terms and images or from the a priori structure of a relationship what its actual injurious content is. It has to be investigated in context. The *early* MacKinnon, the MacKinnon of the *Sexual Harassment of Working Women*, knew that. She really did. She said that it must in every instance be linked to consequences and that we must be able to show that link. The way in which she changed was to say that we don't ever have to show the link to consequences because this is structurally the case. That scares me. It scares me because it means that we have no interpretation to perform. In fact, she has become very, very bitter about the idea of "in-ter-pre-ta-tion," as she puts it – she spits it out. She doesn't want to have to live in a world in which it's a question of "in-ter-pre-ta-tion," and *I* think we have no other choice.

Q. Many of your works are controversial, and so it is no surprise that some scholars would disagree with you. Nancy Fraser, for example, has voiced some criticisms of your work. Are there any misunderstandings or misrepresentations of your work that you would especially like to address at this time?

A. I'm always glad to have Nancy's arguments. I feel that we have a productive disagreement. I guess I'll say one thing about one of the points she regularly makes. Nancy and some other social theorists who are profoundly influenced by the Habermasian school worry that I am always interested in producing new possibilities but that I don't say which possibilities are good to pursue and which are bad to pursue, that I don't have a set of strong norms that would tell us which possibilities to actualize and which not. Certainly, I don't want *all* possibilities realized, so why don't I distinguish among them? What I would answer to that is that when we ask the question, "How ought we to live and what possibilities should we collectively seek to realize?" we always ask it within a given horizon of possibilities that are already established – what is imaginable. What worries me is that we very often make decisions about what life to pursue and what possibilities to realize without ever asking how our very notions of "what is possible," "what is livable," "what is imaginable" are constrained in advance, and maybe in some very politically consequential ways. For instance, say you're in a human rights organization that hasn't thought about the problem of gay and lesbian human rights – violence against gays and lesbians, the radical pathologization or psychiatrization or imprisonment of gays and lesbians. And say you are considering which strategies to pursue in the field but that the field of possibilities is delimited in advance such that gay and lesbian lives are not thinkable within the field. What does it mean to make a normative judgment on that basis when you have not critically interrogated *how* the field of possibility is itself constituted, and constituted through some pretty violent exclusions? It's not as if I wouldn't make such decisions or don't think there are hard decisions to make; what worries me is that the rush to *decision-ism* and to strong normativity very often fails to consider what is meant by some of the very basic terms that it assumes. For example, what is a deciding person? How are decisions made? What is the field of possibilities that is delimited in advance to me? What is outside that field? I worry that there is a critical dimension to political normativity (and even a normative dimension) that is missing, because if there's a violent circumscription of the possible – that is to say, certain lives are not considered lives, certain human capacities are not considered human – what does it mean that we take that for granted as we proceed to decide what we ought and ought not to do? It means that in our effort to be normative we perform a violence and an exclusion for which we are not accountable, and in my view that produces a massive contradiction.

Of course, Martha Nussbaum has also made a very strong attack on me, but I think it actually has nothing to do with my work. It doesn't strike me as an engaged or careful reading, and I presume that it does probably epitomize a certain frustration that a certain kind of liberal American politics has with a critical approach to some of its most important issues. She wants to be able to make strong paternalistic claims about women's conditions; she wants to be able to use the language of universality without interrogating it; she wants to be able to tell us how Indian women suffer; and she wants to be able to, in her words, make "an assault" on local cultures when it is mandated by universal concerns. I see her as being very much opposed to the problem of cultural translation and cultural difference; she thinks they get in the way of strong normative arguments. We can see something like a resurgence of a certain kind of white feminism here that doesn't want to have to hear about difference, that wants to be able to make its strong claims and speak in the name of "reason," and speak in the name of *everyone* without having to hear them, without having to learn what it might mean to hear them. So, I'm sorry about that. It seems to me to be full of a kind of displaced animosity, but I think people can read it for what it is.

Let me make one final comment. You've asked me about difficult writing, and you've asked me whether I think the State has any role in the adjudication of hate speech. These are in effect questions about whether what I write is readable, whether what I am for is translatable into contemporary politics in an obvious or clear way. I think that I probably produce a certain amount of anxiety, or what Foucault calls the politics of discomfort, and I don't do that just to be annoying. For me, there's more hope in the world when we can question what is taken for granted, especially about what it is to be a human, which is a really fundamental question. What qualifies as a human, as a human subject, as human speech, as human desire? How do we circum-scribe human speech or desire? At what cost? And at what cost to whom? These are questions that I think are important and that function within everyday grammar, everyday language, as taken-for-granted notions. We feel that we know the answers. We know what family is, we know what desire is, we know what a human subject is, we know what speech is, we know what is comprehensible, we know its limits. And I think that this feeling of certainty leads to a terrible parochialism. Taking for granted one's own linguistic horizon as the ultimate linguistic horizon leads to an enormous parochialism and keeps us from being open to radical difference and from undergoing the discomfort and the anxiety of realizing that the scheme of intelligibility on which we rely fundamentally is not adequate, is not common, and closes us off from the possibility of understanding others and ourselves in a more fundamentally capacious way.

14

Selected Bibliography of Works by Judith Butler

BOOKS

Subjects of Desire: Hegelian Reflections in Twentieth-Century France (New York: Columbia University Press, 1987, 1999).
Gender Trouble: Feminism and the Subversion of Identity (New York: Routledge, 1990, 1999).
Bodies That Matter: On the Discursive Limits of "Sex" (New York: Routledge, 1993).
Excitable Speech: A Politics of the Performative (New York: Routledge, 1997).
The Psychic Life of Power: Theories in Subjection (Stanford, Calif.: Stanford University Press, 1997).
Antigone's Claim: Kinship Between Life and Death (New York: Columbia University Press, 2000).

FORTHCOMING BOOKS

Precarious Life: Powers of Violence and Mourning (London and New York: Verso, 2004).
Undoing Gender (New York: Routledge, 2004).
Against Ethical Violence (published as *Kritik den Ethischen Gewalt* [Frankfurt: Suhrkamp, 2003] and to be published by Stanford University Press, 2004).

CO-AUTHORED BOOKS

Seyla Benhabib, Judith Butler, Drucilla Cornell, and Nancy Fraser, *Feminist Contentions: A Philosophical Exchange* (London: Routledge, 1995).
Judith Butler, Ernesto Laclau, Slavoj Žižek, *Contingency, Hegemony, Universality. Contemporary Dialogues on the Left* (London: Verso, 2000).

CO-EDITED BOOKS

Judith Butler and Joan W. Scott, *Feminists Theorize the Political* (New York: Routledge, 1997).
Judith Butler, John Guillory, and Kendall Thomas, *What's Left of Theory? New Work on the Politics of Literary Theory* (London: Routledge, 2000).

ARTICLES

"Sex and Gender in Simone de Beauvoir's *Second Sex*." *Yale French Studies* 72 (1986).
"Variations on Sex and Gender. Beauvoir, Wittig and Foucault." In *Feminism as Critique: Essays on the Politics of Gender in Late-Capitalist Societies*, ed. Seyla Benhabib and Drucilla Cornell (Cambridge: Polity Press, 1987).
"Foucault and the Paradox of Bodily Inscriptions." *Journal of Philosophy* 86:11 (1989), pp. 601–7.
"Sexual Ideology and Phenomenological Description: A Feminist Critique of Merleau-Ponty's *Phenomenology of Perception*." In *The Thinking Muse. Feminism and Modern French Philosophy*, ed. Jeffner Allen and Iris Marion Young (Bloomington: Indiana University Press, 1989), pp. 85–100.
"Gender Trouble, Feminist Theory, and Psychoanalytic Discourse." In *Feminism/ Postmodernism*, ed. Linda J. Nicholson (London: Routledge, 1990), pp. 324–40.
"The Force of Fantasy: Mapplethorpe, Feminism, and Discursive Excess." *differences: A Journal of Feminist Cultural Studies* 2:2 (1990), pp. 105–25.
"Imitation and Gender Insubordination." In *Inside Out: Lesbian Theories, Gay Theories*, ed. Diana Fuss (London: Routledge, 1990), pp. 13–31.
"The Nothing That Is: Wallace Stevens' Hegelian Affinities." In *Theorizing American Literature: Hegel, the Sign, and History*, ed. Bainard Cowan and Joseph G. Kronick (London: Louisiana State University Press, 1991). pp. 269–87.
"Gender" entry in *Feminism and Psychoanalysis: A Critical Dictionary*, ed. Elizabeth Wright (Oxford: Blackwell, 1992), pp. 140–5.
"Contingent Foundations: Feminism and the Question of Postmodernism." In *Feminists Theorize the Political*, ed. Judith Butler and Joan W. Scott (London: Routledge, 1990), pp. 3–21, and in Benhabib, Butler, Cornell, and Fraser, *Feminist Contentions: A Philosophical Exchange* (London: Routledge, 1992), pp. 35–54.
"Endangered/Endangering: Schematic Racism and White Paranoia." In *Reading Rodney King/Reading Urban Uprising*, ed. Robert Gooding-Williams (New York: Routledge, 1993), pp. 15–22.
"Against Proper Objects." *differences: A Journal of Feminist Cultural Studies* 6.2 and 6.3 (1994), pp. 1–26.
"Stubborn Attachment, Bodily Subjection: Rereading Hegel on the Unhappy Consciousness." In *Intersections: 19th-Century Philosophy and Contemporary Theory*, ed. David Clarke and Tillotama Rajan (SUNY Press, 1995).

"Sexual Inversions." In *Feminist Interpretations of Michel Foucault*, ed. Susan J. Hekman (Philadelphia: Pennsylvania University Press, 1996), pp. 344–61.

"For a Careful Reading." In *Feminist Contentions: A Philosophical Exchange* (London: Routledge, 1996), pp. 127–43.

"Universality in Culture." In *For Love of Country: Debating the Limits of Patriotism. Martha C. Nussbaum with Respondents*, ed. Joshua Cohen (Boston: Beacon Press, 1996), pp. 43–52.

"Performative Acts and Gender Constitution: An Essay on Phenomenology and Feminist Theory." In *Writing on the Body: Female Embodiment and Feminist Theory*, ed. Katie Conboy, Nadia Medina, and Sarah Stanbury (New York: Columbia University Press, 1997), pp. 401–17. Also in *Performing Feminisms: Feminist Critical Theory and Theatre*, ed. Sue-Ellen Case (Baltimore: Johns Hopkins University Press, 1990).

"Sovereign Performatives in the Contemporary Scene of Utterance." *Critical Inquiry* (Winter 1997).

"Vocabularies of the Censor." In *Censorship and Silencing*, ed. Robert Post (Oxford: Oxford University Press and Getty Foundation, 1998).

"Revisiting Bodies and Pleasures." *Theory, Culture and Society* 16.2 (1999), pp. 11–20.

"Restaging the Universal: Hegemony and the Limits of Formalism"; "Competing Universalities"; "Dynamic Conclusions." In *Contingency, Hegemony, Universality: Contemporary Dialogues on the Left*, with Ernesto Laclau and Slavoj Zizek (London: Verso, 2000), pp. 11–43, 136–81, 263–80.

"Ethical Ambivalence." In *The Turn to Ethics*, ed. Marjorie Garber, Beatrice Hanssen, and Rebecca Walkovitz (New York: Routledge, 2000).

"Conversational Break: A Reply to Robert Gooding-Williams." In *Race: Blackwell Readings in Continental Philosophy*, ed. Robert Bernasconi (Oxford: Blackwell, 2001).

"Style for a Liminal Subject." In *Without Guarantees. Essays in Honour of Stuart Hall*, ed. Angela McRobbie and Paul Gilroy (London: Verso, 2001).

"Is Kinship Always Already Heterosexual?" *differences* 13 (Spring 2002) and in *Left Legalism, Left Critique* ed. Wendy Brown and Janet Halley (Durham, NC: Duke University Press, 2002).

"Doubting Love." In *Take My Advice: Letters to the Next Generation from People Who Know a Thing or Two*, ed. James Harmon (New York: Simon and Schuster, 2002).

"Violence, Mourning, Politics." *Studies in Culture and Sexuality* 4:1. Published in Italian in *Nuovi Argumenti* (July/September 2002) and in French in *Nouvelles Questions Féministes* 22:1 (April 2003).

"Indefinite Detention." In *It's a Free Country: Personal Liberties after 9/11*, ed. Victor Goldberg (New York: RMD Press, 2002).

"Explanation and Exoneration, or What We Can Hear." *Theory and Event* 5:4 (Winter 2002). <http://muse.jhu.edu/journals/social_text/v020/20.Bbutler.html>

"What Is Critique? An Essay on Foucault's Virtue." In David Ingram ed. *The Political. Readings in Continental Philosophy*, ed. David Ingram (Oxford: Blackwell, 2002), pp. 212–26.

"Bodies and Power Reconsidered." In *Deutsche Zeitschrift für Philosophie*, special issue on Foucault, ed. Axel Honneth (forthcoming) and in *Radical Philosophy* 114 (July/August 2003).

"Making Sexuality into an Ethic: Beauvoir on Sade." In *The Cambridge Companion to Simone de Beauvoir*, ed. Claudia Card (Cambridge: Cambridge University Press, 2003).

"Doing Justice to Someone: Sex Reassignment and Allegories of Transsexuality." *GLQ* 7:4 (2001).

"The Charge of Anti-Semitism." *London Review of Books* (August 2003).

"Undiagnosing Gender." In *Transgender Rights: Culture, Politics, and Law*, ed. Shannon Minter and Paisley Currah (Minneapolis: Minnesota University Press, forthcoming).

"Giving an Account of Oneself." *Diacritics* (forthcoming).

INTERVIEWS

"The Body You Want. Liz Kotz Interviews Judith Butler." *Artforum International* (New York, 1992), pp. 82–9.

"Gender as Performance: An Interview with Judith Butler." *Radical Philosophy: A Journal of Socialist and Feminist Philosophy* 67 (Summer 1994), pp. 32–9.

"Performing Gender." In *A Critical Sense: Interviews with Intellectuals*, ed. Peter Osborne (London: Routledge, 1996; reprinted from *Radical Philosophy* 67, 1994).

"On Speech, Race, and Melancholia: An Interview with Judith Butler." *Theory, Culture & Society* 16:2 (1999), pp. 163–74.

"Politics, Power, and Ethics: A Discussion Between Judith Butler and William Connolly." *Theory and Event* 4:2 (2000). <http://muse.jhu.edu/journals/theory_and_event/v004/4.2butler.html>

"Changing the Subject: Judith Butler's Politics of Radical Resignification." With Gary Olson and Lynn Worsham. *JAC* 20:4 (2000), pp. 731–65.

"On Religion, Violence, and Patriotism." *Common Sense* 3:2 (Winter 2002).

"Interview with Judith Butler." *The Believer* (May 2003).

Index